For Reference

Not to be taken from this room

THE
CORPORATE
REPORT CARD

THE CORPORATE REPORT CARD

Rating 250

of America's

Corporations

for the Socially

Responsible

Investor

COUNCIL ON ECONOMIC PRIORITIES

A DUTTON BOOK

DUTTON
Published by Penguin Group
Penguin Putnam Inc., 375 Hudson Street, New York, New York 10014, USA
Penguin Books Ltd., 27 Wrights Lane, London W8 5TZ, England
Penguin Books Australia Ltd., 10 Alcorn Avenue, Toronto, Ontario, Canada M4V 3B2
Penguin Books (N.Z.) Ltd., 182–190 Wairau Road, Auckland 10, New Zealand

Penguin Books Ltd., Registered Offices:
Harmondsworth, Middlesex, England
First published by Dutton, an imprint of Dutton NAL, a member of Penguin Putnam Inc.

First Printing, June, 1998
10 9 8 7 6 5 4 3 2 1

Library of Congress Cataloging-in-Publication data is available.
ISBN 0-525-94287-4

Printed in the United States of America

Contents

v

vi

Introduction

To be of unique value to our owners over the long haul, we must also be of unique value to our consumers, our customers, our fellow employees, and all other stakeholders—over the long haul. The exercise of what is commonly referred to as "corporate responsibility" is a supremely rational, logical corollary of a company's essential responsibility to the long-term interests of its shareowners.

— **Roberto C. Goizueta, late Chairman and CEO,**
Coca-Cola Company

Good corporate citizenship can be a central element in the strategy of highly successful corporations. The results can bring significant benefit to society and build a valuable reputation for the company. This conviction underlay the founding of the Council on Economic Priorities in 1969. And it has inspired the creation of our many innovative programs to aid corporate managers, policy makers, investors and consumers in making informed decisions about how to promote and encourage socially and environmentally responsible management of business.

As more and more people have learned to participate in measurable social change through investing and purchasing practices, CEP has developed new programs to provide the information needed to make influential choices. Several of those programs have laid the groundwork for this inaugural publication of *The Corporate Report Card*, including the Campaign for Cleaner Corporations, the Corporate Conscience Awards, and the *Shopping for a Better World* consumers' guide—which, since its first edition in 1988, has sold over a million copies to consumers who wish to buy from socially responsible companies. Perhaps most directly, however, *The Corporate Report Card* is drawn from CEP's SCREEN Research Service for Investors (covering more than 650 companies in extensive detail) and aims to provide the individual investor with a means of participating effectively in the booming phenomenon of socially responsible investing.

According to a 1997 Social Investment Forum study, $1.2 trillion in assets are under management in the United States in socially and environmentally responsible portfolios, up from $639 billion in 1995, an increase of 85 percent. Nearly one dollar out of every ten invested in U.S. stock markets is socially managed in some fashion, either through screening, filing of shareholder resolutions, or voting proxies. In 1997, for the first time, Lipper Analytical Services gave A or B grades to 20 social investment funds, which also received four- and five-star ratings from Morningstar. This growing phenomenon illustrates that investors are increasingly showing a preference for well managed companies that operate on principles of long-term profitability inextricably linked to social responsibility. What now has entered the lexicon as "socially responsible investing," or SRI, has become a standard service offered to clients by virtually all of the major investment concerns, and many new firms devoted solely to SRI practices have sprung up.

CEP was on the forward edge of this movement when our 1970 study *Paper Profits* (MIT Press), comparing the pollution control records of twenty-four paper and pulp companies, generated prominent coverage in the *New York Times, Wall Street Journal, Business Week,* and

Time. The combined pressure of publicity, environmental concern, and access to CEP's data, brought dramatic improvement (detailed in our update two years later). CEP's *Paper Profits* findings formed the basis for a seminal 1971 paper by Jan Bragdon and John Tepper Marlin that found a high degree of correlation between pollution control and three key measures of profitability. The results were heralded in *Business Week.*

Over the ensuing decades, increasingly sophisticated studies have scrutinized the relationship between companies' social responsibility and the health of their bottom line. A study by Covenant Investment Management in 1993 analyzed the performance of *Business Week* 1000 corporations relative to 36 areas of social concern. The top-scoring 200 companies saw their stock increase in value 100 percent over five years. The bottom-rated firms achieved only a 76.6 percent increase in that period. This study found that shareholder value increased when companies focused on long-term issues, such as improved management, customer loyalty, employee benefits and training, and supplier relations. Shareholder value was lower with the presence of environmental noncompliance, poor labor relations, and unsafe products and workplaces. Studies at Florida International University (1994) and the University of Massachusetts (1988) found strong, statistically significant positive relation-ships between corporate social responsibility and such factors as return on assets and growth in sales. The U-Mass study also found that socially responsible management in such areas as environmental impact and product safety reduces a company's risk of costly litigation and regulatory penalties. Finally, a study conducted jointly by researchers from the Investor Responsibility Research Center (Washington, DC) and Vanderbilt University's Owen Graduate School of Management found in 1995 that there is no penalty for "green" investing; low pollution portfolios often achieve better returns than both high pollution portfolios and the Standard & Poor's (S&P) 500 index.

Building on this tradition, CEP now introduces our *Corporate Report Card*, produced on the principle that individual investors, armed with information, can help to create an incentive for corporations to change environmentally or socially damaging business practices. With *The Corporate Report Card*, we will provide individual investors with information based on our SCREEN research, and hope to encourage you not only to use this information to seek SRI funds for investment opportunities but also to require your investment managers to look at a given company's performance on social and environmental issues before recommending that company for investment or adding to your portfolio.

In evaluating the financial performance of SRI, long-term thinking is key. SRI does not assure good, or even average, financial returns. Some well known SRI funds have significantly unde performed the S&P 500 and the most relevant benchmark standards. It is important to seek social investment advice from knowledgeable, well-qualified investment professionals. Review their investment track record and compare it with the relevant benchmark, such as the Dow Jones Industrial Average, the S&P 500 and the Lipper Balanced (Benchmark Average). Review carefully your financial needs and objectives and the exposure to risk appropriate for your investment portfolio. You have every right to expect a competitive return on your investments.

The participation of more and more people in SRI, and in consumer activism, has resulted in a myriad of informed investment decisions that have already made a significant difference in the policies and practices of major multinational corporations. Within the last few years alone, **The Gap** responded to a nationwide boycott by agreeing to independent monitoring at its subcontractor in El Salvador. PepsiCo withdrew from Burma in January 1997, following an intense five-year effort that included principled purchasing campaigns by city and state governments and universities. These successful campaigns alerted other companies, such as **Avon** and **Toys "R" Us**, to establish proactive codes of conduct for their overseas operations and lead efforts to develop a universal standard for a safe workplace and a system to certify compliance. In 1996, after community leaders raised concerns about environmental damage in the Silicon Valley and New Mexico, a coalition of socially-conscious shareholders voiced dismay over **Intel**'s rapid expansion given its past environmental performance. Their resolution citing "community environmental hazards" was withdrawn when Intel agreed to a series of meetings with community organizations and issued a new environmental policy statement. Also in 1996, **Dominion Resources**, the eleventh largest electric utility in the nation, was listed for the second year as a poor environmental performer by CEP's Campaign for Cleaner Corporations (C-3). The company had increasing sulfur dioxide emissions (a major source of acid rain) and no formal environmental policy or disclosure guidelines. By year-end, Dominion met with CEP, enlisting staff help with formulating a corporate policy that commits the company to: community involvement, pollution prevention, alternative energy development and conservation, and the creation of a comprehensive environmental management system. Through 1996, every corporate polluter named to C-3 since 1992 (23 in all) has sat down with CEP to discuss their performance and negotiate change. All have implemented significant improvements as a result.

Profitability and social conscience are increasingly the hallmarks of some of the major multinationals. In 1996, for the second consecutive year, shareowners in the **Coca-Cola Company** received a return on investment of more than 40 percent. Coca-Cola won a CEP Corporate Conscience Award in 1995 for its continuing focus on equal opportunity. The company's steady promotion of women and people of color, and purchase programs with minority- and women-owned businesses totaling $1 billion annually, are solid evidence of that commitment. Over a ten year period, from 1987 to 1997, Coca-Cola's total return on investment averaged 31 percent.

The **Hewlett-Packard Company**, another Corporate Conscience Award winner and CEP Honor Roll company, during the same period had an annualized shareholder ROI of 17 percent. Fiscal Year 1997 earnings were up 21percent. In 1996, HP and its foundation donated nearly $72 million in cash and equipment (1.3 percent of pretax earnings), involved company volunteers in educational outreach around the world, and made institutional commitments to environmentally sound operations.

Hewlett-Packard has earned a place on CEP's Honor Roll because it achieved a "grade point average" of 3.6. Companies with a 3.2 or higher GPA, and with no F's and at least seven of the eight categories rated, make the list. Coca-Cola also made the Honor Roll, with a 3.4 grade point average. A full list of companies in this book achieving the Honor Roll follows the introduction.

Such has been the proven success of socially responsible management that major investment houses, such as **Merrill Lynch**, the **U.S. Trust Company**, **Rockefeller & Company**, and **Neuberger & Berman**, have added social screening to their line-up of services. Other major institutional investors, like the New York City Employee Retirement System and the United Methodist Church's General Board of Pension and Health Benefits, actively vote their proxies and introduce proxy resolutions on social and environmental issues, often in conjunction with the New York–based Interfaith Center on Corporate Responsibility (ICCR). Ethical investment pioneers like **Dreyfus Third Century** and **Pax World Fund** continue to thrive, providing a way for people to invest according to not only return on investment but also an increasingly relevant set of criteria — their own values. SRI has become a mainstream opportunity.

CEP therefore has prepared this *Corporate Report Card* to provide the individual investor and those interested generally in the environmental and social business practices of major corporations with information on which to base their buying and investing practices. *The Corporate Report Card* will enable you to minimize risk by supporting well-managed companies with strong reputations for bold and innovative efforts to be good corporate citizens. Your letters to CEOs telling them why you won't invest in a socially *irresponsible* company will encourage its leadership to help turn around poor performers. And your letters recognizing socially responsible companies encourage corporate management to excel.

What kind of corporate policies and practices might you look for to invest wisely and responsibly? We recommend that you consider general benchmarks like these:

◆ Board-level responsibility for environmental stewardship that ensures proactive programs above and beyond compliance with the law, early action as environmental threats are identified and before regulations are in effect, and emissions per unit of production well below average for a given company's industry

◆ Fair employment practices that ban discrimination based on gender, race, sexual orientation, or disability, and that promote diversity

◆ Family benefits that enhance a company's personnel to fulfill dual work/family roles well

◆ Generous charitable giving that partners corporate expertise with community leadership to address local problems

◆ Meaningful codes of conduct or adherence to a universal standard for subcontractors that seek to do away with "sweatshop" abuses by assuring at least minimum wage, banning child labor that deprives children of their education, and robust independent monitoring such as certification to SA 8000, the new universal standard for human rights and labor practices

◆ Full disclosure of objective evidence of corporate social performance

CEP has included in *The Corporate Report Card* several of the largest corporations in each of a wide range of industries. Among them are food, clothing, automobile, computer technology, utilities, oil, and pharmaceutical companies. Each company is objectively rated on eight key issues: environment, workplace, family benefits, minority advancement, women's advancement, community outreach, charitable giving, and social disclosure. The resulting 250 profiles, drawn from CEP's SCREEN Research Service for Investors, afford a fascinating look at these corporations, whose policies and programs directly affect millions of lives.

The complete SCREEN Research database covers 450 *additional* companies, featuring profiles that provide more extensive data/information on each corporation. SCREEN Service updates and special analytical reports are issued quarterly.

To aid you further in your decision-making, CEP offers the experience of two other above mentioned programs, our Corporate Conscience Awards, and our Campaign for Cleaner Corporations (C3). The C3 annually identifies some of the nation's weakest companies on corporate environmental performance by comparative analysis of companies in the same environmentally hazardous industry. Final selections are made by a blue ribbon panel of judges. Working with a nationwide coalition of environmental groups that includes Greenpeace, Friends of the Earth, and 20/20 Vision, CEP makes recommendations for improvement of company policies and practices. Since 1992, all twenty-two companies identified by C3 have sat down at the table with CEP to discuss substandard environmental performance and negotiated ways to change by instituting the recommended significant improvements. For example, in 1992, after **General Motors** was listed as an egregious polluter, the company met with CEP and an independent panel of judges. By 1994, GM became the third Fortune 500 company to join the Coalition for Environmentally Responsible Economies, which works to address environmental problems, and its CEP rating had risen from a D to a B. Continuing this enormously effective program in 1998, CEP has just evaluated the transportation industry and has refined our evaluation approach to rank companies from the best to the worst in a given industry. The best performing petroleum company in our study was **Sun Company**, the first Fortune 500 company to join CERES.

The Corporate Conscience Awards (CCA) were created in 1987 to recognize corporations demonstrating good citizenship. Companies based anywhere in the world where CEP has research partners (e.g., United Kingdom, Germany, Belgium, India and Japan) are now eligible for consideration. CEP conducts exhaustive research to locate companies that have instituted corporate initiatives, both proactive and reactive, to act for social good in employee empowerment, community service and development, environmental stewardship, global ethics and human rights. The recipients often lead the way in implementing both global and local changes that improve the quality of life for many millions of people around the world and for communities in their own backyards.

One of our 1997 honorees, the **Co-operative Bank plc** of the U.K., received the Global Ethics award for its leadership in the international campaign to outlaw the production and use of landmines; a recipient of the Community Involvement award, **Community Pride Food Stores**, made a tremendous impact at its local level by providing a nearby grocery source in inner-city neighborhoods, and improving the lives of customers, employees and neighborhood children through education, employment benefits and special services.

The recipients of the 12th Annual Corporate Conscience Awards (1998) include:

◆ *For long-term efforts with measurable results*—**Dollar General Corporation**, for its strong support of literacy, education, and self-sufficiency training programs for public assistance recipients; **Avon Products, Inc.**, for its highly successful promotion of the value of diversity to corporate success and for its exceptional record of advancing women to leadership and executive positions; and **British Airways**, recognizing its long-standing excellent example in environmental reporting and accountability, and new leadership in the Tourism for Tomorrow program, designed to encourage more responsible management of the highly environmentally and economically destructive tourism industry.

◆ *Pioneer Awards (initiatives with promise but too new for a track record)*—**General Mills**, and its partners, **Stairstep, Inc.**, **Glory Foods**, and **U.S. Bancorp**, for creation of **Siyeza**, a new frozen food manufacturing facility in Minneapolis, which will employ inner-city residents and ultimately transfer ownership of the facility to the employees; **British Petroleum**, for its courageous stand in publicly recognizing that global climate change is a reality, and that precautionary steps to curb greenhouse gasses must be taken now; **Ecomat** dry cleaners and laundromats, for the company's elimination from the dry-cleaning process of perchlorethylenes, or "percs"—a probable human carcinogen; and **Oticon A/s**, a Danish manufacturer of hearing aids, for its progressive initiatives in organizational structure that promote both employee development (including employee definition of projects and of their own jobs) and environmental improvements. A list of all previous Award winners appears at the end of the introduction.

The globalization of business has meant tremendous opportunity for American companies manufacturing and sourcing goods abroad, along with increased pressure on those producing at home to remain competitive. Consumers benefit from an ever-increasing array of products as companies compete among themselves on price and quality. Yet the workers at the center of the global marketplace are ever more at risk of exploitation.

After two years of solid research, the Council on Economic Priorities has compiled and evaluated a solid body of information on upwards of 200 major American corporations which source and manufacture products internationally. Our report on international sourcing— International Social Responsibility Research Servic —is offered in conjunction with our SCREEN Research Service.

CEP surveyed 360 companies in more than 40 industries, asking for copies of sourcing guidelines for labor rights (also known as "codes of conduct") and for detailed information on the way those codes are monitored. Of these, 135 companies responded; 225 refused to disclose or did not respond.

Of the responding companies, the companies with the highest rated codes of conduct and also innovators in monitoring programs include Toys R Us, Reebok, Phillips-Van Heusen, The Gap and Levi Strauss. Companies with impressive monitoring programs include Avon, Eileen Fisher, OTTO Versand, Liz Claiborne and LL Bean.

Companies responding to CEP's survey without sourcing guidelines include Eli Lilly, Texaco and Whirlpool. Some examples of companies that refused to disclose or did not respond include AT&T, McDonalds and Walgreen. For a full listing of the companies and how they responded, please contact CEP.

Beginning in late 1998, our SCREEN Research Service will identify companies that have had facilities and/or suppliers certified for compliance with Social Accountability 8000. An international standard for safe and fair working conditions, SA8000 (SA8000) was developed by CEP Accreditation Agency (CEPAA), in a consensus-based process involving an Advisory Board whose members represent major companies, human rights organizations, unions and professional auditors. Third-party independent audits by certification bodies accredited by CEPAA will begin in mid-1998 the process of facility-by-facility verification.

In *The Corporate Report Card*, you will find detailed information about companies that adhere to progressive policies and those that do not. We designed this book to equip you to select investments in those corporations which are socially responsive to all their stakeholders—employees, neighbors, investors, consumers, and the environment. A Ratings Key and Table of Criteria are provided following the introduction, to guide you through the Report Card. Should you want further information on any company presented here—or not presented here—please contact CEP. We'll either get the information for you from our SCREEN Research Service or guide you to a good resource. We hope you will find this publication valuable to you in your quest to influence the creation of a better world, and we hope you will join with us in hopeful activism and embrace the possibility of positive change. As once expressed by Edwin Land, founder of the Polaroid Corporation:

Neither organisms nor organizations evolve slowly and surely into something better, but drift until some small change occurs which has immediate and overwhelming significance. The special role of the human being is not to wait for these favorable accidents, but deliberately to introduce the small change that will have great significance.

CORPORATE CONSCIENCE AWARDS

Each year, the Council on Economic Priorities presents our Corporate Conscience Awards, honoring companies for outstanding achievements and pioneering programs in environmental stewardship, employee empowerment and diversity, community partnerships and global ethics. An independent panel of judges chooses the winners and they are honored at a gala awards ceremony in New York City.

Corporate Conscience Award–winning companies:

1998

Environmental Stewardship
British Airways

Pioneer Award in Environmental Stewardship
British Petroleum
Ecomat

Community Partnership
Dollar General Stores

Pioneer Award in Community Partnership
General Mills, Inc.

Employee Empowerment/Diversity
Avon Products, Inc.

Pioneer Award in Employee Empowerment/Diversity
Oticon A/s

1997

Environmental Stewardship
Novo Nordisk (Denmark)
J. Sainsbury, plc (United Kingdom)
Wilkhahn Wilkening (Germany)

Community Involvement
W. K. Kellogg Foundation and the Kellogg Company
Community Pride Food Stores, Inc.

Employee Relations
Cooperative Home Care Associates, Inc.

Global Ethics
The Co-operative Bank, plc (United Kingdom)

Pioneer Award in Global Ethics
Toys "R" Us
Sporting Goods Manufacturing Association,
Soccer Industry Council of America, and the
World Federation of the Sporting Goods Industry

International Commitment
Levi Strauss & Co.

1996

Environmental Stewardship
Enron
Natural Cotton Colours, Inc.
Otto Versand (Germany)

Community Involvement
Pfizer Inc.
Working Assets Funding Service
Fuji Xerox Co., Ltd. (Japan)

Employer Responsiveness
Hewlett-Packard Company

Equal Employment Opportunity
Fannie Mae

Child Labor Initiatives
Veillon S.A. (Switzerland)

International Human Rights
Starbucks Coffee Company

1995

Environmental Stewardship
New England Electric

Community Involvement
Colgate-Palmolive
The Timberland Company

Equal Employment Opportunity
The Coca-Cola Company

Responsiveness to Employees
Polaroid Corporation

Global Ethics
Merck & Company

1994

Silver Anniversary Awards
Large: Xerox Corporation
Small: Shorebank Corporation

Community Involvement
Brooklyn Union Gas Company

Environmental Stewardship
Large: S.C. Johnson & Son, Inc.
Small: Stonyfield Farm, Inc.

Responsiveness to Employees
SAS Institute

International Commitment
Levi Strauss & Co.

1993

Community Involvement
The Clorox Company

Responsiveness to Employees
Merck & Co., Inc.
Quad/Graphics Inc.

Equal Employment Opportunity
Pitney Bowes Inc.

Environmental Stewardship
Large: Digital Equipment Corporation
Small: Aveda Corp.

Conversion Award
Galileo Electro-Optics Corporation
Kaman Aircraft
Kavlico

Science Applications International Corp.

1992

Charitable Contributions
Large: US West, Inc.
Small: Tomís of Maine

Community Involvement
Supermarkets General Holdings Corporation and
The Prudential Insurance Company of America

Responsiveness to Employees
Donnelly Corporation

Equal Employment Opportunity
General Mills, Inc.

Environmental Stewardship
Large: Church & Dwight Company, Inc.
Small: Conservatree Paper Company

Special Recognition for Innovative Benefit
Lotus Development Corporation

1991

Charitable Contributions
Large: H.B. Fuller Company
Honorable Mention: The Stride Rite Corporation
Small: Foldcraft Company

Community Involvement
Time Warner Inc.

Responsiveness to Employees
Kellogg Company

Equal Employment Opportunity
Hallmark Cards, Inc.

Environmental Stewardship
Large: Herman Miller, Inc.
Honorable Mention: H.J. Heinz Company
Small: Smith & Hawken

1990

Charitable Contributions
Cummins Engine Company, Inc.
Honorable Mention: Patagonia, Inc.

Community Involvement
Xerox Corporation

Responsiveness to Employees
Pitney-Bowes, Inc.
Honorable Mention: Fel-Pro, Inc.

Equal Employment Opportunity
US West, Inc.

Environmental Stewardship
American Telephone & Telegraph Company

1989

Charitable Contributions
Dayton Hudson Corporation
Honorable Mention: Newman's Own, Inc.

Community Involvement
Digital Equipment Corporation

Responsiveness to Employees
Federal Express Corporation

Equal Employment Opportunity
Eastman Kodak Company

Environmental Stewardship
Applied Energy Services, Inc.
Honorable Mention: H.B. Fuller Company

1988

Charitable Contributions
Ben & Jerry's Homemade, Inc.

Fair Employment
Xerox Corporation
Gannett Company, Inc.

Family Concerns
IBM Corporation

Opportunities for People with Disabilities
General Mills, Inc.

Community Action (Job Development)
  Best Western International, Inc.
  South Shore Bank

Education (Literacy)
  Gannett Company, Inc.

Environmental Stewardship
  3M

Animal Rights
  Procter & Gamble Company

Disclosure
  Kellogg Company

1987

Charitable Contributions
  Polaroid Corporation

Sara Lee Corporation
General Mills, Inc.

Equal Employment Opportunity
  Avon Products, Inc.

Family Concerns
  Procter & Gamble Company

Community Action
  IBM Corporation
  Amoco Corporation

Disclosure
  Johnson & Johnson
  Ford Motor Company

South Africa
  Polaroid Corporation

....

CEP's Honor Roll Companies

Of the 250 companies rated by CEP in Corporate Report Card, the 23 listed below earned a grade-point average of 3.2 or higher, with at least 7 of the 8 categories having been rated. Companies with an F or more than one N were not considered.

For our Honor Roll, CEP has weighted all categories of social performance equally. If you feel especially committed to one issue, you may want to look carefully at a company's specific grade on that issue rather than at whether the company has attained the Honor Roll listing.

Adolph Coors Company
Avon Products, Inc.
BankAmerica Corporation
BankBoston Corporation
Baxter International
Ben & Jerry's Homemade
Bristol-Myers Squibb
Brooklyn Union
Chevron Corporation

Citicorp
Coca-Cola Company
Colgate-Palmolive
Dole Food Company
General Electric
Hewlett-Packard
International Business
  Machines
Johnson & Johnson

Kellogg Company
Merck & Company
PepsiCo Inc.
Pfizer Inc.
Polaroid Corporation
Sun Company
Xerox Corporation

Ratings Key

CEP assigns performance grades in eight corporate responsibility issues areas. All social issue area grades are assigned based on a comparison of all companies in CEP's database. Environment grades, however, are relative to the company's industry sector. The general characteristics of CEP's grades are as follows:

A   Outstanding performance in the issue area as defined by the ratings key
B   Above average performance
C   Moderate performance or mixed record
D   Below average performance
F   Poor performance; little evidence of a good record
N   Insufficient information on which to base a rating, unless otherwise noted. For most Retail and Service industries, CEP does not assign environment grades
REV   Indicates that the grade is currently under review by CEP
?   The grade is based on partial information; type of information used for the grade is outlined in each category below

Note: Ratings are assigned to companies relative to the average performance of the sample being studied; the sample is ranked and divided into roughly 20 percent segments. Wherever possible, CEP has sought to distribute the companies equally among these ratings.

Occasionally, there may be information in the text that seems to contradict a grade. This is usually the result of information surfacing through CEP's data search that does not systematically fit into the grading methodology.

ENVIRONMENT

Companies are evaluated in 10 areas of corporate environmental performance:

1. *Environmental Impact:* The Toxic Release Inventory, Emergency Response Notification System, Aerometric Information Retrieval System databases and compliance data are normalized against company sales information. References to increases or decreases in the profiles are based on normalized, not raw data. This indicator is created by weighting, then combining average total releases over a time period with percent change. The environmental impact portion of the rating is based on domestic operations.

2. *Environmental Policy:* Each company's policy is analyzed using the following five indicators — signature on the policy, communication, general commitments, policy updating elements, and progressive commitments.

3. *Corporate Environmental Commitment:* Top-level commitment is determined by the following four indicators—Board of Director's committee/personnel with environmental responsibility, presence of an integrated environmental management system, voluntary principles the company has adopted, and its international policy on environmental standards.

4. Environmental Audits: Six indicators are considered for this criterion— presence of environmental audit program, worldwide applicability of the program, internal audit training program, third party verification of the audit program, corrective action program/elements, and public availability of the results.

5. Employee Training/Accountability: Four indicators are assessed — environmental, health and safety (EH&S) training program/applicability, company EH&S awareness measures, internal EH&S awards, and employee EH&S accountability measures.

6. Waste Management and Pollution Prevention: Indicators for this criterion include pollution prevention policy, pollution prevention program and elements, and company annual reduction goals.

7. Supplier Relationship: This criterion measures how a company incorporates and promotes environmental responsibility regarding its suppliers. Indicators include: waste vendor selection and monitoring criteria, supplier selection criteria, presence of a technical assistance program for suppliers, procurement guidelines for purchasing decisions.

8. Product Stewardship: This criterion measures a company's commitment to managing the entire life cycle of its products. Indicators include: written commitment to product stewardship, existence of a corporate product stewardship review board/team, product evaluation impact categories, and types of product stewardship programs.

9. Resource/Energy: Use: A company's approach towards raw materials and energy consumption constitutes this criterion. Indicators include materials reduction policy, natural resource use programs, corporate energy policy and a company's energy reduction goals.

10. Corporate Environmental Report: CEP researchers analyze a company's corporate environmental report (CER) with respect to the following indicators: CER frequency, guidelines, verification, environmental issues scope and depth, and extent of environmental impact data inclusion.

A company received a complete grade if it answered CEP's environment questionnaire or made changes to its draft profile. A company also received a complete grade if the following was available: a corporate environmental report, corporate environmental policy, publicly available environmental impact data, and secondary source information pertaining to corporate environmental commitment and environmental audit criteria.

A company received a partial grade — indicated by a "?" — if it did not respond to either the CEP questionnaire or draft, or if CEP researchers were unable to obtain secondary source information for the company.

A company received an N if it did not respond to either the CEP questionnaire or the draft profile, and if there was no information available through secondary sources.

WOMEN'S ADVANCEMENT

Using information provided by the company and external sources, CEP analyzes the representation of minorities on a company's board of directors, and among corporate officers, officials and managers, and the top 25 paid employees at a company. CEP also looks at minorities programs and purchasing from minority-owned businesses. The average and standard deviation of the numbers in each category are computed and normalized using a weighted system. The numbers are then combined into a company's total score. The scores are then evenly distributed across the sample from the top 20 percent (A's) through to the bottom 20 percent (F's).

For women's advancement, the "?" notation indicates that the grade was determined using only representation numbers on the Board and among Corporate Officers.

MINORITY ADVANCEMENT:

Using information provided by the company and external sources, CEP analyzes the representation of minorities on a company's board of directors, and among corporate officers, officials and managers, and the top 25 paid employees at a company. CEP also looks at minorities programs and purchasing from minority-owned businesses. The average and standard deviation of the numbers in each category are computed and normalized using a weighted system. The numbers are then combined into a company's total score. The scores are then evenly distributed across the sample from the top 20 percent (A's) through to the bottom 20 percent (F's).

For minority advancement, the "?" notation indicates that the grade was determined using only representation numbers on the Board and among Corporate Officers.

CHARITABLE GIVING

Total worldwide cash donations (including direct corporate giving, foundation giving, and matching gifts) for the most recent year is figured as a percentage of the average of three previous years' pretax worldwide earnings. For companies taking a loss for two or more of the last three years, no calculation was made and their rating is an NR.

In-kind (non-cash) giving is also considered, though at a portion of its reported cash value. A substantial increase or decrease in the total value of a company's charitable giving may affect the company's rating by as much as one letter grade. A "?" notation in this area indicates that the rating is based on information from years prior to 1996.

The average and standard deviation of the combined giving are computed and normalized using a weighted system. The numbers are then combined into a company's total score. The scores are then evenly distributed across the sample from the top 20 percent (A's) through to the bottom 20 percent (F's).

General ranges correspond to the following grades:

A 1.7 percent or more of net pretax arnings given to charity.

B 1.1 percent up to but not including 1.7 percent of net pretax earnings given to charity.

C 0.7 percent up to but not including 1.1 percent of net pretax earnings given to charity.

D 0.4 percent up to but not including 0.7 percent of net pretax earnings given to charity.

F Less than 0.4 percent of net pretax earnings given to charity.

COMMUNITY OUTREACH

CEP evaluates three areas of community involvement efforts: 1) volunteer programs; 2) investment in housing and businesses in low-income neighborhoods, school partnerships, and other comparable programs; and 3) internal management systems (e.g. community needs assessment, program evaluations, organization of staff), which was weighted least in importance. Each area was rated according to the scale of the program and commitment of company resources (e.g. financial, personnel), the range and organization of program components, the systems for measuring impact on the community, and improvements achieved. Characteristics of the ratings are as follows:

A 1) Volunteer programs are strategically organized, with great depth and breadth of involvement; 2) community investment programs, school partnerships, and comparable programs that are large-scale or innovative and include a broad range of program components; and 3) systems for measuring programs' impact and/or internal management systems are sophisticated.

B 1) Voluntary programs are substantial; 2) community investment, school partnerships, and/or comparable programs are sizable, with several components; and 3) systems for measuring programs' impact and/or internal management systems are established.

C 1) Volunteer programs are modest; 2) community investment and other programs are modest in size with a limited range of components; and 3) some evidence of internal management and/or metric systems.

D 1) Little or no evidence of volunteer programs; 2) little or no evidence of community investments or programs; and community investments or programs are single-faceted; and 3) little or no evidence of internal management or metric systems.

F 1) Significant negative impact on local communities; 2) little or no evidence of programs designed to benefit community.

Note: Ratings in this category apply to U.S. operations only. Citizen campaigns related to environmental issues or other issues CEP rates will be considered in the relevant category.

FAMILY BENEFITS

CEP rates companies on a numerical scale that measures the extent and balance of family benefits offered in four major areas:

I. Medical Insurance: health insurance coverage for family

II. Dependent Care & Day Care: child, elder, and disabled-dependent care resource and referral services and subsidies; on- and near-site day care centers

III. Flexibility: part-time return to work following parental leave, flextime, compressed work week, job-sharing and work-at-home

IV. Leave: maternity, paternity, family and personal

The company receives a rating based on its composite score in relation to other companies under consideration. The

"Family Benefits Categories" section on the profile reflects the company's scores in these different areas.

If a benefit is in an experimental stage or in process of being implemented, CEP counts it as a "yes." A benefit still in research stage is counted as a "no." The size of the company and type of industry are also considered. A benefit granted through "departmental discretion" or on a "case-by-case basis" is counted as a "no" for large companies. Only a company-wide written policy is considered to adequately address prevention of discrimination. For small companies, however, handling employee needs on a case-by-case basis is common. CEP credits case-by-case benefits for small companies only.

Note: Ratings in this category apply to U.S. operations only.

WORKPLACE ISSUES

Companies are evaluated in five work-related areas:

I. Medical Coverage: health insurance coverage

II. Pension Coverage: retirement plans, company contributions to plan

III. Workplace Safety: worker injury rates, OSHA violations, ergonomic and other worker safety programs

IV. Worker Involvement/Development: profit sharing, employee stock ownership, bonus plans, in-house skills/literacy/career training, tuition reimbursement, fitness/wellness programs, employee assistance program

V. Displaced Worker Assistance: No-layoff policy, relocation assistance, severance pay, out placement services, job training assistance

Companies are rated based on a weighted average of their performance in each of these categories. The size of the company and type of industry are also considered. The "Workplace Categories" section on the profile reflects the company's scores in these different areas.

A "?" notation next to a grade in this category indicates that the grade is based solely on the company's safety performance as indicated by information obtained from OSHA. CEP evaluates a company's OSHA data relative to the data for other companies in its industry sector that are also under consideration. Companies given a grade with a "?" in this issue area did not respond to CEP's questionnaire.

Note: Ratings in this category apply to U.S. operations only.

DISCLOSURE OF INFORMATION

CEP measures corporate disclosure on the issue areas it tracks and rates by considering two areas. First, how the company discloses to CEP through responses to questionnaires and documents provided. Secondly, through the level of information that is available to CEP through secondary sources.

A Company provides complete and current materials on its social programs and policies either by fully completing CEP's questionnaire or by providing comparable information in printed matter or phone interviews.

B Company provides extensive yet incomplete information on its social programs and policies either by partially completing CEP's questionnaire or by providing comparable information in printed matter or phone interviews. At least two questionnaire responses plus significant outside information was available to CEP researchers.

C Company provides some specific information on social programs and policies though many key questions left unanswered. Company responded to half the questionnaires CEP sent them, or substantial information from other sources was available to CEP researchers.

D Company answers few questions or comments on programs and policies only in general terms. Thus, response is not detailed enough to give any real indication of the company's performance. No responses and some additional information were available to CEP researchers.

F Company provides only the most basic information: an annual report, proxy statement and 10-K, or less. No responses to CEP questionnaires and a minimal amount of additional

information were available to CEP researchers.

Please Note: Most sales and employee figures are from fiscal 1996. Charitable giving figures are the most recent made publicly available by the companies through 1996. EEO data are gathered from the most recent company documents available as of July 1997. Many companies, such as Dayton Hudson, Microsoft, and Johnson & Johnson, not only provided data requested by CEP but additional information as well. Some companies, such as Rubbermaid (household products and toys), Stanley Works (hand tools), and PPG Industries (plate glass) chose not to disclose any information to CEP; some did not provide even their current annual report after repeated requests.

Unless the company provided more recent information, CEP used the 1994 data from reports of the Environmental Protection Agency's Toxic Release Inventory (TRI).

For corporate military contract, CEP checked those appearing among the Top 100 Worldwide Weapons Contractors and the Top 100 Defense Contractors to the Pentagon; most recent data drawn from lists available by 1997 and 1996, respectively.

Abbott Laboratories

STOCK SYMBOL: ABT
STOCK EXCHANGES: NY, B, C, CH, P, PH

Environment	D
Women's Advancement	B
Minority Advancement	A
Charitable Giving	C
Community Outreach	A
Family Benefits	NR
Workplace Issues	B?
Social Disclosure	A

Abbott Laboratories, based in Abbott Park, Illinois, is one of the world's largest international health care companies. In 1996, Abbott had sales of over $11 billion and 50,241 employees.

Environment: Abbott Laboratories does not currently publish a corporate environmental report. The company has a pollution prevention policy and is very active in pollution prevention and waste management initiatives, devising methods to reduce waste at the source. Abbott Laboratories extends support to the communities where its facilities are located, underwriting lectures and workshops covering a variety of environmental topics. Abbott Laboratories believes in product stewardship and promotes safe handling and use of products to its customers and seeks ways to minimize the amount of packaging it utilizes without jeopardizing the quality of the product. The company also seeks ways to minimize waste as well as the use of natural resources early in the product design phase.

Abbott Laboratories' average total toxic releases and transfers during the years 1993–1994 were less than the industry sample average. Emissions decreased by about a fifth during those years, a better than average performance.

In November 1997, the Lake County Forest Preserve District Board of Commissioners presented Abbott with the National Society of Park Resources award for corporate citizenship in the field of parks and recreation. Abbott made a $500,000 pledge toward the construction of the Greenbelt Center for Culture and Urban Environmental Education near North Chicago. In May, 1996, Abbott Laboratories agreed to pay $600,000 to settle a complaint that it discharged contaminants into ' Lake Michigan between 1991 and 1995.

EEO: In 1996, Abbott Laboratories achieved a higher than average rating in both diversity categories, placing them easily in the top third of S&P 500 companies. One woman and one minority served on Abbott Laboratories's 13-member board. Of 38 corporate officers at the company, four were women and three were minorities, while four of the top 25 paid employees were women, and three were minorities.

The company is a member of the Chicago Area Partnerships, a group of corporate, government, and community representatives committed to eliminating the "glass ceiling." Abbott policy expressly prohibits discrimination on the basis of sexual orientation.

Community Involvement: In 1996, Abbott Laboratories' charitable giving totaled $9.5 million in cash, which was equal to 0.36 percent of the company's pretax earnings for that year. In terms of the actual dollar amount donated by the company, the level of cash contributions in 1996 represented a decrease of 11.58 percent from that of 1995, which was 0.40 percent of the company's earnings for that year. The company's in-kind giving—the donation of products or services—came to a total of $35.5 million in 1996.

Abbott encourages employees to volunteer in their communities and conducts a variety of educational programs, many of which are designed to interest girls and minorities in science careers. Abbott has contributed over $1.2 million to develop AIDS education programs.

Workplace Information: OSHA records indicate that Abbott was inspected four times from 1994 to 1996. Violations included one classified as "serious" for an average of $431 in fines per inspection. In comparison, the median amount of fines per inspection for other medical and cosmetic companies was $2266.

Legal Proceedings: Abbott recently faced a number of antitrust lawsuits alleging that the company, along with other major U.S. manufacturers, fixed the prices of its infant formulas. In June 1996, Abbott settled 17 of the suits for over $25 million in cash and $7.5 million in products. Abbott reports that the settlement required no change in its business practices and constitutes no admission of guilt or wrongdoing. The company is also facing 114 prescription pharmaceutical pricing antitrust cases in federal court and 19 in state courts. To date, it has won all of the cases that went to trial.

Advanced Micro Devices

STOCK SYMBOL: AMD
STOCK EXCHANGES: NY, B, CH, PH, P

Environment	B
Women's Advancement	N
Minority Advancement	N
Charitable Giving	C
Community Outreach	B
Family Benefits	N
Workplace Issues	C?
Social Disclosure	B

Based in Sunnyvale, California, in 1969, as a supplier of integrated circuits for the personal computer and communications markets, AMD has grown into a worldwide organization with revenues of $2.4 billion in 1997 and more than 12,700 employees. The company conducts advanced process technology development, new product prototyping, and pilot production activities at its Submicron Development Center in Sunnyvale, and owns and operates three manufacturing facilities in Austin, Texas.

Environment: AMD has an environmental policy and a corporate environmental report, which is updated annually. AMD has implemented an integrated environmental management system and provides environmental health and safety (EH&S) training to all employees. It also considers contribution towards EH&S goals in the job performance reviews of EH&S staff and presents awards to employees for their contribution to environmental issues.

AMD has a written pollution prevention policy and has initiated a companywide pollution prevention program, which establishes annual reduction goals for solid waste. Although the company does not have a corporate policy on community involvement relating to local environmental concerns, the Austin site holds quarterly Neighborhood Meetings on environmental concerns. AMD does not have a written policy on product stewardship, but has provided information to customers on life-cycle impact analysis, with the objective of reducing the environmental impacts of certain products.

Advanced Micro Devices' average toxic releases and transfers during the years 1994–1996 were less than the industry sample average. However, its emissions increased by an average of a third annually during those years, a below average performance.

EEO: In 1996, Advanced Micro Devices' eight-member board of directors and eight corporate officers included no women or minorities.

In June 1994, AMD extended medical and dental benefits to the partners of its gay and lesbian employees. The company explicitly prohibits discrimination on the basis of sexual orientation and includes gay and lesbian issues in diversity awareness training.

Community Involvement: In 1996, AMD's charitable giving totaled $3.1 million in cash. In terms of the actual dollar amount donated by the company, the level of cash contributions in 1996 represented an increase of 32.26 percent from that of 1995, which was 1.23 percent of the company's earnings for that year. The company's in-kind giving—the donation of products or services—came to a total of $650,000 in 1996.

AMD implemented a volunteer program in 1995. Approximately 10 percent of the employees are involved with the program, which includes clean-up projects, food sorting, convalescent home visits, and staff benefits for nonprofit organizations. The program also utilizes intra-office e-mail to inform employees about volunteer activities.

Workplace Information: AMD reports that it was not issued any violations by OSHA during 1996, and that violations resulting from a 1995 inspection were contested by the company and withdrawn.

AMD's innovative benefits include a "dream vacation"—a paid week and $4,000 in spending money—awarded to nonexempt employees after seven years of service. Exempt employees can take a two-month paid sabbatical after seven years. The company has offered profit-sharing for more than two decades (10 percent of pretax profits) and gives cash incentives for perfect attendance.

International: AMD has test and assembly facilities in Penang, Malaysia; Singapore; and Bangkok, Thailand. It is also developing a plant in Suzhou, China, and Dresden, Germany. An AMD-Fujitsu joint venture operates two facilities in Aizu-Wakamatsu, Japan.

Legal Proceedings: In 1995, Intel and AMD resolved several long-standing legal battles involving alleged patent infringement and breach of contract issues.

H.F. Ahmanson

STOCK SYMBOL: AHM
STOCK EXCHANGES: NY, B, CH, PH, P

Environment	N
Women's Advancement	A
Minority Advancement	A
Charitable Giving	N
Community Outreach	D
Family Benefits	N
Workplace Issues	N
Social Disclosure	B

H. F. Ahmanson, headquartered in Irwindale, California, is one of the largest residential real estate services, and was organized in 1928 to provide the public with mortgage loans, mortgage-backed securities and investment securities. Home Savings of America, a federally chartered bank, generates virtually all of the company's consolidated revenue and is the largest savings institution in America. In 1996, H. F. Ahmanson had income of $3.7 billion and approximately 9,500 employees.

Environment: Ahmanson's recycling program extends beyond the usual items to include oil and antifreeze from its warehouse operations. Its offices use various recycled paper products and have committed to the EPA's Green Lights program.

EEO: In 1996, H.F. Ahmanson achieved a higher than average rating in both diversity categories, placing them easily in the top third of S&P 500 companies. Two women and three minorities served on H.F. Ahmanson's 13-member board. Of 1,103 corporate officers at the company, 552 were women and 259 were minorities, while seven of the top 26 paid employees were women, and two were minorities.

H.F. Ahmanson is one of only three companies among the nation's 500 largest that have more than one woman among the five top officers. H.F. Ahmanson gives loans for affordable housing to minority group members and has committed itself to a standard of diversity in its senior management and board.

H.F. Ahmanson has developed special programs for the recruitment of both women and minorities.

Community Involvement: In 1977, Home Savings established a Community Outreach Department, where managers in Los Angeles, Oakland, Chicago, Miami and New York work with neighborhoods to improve current conditions and prevent future problems. In order to monitor its ongoing fair lending programs, a Community Reinvestment Committee of 13 members was formed in 1990.

Home mortgage lending (HMDA) data, compiled and analyzed by CANNICOR, indicates that Home Savings has generally been successful in reaching blacks and Hispanics, particularly with loans for refinancing, which account for 53 percent of its total lending. The data shows the company lending below industry rates to low-income blacks for purchase, however. Home Savings reports that its $1.3 billion in residential loans in low-income areas makes it the largest lender to such communities in California. Ahmanson has been honored by the United Way for Corporate Leadership and been given the Bellringer Award for Corporate Community Involvement. The Office of Thrift and Supervision rates Ahmanson as Outstanding.

When its South Vermont branch was destroyed in the Los Angeles riots in 1992, Home Savings built an expanded facility on the same site using community contractors. The company's Career Awareness Program (CAP) has encouraged more than 26,000 inner-city high school students to graduate by providing them job training sessions, scholarships, workshops and consideration for employment. Last year the company awarded $4,000 scholarships to 114 students and permanently hired 80 of the 450 persons it received through the program. Five percent of Ahmanson's work force are CAP graduates.

Workplace Information: The records of the Occupational Safety and Health Administration indicate that H.F. Ahmanson was not inspected from 1994 to 1996. Consequently no fines or violations were assessed to the company.

Air Products and Chemicals

Stock Symbol: APD
Stock Exchanges: NY, B, Ch, P, Ph

A ir Products and Chemicals, based in Allentown, Pennsylvania, is one of the largest distributors of gases (oxygen, nitrogen, helium, hydrogen, etc.) used in industrial applications. It also produces chemical intermediates and is involved — through joint ventures—in cogeneration and flue gas desulphurization. In 1997, company revenues were $4.6 billion and employees numbered 16,600.

Environment	C
Women's Advancement	F
Minority Advancement	C
Charitable Giving	B
Community Outreach	B
Family Benefits	N
Workplace Issues	C?
Social Disclosure	A

Environment: Air Products and Chemicals has an environmental policy and a corporate environmental report, which is updated annually and is available on the internet. Air Products and Chemicals has implemented an integrated environmental management system and provides environmental health and safety (EH&S) training to all employees. It also considers contribution towards EH&S goals in the job performance reviews of EH&S staff and facility staff.

Air Products and Chemicals has a written pollution prevention policy and has initiated a company-wide pollution prevention program, which establishes annual reduction goals for point sources and solid waste. The company also has a corporate policy on community involvement relating to local environmental concerns. Seventeen facilities have community advisory panels. Air Products and Chemicals has a written policy on product stewardship and evaluates its products with the objective of reducing their life-cycle impacts on the environment. Internationally, Air Products and Chemicals monitors SARA Title III, or equivalent emissions and follows US regulations in the US and local regulations abroad.

Air Products & Chemicals' average toxic releases and transfers during the years 1994–1996 were higher than the industry sample average. Emissions increased by an average of over three-quarters annually during those years, the worst performance in the sample. APD reports this increase is due to the addition of new chemicals to the TRI list by the EPA.

EEO: In 1996, Air Products & Chemicals' 13-member board of directors included one woman and one minority. Of 33 corporate officers at the company, one was a woman and two were minorities. No women or minorities ranked among the 25 highest paid employees at the company. According to *Cracking the Corporate Closet* (Harper Business, 1995), Air Products' gay and lesbian employee association, which was formed in 1992, participates in diversity education programs.

Air Products & Chemicals operates recruitment programs, support networks, and maintains diversity goals for both women and minorities.

Community Involvement: The Air Products Foundation supports education primarily in the form of grants to the engineering and business departments of colleges and universities. The company has also participated in public and private ventures to rehabilitate abandoned and condemned properties in Allentown, Pennsylvania, the location of its headquarters. The company has no formal employee volunteer program but reports that 70 percent of employees volunteer time in the community. Through its "Growing With Science" educational partnership program, Air Products and Chemicals works with an inner-city elementary school to promote interest in math and science.

Workplace Information: Air Products and Chemicals' Recordable Injury Rate declined to well below the chemical industry average: 1.25 injuries per 200,000 work hours. OSHA records indicate that Air Products and Chemicals was inspected ten times from 1994 to 1996. Violations included 25 classified as "serious" for a total of $31,805 in fines, an average of $3,180 per inspection. In comparison, the median amount of fines per inspection for other extractive companies was $2,941.

International: Air Products and Chemicals has half-, majority-, or wholly-owned subsidiaries in Brazil, China, Dubai, Korea, Mexico, Singapore, South Africa, and United Arab Emirates.

Weapons Contracts: In 1994, Air Products had $7.5 million in non–weapons-related sales to the Department of Defense (0.2 percent of total revenues).

Alberto-Culver

STOCK SYMBOL: ACV, ACVA
STOCK EXCHANGES: NY, B, CH, PH, P

Environment	C
Women's Advancement	A
Minority Advancement	F
Charitable Giving	N
Community Outreach	D
Family Benefits	F
Workplace Issues	C
Social Disclosure	B

Chicago-based Alberto-Culver is a tightly-held company run by four family members, who serve on both the board and in the highest levels of management. The family controls over 50 percent of voting stock. Alberto-Culver manufactures a range of consumer products, including Alberto VO5, Consort, Mrs. Dash, SugarTwin, and Static Guard. Its Sally Beauty Company subsidiary operates nearly 1,800 international cash-and-carry beauty supply stores. In 1997, Alberto-Culver had sales of $1.78 billion and approximately 11,000 employees.

Environment: Alberto-Culver does not have a written environmental policy, does not produce a corporate environmental report, and has no corporate environment department. The company has no required environmental guidelines for suppliers, other than for hazardous waste disposal. Alberto-Culver is not a participant in EPA's Green Lights energy efficiency program, but does constantly monitor energy use for economic reasons. From 1991 to 1995, the company achieved a ten percent reduction in energy usage. The company does not participate in EPA's WasteWi$e program, and has made only limited progress in reducing its packaging volume. However the company reports that it has traditionally done little boxing or shadow boxing, and redesigned a number of shipping cartons in 1997 to reduce corrugated usage. In the face of new state regulations that control volatile organic compounds (VOCs), the company has been forced to consider the environmental impact of its hair sprays.

Alberto-Culver's average total toxic releases and transfers during the years 1993–1994 were less than the industry sample average. Emissions decreased by about a fifth during those years, an average performance.

EEO: In 1996, Alberto-Culver's board totaled 12 directors (11 in 1997), including two women, both members of the company's founding family, and no minorities. Four of a total of 24 corporate officers were women, and none were minorities. Additionally, four women and no minorities were among the 24 employees with the highest salaries at the company. Alberto-Culver provides recruitment and mentoring programs for women and minorities, and bans discrimination based on sexual orientation.

Alberto-Culver maintains diversity goals for the levels of women and minorities at the company, and operates recruitment programs as a means to reach those goals.

Community Involvement: Alberto-Culver gives to charity directly; however, the company will not disclose giving figures to CEP. The company generally supports organizations in areas with large Alberto-Culver employee populations.

Family Benefits: The company provides 12-week paid medical leaves and extended nonpaid leaves with management approval. Alberto-Culver also offers such flexible scheduling options as job sharing and part-time return to work following leave, as well as child care resource and referral services at some locations. The company is implementing flexible spending accounts for elder/child care and noncovered medical expenses.

Workplace Information: The records of the Occupational Safety and Health Administration indicate that Alberto-Culver was not inspected from 1994 to 1996. Consequently no fines or violations were assessed to the company.

Animal Testing: Alberto-Culver conducts animal testing on new products that come in contact with the skin or may be accidentally ingested. The company maintains that 96 percent of personal care products have not been tested in the past five years (or ever) on animals. Whenever possible, the company uses human subjects and computer analysis to replace animal testing.

In September 1992, the company pledged $250,000 over six years to support the Johns Hopkins Center for Alternatives to Animal Testing.

5

Albertson's, Inc.

STOCK SYMBOL: ABS
STOCK EXCHANGES: NY, B, CH, P

Environment	N
Women's Advancement	B
Minority Advancement	B
Charitable Giving	F
Community Outreach	C
Family Benefits	N
Workplace Issues	C?
Social Disclosure	B

Boise, Idaho–based Albertson's is one of the nation's largest food and drug retailers. It operates approximately 790 stores in 19 western, midwestern, and southern states. In 1996, Albertson's had $13.8 billion in revenue and 88,000 employees. The company was named the "most admired" supermarket company in a recent *Fortune* survey of corporate executives.

Environment: Albertson's has a formal environmental policy. The company participates in EPA's Green Lights program for lighting efficiency and was recognized as among the "best and brightest" in 1995 for its progress. It has not joined EPA's WasteWi$e initiative, but it has an extensive recycling program. The company is exploring the use of vegetable waste for composting and conversion to animal feed, which, if successful, would eliminate 30 percent of its off-site waste. Albertson's has a policy against distributing milk from cows treated with bovine growth hormone.

EEO: In 1996, Albertson's achieved a higher than average rating in both diversity categories. Two women and three minorities served on Albertson's 15-member board. Of 67 corporate officers at the company, four were women and none were minorities, though two African Americans were recently promoted to district sales manager positions, which are on the officer track. One of the top 25 paid employees was a woman. Albertson's operates mentoring programs, apprenticeship programs, recruitment programs, maintains diversity goals, and gives special consideration for management training to both women and minorities.

Between 1989 and 1993, Albertson's twice settled charges of discrimination against women and minorities. To address these concerns, the company created the Human Resources and Diversity Department; introduced job posting, mentoring, and diversity awareness training; and is now more forthcoming with EEO data. In 1996, a Florida woman filed suit against the company claiming that women were rarely promoted to management positions.

Community Involvement: In 1996, Albertson's charitable giving totaled $2.5 million in cash, which was equal to 0.31 percent of the company's pretax earnings for that year.

Workplace Information: According to the Occupational Safety and Health Administration's records, Albertson's was inspected 64 times from 1994 to 1996. The OSHA inspectors' citations included nine violations classified as "willful" or "repeat" and 102 violations classified as "serious." A total of $44,178 in fines, averaging $690 per inspection, was assessed to the company following the inspections. In comparison, the median amount of fines per inspection for other companies in the food, beverage, and household products industries was $1,515.

In July, 1997, the National Labor Relations Board issued a complaint against Albertson's following lawsuits the company brought against the United Food and Commercial Workers International and locals. The NLRB described the suits as unlawful and "retaliatory," indicating that the actions taken by the unions are guaranteed under the National Labor Relations Act.

After 18 months of striking, workers for a Rock Springs Albertson's supermarket reluctantly accepted in April of 1996 a new three year contract. The strike began on October 8, 1994 when workers and the company were unable to come to a compromise regarding seniority and shift preferences. The new contract explicitly addresses these issues for six months, after which a letter of understanding is to take effect giving latitude to workers who feel they are being mistreated.

Product Quality: In 1995, Albertson's was honored by the International Association of Milk, Food and Environmental Sanitarians for the cleanliness of its stores.

Legal Proceedings: In July 1995, Albertson's cooperated fully with the Tulare County, California, district attorney's office investigation, and settled amicably charges of unfair trade practices, including producing misleading advertisements and charging incorrect prices on bulk and packaged goods.

Alcan Aluminium Limited

STOCK SYMBOL: AL

STOCK EXCHANGES: NY, B, C, CH, P, PH

Environment	C
Women's Advancement	D?
Minority Advancement	F?
Charitable Giving	D?
Community Outreach	N
Family Benefits	N
Workplace Issues	B?
Social Disclosure	D

Based in Montreal, Quebec, Alcan is a world leader in bauxite mining, alumina refining, and aluminum smelting, manufacturing, and recycling. In 1996, the company had revenues of $5.6 billion and 39,000 employees, 28 percent of them based in Canada.

Environment: Alcan Aluminium has an environmental policy and a corporate environmental report, which is updated every three to four years. The company has implemented an integrated environmental management system and provides environmental health and safety (EH&S) training to all employees whose work has potential to result in significant environmental impacts. Alcan has a written pollution prevention policy and has initiated a company-wide pollution prevention program. The company also has a corporate policy on community involvement relating to local environmental concerns and has established community advisory panels at less than 5 percent of its facilities. Alcan has a written policy on product stewardship, and evaluates its products with the objective of reducing their life-cycle impacts on the environment. Alcan's Aluminum Vehicle Technology system provided General Motors with the design flexibility to develop the EV1, the first production electric vehicle in North America to feature an all-aluminum structure. Alcan has an environmental audit program with worldwide standards/applicability. Internationally, Alcan does not monitor SARA Title III, or equivalent emissions, and it adheres to local regulations or company minimum standards, whichever is stricter.

Alcan Aluminium's average toxic releases and transfers during the years 1993–1994 were the lowest compared to an industry sample. Furthermore, its emissions decreased by more than a fourth during those years, the best performance within the industry sample.

EEO: In 1996, Alcan Aluminium's 12-member board of directors included one woman and no minorities. Of 15 corporate officers at the company, none were women or minorities.

Community Involvement: In 1995, Alcan gave $2.5 million in direct giving, 0.45 percent of average pretax profits, and $3 million in in-kind giving to charitable organizations. The company supports numerous community development initiatives, grants to universities, and an environmental program at the Young Entrepreneurship Primary School in Brazil.

Family Benefits: The company offers on-site day care, part-time return to work after parental leave, job-sharing, flextime, and work-at-home arrangements at some facilities.

Workplace Information: The records of the Occupational Safety and Health Administration indicate that Alcan Aluminium underwent three health and safety inspections from 1994 to 1996. The violations reported by OSHA as a result of the inspections include 11 classified as "serious." The company was required to pay an average of $1,003 per inspection totaling $3,010. In comparison, the median amount of fines per inspection for other companies in the extractive business was $2,941.

International: With operations and sales offices in 30 countries — including India, China, Thailand, Malaysia, Ghana, Brazil, and Uruguay — Alcan is the most international aluminum company. International sales accounted for 86 percent of Alcan's 1995 total sales. The company is in the process of adopting an international code of conduct that will cover health and safety standards, child labor, forced and bonded labor, minimum wage, and environmental protection.

Weapons Contracts: In 1994, the company had $835,000 in U.S. Department of Defense contracts, $32,000 of which was related to weapons.

7

Allergan, Inc.

STOCK SYMBOL: AGN
STOCK EXCHANGES: NY, P

Environment	A
Women's Advancement	C?
Minority Advancement	N
Charitable Giving	N
Community Outreach	N
Family Benefits	N
Workplace Issues	N
Social Disclosure	C

Headquartered in Irvine, California, Allergan is a leading provider of specialty therapeutic eye care products and also produces niche pharmaceutical products in skin care and movement disorders. In 1996, the company had over $1.1 billion in sales and employed approximately 6,100 people worldwide. Between 1980 and 1989, the company was operated as a wholly-owned subsidiary of SmithKline Beecham.

Environment: Allergan has an environmental policy and a corporate environmental report, which is updated biennially and will be available on the internet in 1998. The company has implemented an integrated Environmental Management System and provides environmental health and safety (EH&S) training to all employees. Allergan also considers contribution towards EH&S goals in the job performance reviews of all manufacturing and research and development employees, which includes EH&S staff and facility staff. The company presents awards to employees for their contribution to environmental issues. Allergan has written a pollution prevention policy and has initiated a company-wide pollution prevention program, which established reduction goals for point sources, fugitive emissions, and solid waste. It has a corporate policy on community involvement relating to environmental concerns, and three of its facilities have Community Advisory Panels.

Allergan has a written commitment to product stewardship and a product stewardship review board that evaluates its products with the objective of reducing their life-cycle impacts on the environment. In the selection of suppliers, Allergan conducts or reviews environmental audits on suppliers' facilities, evaluates environmental management systems of suppliers, and determines whether suppliers have necessary permits. The company has an environmental audit program with worldwide standards/applicability. In 1996, 50 percent of U.S. and international facilities were audited. The company monitors SARA Title III or equivalent emissions in non-U.S. operations and follows Allergan international standards and local regulations worldwide. Allergan standards are made up of applicable U.S., European, and best management practices.

Allergan has no reportable toxic emmissions under Environmental Protection Agency regulations.

EEO: In 1996, Allergan, Inc.'s 12-member board of directors included one woman. Of 16 corporate officers at the company, two were women.

Workplace Information: The records of the Occupational Safety and Health Administration indicate that Allergan, Inc. was not inspected from 1994 to 1996. Consequently no fines or violations were assessed to the company.

Less than half of Allergan's 6,000 employees are based in the U.S. The company's domestic workforce is not unionized. In accordance with recent industry trends, Allergan has experienced major restructuring leading to workforce reductions. In 1996, the company announced a restructuring plan which will involve the elimination of 450 jobs, approximately eight percent of its total workforce.

In July 1996, an Orange County Court ruled in favor of Allergan in a case where a former regulatory-affairs manager accused the company of wrongful termination after raising concerns about the safety of a soft-lens disinfectant kit. In a nine to three vote, the jury found that the company was not guilty of wrongful termination.

8

Aluminum Company of America

STOCK SYMBOL: AA
STOCK EXCHANGES: NY, B, C, CH, P, PH

Environment	B
Women's Advancement	B?
Minority Advancement	B?
Charitable Giving	B
Community Outreach	N
Family Benefits	N
Workplace Issues	B?
Social Disclosure	C

Based in Pittsburgh, Pennsylvania, the Aluminum Company of America (Alcoa) is the world's largest producer of aluminum and alumina. In 1996, the company had $13.1 billion in sales and 72,000 employees.

Environment: Aluminum Company of America (Alcoa) has a written environmental, health and safety policy and a corporate environmental, health and safety report, which is updated annually. The company has implemented an integrated environmental management system. Alcoa has a written pollution prevention policy and has initiated a company-wide pollution prevention program, which establishes annual reduction goals for solid waste. The company also has a corporate policy on community involvement relating to local environmental concerns and has established community advisory panels at approximately five percent of its facilities. The company presents awards to employees for their contribution to environmental issues. Alcoa evaluates its products with the objective of reducing their life-cycle impacts on the environment. Ford, GM and Chrysler have asked their aluminum, steel and plastic suppliers to help them create a holistic ecological profile of today's mid-size passenger vehicles as basis for future improvements. As a result, Alcoa organized and conducted a comprehensive life cycle inventory of primary and secondary aluminum processing, in collaboration with the Aluminum Association. The company participated in EPA's 33/50 and Green Lights Programs.

Aluminum Co. of America's average toxic releases and transfers during the years 1993–1994 were less than the industry sample average. However, its emissions increased by a fifth during those years, the worst performance within the industry sample.

Alcoa received the World Environment Center's Gold Medal for International Corporate Environmental Achievement in 1996, presented annually in recognition of a multinational corporation's outstanding and well-implemented worldwide environmental policy.

EEO: In 1996, two women and one minority served on Aluminum Co. of America's 11-member board. Of 22 corporate officers at the company, one was a woman and one was a minority; in 1997, two women and one minority were among 27 corporate officers.

In June, 1995, Alcoa was named as the defendant in a class action suit brought by employees and prospective employees who claim the company practiced discrimination on the basis of race and gender. Alcoa maintained that it did not violate state or Federal law. In January 1995, a former employee of Alcoa's Warrick Operations in Indiana was awarded more than $230,000 in back pay by a federal judge who ruled that she was fired as retaliation for sexual discrimination complaints.

Community Involvement: In 1996, Alcoa's contributions to various charitable institutions included cash donations totaling $12.9 million, or 1.2 percent of its earnings before taxes for the same year. Approximately one quarter of the Alcoa Foundation's contributions towards education is made through the company's matching gifts program. Alcoa Foundation supports academic excellence and opportunities for students from diverse backgrounds and experiences to succeed through education.

Workplace Information: OSHA records indicate that Alcoa was inspected 30 times from 1994 to 1996. Violations include one classified as "repeat" and 69 classified as "serious" for $55,179 in fines. In 1996, Alcoa negotiated a six-year contract (with wage increases and improved benefits) with the United Steelworkers of America and the Aluminum, Brick and Glass Workers International Union National Bargaining Council.

Weapons Contracts: In 1994, Alcoa had $3.6 million in military contracts with the Department of Defense, $1.6 million of which was related to nuclear weapons systems.

International: At the company's 1996 annual meeting, five workers from Alcoa Fujikura's auto parts plant in Mexico charged that the plant's wages are low, that work conditions are unsafe, and that Alcoa disciplined workers for union organizing.

9

Amdahl Corporation

STOCK SYMBOL: AMH
STOCK EXCHANGES: AS, B, CH, P, PH

Environment	B
Women's Advancement	F
Minority Advancement	A
Charitable Giving	N
Community Outreach	B
Family Benefits	N
Workplace Issues	N
Social Disclosure	B

Amdahl, based in Sunnyvale, California, manufactures and sells IBM-compatible computer systems. With revenues of $1.6 billion in 1996 and 8,000 full-time employees, Amdahl has expanded its lines of computers to include software products, educational and professional services, and hardware maintenance services. Amdahl manufactures its computers in California and Ireland. Presently, 44 percent of Amdahl's outstanding common stock is owned by Fujitsu Limited, a major Japanese computer system manufacturer. Many subsystems and components used in the computers are manufactured by Fujitsu.

Environment: Amdahl has an environmental policy and will be implementing Environmental Management principles consistent with those of ISO 14000. The company provides Environmental Health and Safety (EH&S) training to all employees and considers contribution towards EH&S goals in the job performance reviews of all employees and presents awards to employees for their contribution to environmental issues.

Amdahl has written a pollution prevention policy and has initiated a company-wide pollution prevention program, which establishes reduction goals for solid waste. It has also implemented a corporate policy on community involvement relating to environmental concerns.

In 1996, 100 percent of Amdahl's U.S. facilities were audited under the company's environmental audit program. Internationally, the company follows U.S. regulations in the U.S. and local regulations abroad.

Amdahl's average toxic releases and transfers during the years 1993–1994 were high relative to its industry sample, indicating a below average performance. Although its emissions decreased slightly during those years, its performance was still below average within the industry sample.

EEO: In 1996, Amdahl Corp.'s ten-member board of directors included no women and three minorities. Of 15 corporate officers at the company, one was a woman and one was a minority. One woman and one minority also ranked among the 25 highest paid employees at the company.

Community Involvement: The Amdahl Corporation received two Presidential Citations in the 1997 President's Service Awards, for its Teacher Link program and its Read to Succeed program. Teacher Link matches each participating school with a technologically knowledgeable employee volunteer who helps the school develop a training program for software and hardware the school owns or is planning to purchase. In developing the training program, the employee and school consider the specific needs of the school, with the overall goal of incorporating the available technology in class.

The Read to Succeed program recognizes students for their reading achievements and teachers for their impact on the community. The program encourages children to read, and encourages teachers to develop individual reading goals for their students. The company publishes a Read to Succeed newsletter monthly or bi-monthly. Yale University and the Oakland Athletics have since initiated their own Read to Succeed programs.

Workplace Information: According to the Occupational Safety and Health Administration's records, Amdahl Corp. was not inspected from 1994 to 1996. Consequently no violations or fines were assessed to the company.

Weapons Contracts: In 1994, Amdahl had $39 million in contracts with the U.S. Department of Defense, $102,000 of which was for weapons-related systems.

Additional Information: Our Japanese partner organization, Asahi Foundation, has analyzed Fujitsu Limited, which has a substantial stake in Amdahl. Fujitsu receives strong marks for community involvement and charitable contributions, but poor grades on the well-being of employees and responsiveness to consumers.

Amerada Hess Corporation

STOCK SYMBOL: AHC

STOCK EXCHANGES: NY, To, B, C, CH, P, PH, MO

Environment	C
Women's Advancement	F?
Minority Advancement	N
Charitable Giving	N
Community Outreach	N
Family Benefits	N
Workplace Issues	A?
Social Disclosure	C

Amerada Hess, headquartered in New York City, was formed by the 1969 merger of Hess Oil and Chemical and Amerada Petroleum. The company is involved in the exploration, development and production of natural gas and crude oil, as well as the manufacture of petroleum products. The company's operations are conducted in the U.S., Canada, Denmark, Gabon, Indonesia, Kazakhstan, Thailand, and the United Kingdom and Norwegian sectors of the North Sea. In 1996, revenues reached $8.2 billion. Hess employs just over 9,000 persons.

Environment: Amerada Hess Corporation has an environmental policy but does not currently publish a corporate environmental report (CER). However, the company is in the process of designing its first U.S. CER, which is planned for publication by mid-1998. Hess is also in the process of fully integrating its environmental management system. The company provides environmental, health, and safety training for all its employees. In addition to awareness training, Hess requires each employee to review the Corporation's Business Practice Guide, which encourages each employee to report violations of environmental and safety laws or policies. It further provides a toll free number to report anonymously, if preferred. Amerada Hess has a written pollution prevention policy, but has not yet initiated a company-wide pollution prevention program.

Hess does not have a corporate policy on community involvement relating to local environmental concerns, and does not have any community advisory panels. However, the Corporate Vice President for Environmental Affairs is directly involved with every reported environmental concern and ensures that local environmental concerns are addressed by the Corporation's business units. The Corporation also maintains dialogue with many individuals as well as local community civic and environmental organizations. Amerada Hess does not have a written policy on product stewardship , but evaluates its products with the objective of reducing their life-cycle impacts on the environment. The Company is a sponsor for the Wildlife Conservation Society and the Tri-State Bird Sanctuary. It also participated in EPA's 33/50 Program and EPA's Natural Gas Star Emissions Reduction Program for Exploration & Production Facilities.

Amerada Hess's releases and transfers were below average for both 1993 and 1994, compared to an industry sample. The company decreased its emissions by 40 percent between 1993 and 1994, a better than average performance within the sample.

In late 1996, the Hess Oil Virgin Islands Corporation unit pleaded guilty to knowingly transporting 600,000 pounds of benzene-containing "spent" refinery catalyst as "nonhazardous waste" to a cement company in Arizona; the benzene, at levels up to 85 times the EPA limit, was burnt off in the production of cement. The company agreed to pay $5.3 million in fines and restitution. The company states that it has since implemented a waste management program to prevent this kind of occurrence.

EEO: In 1996, Amerada Hess's 16-member board of directors included one woman and no minorities.

Community Involvement: Amerada Hess did not provide CEP with any information regarding corporate contributions or community involvement; researchers were unable to find the information in other sources.

Workplace Information: OSHA records indicate that Hess was inspected four times from 1994 to 1996. Violations included six classified as "serious" for a total of $9,187 in fines, averaging $2,296 per inspection. In comparison, the median amount of fines per inspection for other extractive companies was $2,941.

Additional Information: AHC received $6.2 billion in tax exemptions from the Virgin Islands through its HOVIC subsidiary from 1966 to 1990. However, the benefit from Hess to the Virgin Islands economy over the same time period was estimated to be only $1.7 billion. The current agreement between Hess and the Virgin Islands government expires in 2010.

American Stores

STOCK SYMBOL: ASC
STOCK EXCHANGES: NY, B, CH, PH, P

Environment	A
Women's Advancement	D?
Minority Advancement	B?
Charitable Giving	N
Community Outreach	B
Family Benefits	N
Workplace Issues	N
Social Disclosure	C

American Stores, based in Salt Lake City, Utah, is the second largest food retailer in the U.S. and operates one of the country's largest networks of drugstore outlets. In recent years, the company has sought more centralized control of its holdings which include Acme Markets, Jewel Osco, Lucky Stores, Sav-on, Super Saver and RxAmerica. In total, American operates 1,650 stores in 26 Western, Midwestern and Northeast states. In fiscal year ending in January 1997, the company had revenues of $18.6 billion and approximately 127,000 employees.

Environment: American reports that it has identified environmental contamination sites related to underground petroleum storage tanks at several of its facilities. The company expects the costs incurred to remediate these sites will be immaterial.

EEO: In 1996, American Stores' board totaled 12 directors, including one woman and two minorities, while two of a total of 24 corporate officers were women, and none were minorities.

In December, 1993, American Stores settled a sex-discrimination class action suit filed against its Lucky Stores grocery chain for $107.3 million. The judge presiding at the trial found Lucky Stores liable for sex discrimination in its job assignments, promotions, distribution of hours and full-time work. The suit, originally filed in 1988, attained class action on behalf of 20,000 women. About 14,000 current and former employees shared in the damages.

Community Involvement: American Stores reports that it operates a formal giving program through the American Stores Charitable Foundation, in addition to making grants directly from the company's operating divisions. The company places priority on the areas of education and scholarships, food banks, and health and human services organizations such as the United Way.

Workplace Information: The records of the Occupational Safety and Health Administration indicate that American Stores was not inspected from 1994 to 1996. Consequently no fines or violations were assessed to the company. As complaints about the health and safety conditions of a company's facility can frequently prompt an inspection, a lack of inspections may indicate that American Stores has a relatively safe and healthy working environment.

Additional Information: In 1996, certain share-holders pressed the company to eliminate its retirement plan for non-employee directors. Although the company urged shareholders to reject the proposal, management will review the matter internally.

American Telephone & Telegraph

STOCK SYMBOL: T

STOCK EXCHANGES: NY, B, C, CH, P, PH

Environment	B
Women's Advancement	C?
Minority Advancement	B?
Charitable Giving	B?
Community Outreach	A?
Family Benefits	N
Workplace Issues	C?
Social Disclosure	C

AT&T, headquartered in New York City, is a global provider of telecommunications services and equipment manufacturing. The company employs over 130,000 persons and in 1996 had revenues of over $52 billion.

Environment: AT&T has an environmental policy and a corporate environmental report. AT&T has implemented an integrated environmental management system and provides environmental health and safety (EH&S) training to employees. The company also presents awards to employees for their contribution to environmental issues and has a corporate policy on community involvement relating to local environmental concerns. In the selection of suppliers, AT&T requires suppliers to follow the company's environmental guidelines as a contract condition.

AT&T is the only company within CEP's industry sample of telecommunications companies that have reportable toxic emissions. Emissions decreased by about a third from 1993 to 1994.

In October 1997, the Virgin Islands government filed an environmental damage lawsuit against AT&T. The lawsuit alleges that AT&T and its contractor, A&L Underground, Inc., caused extensive damage to fragile coral reefs and marine wildlife during an underground cable project off St. Croix. "The suit should send an unmistakable signal that this government will not tolerate violations of its environmental laws," claimed the governor after the suit's announcement, adding that AT&T must "answer for such illegal degradation of our precious natural assets."

EEO: In 1996, AT&T's ten-member board of directors included one woman and one minority.

Recently AT&T implemented a program where each division of the company is required to design a plan for increasing the ranks of African-Americans and women in management. The program includes comparisons to hiring practices with those of the company's competitors. Since the program was instituted, the numbers of African-Americans and women in senior management has doubled.

AT&T is a sponsor of the National Foundation for Women Business Owners report. In 1975, AT&T became the first corporation to include sexual orientation in its nondiscrimination policy. Later it added a support group for gay and lesbian empoyees.

Community Outreach: In 1995, AT&T's contributions to various charitable institutions included cash donations totaling almost $50 million.

The AT&T Foundation contributes to education through its "Learning Network" initiative that works to bring communications technology into classrooms. The Learning Network makes grants to programs that intend to increase the involvement of families in education, support educators, and encourage life-long learning and collaboration within communities.

In 1997, AT&T granted every employee around the world one paid workday to engage in community service; this program will result in a contribution of over 1,000,000 volunteer hours this year. The company also encourages volunteerism among employees through its Caring & Sharing Volunteers program.

Workplace Information: OSHA records indicate that AT&T was inspected 21 times from 1994 to 1996. Violations included 34 violations classified as "serious" for a total of $24,210 in fines, averaging $1,152 per inspection. In comparison, the median amount of fines per inspection for other electronic manufacturing companies was $1,347.

Weapons Contracts: In 1995, AT&T was ranked 73 in the list of top worldwide defense companies with revenue of $422 million from its activity in defense electronics and communications systems. Defense represented 0.5 percent of its overall revenue. AT&T was the 22nd-largest contractor to the U.S. Department of Defense in 1996 with contracts worth $529 million. On September 30, 1993, AT&T formally ended its contract to operate Sandia National Laboratories where tests are conducted for nuclear weapons development, arms control verification and nuclear waste transportation for the Department of Energy.

Ameritech

STOCK SYMBOL: AIT
STOCK EXCHANGES: NY, B, PH, P, CH

Environment	N
Women's Advancement	A
Minority Advancement	A
Charitable Giving	C
Community Outreach	A
Family Benefits	B
Workplace Issues	D?
Social Disclosure	A

Chicago, Illinois–based Ameritech (formerly American Information Technologies Corporation) consists of five Bell telephone companies in the Great Lakes: Illinois Bell, Indiana Bell, Michigan Bell, Ohio Bell, and Wisconsin Bell. In addition to local telephone service, Ameritech offers cellular, paging, long distance, cable TV, security monitoring, internet services, and managed communications services. Ameritech focuses its international investments in Europe; these include communications providers for Belgium, Denmark, and Hungary; a cellular service provider in Norway, and a business directory provider in Germany. In 1997, Ameritech had sales of $16 billion and the company had over 74,000 employees.

Environment: Ameritech does no manufacturing, and produces no process waste. In 1990, the company formed an environmental task force which recommended programs to conserve energy in all offices, encourage commuter pools and use of public transportation, and recycle outdated telephone books. The telephone book publishing subsidiary coordinates used-book collections with municipalities, works with a paper manufacturer to recycle directories, and uses soy-based inks and recycled content paper.

EEO: In 1996, Ameritech achieved a higher than average rating in both diversity categories, placing them easily in the top third of S&P 500 companies. Three women and two minorities served on Ameritech's 13-member board. Of 16 corporate officers at the company, three were women and one was a minority, while four of the top 25 paid employees were women (five in 1997), and two were minorities.

Although Ameritech does not have any special programs for banking with minority-owned banks, it indicates that the company conducts finance activities with minority-owned banks within its five-state region.

Community Involvement: In 1996, Ameritech's charitable giving totaled over $25 million in cash, which was equal to 0.76 percent of the company's pretax earnings for that year. Contributions in 1995 were also at 0.76 percent of pretax earnings. Ameritech was listed as the second top corporate contributor to the area of Civic and Public Affairs in 1995 by the Corporate Giving Watch.

Ameritech states that it considers volunteerism to be important; more than 10,000 employees volunteer time and skills to nonprofit and education-related organizations annually.

Workplace Information: OSHA records indicate that Ameritech underwent 20 inspections from 1994 to 1996. The violations reported by OSHA as a result of the inspections include three classified as "willful" or "repeat" and 39 classified as "serious." Ameritech reports that 9 inspections in 1997 turned up one "serious" violation for fines under $2,000.

In early 1996, Communications Workers of America filed eleven unfair labor practice charges with the NLRB against Ameritech. Lori Everts, a vice president with CWA Local 4900 in Indianapolis, stated that CWA has "a lot of little issues" over the company's interpretation of a contract ratified several months earlier. About 30,000 company employees are CWA members.

In August, 1997, the International Brotherhood of Electrical Workers pushed the Illinois Commerce Commission not to allow Ameritech's proposed purchase of a company owned by Sprint, citing a concern over the quality of service in some areas. The union has been critical of the company's policy in hiring the Sprint workers, which requires the workers to apply as new employees at Ameritech, thus losing the pension credit they had accumulated while working at Sprint.

The IBEW has alleged that Ameritech was guilty of election violations in conducting "captive audience" sessions that the union claims worked to mislead or intimidate employees before an organization vote at the SecurityLink unit of Ameritech. The CWA claims that Ameritech used similar tactics in a vote at a Wisconsin cellular unit that was narrowly lost by the union. Ameritech reported to CEP that the above labor issues are "over with."

Amoco Corporation

STOCK SYMBOL: AM
STOCK EXCHANGES: NY, TO, B, C, CH, PH, P

Environment	B
Women's Advancement	B?
Minority Advancement	B?
Charitable Giving	C
Community Outreach	C
Family Benefits	B
Workplace Issues	F
Social Disclosure	A

Amoco, headquartered in Chicago, Illinois, is the fifth-largest U.S. oil company, and North America's largest producer of natural gas. In 1996, the company had sales of $32.1 billion and 41,723 employees.

Environment: Amoco Corporation has an environmental policy and publishes a corporate environmental report, which is updated annually, follows the Public Environmental Reporting Initiative (PERI), and is available on the internet. Amoco has implemented an integrated environmental management system and provides environmental health and safety (EH&S) training to all employees. Amoco has a written pollution prevention policy, and reports that site-specific programs are in place instead of a company-wide pollution prevention program. The company also has a corporate policy on community involvement relating to local environmental concerns, and currently has community advisory panels at 18 of its facilities. Amoco has a written policy on product stewardship and evaluates some of its products with the objective of reducing their life-cycle impacts on the environment. It also participated in EPA's 33/50 and Green Lights programs.

Amoco's average toxic releases and transfers during the years 1993–1994 were less than the industry sample average. Furthermore, its emissions decreased by almost a half during those years, the best performance within the industry sample. The company ranked 6th out of 15 for CEP's Campaign for Cleaner Corporations' 1997 Petroleum Refining Report.

Amoco was the first U.S. refiner/marketer to announce it won't blend MMT into its conventional gasoline grades, despite the lifting of the U.S. ban on the octane additive. However, Amoco will not sign an Environmental Defense Fund–led coalition's pledge to remain "MMT-free."

Amoco agreed to pay a penalty of $216,000 and complete its $13 million effort to reduce air emissions of chemicals from wastewater ponds at its Joliet, IL chemical plant by December, for distributing a chemical without proper safety information.

EEO: In 1996, Amoco Corp.'s 15-member board of directors included two women and three minorities. Of 47 corporate officers at the company, five were women. Charles Walker, executive director of the National Society of Blacks in Engineering, described Amoco as an industry leader in minority recruitment.

Community Outreach: Amoco Corp.'s charitable contributions totaled $24 million in cash in 1996. The $24 million cash-giving figure represented the equivalent of 0.61 percent of the company's pretax earnings for the same year, and a decrease of 0.06 percent from the company's cash contributions in 1995. In 1995, the company donated 1 percent of its pretax earnings.

As a part of its support for education, Amoco pledged more than $7 million in hands-on science programs and economics education in April, 1997. The foundation provides some support for employee and retiree volunteer programs, and AmoCARES (Concerned Amoco Retirees Engaged in Service) donates approximately $2 million in volunteer services annually. In 1996, about $650,000 was given to organizations at which employees volunteered. Five percent of company employees are currently involved with Amoco's 15-year old volunteer program.

Family Benefits: Amoco makes on-site or near-site child care, a resource/referral service, and a subsidy for child care available to employees with children. Amoco reports that it also offers adoption reimbursement, 26 weeks of family/medical leave, paid time to care for ill family members, and reimbursement for child care expenses made necessary by work-related travel or late meetings. The company also offers such flexible scheduling options as a compressed work week, work-at-home arrangements, flextime, and job sharing.

Workplace Information: OSHA records indicate that Amoco was inspected 20 times from 1994 to 1996. Violations included 93 classified as "serious" for a total of $73,712 in fines.

AMP, Inc.

STOCK SYMBOL: AMP
STOCK EXCHANGES: NY, B, C, CH, P, PH

Environment	A
Women's Advancement	D?
Minority Advancement	F?
Charitable Giving	F
Community Outreach	D
Family Benefits	N
Workplace Issues	D?
Social Disclosure	B

Headquartered in Harrisburg, Pennsylvania, AMP manufactures electrical and electronic connecting devices. In 1997, the company had 45,000 employees and sales of $5.75 billion. AMP has recently expanded its operations in Europe and the Pacific Rim.

Environment: AMP Inc. has an environmental policy and a biennial corporate environmental report, available on the internet. AMP Inc. has implemented an integrated environmental management system and provides environmental health and safety (EH&S) training to all employees. It also considers contribution towards EH&S goals in the job performance reviews of EH&S and facility staffs, executives, and managers. AMP Inc. has a pollution prevention policy and program, which establishes reduction goals for point sources. The company also has a written policy on product stewardship. The company has an environmental audit program, which has worldwide standards and applicability and third party evaluation. AMP Inc. does not make the audit findings available to the public.

AMP's toxic releases and transfers were below average for both 1993 and 1994 compared to its industry sample (in terms of emissions/$ sales). Emissions decreased by over four fifths between 1993 and 1994, the fourth best performance within the industry sample.

The Electronic Industries Association's (EIA) Environmental Progress Awards Selection Committee presented AMP with the 1998 Corporate Award for its outstanding achievement in the development of their Design for Environment program.

EEO: Among the companies surveyed by CEP, the average representation of women and minorities on S&P corporate boards was 10.8 percent and 7.5 percent, respectively. In comparison, AMP, Inc. had one woman and no minorities on its 12-member board.

In 1996, a shareholder resolution, sponsored by the Interfaith Center on Corporate Responsibility, proposing that AMP report on its board inclusiveness, was withdrawn by the sponsors, generally indicating that an agreement has been reached with management.

Community Involvement: In 1996, AMP, Inc.'s charitable giving totaled $1.2 million in cash ($1.4 in 1997), which was equal to 0.27 percent of the company's pretax earnings for that year. In terms of the actual dollar amount donated by the company, the level of cash contributions in 1996 represented an increase of 50 percent from that of 1995, which was 0.18 percent of the company's earnings for that year.

Workplace Information: In May, 1996, AMP, Inc. asked all 18,000 of its U.S. employees to take a week off work without pay as a result of a decrease in demand for the electrical connectors it manufactures. In eight of the previous 21 years, the company had made similar requests, and the effort may offset any potential need for layoffs.

The records of the Occupational Safety and Health Administration indicate that AMP, Inc. underwent 11 health and safety inspections from 1994 to 1996. The violations reported by OSHA as a result of the inspections include 28 classified as "serious." The company was required to pay $20,410 as a result of its violations, averaging $1,855 per inspection. In comparison, the median amount of fines per inspection for other companies in the electronic manufacturing industries was $1,347.

Weapons Contracts: AMP has consistently derived 5 percent of its net sales (although in 1994 they fell to 3 percent) from aerospace and military operations. Its military contracts—which include providing electronic systems for the Minuteman missile—are handled by Matrix Science Corporation, which the company acquired in 1988, and sold in 1997.

AMR Corporation

STOCK SYMBOL: AMR
STOCK EXCHANGES: NY, B, C, CH, P, PH

Environment	B
Women's Advancement	C
Minority Advancement	B
Charitable Giving	F
Community Outreach	C
Family Benefits	N
Workplace Issues	D?
Social Disclosure	C

AMR, based in Fort Worth, Texas, is the holding company for American Airlines, one of the nation's largest airlines. It also owns the SABRE Group, a group of information technology companies that includes Sabre Travel Information Network, Sabre Computer Services, Sabre Decision Technologies, and Sabre Interactive. In 1996, AMR had 88,900 employees and revenues of $17.7 billion.

Environment: American Airlines made environmental concerns an integral part of its business planning. The airline has extensive recycling programs at most locations, and purchased $79.1 million worth of recycled materials in 1994 (more than twice the 1993 levels). Through its Waste Not, Earn A Lot program, employees recommend operating changes that improve environmental performance. A member of the EPA's Green Lights, the company is six years ahead of government mandates to modernize aircraft and reportedly has the most quiet and fuel-efficient fleet in the industry.

From 1990 to 1994, accidental spills released 22,000 pounds of materials into the environment.

EEO: In 1996, AMR Corporation's 12-member board of directors included one woman and three minorities. Of 51 corporate officers at the company, five were women and none were minorities. Two women also ranked among the 25 highest paid employees at the company.

The leading gay travel publication, *Out and About*, picked AMR in 1995 and 1996 for its efforts and involvement in the gay community. The airline is the first US carrier to include gays and lesbians in its written employment nondiscrimination guidelines. The airline also holds membership in the International Gay Travel Association (IGTA).

Its Supertrack system requires all officers to create cross-functional development plans for high-potential minority and women candidates from middle management upwards. An advisory council serves to educate and mentor women who are interested in nontraditional jobs.

Community Involvement: In 1996 AMR Corporation announced that it would donate $1 million to two organizations that served children living with life-threatening illnesses. Community development, including environmental programs and economic development initiatives, is also one of AMR's priorities.

Workplace Information: According to the Occupational Safety and Health Administration's records, AMR Corporation was inspected 16 times from 1994 to 1996. AMR's violations included two classified as "willful" or "repeat" and 27 classified as "serious." A total of $9,091 in fines, averaging $568 per inspection, was assessed to the company following the inspections. In comparison, the median amount of fines per inspection for other companies in the service industry, such as banks and communications companies, was $573.

President Clinton halted a strike by American Airlines pilots after 24 minutes on February 15, 1997. The pilots had rejected a deal which would have included a five percent raise over four years plus stock options when the company reported record earnings of $1 billion in 1996, and American would not agree to the 11 percent raise over the same time span and option deal the pilots wanted. At an average of approximately $120,000 a year, American's pilots were already the highest paid in the industry. The pilots were also concerned about company intentions to replace the turboprops of its American Eagle subsidiary with jets. American Eagle pilots are paid considerably less than AA pilots, and the striking pilots feared that many of their short-haul routes would be taken over by American Eagle once the relatively uncomfortable turboprops were replaced.

Legal Proceedings: American Airlines, along with seven other carriers, settled Justice Department charges of price-fixing between 1988 and 1992. Fares at various airlines increased over $1 billion during those years.

🏅 Anheuser-Busch

STOCK SYMBOL: BUD
STOCK EXCHANGES: NY, B, PH, P

Environment	A
Women's Advancement	B
Minority Advancement	A
Charitable Giving	B
Community Outreach	B
Family Benefits	N
Workplace Issues	B?
Social Disclosure	A

Anheuser-Busch (A-B), based in St. Louis, Missouri, focuses primarily on brewing beer, making aluminum cans, and running theme parks, having recently spun off its bakeries and closed Eagle Snacks. In 1996, the company had revenues of $10.9 billion and 42,529 employees.

Environment: Breweries produce large amounts of waste water and volatile organic compounds(VOCs). A-B participates in innovative pollution prevention projects, including President Clinton's Project XL— a program which encourages businesses to voluntarily lower their emissions beyond legal requirements. The company has extensive environmental management systems in place, including audits, policy, reporting, community involvement and employee training. Through its waste minimization programs, solid waste has been halved since 1991.

The company's toxic release inventory (TRI) is the worst in the alcoholic beverage industry. A-B notes, however, that about 80 percent of the TRI is attributable to can-making operations, which other brewers do not have.

EEO: In 1996, Anheuser-Busch achieved a higher than average rating in both diversity categories, placing them easily in the top third of S&P 500 companies. Two women and five minorities served on Anheuser-Busch's 17-member board. Of 58 corporate officers at the company, four were women and four were minorities.

Anheuser-Busch representatives serve on many committees that promote equal employment opportunities. The company is on the Employer Subcommittee of the President's Committee on Employment of People with Disabilities. A-B also received a 1995 award from the NAACP.

In 1996, a bottler for Anheuser-Busch sued the company supervisor for gender discrimination.

Community Involvement: In 1996, Anheuser-Busch's charitable giving totaled $28 million in cash, which was equal to 1.48 percent of the company's pretax earnings for that year. In terms of the actual dollar amount donated by the company, the level of cash contributions in 1996 was identical to that of 1995, which was 1.92 percent of the company's earnings for that year.

Anheuser-Busch, through its Foundation and corporate funds, supports organizations involved primarily in higher education, health care, and programs for minorities and youth. In 1997, the Foundation gave a $1.5 million gift to the Harris-Stowe State College, a predominantly black institution, for expansion of the campus. The company has been a major sponsor of The College Fund (formerly The United Negro College Fund), the Lou Rawls Parade of Stars telethon, and the National Urban League.

Anheuser-Busch has sponsored many programs and campaigns to promote alcohol awareness.

Workplace Information: All of A-B's brewery employees belong to the International Brotherhood of Teamsters, netting them high hourly wages and good job security. The union is generally happy with the company's labor relations and optimistic about settling occasional disputes.

The records of the Occupational Safety and Health Administration indicate that Anheuser-Busch underwent eight health and safety inspections from 1994 to 1996. The violations reported by OSHA as a result of the inspections include two classified as "serious." The company was required to pay $3,520, or an average of $440 per inspection, as a result of its violations. In comparison, the median amount of fines per inspection for other companies in the food, beverage, and household products industries was $1,515.

Apple Computer, Inc.

STOCK SYMBOL: AAPL
STOCK EXCHANGE: NNM

Environment	C
Women's Advancement	B
Minority Advancement	C
Charitable Giving	D
Community Outreach	C?
Family Benefits	N
Workplace Issues	A?
Social Disclosure	B

Based in Cupertino, California, Apple Computer is America's second largest computer manufacturer, with sales of $9.8 billion in 1996 and a total of 10,896 employees worldwide. The company designs, manufactures, and markets microprocessor-based personal computers and related products.

Environment: Apple has an environmental policy, but does not publish a corporate environmental report. Apple has implemented an integrated environmental management system and provides environmental health and safety (EH&S) training to employees. It also presents awards to employees for their contribution to environmental issues. Apple does not have a written pollution prevention policy or a company-wide pollution prevention program; however, the company has established annual reduction goals for solid waste. The company also has a corporate policy on community involvement relating to local environmental concerns; however, it does not have any community advisory panels.

Apple does not have a written policy on product stewardship, but states that it does evaluate its products with the objective of reducing their life-cycle impacts on the environment. In the selection of suppliers, Apple conducts or reviews environmental audits on suppliers' facilities and determines whether the supplier has necessary permits. The company has an environmental audit program, which has worldwide standards and applicability. Internationally, Apple Computer follows US regulations in the US and local regulations abroad. Apple does not have any reportable toxic emissions.

EEO: In 1996, Apple Computer, Inc.'s seven-member board of directors included one woman and one minority. Of ten corporate officers at the company, two were women and none were minorities.

Apple sponsored a forum in 1996 given by PROGRESS, (the Professional Gay, Lesbian and Bisexual Related Employee Support Summit) on a variety of workplace issues, such as the extension of benefits to gay employees and domestic partners and other equal workplace rights. To reduce harassment in the workplace, the company has assigned leaders to enforce a "zero tolerance" policy, and holds managers responsible in performance reviews. In 1994, Elizabeth Birch, the director of worldwide litigation and human resources at Apple, resigned to become the head of the Human Rights Campaign Fund, the largest gay and lesbian rights organization, based in Washington, D.C.

In 1994, Texas county commissioners threatened to rescind a $750,000 tax break because Apple extended its benefits to gay couples, but Apple held its policy.

Community Involvement: In 1994, Apple Computer, Inc. made $1 million in cash contributions to charitable institutions, the equivalent of 0.20 percent of the company's earnings before taxes that year. The company also made in-kind donations of products and services totaling $6 million in the same year.

The vast majority of Apple's philanthropic giving is in non-monetary support, primarily in the form of donated computers, training, and support. The company is also particularly interested in K-12 programs for at-risk children. Apple is part of a collaboration to provide 106,000 K-12 schools with web pages along with IBM K-12 Education, Vanderbilt University, and Computers for Education. The web pages will have the capacity to host over three million teacher pages and 50 million student pages.

Recipients of donations from Apple must adhere to the company's internal nondiscrimination policies.

Workplace Information: OSHA records indicate that Apple was inspected twice from 1994 to 1996, receiving only incidental violations and $635 in fines, averaging $317 per inspection. In comparison, the median amount of fines per inspection for other companies in the electronic manufacturing industries was $1,347.

In 1994, Apple restructuring led to the termination of approximately 1,760 jobs. In 1993, the company cut its workforce by 2,500 employees.

Applied Materials

STOCK SYMBOL: AMAT
STOCK EXCHANGE: NNM

Environment	B
Women's Advancement	C
Minority Advancement	A
Charitable Giving	A
Community Outreach	B
Family Benefits	A
Workplace Issues	B
Social Disclosure	A

Founded in 1967, Applied Materials was the first semiconductor fabrication equipment maker to reach $1 billion in sales, which it achieved in 1993. The Santa Clara, California-based company now controls about 30 percent of the market, deriving nearly two-thirds of its revenues outside the U.S. Revenues for 1996 were over $4 billion. AMAT has about 11,400 employees.

Environment: Applied Materials has an environmental policy and has implemented an integrated environmental management system. The company provides Environmental Health and Safety (EH&S) training to all employees. Applied Materials has written a pollution prevention policy and has initiated a company-wide pollution prevention program, which establishes reduction goals for point sources, fugitive emissions, and solid waste. Applied Materials recently formed a Green Initiative within the company that allows it to strategically address the environmental impact of its entire product line. The company also has a corporate policy on community involvement relating to environmental concerns. Applied Materials has no reportable toxic emissions.

AMAT was one of the first Silicon Valley companies to completely phase out Ozone Depleting Chemicals well before the mandated Clean Air Act deadline. AMAT's Emergency Response Program recently won the Peninsula Conservation Center Foundation Award, being recognized for going beyond regulatory requirements and contributing to overall employee awareness of safety and environmental concerns. The company is an active member of the Business Environmental Network in Silicon Valley and provides support to a number of environmental organizations.

Applied Materials' average toxic releases and transfers during the years 1994–1996 were the lowest compared to the industry sample. Furthermore, its emissions decreased by more than four-fifths during those years, one of the best performances within the industry sample.

EEO: In 1996, AMAT's board totaled nine directors, including one woman and one minority, while one of a total of 29 corporate officers was a woman, and 11 were minorities. AMAT operates mentoring programs, recruitment programs, and support networks for both women and minorities.

Community Involvement: In 1996, AMAT's charitable giving totaled $4.5 million in cash, which was equal to 0.49 percent of the company's pretax earnings for that year. In terms of the actual dollar amount donated by the company, the level of cash contributions in 1996 represented a decrease of 40 percent from that of 1995, which was 0.64 percent of the company's earnings for that year. The company's in-kind giving — the donation of products or services — came to a total of $4 million in 1996. Applied Materials reports that it "was the founder, and remains committed to, Joint Venture: Silicon Valley Network, The 21st Century Education Initiative's Challenge 2000, and CHARITech's Center on Corporate Citizenship."

Workplace Information: The records of the Occupational Safety and Health Administration indicate that AMAT was not inspected from 1994 to 1996. Consequently no fines or violations were assessed to the company.

Employees of Austin-based subsidiary, Applied Manufacturing and Engineering Technology, are expected to spend 20 percent of their time exploring enhancement possibilities for products and processes. CEO James Morgan has eschewed such executive perks as reserved parking and luxurious offices.

Weapons Contracts: In 1994, AMAT received Defense Department contracts worth $4.7 million (less than 0.5 percent of total revenues). These contracts were not weapons-related.

International: AMAT created a wholly-owned Japanese subsidiary in 1979 and now derives half its revenues from that market. The company relies mainly on local talent and reports that the primary characteristic that distinguishes it from other firms is its efforts to promote women to senior positions.

Armstrong World Industries

STOCK SYMBOL: ACK
STOCK EXCHANGES: NY, B, CH, P, PH

Environment	B
Women's Advancement	F
Minority Advancement	B
Charitable Giving	A
Community Outreach	D
Family Benefits	D
Workplace Issues	A
Social Disclosure	A

A rmstrong, based in Lancaster, Pennsylvania, is a leading manufacturer of interior furnishings, including floor coverings and building and industry products. In 1997, Armstrong had 10,500 employees and sales of $2.2 billion.

Environment: Armstrong has a formal corporate environmental policy, environmental operating principles, and an annual environmental, health, and safety report available to the public. In 1997, the company completed 20 environmental facility audits.

A participant in EPA's 33/50 program, the company surpassed its 50 percent reduction goal in 1991. Despite a 14 percent increase in sales from 1991 to 1995, the company's solid waste generation has dropped 42 percent and its Bright Light$ program, based on EPA's Green Lights, has saved 6 million kwh of power since its 1992 inception.

EEO: In 1996, Armstrong World Industries' eight member board of directors included no women and two minorities. Of 18 corporate officers at the company, one was a woman and none were minorities. The company reports that in 1997, the board increased to nine members, and a second woman joined the ranks of corporate officers.

Armstrong World Industries was selected by the U.S. Department of Labor to receive the 1996 Exemplary Voluntary Efforts Award. The Award recognizes the corporation as one of the country's leaders in equal employment opportunity practices.

Community Involvement: Armstrong World Industries' charitable contributions totaled $1.95 million in cash in 1996. The $1.95 million cash-giving figure represented the equivalent of 0.80 percent of the company's pretax earnings for the same year.

The Armstrong Foundation considers higher education and community funds to be its primary areas of focus. In 1997, the foundation gave $550,000 to the United Way of Lancaster County in Lancaster, Pennsylvania. Other grants given that year include $161,546 to the

National Merit Scholarship Corporation in Evanston, Illinois, and $95,000 to Millersville University in Pennsylvania.

Family Benefits: Armstrong offers such flexible scheduling options as a compressed work week, work-at-home arrangements, flextime, job sharing, and part-time return to work following leave.

Workplace Information: OSHA records indicate that Armstrong was inspected three times from 1994 to 1996, receiving only one "serious" violation and a total of $1,625 in fines. Armstrong reports that it was inspected four times in 1997, and received no citations or fines.

A subsidiary of Armstrong merged with Dal-Tile International in December, 1995, after which Dal-Tile laid off 202 workers from the former subsidiary with just one week of severance pay. Armstrong, which retained 34 percent ownership of the merged company, claims the decision was entirely that of Dal-Tile.

International: Armstrong has recently constructed a ceiling manufacturing plant in Shanghai, China.

Product Information: Though Armstrong has ceased producing asbestos-containing products, it remains embroiled in the ongoing liability litigation. In May 1996, 20 companies including Armstrong agreed to pay $200 million to settle current claims and $1.3 billion to settle future claims. An appeals court rejected the class action settlement.

A finalist in 1992 and 1993, Armstrong earned the Malcolm Baldrige National Quality Award in 1996.

Ashland Inc.

STOCK SYMBOL: ASH
STOCK EXCHANGES: NY, B, C, CH, P, PH

Environment	B
Women's Advancement	F?
Minority Advancement	C?
Charitable Giving	A
Community Outreach	N
Family Benefits	N
Workplace Issues	C?
Social Disclosure	C

Based in Russell, Kentucky, Ashland Inc. is a diversified energy corporation. One of the nation's largest independent refiners, the company markets gasoline, motor oil, and other petroleum products. Ashland is also the largest North American distributor of chemicals and plastics. It produces natural gas and crude oil (Valvoline) and has interests in two coal companies. In 1996, revenues were $12.1 billion, and the company had 36,100 employees.

Environment: Ashland Inc. has an environmental policy and a corporate environmental report, which is updated annually and is available on the internet. The company has implemented an integrated environmental management system and provides environmental health and safety (EH&S) training to all employees. It also considers contribution towards EH&S goals in job performance reviews for all employees, and presents awards to employees for their contribution to environmental issues. Ashland has a written pollution prevention policy and has initiated a company-wide pollution prevention program. The company also has a corporate policy on community involvement relating to local environmental concerns, and currently has community advisory panels at eight of its facilities. Ashland has a written policy on product stewardship and evaluates its products with the objective of reducing their life-cycle impacts on the environment.

Ashland is a member of the Wildlife Habitat Council, a non-profit organization established in 1988 by corporations and conservation groups. Ashland has established three sites to protect, preserve and enhance native wildlife in Kentucky and Louisiana, and a fourth site is being considered. The company also participates in EPA's WasteWi$e, 33/50, and Green Lights Programs.

Ashland Oil's average toxic releases and transfers during the years 1994–1996 were less than the industry sample average. Emissions decreased by an average of close to one tenth annually during those years, an above average performance. The company ranked fifth out of 15 for CEP's Campaign for Cleaner Corporations' 1997 Petroleum Refining Report.

Rather than install a safety system that would prevent hydrogen fluoride (HF) from being vaporized, Ashland opted to pay an $800,000 fine. When released into the air, HF forms a toxic cloud that can cause serious respiratory damage and death as far as six miles from the site of vaporization.

EEO: In 1996, Ashland Inc.'s board totaled 16 directors, including one woman and one minority, while none of a total of 25 corporate officers were women, and none were minorities. Ashland offers diversity awareness training and maintains recruitment and apprenticeship programs for minorities.

Community Involvement: In 1996, Ashland Inc.'s charitable giving totaled $5 million in cash, which was equal to 1.61 percent of the company's pretax earnings for that year.

Workplace Information: The records of the Occupational Safety and Health Administration indicate that Ashland Inc. underwent one health and safety inspection from 1994 to 1996. The violations reported by OSHA as a result of the inspection include four classified as "serious." The company was required to pay $270 as a result of its violations. In comparison, the median amount of fines per inspection for other companies in the extractive business was $2,941.

Weapons Contracts: In 1994, Ashland had $23.8 million — or 0.2 percent of total revenues for the year — in fuel-related contracts with the Department of Defense.

Legal Proceedings: In May 1994, Ashland Chemical was one of ten companies found guilty of negligence in a toxic exposure suit brought by 600 former and current Lockheed workers who suffered physical ailments from working with certain chemicals during the 1970s and 1980s. According to the ruling, the companies failed to provide sufficient warnings about usage in their product packaging and in material safety data sheets.

Atlantic Richfield Corporation

STOCK SYMBOL: ARC
STOCK EXCHANGES: NY, TO, B, C, CH, PH, P

A tlantic Richfield Corporation (ARCO), based in Los Angeles, California, is the sixth-largest oil company in the US, and the leading gas retailer on the West Coast. ARCO also has natural gas, chemical, and coal operations. In 1996, sales were $18.6 billion, and ARCO employed 22,800 people.

Environment	REV
Women's Advancement	B?
Minority Advancement	D?
Charitable Giving	B
Community Outreach	B
Family Benefits	N
Workplace Issues	A?
Social Disclosure	B

Environment: Atlantic Richfield Corporation has an environmental policy and publishes a corporate environmental report, which is updated periodically, and is available on the internet. ARCO has implemented an integrated environmental management system and provides environmental health and safety (EH&S) training to all employees, including consultants/contractors. At ARCO, EH&S awareness is promoted through Corporate Environmental Achievement Awards, Waste Minimization Awards, and Safety Awards. ARCO has initiated a companywide pollution prevention program. The company also has a corporate policy on community involvement relating to local environmental concerns, and currently has community advisory panels at all of its facilities. ARCO has a written policy on product stewardship and evaluates some of its products with the objective of reducing their life-cycle impacts on the environment. The company has a partnership with the World Wildlife Fund. It also participated in EPA's Green Lights and 33/50 Programs.

Atlantic Richfield's average toxic releases and transfers during the years 1993–1994 were less than the industry sample average. Although emissions decreased by about five percent during those years, its performance was still below average within its industry sample. The company ranked last for CEP's Campaign for Cleaner Corporations' (C-3) 1997 Petroleum Refining Report. It was placed on C-3's "worst performer" list.

According to a 1997 shareholder proposal, ARCO has paid several million dollars to an oil company owned by the Burmese military junta for seismic data and exploration rights to two off-shore blocks. ARCO vice-president Roger Truitt attended a ceremony involving Myanmar's (Burma's) national oil and gas company; ARCO reports that the ceremony was attended by a number of industry and government people. Also present were the chief of secret police and a member of the junta who had threatened to kill Nobel peace prize–winner Aung San Suu Kyi the previous week.

In 1996, Arco acknowledged responsibility for an estimated 10,000 gallon petroleum spill from a ruptured pipeline endangering wildlife in the Long Beach channel, and agreed to pay for all costs of cleanup. ARCO reports that the cleanup proceeded quickly with minimal impact on the environment and wildlife.

EEO: In 1996, Atlantic Richfield's 14-member board of directors included two women and one minority. Of 18 corporate officers at the company, two were women and none were minorities. As an employer of minorities, Atlantic Richfield ranked higher than any other company surveyed by *The Oil Daily* in December, 1996, though few minorities appear to have reached the ranks of senior managment. The company was also one of the largest employers of women. Minorities make up 29 percent of ARCO's workforce.

Community Involvement: Atlantic Richfield's charitable contributions totaled $33 million in cash in 1996. The $33 million cash-giving figure represented the equivalent of 1.22 percent of the company's pretax earnings for the same year, and a decrease of 6.06 percent from ARCO's cash contributions in 1995. In 1995, ARCO donated 1.52 percent of its pretax earnings.

Approximately $5.7 million of the $10 million in grants given by the ARCO foundation in 1995 was given through matching grants and volunteer grants. The foundation typically gives priority to employee programs over direct grants to reinforce employee and retiree support of community causes. In March, 1997, Atlantic Richfield presented $10 million to the Walt Disney Concert Hall project in Los Angeles. The Hall, which has been facing financial difficulties, would become the home of the Los Angeles Philharmonic.

Workplace Information: OSHA records indicate that Atlantic Richfield was inspected once from 1994 to 1996. Violations included one classified as "serious" for a total of $600 in fines.

23

Avery Dennison Corporation

STOCK SYMBOL: AVY
STOCK EXCHANGES: NY, CH, P

Environment	D
Women's Advancement	F
Minority Advancement	F
Charitable Giving	N
Community Outreach	N
Family Benefits	N
Workplace Issues	F?
Social Disclosure	C

Based in Pasadena, California, Avery Dennison Corporation is a major producer of self-adhesive materials. It also is a market leader in office products under the Avery and Dennison brands (the two companies merged in 1990), manufacturing tags for the retail industry, labels for consumer products, and pressure-sensitive stamps for the postal service. The company has operations in 27 countries (Western Europe, Asia Pacific, Latin America). In 1996, revenues were $3.2 billion and there were 15,800 employees worldwide.

Environment: Avery Dennison did not respond to CEP's environmental questionnaire and does not publish a corporate environmental report. The company does consider contribution towards EH&S goals in the job performance reviews of managers. In the selection of suppliers, Avery Dennison conducts or reviews environmental audits on suppliers' facilities. The company has an environmental audit program, but does not make audit findings available to the public.

Avery Dennison's average total toxic releases and transfers during the years 1993–1994 were less than the industry sample average. Emissions decreased slightly during those years, a below average performance.

In June, 1993, its Fasson Merchant Products division was fined $15,000 for excessive organic compound emissions and failure to properly maintain pollution control equipment. The company's 1994 10-K Report states that Avery Dennison "has made a substantial investment in solvent capture and control units, and solvent-free systems" during the past several years.

EEO: In 1996, Avery Dennison Corp.'s board totaled 12 directors, including one woman and one minority.

Community Involvement: The Corporate Giving Directory reports that Avery Dennison's mode of corporate giving is a general support program through which it funds "programs and projects which address specific community challenges and needs…in which self-support or broad-based community support is the ultimate goal or objective." Preference in funding is given to organizations at which employees are active participants.

Workplace Information: The records of the Occupational Safety and Health Administration indicate that Avery Dennison Corp. underwent five health and safety inspections from 1994 to 1996. The violations reported by OSHA as a result of the inspections include seven classified as "serious." The company was required to pay $8,805 as a result of its violations. The average amount of fines per inspection was $1,761; in comparison, the median amount of fines per inspection for other companies in the extractive business was $2,941.

The company offers defined benefit and defined contribution savings plans, and participation in an ESOP (for non-union employees).

Avon Products, Inc.

STOCK SYMBOL: AVP
STOCK EXCHANGES: NY, B, C, CH, P, PH

Environment	A
Women's Advancement	A
Minority Advancement	A
Charitable Giving	A
Community Outreach	C
Family Benefits	B
Workplace Issues	A
Social Disclosure	A

Based in New York City, Avon is a leading manufacturer and distributor of beauty products, fragrances, jewelry, and gift products. In 1996, the company had sales of $4.8 billion and 31,800 employees, 75 percent of whom are based outside the U.S. International sales account for nearly 65 percent of total revenues.

Environment: Avon has an environmental policy and a corporate environmental report, which is updated annually. The company has implemented an integrated environmental management system and provides environmental health and safety (EH&S) training to all employees. Avon has written a pollution prevention policy and has initiated a company-wide pollution prevention program, which establishes reduction goals for point sources and solid waste. Avon has a written commitment on product stewardship, a product stewardship review board, and evaluates its products with the objective of reducing their life-cycle impacts on the environment. In the selection of suppliers, Avon will only work with suppliers who are not knowingly out of compliance with local laws and regulations. Avon also has a corporate policy on community involvement relating to environmental concerns.

Avon's average total toxic releases and transfers during the years 1994–1996 were below the industry sample average. Emissions decreased an average of about two-fifths annually during those years, the best performance in the sample.

EEO: In 1996, four women and two minorities served on Avon's 13-member board. Nine of the top 25 paid employees were women, and two were minorities. In January, 1997, Avon was presented with the Catalyst Award for their women/minority advancement efforts.

The company utilizes the "slating process", a high potential job selection process used to expand the pool of internal candidates for open positions. By incorporating slating, the company reports that "the pool of high potentials is screened to ensure adequate representation of minorities and women." The company also reported that it formed a Communication Systems and Managing Diversity Program to encourage employees to support diversity.

In 1996, Avon purchased over $144 million in goods and services from women- and minority-owned businesses.

Community Involvement: In 1996, Avon's charitable giving totaled $13.4 million in cash, which was equal to 2.63 percent of the company's pretax earnings for that year. The company's in-kind giving—the donation of products or services—came to a total of $6.3 million in 1996.

In 1992, Avon created the Worldwide Fund for Women's Health, a global web of programs intended to raise money for, and improve education and awareness of women's most crucial health issues. Avon also initiated a campaign against breast cancer in six countries; in the United States this Breast Cancer Awareness Crusade is contributing millions of dollars to community breast cancer education programs and to early detection services. Although AVON does not currently run a volunteer program for its employees, it is developing a volunteer policy.

Workplace Information: The records of the Occupational Safety and Health Administration indicate that Avon was not inspected from 1994 to 1996. Consequently Avon received no fines or violations.

For the past several years, Avon has been named one of the 100 best companies for working women according to *Working Mother* magazine.

International: In 1997, Avon adopted new supplier standards that prohibit prison, forced, and child labor by all contractors and suppliers. The standards take a stronger position on child labor than on working hours. Avon was instrumental in the development of SA8000, the first international standard on labor rights for companies subcontracting their manufacturing.

Animal Testing: Avon completely eliminated company animal testing in 1990.

Baltimore Gas & Electric

STOCK SYMBOL: BGE
STOCK EXCHANGES: NY, B, C, CH, P, PH

Environment	C
Women's Advancement	C
Minority Advancement	B
Charitable Giving	C
Community Outreach	C
Family Benefits	N
Workplace Issues	B?
Social Disclosure	B

Baltimore Gas & Electric (BG&E) and its subsidiaries are principally involved in producing, purchasing, and selling electricity and purchasing, transporting, and selling natural gas. BG&E, headquartered in Baltimore, Maryland, owns and operates seven steam-electric generating plants in Maryland and maintains a partial interest in three generating facilities in Pennsylvania. In 1996, the company had 9,279 employees and revenues of $3.1 billion.

Environment: During this decade, carbon dioxide emissions from BG&E's fossil-fuel plants will increase about 32 percent, the second largest projected increase among the 25 largest utilities CEP studied. The company's sulfur dioxide emissions are slightly better than the industry average, while its nitrogen oxide emissions are worse. BG&E does not plan to develop additional renewable energy capacity in its service area for at least ten years. The company's generation mix is primarily of coal and nuclear sources.

The company projects that its Conserve 2000 program will reduce overall projected peak energy load by 16 percent. In 1992, the company offered a $100 rebate to customers who exchanged gasoline-powered lawnmowers for electric-run models built by Black & Decker. That year, BG&E also added 100 natural gas-powered vehicles to its fleet. The utility has joined Chrysler and Westinghouse in a consortium with the state of Maryland to conduct electric vehicle research.

In June 1991, BG&E began a program to safely relocate ospreys that have nested on company utility poles.

EEO: In 1996, BG&E's board totaled 14 directors, including two women and two minorities, while one of a total of 18 corporate officers was a woman, and one was a minority.

BG&E is one of several hundred companies that have begun implementing programs under a voluntary pledge with the U.S. Department of Labor's Women's Bureau. The company has begun a career advancement program and pilot mentoring program for female employees in compliance with its pledge.

In 1996, Baltimore Gas & Electric purchased over $70.3 million in goods and services from women- and minority-owned businesses. The company's total purchasing for that year was $839 million.

Community Involvement: Baltimore Gas & Electric's charitable contributions totaled about $4.1 million in cash in 1996, and $149,720 in in-kind donations. The $4.1 million cash-giving figure represented the equivalent of 0.87 percent.

In 1996, BG&E began a pilot program directed at assisting low-income Baltimore-City residents with their utility bills. While similar programs in other states are usually the result of legislation or mandates from regulatory agencies, cooperation in the plan is voluntary. Under the pilot program, 350 low-income residents will pay as little as 25 percent of their regular bill.

Workplace Information: In 1997, the International Brotherhood of Electrical Workers claimed that the inclusion of only production and maintenance workers in a lost election bid was a violation of fair labor practices by BG&E. The union also claims BG&E bribed workers with the prospect of higher wages after a planned merger with Potomac Electric Power Company.

According to the Occupational Safety and Health Administration's records, BG&E was inspected two times from 1994 to 1996. The OSHA inspectors' citations included two violations classified as "serious." A total of $2,875 in fines, averaging $1,437 per inspection, was assessed to the company following the inspections. In comparison, the median amount of fines per inspection for other companies in the utilities industry was $2,625.

Nuclear Power: BG&E derives about half of its electricity from nuclear power.

🎖 BankAmerica Corporation

STOCK SYMBOL: BAC
STOCK EXCHANGES: NY, B, C, CH, PH, P

Environment	A
Women's Advancement	A
Minority Advancement	A
Charitable Giving	C
Community Outreach	A
Family Benefits	C
Workplace Issues	A
Social Disclosure	A

BankAmerica, headquartered in San Francisco, California, provides banking and other financial services throughout the United States and in selected international markets to consumers and business customers, including corporations, governments, and other institutions. BankAmerica is one of the three largest bank holding companies in the United States, with total assets of $250.8 billion. In 1996, BankAmerica had income of $22 billion and nearly 100,000 employees.

Environment: BankAmerica is the first major bank to establish a comprehensive environmental policy that affects loan decisions, which it began in 1991. Through the program, the bank checks a potential borrower's compliance record and looks for positive environmental effects. According to the company, it places restraints on what the credit can be used for. One example is that a loan to a forest products company stipulated that the debt could not be paid by logging in environmentally sensitive areas. The bank reports that in 1993 it rejected six loans on environmental grounds, but for business reasons cannot disclose any names. BankAmerica's potential suppliers are asked if they are certified or are planning to be certified under ISO 14001, although they are not required to be certified at this time.

In addition to setting standards for groups it does business with, BankAmerica has instituted strong internal programs. BankAmerica is an endorser of the CERES principles and is one of the few in its industry that publishes an annual environmental report. From 1994 to 1996, the company reduced paper use by 26 percent. In 1997, EPA named BankAmerica its "Partner of the Year" for energy reduction achievements in the Green Lights program.

From 1991 to 1993, BankAmerica donated $6 million worth of its $2.4 billion Latin American debt to rainforest conservation projects in the region, the largest gift of its kind. Other charitable gifts to environmental causes include a $500,000 grant to the California Institute of Technology to study atmospheric pollution.

EEO: Women make up 69 percent of the bank's workforce, and minorities 41 percent. The diversity training and communications efforts also include gay issues. The company supports a purchasing program with minority entrepreneurs and women business owners.

Community Involvement: BankAmerica Corporation's charitable contributions totaled $29.8 million in cash in 1996, and $2.4 million in in-kind donations. The $29.8 million cash-giving figure represented the equivalent of 0.62 percent of the company's pretax earnings for the same year, and a decrease of 6 percent from the company's cash contributions in 1995, when it contributed 0.65 percent of its pretax earnings

The foundation supports both through grants and loans areas such as health, human resources, community and economic development, education, culture and arts. Support is also given for special programs developed by the foundation. BankAmerica's Volunteer Network allows salaried employees time off work with pay to participate in the company's volunteer activities. In 1996, BankAmerica won an Award for Excellence in Corporate Community Service from the Points of Light Foundation. BankAmerica's employee volunteer program has vowed to complete 1.25 million hours of community volunteer service by the year 2000. Also in 1996, the company won a United Way Spirit Award and a Corporate Business Ethics Award from *Business Ethics* magazine for its commitment to the environment, community reinvestment and high ethical standards. BankAmerica was rated in 1995 with an outstanding Record of Meeting Credit Needs. BankAmerica's Board of Directors actively considers the Community Reinvestment Act (CRA) in their planning process and regularly reviews CRA activities.

Workplace Information: According to the Occupational Safety and Health Administration's records, BankAmerica Corporation was not inspected from 1994 to 1996. Consequently no violations or fines were assessed to the company.

⚫ BankBoston Corporation

STOCK SYMBOL: BKB
STOCK EXCHANGES: NY, B, C, CH, PH, P

Environment	N
Women's Advancement	A
Minority Advancement	A
Charitable Giving	B
Community Outreach	A
Family Benefits	C
Workplace Issues	A
Social Disclosure	A

BankBoston provides retail, corporate and international banking services. Its banking subsidiaries operate throughout the U.S. and 23 foreign countries. The firm, headquartered in Boston, Massachusetts, employs 22,898 employees and had assets of $69 billion as of December 31,1997.

EEO: In 1996, BankBoston Corp. achieved a higher than average rating in both diversity categories, placing them easily in the top third of S&P 500 companies. One woman and three minorities served on BankBoston's 18-member board. Of 6,172 corporate officers at the company, 3,101 were women and 600 were minorities, while three of the top 25 paid employees were women, and one was a minority.

Also in 1996, BankBoston purchased over $11.3 million in goods and services from women- and minority-owned businesses.

BankBoston offers mentoring programs, apprenticeship programs, recruitment programs, support networks, and maintains diversity goals for both women and minorities. It has also set up affinity groups and organizes forums on workplace diversity.

Community Involvement: In 1996, BankBoston's charitable giving totaled $11.4 million in cash, which was equal to 1.01 percent of the company's pretax earnings for that year. In terms of the actual dollar amount donated by the company, the level of cash contributions in 1996 represented a decrease of 16 percent from that of 1995, which was 0.94 percent of the company's earnings for that year. The company's in-kind giving—the donation of products or services—came to a total of $900,000 in 1996.

BankBoston provided $26 million in financing for Ruggles Center, the largest development in the history of Roxbury and the largest minority-owned real estate development in the country. Announced on Martin Luther King Day in 1992, the project provided some 2,000 construction jobs and potentially as many as 3,000 permanent jobs to Roxbury. The company has also contributed more than $500,000 in funds to Community Development Corporations. BankBoston has gained recognition from the Small Business Administration as a Certified Lender and was among the first to be named a Preferred Lender.

The BankBoston Charitable Foundation administers employee programs, the Employee Matching Gifts Program and the Golden Eagle Volunteer of the Year Awards. The two main areas of interest are economic opportunity and education. The bank offers programs to improve neighborhoods, restore or create affordable housing, support entrepreneurship and small business development. The company operates the Eagle Corps volunteer program to facilitate employee volunteerism. Through its partnership school programs, BankBoston supports public education. The bank is also committed to adult education, employment and job training, and food and shelter assistance.

Family Benefits: BankBoston makes a resource/referral service for child care available to employees with children. The company also offers a Snowy Day program, which provides free on-site child care at six locations on days that schools are closed in New England due to snow. The company is also a member of the American Business Collaboration, a group of companies planning to invest over $100 million in dependent care projects by the year 2000.

The company offers such flexible scheduling options as a compressed work week, work-at-home arrangements, flextime, job sharing, and part-time return to work following leave.

Workplace Information: The records of the Occupational Safety and Health Administration indicate that BankBoston Corp. was not inspected from 1994 to 1996. Consequently no fines or violations were assessed to the company. In comparison, the median amount of fines per inspection for other companies in the service industry, such as banks and communications companies, was $573.

International: Since opening its first international office in 1917, BankBoston's global network has grown to be the third largest among U.S. banks.

Bankers Trust

STOCK SYMBOL: BT

STOCK EXCHANGES: NY, B, C, CH, PH, P

Environment	N
Women's Advancement	F
Minority Advancement	B?
Charitable Giving	B
Community Outreach	B
Family Benefits	C
Workplace Issues	D
Social Disclosure	B

Bankers Trust is a commercial and wholesale banking firm headquartered in New York City. In 1996, Bankers Trust had income of $9.5 billion. The company has approximately 15,200 employees and has offices in nearly 50 countries.

Environment: The firm established an environmental service group, a team of professional individuals devoted to public utilities who assist companies facing environmental responsibility. It also supplies funds to help manage hazardous waste clean-ups.

EEO: In 1996, Bankers Trust's board totaled 12 directors, including one woman and one minority. None of the seven corporate officers were women and none were minorities.

Bankers Trust offers Support Networks and maintains diversity goals for its female employees. Almost half of Bankers Trust's employees are women.

Community Involvement: Bankers Trust's charitable contributions totaled $9.5 million in cash in 1996. The $9.5 million cash-giving figure represented the equivalent of 1.09 percent of the company's pretax earnings for the same year, and a decrease of 9 percent from the company's cash contributions in 1995. In 1995, the company contributed 3.05 percent of its pretax earnings for that year to charity.

Bankers Trust launched a $15 million fund to support community development corporations in New York City. Community development is the main focus area for funding. Through the bank's Volunteer Assistance Fund and the Matching Gifts Program, Bankers Trust supports different groups for community development. The Federal Reserve Bank of New York recognized BT's support with a recent rating of "outstanding" for its compliance with the Community Reinvestment Act (CRA). Bankers Trust launched the $15 million Neighborhood 2000 Fund. This fund will support approximately 50 established nonprofit neighborhood-based community development corporations working to rebuild low- and moderate-income neighborhoods throughout New York City. The primary focus of the bank's philanthropic effort is community development in distressed neighborhoods. BT Foundation's grant support in this area reached over $1.6 million in 1995. BT Foundation's strategy for community revitalization in targeted neighborhoods also includes grants for education, health and environmental projects totaling $986,000. Combined, these grants represent a total investment of $2.6 million in nonprofits working in low- and moderate- income neighborhoods. In 1993, BT established the Bankers Trust Non Profit Property Management Excellence Awards. The bank's Volunteer Assistance Fund involves the bank's workforce in targeting the contributions program. BT promotes economic mobility for members of minority groups through different programs and training.

Family Benefits: Bankers Trust makes on-site or near-site child care, a resource/referral service, and a subsidy for child care available to employees with children.

The company also offers such flexible scheduling options as a compressed work week, work-at-home arrangements, flextime, and job sharing.

Workplace Information: According to the Occupational Safety and Health Administration's records, Bankers Trust New York Corp. was not inspected from 1994 to 1996. Consequently no violations or fines were assessed to the company. In comparison, the median amount of fines per inspection for other companies in the service industry, such as banks and communications companies, was $573.

International: A 1995 shareholder resolution filed by religious investors with Bankers Trust, Chase Manhattan, and J.P. Morgan, asks the banks to report on their official position concerning "structural adjustment programs" in developing countries, and to analyze the effect these have on debtor countries' people, economy, and ability to repay debt.

C.R. Bard

Environment	F
Women's Advancement	D?
Minority Advancement	C?
Charitable Giving	A
Community Outreach	B
Family Benefits	N
Workplace Issues	N
Social Disclosure	C

C.R. Bard, based in Murray Hill, New Jersey, is a leading manufacturer of vascular, urological, encological, and surgical products. In 1980, Bard introduced the first heart catheter, a balloon-like device that is placed within blocked arteries and inflated to clear the passageway. The product helped spark strong financial performance though it was subsequently the focus of considerable adverse publicity. In 1996, total revenues for the company climbed to $1.2 billion and its employment figures stood at approximately 9,800.

Environment: C.R. Bard did not provide a response to CEP's environment questionnaire in 1997. The company does not currently publish a corporate environmental report.

C.R. Bard's average total toxic releases and transfers during the years 1993–1994 were the highest in the industry sample. Emissions decreased, however, by about a fifth during those years, a better than average performance.

EEO: In 1996, C.R. Bard's 13-member board of directors included one woman and one minority. Of a total of 20 corporate officers working at the company in the same year, two were women and none were minorities.

Community Involvement: In 1996, C.R. Bard's charitable giving totaled $2.1 million in cash, which was equal to 2.04 percent of the company's pretax earnings for that year. In 1995, Bard contributed 1.70 percent of the company's earnings for that year. The percentage increase reflects a drop in earnings for the company; cash contributions stayed at the same amount. The company's in-kind giving — the donation of products or services — came to a total of $1.9 million in 1996.

Some organizations to which Bard has donated include the American Foundation for Urologic Disease, the Cardiovascular and Interventional Radiology Research and Education Foundation, the National Medical Fellowships, Inc., the University of Texas–Houston, and Youth for Understanding International Exchange. The matching gifts program accounts for one-eighth of total foundation giving, the majority of which goes to education. The foundation has an allocation for each state; a committee at each location makes decisions about local donations.

Family Benefits: C.R. Bard did not provide CEP with any information on family benefits in 1997.

Workplace Information: The records of the Occupational Safety and Health Administration indicate that C.R. Bard was not inspected from 1994 to 1996. Consequently no fines or violations were assessed to the company. As inspections are most commonly called in response to a complaint regarding the health or safety conditions at a company or one of its facilities, a lack of inspections may be an indicator of a relatively sound workplace in terms of safety and health. However, it is not particularly unusual for OSHA to report that it has not inspected a company over the course of several years.

Barnett Banks

STOCK SYMBOL: BBI
STOCK EXCHANGES: NY, B, CH, P

Environment	N
Women's Advancement	A
Minority Advancement	B
Charitable Giving	B
Community Outreach	C
Family Benefits	C?
Workplace Issues	C?
Social Disclosure	A

With assets of $38.3 billion, Jacksonville, Florida–based Barnett Banks is the largest bank holding company in Florida and the 21st largest in the U.S. The company operates 31 banks, including 621 banking offices in Georgia and Florida. It also owns seven nonbanking affiliates that provide trust management, brokerage, and mortgage banking services. In 1996, Barnett had 22,179 employees and revenues of $3.8 billion.

EEO: In 1996, Barnett Banks' achieved a higher than average rating in both diversity categories, placing them easily in the top third of S&P 500 companies. Two women and two minorities served on Barnett Banks' 14-member board. Of 303 corporate officers at the company, 87 were women and 20 were minorities, while four of the top 25 paid employees were women, and none were minorities.

Barnett Bank's workplace initiatives include diversity awareness workshops, a Diversity Report Card, a diversity council and an independent arbiter.

Barnett Banks offers mentoring programs, recruitment programs, support networks, maintains diversity goals, and gives special consideration for management training to both women and minorities.

Community Investment: Barnett Banks' charitable contributions totaled $10 million in cash in 1996, and $2 million in in-kind donations. The $10 million cash-giving figure represented the equivalent of 1.10 percent of the company's pretax earnings for the same year, and was identical to the company's cash contributions in 1995. In 1995, the company contributed 1.22 percent of its pretax earnings for that year to charity.

Barnett Banks was one of the corporations that on May of 1996 unveiled a statewide scholarship program—Take Stock in Children—aimed at providing scholarships and mentoring to thousands of school children in Florida, contributing $2 million.

In June 1992, Barnett set a five-year goal of more than $2 billion for residential and business loans in low- and moderate-income communities. Barnett's Home Ownership Made Easy (H.O.M.E.) program, which has financed 1,393 mortgages totaling nearly $72 million, provides low- and middle-income families with below-market rates, easier down payment terms, and lower closing costs.

Family Benefits: Barnett Banks ranked in the top ten of *Working Mother* magazine's 1994 list of 100 best companies for mothers, and has been included in the magazine's subsequent top 100 issues. The company's impressive child care services operate three care centers serving over 450 children, have a kindergarten learning center at headquarters, and provide various backup care and after-school, holiday, and summer programs.

The bank also offers a wide assortment of flexible work arrangements, including a compressed work week, work-at-home arrangements, flextime, and job sharing. Barnett has a full-time work/family coordinator.

Workplace Information: According to the Occupational Safety and Health Administration's records, Barnett Banks was not inspected from 1994 to 1996. Consequently no violations or fines were assessed to the company.

Working Mother magazine reports that turnover among hourly employees dropped from 32 to 25 percent in 1992, indicating an overall increase in workplace satisfaction among hourly employees at the company.

31

Bausch & Lomb Inc.

STOCK SYMBOL: BOL
STOCK EXCHANGES: NY, B, CH, PH, P

Environment	B
Women's Advancement	B
Minority Advancement	B
Charitable Giving	A
Community Outreach	C
Family Benefits	N
Workplace Issues	F?
Social Disclosure	A

N ow over 140 years old, Bausch & Lomb makes optical products such as sunglasses, binoculars, and telescopes; its health care business includes eye care products, dental implants, and hearing aids. Based in Rochester, New York, Bausch & Lomb has 13,000 employees and in 1996 sales reached $1.9 billion.

Environment: Bausch & Lomb does not currently publish a corporate environmental report, but has an environmental policy and has implemented an integrated environmental management system (EMS), which is in the process of being updated. Bausch & Lomb provides Environmental Health and Safety (EH&S) training to EH&S staff, facility staff, and other employees as needed. The company also considers contribution towards EH&S goals in the job performance reviews of EH&S staff and line managers in some business units. Bausch & Lomb has a written pollution prevention policy and a company-wide pollution prevention program. It does not have a written commitment to product stewardship, but life-cycle impact evaluations of some products occurs on a decentralized basis. Bausch & Lomb has an environmental audit program with worldwide standards/applicability. In 1996, 20 percent of U.S. facilities and 17 percent of international facilities were audited. Internationally, the company states that it follows U.S. regulations in the US and abroad unless local regulations are stricter.

Bausch & Lomb's average total toxic releases and transfers during the years 1994–1996 were slightly higher than the industry sample average. Emissions decreased by an average of about a fifth annually during those years, a better than average performance.

EEO: In 1996, two women and one minority served on Bausch & Lomb Inc.'s 11-member board. Of 21 corporate officers at the company, two were women and one was a minority. Two of the top 25 paid employees were women, and one was a minority.

Bausch and Lomb is one of over 100 companies that have joined the ranks of the the U.S. Department of Labor's Working Women Count Honor Roll. Members of the honor roll pledge to introduce programs and practices to improve conditions for women in the workplace. Bausch and Lomb committed to improving its performance in providing pay and benefits for its female employees.

Bausch & Lomb Inc. offers mentoring programs, recruitment programs, support networks, maintains diversity goals, and gives special consideration for management training to both women and minorities.

Community Involvement: In 1996, Bausch & Lomb Inc.'s charitable giving totaled $2.6 million in cash, which was equal to 1 percent of the company's pretax earnings for that year. The dollar amount of cash contributions in 1996 represented an increase of 5.70 percent from that of 1995, which was 1.55 percent of the company's earnings for that year. The company's in-kind giving—the donation of products or services—came to a total of $1.3 million in 1996.

Bausch & Lomb, in collaboration with Prevent Blindness America, started a program in 1994 called Making the Grade. This program provides free and accurate eye exams for children in schools in twenty-five cities throughout the country.

Workplace Information: OSHA records indicate that Bausch & Lomb was inspected once from 1994 to 1996. Violations included eight classified as "serious" for a total of $6,555 in fines, or $819 per inspection. In comparison, the median amount of fines per inspection for other cosmetics and health products companies was $2,266.

Animal Testing: Bausch & Lomb contracts with outside labs for tests on an undisclosed number of animals per year. The tests are generally for products to be used in the eye. The company is a major contributor to Johns Hopkins' Center for Alternatives to Animal Testing, donating $100,000 yearly.

32

⚜ Baxter International

STOCK SYMBOL: BAX
STOCK EXCHANGES: NY, B, C, CH, PH, P

Environment	A
Women's Advancement	A
Minority Advancement	A
Charitable Giving	A
Community Outreach	B
Family Benefits	B
Workplace Issues	A
Social Disclosure	A

Baxter International, based in Deerfield, Illinois, is the world leader in the manufacture of medical products. It has more than 40 facilities in the U.S. and operations in 21 other countries. In 1996, the company had 37,000 employees and sales of $5.4 billion.

Environment: Baxter International, a CERES signatory, has an environmental policy and a corporate environmental report (CER), which is updated annually. Baxter's CER is notable for its environmental financial statement, which estimates its income, savings and cost-avoidance from environmental management. For 1996, Baxter's environmental initiatives saved the company $11 million. International consulting firm Arthur D. Little states that Baxter's environmental management systems reflect a "state-of-the-art" approach for major companies with environmental challenges comparable to Baxter's. Baxter established state-of-art (SOA) environmental management standards in 1991. Environmental programs within Baxter are certified SOA when an evaluator from outside the unit being evaluated determines that the program has met all applicable SOA standards. In 1997, Baxter established environmental, health and safety goals for the year 2005. Baxter predicts that meeting these goals will save the company $125 million a year.

Baxter has a written pollution prevention policy and program which establishes annual reduction goals for point sources, secondary sources, fugitive emissions, and solid waste. The company requires each of its facilities to have an EH&S community outreach program. Baxter has a written policy on product stewardship and evaluates its products with the objective of reducing their life-cycle impacts on the environment. Baxter has developed checklists, training and life-cycle tools to use in assessing the EH&S impact of its products. During the past year and a half, the company undertook a review and evaluation of all its environmental, health & safety policies, reworking them so that they apply to operations worldwide.

Baxter International's average total toxic releases and transfers during the years 1993–1994 were less than the industry sample average. Emissions decreased slightly during those years, a better than average performance.

Baxter, along with Sony Display Devise, is among the first companies to be ISO 14001 certified in Singapore by the Productivity and Standards Board. Baxter won over 20 awards for environmental initiatives in 1996.

EEO: In 1996, three women and two minorities served on Baxter International's 13-member board. Of 22 corporate officers at the company, one was a woman and four were minorities, while two of the top 25 paid employees were women, and four were minorities.

"Baxter Women Inc." (BWI), an internal group organized by the company, was designed to address the "glass ceiling" issue and identify where and why it exists at Baxter. The committee collects data on women's representation and has developed programs to encourage improvement. The Glass Ceiling Commission cited Baxter for an initiative that holds managers individually accountable for recruiting, retaining, and promoting minorities and women.

Community Involvement: Baxter International's charitable contributions totaled $4.5 million in cash in 1996 and $21 million in in-kind donations. The $4.5 million cash-giving figure represented the equivalent of 0.57 percent of the company's pretax earnings for the same year, and a decrease of 27 percent from the company's cash contributions in 1995. In 1995, Baxter donated 0.86 percent of its pretax earnings.

In 1996, Baxter International, with three other drug companies, offered to give $600 million to hemophiliacs who became infected with the AIDS virus by using tainted hemoglobin products that were distributed by Baxter in the early 1980s.

Workplace Information: From 1994 to 1996, Baxter was cited by OSHA only for violations classified as "other," the least egregious type of violation, for a total of $7,000 in fines.

33

Becton Dickinson

STOCK SYMBOL: BDX
STOCK EXCHANGES: NY, B, C, CH, P, PH

Environment	B
Women's Advancement	F
Minority Advancement	F
Charitable Giving	N
Community Outreach	C
Family Benefits	N
Workplace Issues	C?
Social Disclosure	B

Becton Dickinson, based in Franklin, New Jersey, is engaged principally in the manufacture and sale of a broad line of medical supplies and devices and diagnostic systems used by health care professionals, medical research institutions and the general public. The company's operations consist of two worldwide business segments: medical supplies and devices, and diagnostic systems. For the year ending September 30, 1997, Becton Dickinson had revenues of $2.8 billion and 18,900 employees worldwide.

Environment: Becton Dickinson has an environmental policy and provides environmental health and safety (EH&S) training to all EH&S staff and facility staff. The company does not have a written commitment to product stewardship, but states that it does evaluate products with the objective of reducing their life-cycle impacts on the environment to benefit human health and social welfare. Becton Dickinson has an environmental audit program with worldwide standards and applicability and is evaluated by a third party. Internationally, the company follows U.S. regulations in the U.S. and local regulations abroad, unless they determine that the local rules do not protect human health and the environment.

Becton Dickinson's average total toxic releases and transfers during the years 1993–1994 were slightly below the industry sample average. Emissions increased by about a fifth during those years, a below average performance.

EEO: In 1996, Becton Dickinson had one woman and no minorities on its 12-member board, and has since replaced a male board member with a second woman. Additionally, the company's total of 21 corporate officers included two women and no minorities, while the company counted one woman and no minorities among the 25 highest paid employees, though now one minority is included in that employee group.

In 1997, Becton Dickinson purchased over $4.8 million in goods and services from women- and minority-owned businesses.

Becton Dickinson maintains diversity goals for both women and minorities.

Community Involvement: Becton Dickinson reports that its "Good Works" program is twofold. At the global level, the company invests in public and preventive health care initiatives that address unmet needs with viable, cost-effective solutions. At the local level, the company's focus broadens beyond health care to programs that improve the quality of life in the communities in which its employees live and work. In all cases, the company seeks partners who share their commitment to innovative, cost-effective solutions that nurture creativity and demonstrate results.

In 1995, Becton, Dickinson and Company donated $1 million to help create the Becton Dickinson Diabetes Interdisciplinary Research Program at the University of Texas Southwestern.

Workplace Information: The records of the Occupational Safety and Health Administration indicate that Becton Dickinson underwent three health and safety inspections from 1994 to 1996. The violations reported by OSHA as a result of the inspections include six classified as "serious." The company was required to pay $6,250 as a result of its violations, or $2,083 per inspection. In 1997, Becton Dickinson reports that it was inspected five times, receiving five "serious" violations and a total of $2,124 in fines, or $425 per inspection. In comparison, the median amount of fines per inspection for other companies in the drug, cosmetics, and medical supplies industries was $2,266.

Bell Atlantic

STOCK SYMBOL: BEL
STOCK EXCHANGES: NY, B, CH, P, PH

Environment	N
Women's Advancement	B?
Minority Advancement	A?
Charitable Giving	D
Community Outreach	D?
Family Benefits	N
Workplace Issues	C?
Social Disclosure	C

B ell Atlantic, headquartered in Philadelphia, Pennsylvania, became the second largest US phone company, after AT&T, when it merged with NYNEX in 1997. In 1996, the corporation provided local phone services in the mid-Atlantic, such as consumer marketing, directory information, Internet access, long distance wireless, and others. Sales in 1996 totaled $13 billion and there were 62,600 employees.

Environment: Bell Atlantic does no manufacturing and produces no process waste. Three of its telephone subsidiaries have been designated potentially responsible parties at five EPA Superfund sites. Since 1990, its annual reports and other shareholder communications are printed on 10 percent post-consumer recycled paper. The company encourages telecommuting and 2,000 employees work from home at least some of the time. Telecommuting reduces fuel consumption and air pollution. Its Yellow Pages directories are recyclable and printed on recycled paper if possible. The company works with communities on setting up phone book recycling programs, and maintains three reclamation centers for recycling plastic, copper and other materials from used telephone equipment. It is a member of the EPA's Green Lights voluntary energy-efficiency program.

EEO: In 1996, Bell Atlantic Corp.'s 15-member board of directors included two women and two minorities. Of 15 corporate officers at the company, two were women and one was a minority; 26 percent of the company's workforce were minorities, 19 percent of whom were in executive positions. In 1996, the National Minority Business Council named Bell Atlantic its "Outstanding Corporate Business."

In 1996, 48 current and former employees of Bell Atlantic from Washington, D.C., Virginia, and Maryland, filed a lawsuit against the company alleging racial discrimination in promotions, training, and work assignments. The workers alleged a pattern of bias which had been driving African-Americans into lower paying jobs with little opportunity for advancement. The plaintiffs' lawyer claimed that black employees at Bell Atlantic tended to be assigned the most physical work, were given inferior equipment, and were assigned lower level tasks than white workers. Some of the plaintiffs had made previous complaints; in cases where government investigations were completed, there were no findings of racial discrimination, and no government agency has intervened in the suit.

In 1996, an ICCR-sponsored shareholder resolution, asking that Bell Atlantic distribute an EEO report, was withdrawn by the sponsors when the company agreed to the terms.

Community Involvement: Bell Atlantic Corp.'s charitable contributions totaled $13.8 million in cash in 1996. The $13.8 million cash-giving figure represented the equivalent of 0.50 percent of the company's pretax earnings for the same year, and was identical to the company's cash contributions in 1995. In 1995, the company contributed 0.46 percent of its pretax earnings for that year to charity.

In April, 1997, Bell Atlantic and NYNEX pledged that they would give a total of more than $50 million through the year 2000 to community-based programs for after-school day-care. The companies, which made the announcement following the conclusion of the President's Summit for America's Future, plan to support programs that will provide children with safe, stimulating, and nurturing environments. They also announced that they will provide $1.6 million in products, services, and internet training to Summit participants.

Workplace Information: OSHA records indicate that Bell Atlantic was inspected 11 times from 1994 to 1996. Violations included 12 violations classified as "serious" for a total of $13,780 in fines, $1,253 per inspection. In comparison, the median amount of fines per inspection for other companies in the service industry, such as banks and communications companies, was $573.

BellSouth Corporation

STOCK SYMBOL: BLS
STOCK EXCHANGES: NY, B, Cн, P, Pн

Environment	N
Women's Advancement	B?
Minority Advancment	A?
Charitable Giving	D
Community Outreach	B
Family Benefits	N
Workplace Issues	B?
Social Disclosure	B

BellSouth Corporation, based in Atlanta, Georgia, provides local telephone service to 23 million customers through its subsidiary BellSouth Telecommunications to nine Southern states in its region. BellSouth Cellular is the third-largest supplier of cellular telephone service in the U.S. with over four million customers. BellSouth International provides cellular service to nearly two million customers worldwide. For 1997, the company reported consolidated revenues of nearly $21 billion and had 81,000 employees.

Environment: BellSouth does no manufacturing and produces no process wastes. It is a participant in the "Buy Recycled" Business Alliance, a voluntary coalition of large U.S. companies formed to expand markets for recycled products. BellSouth is also a participant in the EPA's Green Lights program to reduce energy consumption, and Wastewise, another EPA initiative aimed at goal-driven waste minimization. In 1996, BellSouth was one of 17 companies to earn the EPA's highest award for sustained leadership in waste prevention. The company has 54 vehicles in its fleet which are powered using compressed natural gas and plans to trial the use of electric vehicles in 1998.

EEO: In 1996, BellSouth Corp. achieved a higher than average rating in both diversity categories, placing them easily in the top third of S&P 500 companies. Two women and two minorities served on BellSouth Corp.'s 12-member board. Of 49 officers at BellSouth and its subsidiaries, four are women and three are minorities.

Community Involvement: In 1996, BellSouth Corp.'s charitable giving totaled $21 million in cash, which was equal to 0.46 percent of the company's pretax earnings for that year. The company's charitable contributions budget for 1997 is $24 million, an increase of 14 percent. The company's in-kind giving — the donation of products or services — came to a total of $500,000 in 1996.

The BellSouth Foundation's mission statement is "to improve education in the South by stimulating fundamental change in primary and secondary education that will result in active learning and improved outcomes for all students." One half of the foundation's contributions are open grants to organizations like the National Board for Professional Teaching Standards

and the Memphis City Public Schools; the money supports programs as varied as teaching standards reform and conflict resolution training for students.

Company programs to support student preparation for work include job shadowing, student hiring programs, teachers in the workplace; other company community programs include student mentoring, local chamber development grants, and school-business partnerships. The company won Vice President Al Gore's Hammer Award for its student preparation programs.

BellSouth employees and retirees volunteer approximately 12 million hours of volunteer service.

Workplace Information: The records of the Occupational Safety and Health Administration indicate that BellSouth Corp. underwent five health and safety inspections from 1994 to 1996. The violations reported by OSHA as a result of the inspections include two classified as "serious." The company was required to pay $780 as a result of its violations, $156 per inspection. In comparison, the median amount of fines per inspection for other companies in the service industry, such as banks and communications companies, was $573.

The NLRB filed a complaint against both BellSouth and the Communications Workers of America for requiring employees having contact with customers to wear uniforms with both the company's and the union's logos on them regardless of whether the employee is a union member. The company and the union claim no labor laws have been violated. Wearing the uniform was a condition of employment agreed in a 1995 bargaining agreement by both the company and CWA, and was intended as a security measure to help identify employees as official company representatives to telephone customers.

⊕ Ben & Jerry's Homemade

STOCK SYMBOL: BJICA
STOCK EXCHANGES: NNM

Environment	A
Women's Advancement	A
Minority Advancement	A
Charitable Giving	A
Community Outreach	A
Family Benefits	A
Workplace Issues	B
Social Disclosure	A

Ben & Jerry's, based in Waterbury, Vermont, is the second largest producer of premium ice cream and frozen yogurt. BJICA has 703 employees and revenues of $167 million.

Environment: BJICA was one of the first signatories of the CERES Principles. Its environmental initiatives are pioneering. The company was the first to replace cardboard boxes used to package its Peace Pops with a thin plastic wrapper, saving 165 tons of trash a year. BJICA converts dairy waste into valuable byproducts. The company requires that its suppliers pledge to never use dairy products with recombinant bovine growth hormone, a controversial substance. It also uses organic fruit in many of its sorbet products.

EEO: Women constitute about 50 percent of Ben & Jerry's senior managers (including its chief financial officer) and 30 percent of its professional staff. Minority representation (3 percent) is nearly double the percentage of minorities in the Vermont population. The company won plaudits from black executives when it selected African-American Robert Holland, Jr., to replace CEO Ben Cohen. BJICA is listed in *The 100 Best Companies for Gay Men and Lesbians* (Pocket Books, 1994) for promoting a supportive culture and for extending benefits to same-sex partners in 1989 (one of the first companies to do so).

Community Involvement: Each year, Ben & Jerry's donates 7.5 percent of its pretax earnings to grassroots organizations working to eliminate discrimination, environmental degradation, poverty, and other social ills. Through its PartnerShop program, the company franchises stores to nonprofit organizations. It also seeks suppliers that have such social objectives as employing formerly homeless individuals or the disabled. Since 1991, BJICA has paid above-market prices for dairy supplies, aiding Vermont's farming community.

Family Benefits: Ben & Jerry's offers paid leave for mothers, fathers, and adopting parents. Its family benefits also include on-site child care, adoption assistance, phased return to work for new mothers, and flextime. A flexible spending account allows employees to apply pretax dollars to uncovered medical expenses or dependent care. BJICA is listed in *Working Mother's* "100 Best Companies for Working Mothers."

Workplace Information: Wages are above average for Vermont, and employees are offered profit-sharing, stock ownership, and savings programs. Employees have access to a free fitness center. BJICA is listed in *The 100 Best Companies to Work for in America* (Currency/Doubleday, 1993). Employee dissatisfaction, however, has risen in recent years because of concerns that the company's commitment to its founding values are waning. In 1995, Ben & Jerry's eliminated its highly touted 7-to-1 executive salary cap.

Social Disclosure: Starting in 1995, the company adopted a systematic social audit, which is disclosed in its annual report. Performed by an independent external auditor, the audit covered indicators such as energy use, female representation, and worker injury rates.

Product Issues: Label space on company products is dedicated to educating consumers about pressing issues. In 1995, the company changed the labels of its Rainforest Crunch to avoid exaggerating the effectiveness of the product in assisting indigenous peoples in Brazil. The company has been criticized for the high fat content of its ice cream and was forced to reformulate its "low-fat" frozen yogurt to satisfy federal regulators.

Legal Proceedings: BJICA faces litigation brought by La Soul Bakery, a former supplier that provided employment for persons recovering from drug addiction. La Soul claims that BJICA's erratic purchasing requirements resulted in its bankruptcy.

Bestfoods

STOCK SYMBOL: BFO
STOCK EXCHANGES: NY, B, C, CH, P, PH

Environment	C
Women's Advancement	C
Minority Advancement	A
Charitable Giving	B
Community Outreach	N
Family Benefits	N
Workplace Issues	A?
Social Disclosure	B

Bestfoods changed its name from CPC International Inc. when CPC spun off its corn refining business into a new company, Corn Products International, Inc. Bestfoods, headquartered in Englewood Cliffs, New Jersey, is a worldwide consumer food and corn refining company with operations in over 60 countries. Two-thirds of the company's 45,000 employees work outside the U.S. In 1997, revenues rose to $8.4 billion.

Environment: Bestfoods publishes a brief environmental statement.The company has eliminated the use of toxic gases such as chlorine and ammonia worldwide. Between 1991 and 1994, the company cut TRI releases by 66 percent.

EEO: In 1996, the company's board totaled 12 directors (in 1997, 14 directors), including two women and one minority, while one of a total of 25 corporate officers was a woman, and two were minorities. Additionally, one woman and two minorities were among the 25 employees with the highest salaries at the company. The company maintains many diversity programs, including recruitment, mentoring and support networks, and minority banking and purchasing. Bestfoods has for many years participated in the INROADS program, providing scholarships and internships to minority youth.

Bestfoods has a policy prohibiting discrimination based on sexual orientation.

Community Involvement: In 1997, Bestfoods made about $21 million in cash and food donations. Cash contributions totaled $16 million in 1996, the equivalent of 1.6 percent of the company's earnings before taxes.

Product donation is done chiefly through its divisions and given primarily to the Second Harvest Food Bank. Bestfoods' giving focus tends to be on larger, well-established organizations, but local contributions sometimes go to smaller, more innovative programs.

Family Benefits: Bestfoods' work/family programs include flexible work arrangements, dependent care referrals, and adoption expense reimbursement.

Workplace Information: Sixty percent of Bestfoods' 17,000 U.S.-based employees are represented by collective bargaining agreements; there have been no significant labor disputes in the past five years.

Bestfoods designates one week each year as "Safety Awareness Week," involving employees in discussing ways to reduce injuries and accidents. The records of the Occupational Safety and Health Administration indicate that Bestfoods underwent one health and safety inspection from 1994 to 1996. The only violations reported by OSHA were classified as "other," the least serious kind of violation. The company was required to pay $370 as a result of its violations. In comparison, the median amount of fines per inspection for other companies in the food, beverage, and household products industries was $1,515.

International: In addition to its North American and European facilities, Bestfoods operates approximately 17 plants in Asia, 25 in Africa and the Middle East, and 21 in Latin America. The company reports that it maintains worldwide health and safety standards equivalent to U.S. requirements and environmental practices based on local requirements.

Animal Testing: Bestfoods uses outside contractors to administer tests on animals of new food ingredients. The company has eliminated animal tests on nonfood items. Bestfoods supports the Johns Hopkins Center for Alternatives to Animal Testing.

Legal Proceedings: In July 1995, the Justice Department initiated an investigation of several companies, including Bestfoods, related to alleged antitrust activity in the marketing of high-fructose corn syrup. In June 1996, Bestfoods agreed to pay $7 million for price-fixing charges. Bestfoods still faces various state actions on this matter.

Additional Information: Bestfoods' Corporate Affairs Committee reviews policies and programs relating to consumer, employee and community relations, health and safety, environment, and business ethics.

Biomet

STOCK SYMBOL: BMET
STOCK EXCHANGES: NNM, PH

Environment	N
Women's Advancement	F?
Minority Advancement	F?
Charitable Giving	D
Community Outreach	C
Family Benefits	F
Workplace Issues	C
Social Disclosure	C

Biomet Inc. designs, manufactures and markets products used primarily by orthopedic medical specialists in both surgical and non-surgical therapy, including reconstructive and trauma devices, operating room supplies, powered surgical instruments, general surgical instruments, arthroscopy products and craniomaxillofacial products and instruments. Biomet, based in Warsaw, Indiana, and its subsidiaries currently distribute products in about 100 countries. In fiscal year ending in May of 1997, Biomet had sales of $535 million and employed approximately 1,800 people.

Environment: Biomet, Inc. did not respond to CEP's environment questionnaire in 1997. Biomet does not currently publish a corporate environmental report.

EEO: Biomet, Inc. turned in a below average performance in the area of diversity in 1996, compared to other S&P 500 companies. Among the companies surveyed by CEP, the average representation of women and minorities on S&P corporate boards was 10.8 percent and 7.5 percent, respectively. In comparison, Biomet, Inc. had one woman and no minorities on its 13-member board.

Community Involvement: In 1996, Biomet, Inc.'s charitable giving totaled $167,000 in cash, which was equal to 0.11 percent of the company's pretax earnings for that year. In terms of the actual dollar amount donated by the company, the level of cash contributions in 1996 represented a decrease of 18 percent from that of 1995, which was 0.13 percent of the company's earnings for that year. The company's in-kind giving — the donation of products or services — came to a total of $66,000 in 1996.

The Biomet foundation makes contributions to the causes of education, hospitals, human services, and general charitable giving. The company participates in the Annual March of Dimes Walk-a-Thon, the Annual United Way Campaign, as well as a Community Adopt-a-School Program. Biomet has also partnered with the Junior Achievement program. As a part of the partnership, the company provides employee volunteers who act as classroom consultants, while other employees volunteer for the annual Junior Achievement phone-a-thon.

Family Benefits: Biomet offers only the 12-week legal minimum under the Family and Medical Leave Act to new mothers and fathers. There are no flexible scheduling options available to salaried employees; however, hourly employees may take advantage of part-time return to work following leave, job sharing, or a compressed work week. Biomet does offer assitance to dependent care centers, but does not have any dependent care subsidies, on-site centers, or resource/referral services for employees.

Workplace Information: The records of the Occupational Safety and Health Administration indicate that Biomet, Inc. was not inspected from 1994 to 1996. Consequently no fines or violations were assessed to the company. In comparison, the median amount of fines per inspection for other companies in the drug, cosmetics, and medical supplies industries was $2,266.

Boeing Company

Environment	N
Women's Advancement	C?
Minority Advancement	F?
Charitable Giving	A
Community Outreach	C?
Family Benefits	N
Workplace Issues	F?
Social Disclosure	F

The Boeing Company, based in Seattle, Washington, is one of the world's major aerospace firms. The company operates in two principal industries: commercial aircraft, and defense and space. Commercial aircraft operations involve development, production and marketing of commercial jet transports and providing related support services to the commercial airline industry worldwide. Defense and space operations involve research, development, production, modification and support of military aircraft and helicopters and related systems, space systems, and missile systems. Defense and military sales are principally through US Government contracts. In 1997, Boeing acquired McDonnell Douglas, the world's leader in military aircraft production. In 1996, Boeing had sales of $23 billion and employed approximately 105,000 people.

EEO: In 1996, Boeing Company's board totaled ten directors, including one woman and no minorities.

Boeing is one of 15 of the nation's 100 largest companies which does not have any minority directors.

Community Involvement: Boeing Company's charitable contributions totaled $36.4 million in cash in 1996. The $36.4 million cash-giving figure represented the equivalent of 2.67 percent of the company's pretax earnings for the same year, and was identical to the company's cash contributions in 1995.

Boeing was one of the top ten corporate contributors in the areas of arts & humanities, health, and social services in 1995, awarding $6 million, $7.4 million, and $7.4 million respectively. In 1994, Boeing gave $27 million through the Boeing Employees Good Neighbor Fund and the company's gift-matching program. Employees volunteered more than one million service hours in 1994 alone to organizations in those communities where Boeing operated. The Boeing Everett site was awarded with the Commuter Challenge Award for its Emergency Ride Home program in 1994 by the Bullitt Foundation.

Workplace Information: According to the Occupational Safety and Health Administration's records, Boeing Company was inspected 14 times from 1994 to 1996. The OSHA inspectors' citations included 121 violations classified as "serious." A total of $190,865 in fines was assessed to the company following the inspections, $1,577 per inspection. In comparison, the median amount of fines per inspection for other companies in similar manufacturing industries was $2,412.

The Seattle Professional Engineering Employees Association filed unfair labor practices charges against Boeing in response to the company's decision to transfer 220 professional and 52 technical employees to a new joint venture. The two sides came to an agreement in April, 1997, wherein employees who refuse to relocate will be guaranteed equivalent positions and pay with Boeing. Those employees accepting the transfer will be given a $15,000 bonus; they will also receive severance pay and recall rights if they decide to return to Boeing.

A Boeing spokesman assured unionized employees of Boeing and McDonnell Douglas Corp. that the merger between the two companies will not affect previously negotiated contracts. All contracts will be honored, and any changes will be negotiated with the appropriate bargaining units.

Weapons Contracts: In 1996, Boeing was number seven in the world among defense firms. That year, Boeing generated $5.5 billion from defense (40.1 percent of its overall business), and had $1.6 billion in prime contracts with the U.S. Department of Defense, making it the eighth largest government contractor in the defense industry.

Since acquiring McDonnell Douglas, Boeing has become the second biggest defense firm in the world after Lockheed Martin.

Boise Cascade Corporation

STOCK SYMBOL: BCC

STOCK EXCHANGES: NY, B, C, CH, P, PH

Environment	F
Women's Advancement	D
Minority Advancement	F
Charitable Giving	N
Community Outreach	D?
Family Benefits	D
Workplace Issues	F
Social Disclosure	B

Boise Cascade, based in Boise, Idaho, is one of the world's largest producers of paper, paper products, and wood products. In 1996 the company had $5.1 billion in sales and 17,820 employees.

Environment: Boise Cascade does not publish a corporate environmental report. Boise Cascade considers contribution towards EH&S goals in the job performance reviews of executives. In the selection of suppliers, the company conducts or reviews environmental audits on suppliers' facilities. Boise Cascade has an environmental audit program, but does not make audit results publicly available. Boise Cascade is in compliance with the American Forest & Paper Association's Sustainable Forestry Initiative.

Boise Cascade's average total toxic releases and transfers during the years 1993–1994 were higher than the industry sample average. Furthermore, its emissions increased by more than a half during those years, the worst performance within the industry sample.

In 1997, environmental groups claimed they discovered a document from Boise Cascade to the U.S. Forest Service asking that it keep the classification of a tract of forest as old growth secret, as the company planned to cut it and feared sabotage. Forest Service officials deny hiding information, but eventually turned over records showing that the Service had inspected the 840-acre grove back in 1992, and had classified the tract as old growth.

Boise Cascade is one of several paper and forest product companies using fast-growing genetically altered trees as a source of wood fiber for its paper mills, currently utilizing 75-foot-tall trees that were planted in 1991. Boise Cascade is also the second largest manufacturer of "engineered" wood products, which do not require the cutting of old-growth trees.

In 1996, the Yakima County Clean Air Authority approved an environmental review of a $4.2 million renovation project that will substantially reduce carbon monoxide, sulfur oxide and particulates emissions from Boise Cascade's Yakima mill. The renovation is part of a 1995 consent decree after Boise Cascade received the largest fine ever given by the authority.

EEO: In 1996, Boise Cascade had two women and no minorities on its 12-member board. Additionally, the company's total of 24 corporate officers included one woman and no minorities. The company counted one woman and no minorities among the 25 highest paid employees.

Boise Cascade was recognized by the Dallas Together, a coalition of businesses, chambers of commerce, and nonprofits, in October, 1996, for achieving specific goals in "partnering with minority firms." Boise Cascade offers recruitment programs, maintains diversity goals, and gives special consideration for management training to both women and minorities

Community Involvement: According to the Corporate Philanthropy Report, Boise Cascade does not disclose giving figures.

Family Benefits: Boise has dependent care financial assistance, flextime for employees, work-at-home options on a limited basis, and spouse reemployment support after employee relocation.

Workplace Information: OSHA records indicate that Boise Cascade underwent 53 inspections from 1994 to 1996. Violations included two classified as "willful" or "repeat" and 141 classified as "serious" for an average of $613 per inspection. In comparison, the median amount of fines per inspection for other companies in the extractive business was $2,941. Boise has adopted a health and safety strategic plan that includes training, equipment design, and ongoing audits. The company claims that it has among the lowest accident-incidence rates in its industry.

Just over one half of Boise's employees are unionized. The company has not experienced a strike since 1988, though members of the Association of Western Pulp and Paper Workers (AWPPW) worked without a collective bargaining agreement throughout most of 1993.

Briggs & Stratton

STOCK SYMBOL: BGG
STOCK EXCHANGES: NY, B, CH, PH, P

Based in Wauwatosa, Wisconsin, Briggs & Stratton is the world's largest producer of automotive locks and air cooled gasoline engines for outdoor power equipment. In 1996 the company had revenues of $1.3 billion and 7,660 employees.

Environment: Briggs & Stratton has no regularly published environmental progress report available to the public, but does provide environmental information in press releases. The company is not a member of any of EPA's voluntary programs for energy conservation, toxics reduction, or waste management, but has recently implemented several of its own "innovative" environmental programs.

Briggs & Stratton uses waste from its Wisconsin based plants to produce 25 percent of the heat at its Menomonee Falls factory. All of the 80 million pounds of aluminum used annually by the company comes from secondary smelters, which produce the material from a variety of sources, such as transmission cases and other castings. Briggs & Stratton also recycles 100 percent of its aluminum scrap and uses recycled cast iron for other engine parts. The company has a water conservation program which treats more than 1.3 million gallons used for cleaning. Oil recovered in the treatment process in recycled.

Half of the company's engineering staff is dedicated to designing cleaner engines that meet new air regulations by the California Air Resources Board. Lawn mowers using such engines can operate under average use for 38 years before producing the emissions equal to driving a new car for one year.

EEO: In 1996, Briggs & Stratton's board totaled nine directors, including no women and one minority.

Environment	C
Women's Advancement	N
Minority Advancement	B?
Charitable Giving	C
Community Outreach	N
Family Benefits	N
Workplace Issues	C?
Social Disclosure	F

Community Involvement: In 1995, Briggs & Stratton made cash contributions of $1.5 million to charitable organizations, or 0.9 percent of its pretax earnings for that year. Briggs & Stratton's support of art and culture is limited to the United Performing Arts Fund, museums and public television. Educational support goes to scholarships for employees' children, colleges, universities, educational funds, precollege programs, and agricultural education.

Workplace Information: The records of the Occupational Safety and Health Administration indicate that Briggs & Stratton underwent seven health and safety inspections from 1994 to 1996. The violations reported by OSHA as a result of the inspections include 13 classified as "serious." The company was required to pay $19,015 as a result of its violations, $2,716 per inspection. In comparison, the median amount of fines per inspection for other companies in similar manufacturing industries was $2,412.

At the end of 1995, Briggs & Stratton started laying off 2,000 hourly workers in Milwaukee, and offering transfers for salaried employees. The company is shifting the jobs to Kentucky and Missouri, where hourly wages are considerably less than in Wisconsin.

Bristol-Myers Squibb Company

STOCK SYMBOL: BMY

STOCK EXCHANGES: NY, B, C, CH, P, PH

Environment	A
Women's Advancement	A
Minority Advancement	B
Charitable Giving	B
Community Outreach	B
Family Benefits	A
Workplace Issues	B
Social Disclosure	A

New York City-based Bristol-Myers Squibb (BMY) has four core business segments: pharmaceuticals, consumer products, nutritional products, and medical devices. In 1996, sales were $15.1 billion, and the company had 49,000 employees.

Environment: Bristol-Myers Squibb has an environmental policy and a corporate environmental report which is updated biennially, is verified by a third party, and is available on the internet. The company has implemented an integrated environmental management system and provides environmental health and safety (EH&S) training to all of its employees. Bristol Myers also considers contribution towards EH&S goals in the job performance reviews of EH&S staff and Facility staff. It has written a pollution prevention policy and has initiated a companywide pollution prevention program, which established reduction goals for point sources, fugitive emissions, secondary sources, and solid waste. The company has a corporate policy on community involvement relating to local environmental concerns and five facilities have community advisory panels. BMY has written a policy on product stewardship, has a product stewardship review board, and evaluates all major products with the objective of reducing their life-cycle impacts on the environment.

Bristol Myers' average total releases and transfers during the years 1994–1996 were less than the industry sample average. Emissions decreased by an average of almost three-quarters annually during those years, the best performance in the sample.

According to an Arthur D. Little survey, BMY product life-cycle reviews have been very successful. By 1996, with reviews for more than half BMY's products completed, the company had identified average savings of $ 300,000 on each review.

In September 1997, Bristol-Myers agreed to pay a $155,000 civil penalty for violating New York State's clean air standards the past two years. However, state officials did acknowledge that Bristol-Myers Squibb had made improvements in its environmental performance in recent years.

EEO: Two women and one minority served on BMY's ten-member board. Of 35 corporate officers at the company, four were women and three were minorities. Two of the top 25 paid employees were women.

Community Involvement: BMY's charitable contributions totaled $23 million in cash in 1996, and $38 million of in-kind donations. The $23 million cash-giving figure represented 0.57 percent of the company's pretax earnings. In 1995, the company contributed 0.96 percent of its pretax earnings to charity.

BMY's Women's Health Initiative, through which Bristol-Myers donated $1.5 million in 1996, supports programs that increase women's access to information to make better informed decisions about their health.

Workplace Information: OSHA records indicate that Bristol-Myers Squibb Co. was inspected once in 1996. BMY only received violations classified as "other," the least egregious type of violation, and no fines. BMY has a formal grievance procedure for nonunion employees, who make up 95 percent of its workforce.

International: BMY has adopted a code of conduct for its suppliers covering health and safety standards and environmental protection. The code does not address the use of child labor, forced or bonded labor, minimum wage, or other workers' rights issues.

Animal Testing: From 1994 to 1995, the company's use of laboratory animals declined by approximately seven percent. Pharmaceutical and health care products were responsible for 99.63 percent of total animal use. The company's corporate Animal Welfare Committee addresses animal testing alternatives.

Legal Proceedings: In early 1996, a woman blaming health problems on leaky BMY silicone breast implants was awarded $1.5 million in compensatory damages. In 1995, BMY settled a $28 million class action breast implant suit — which covered approximately 3,000 women in Quebec — out of court.

43

⚙ Brooklyn Union

STOCK SYMBOL: KSE
STOCK EXCHANGES: NY, CH, PH

Environment	C
Women's Advancement	A
Minority Advancement	B
Charitable Giving	N
Community Outreach	A
Family Benefits	B
Workplace Issues	A
Social Disclosure	A

Founded in 1895, Brooklyn Union serves 1.2 million metered customers in the Brooklyn, Queens, and Staten Island boroughs of New York City. KeySpan Corporation is the holding company for Brooklyn Union. In February, 1998, the New York State Public Service Commission approved the creation of a new energy company that results from the combination of KeySpan and the Long Island Lighting Company. The fifth largest gas utility in the U.S., BU has operations in gas distribution, exploration, and production, with investments in gas cogeneration and pipeline/storage projects. In 1996, the company had 3,336 employees and revenues of $1.4 billion.

Environment: Brooklyn Union reported in 1996 that environmental cleanup at two manufactured gas plant sites it formerly operated is expected to cost about $34 million. The company initiated a recycling/environmental task force in May 1993 to address recycling, energy conservation, and support of local recycling/environmental groups. It had earlier built several natural gas fueling stations and converted more than 150 city-owned vehicles.

The Bright Futures project, cofounded with New York City Technical College, recycles laser printer toner cartridges and uses the funds to support environmental programs in local schools.

EEO: Two women are among 12 corporate officers. One woman and one African-American man serve on the nine-member board. Two women are among the company's 25 highest paid. The company has banking programs with minority banks, and purchases more than $2 million annually from women- and minority-owned firms. In 1993, BU signed a 10-year, $40 million contract with ICC Corporation, a minority-owned natural gas supplier, and it has since added more minority suppliers. BU is the first utility in New York State to sign long-term contracts with minority-owned suppliers. The company provides diversity training and bans discrimination based on sexual orientation.

Community Involvement: No new giving information is available. In 1994, BU donated cash gifts of approximately $2 million and about $400,000 in products and services to charitable causes. Brooklyn Union is a pace-setter in organizing community development programs that link employee volunteerism (more than one-third volunteer) and funding to foster small business start-ups and housing rehabilitation in run-down neighborhoods. The company's "Cinderella Project," initiated in 1966, has invested in the rehabilitation of properties to help stabilize housing and support local development. The project's Area Development Fund (ADF) supplies flexible funding for a wide array of housing and business venture projects developed in association with local development corporations. The ADF director estimates that ADF support of $8.6 million in investments has helped leverage $300 million to create 3,000 housing units, 24 industrial and commercial facilities, and over 100 permanent jobs.

Brooklyn Union's service area is home to more than 90 distinct ethnic and cultural groups. Its cross-cultural outreach programs have earned the company several awards.

Family Benefits: Flexible scheduling includes job-sharing, part-time return to work after maternity leave, and work-at-home. Resource and referral help is available for child care, and BU offers a child care subsidy to parents making less than a certain amount a year.

Workplace Information: BU is 63 percent unionized, primarily by the Utility Division of the TWU. There is a grievance procedure for nonunion employees. A full range of benefits includes profit-sharing, ESOP, employee stock purchase plan, 401(k) with company match, tuition reimbursement, in-house training, and fitness/wellness programs. Over the last few years, the company has instituted safety programs such as lead exposure control, hearing conservation, bloodborne pathogens exposure control, and respiratory protection.

Burlington Resources

STOCK SYMBOL: BR

STOCK EXCHANGES: NY, CH, PH, P

Environment	N
Women's Advancement	C?
Minority Advancement	N
Charitable Giving	A?
Community Outreach	N
Family Benefits	N
Workplace Issues	N
Social Disclosure	F

Burlington Resources was created in 1988 when railroad giant Burlington Northern spun off its natural resource holdings, acquired largely through the railroad land grant program of the late 1800s. Burlington, headquartered in Houston, Texas, has approximately 1,800 employees and in 1997 had $2 billion in revenue.

Environment: Burlington Resources does not publish a corporate environmental report, and does not have a written environmental policy.

Burlington was one of a dozen corporations to contribute $1 million or more to the Nature Conservancy's "Last Great Places" preservation campaign in 1992.

EEO: In 1996, Burlington Resources' board totaled ten directors, including one woman and no minorities.

In 1996, a shareholder resolution on board inclusiveness sponsored by the Interfaith Center on Corporate Responsibility was withdrawn by its proponents. The resolution proposed that the company make greater efforts to find qualified women and minority candidates for nomination to the board. Generally, the withdrawal of a resolution indicates that the company management has agreed to do much of what is requested.

Community Involvement: In 1994, Burlington Resources made $1.7 million in cash contributions to charitable institutions, the equivalent of 1.89 percent of the company's earnings before taxes that year.

Technical colleges and educational programs related to the mining industry are given high priority in the Burlington Resources Foundation's education giving.

However, support is not given for the expansion of a student body or for scholarships. The foundation does not supply grants for computers or computer-related projects.

Family Benefits: Burlington Resources did not provide CEP with any information regarding family benefits issues in 1997.

Workplace Information: According to the Occupational Safety and Health Administration's records, Burlington Resources was not inspected from 1994 to 1996. Consequently no violations or fines were assessed to the company. As inspections can frequently be called in response to a complaint regarding the health or safety conditions at a company, a lack of inspections can be an indicator of a relatively safe and healthy workplace. A lack of inspections over several years is not especially unusual.

Burlington provides pension funds through a defined benefit plan. The company has an employee assistance program that assists workers with substance abuse and other personal problems.

Campbell Soup

STOCK SYMBOL: CPB

STOCK EXCHANGES: NY, To, B, CH, P, PH

Environment	C
Women's Advancement	B
Minority Advancement	A
Charitable Giving	A
Community Outreach	C
Family Benefits	C
Workplace Issues	D
Social Disclosure	A

Founded in 1869 in Camden, New Jersey, Campbell Soup Company is the largest manufacturer of canned soups in the world. The company is also well known for its Pepperidge Farm crackers and cookies, Godiva chocolates, Swanson frozen dinners, Prego spaghetti sauce, and Vlasic pickles. Sales in 1997 were $7.96 billion. Campbell has approximately 37,000 employees.

Environment: Campbell's brief environmental policy focuses on recycling and environmentally friendly packaging. The company does not publish an environmental progress report but has a corporate environmental handbook. Campbell audits 100 percent of its facilities annually both in the U.S. and abroad. Audit results are not available to the public.

Campbell's toxic releases have declined only 5 percent from 1990 through 1994, to 489,483 pounds, slightly better than the food industry average.

The company requires its vendors to use a minimum of 25 percent post-consumer recycled content in glass jars. Campbell runs a companywide recycling program and source reduction programs to cut down on waste and effluents. A participant in the CONEG Challenge for improved packaging, the company eliminated heavy metal inks and reduced package size.

In 1997, Campbell's achieved an 81 percent recycle rate of solid waste generated in its manufacturing facilities.

EEO: In 1996, Campbell Soup achieved a higher than average rating in both diversity categories, placing them easily in the top third of S&P 500 companies. Two women and two minorities served on Campbell Soup's 15-member board. Of 23 corporate officers at the company, two were women and three were minorities. Two of the top 26 paid employees were women and three were minorities. Campbell provides diversity training and has a written policy banning discrimination based on sexual orientation. Management job reviews include assessment of progress toward affirmative action goals.

Community Involvement: In 1995, Campbell Soup's contributions to various charitable institutions included cash donations totaling $1.5 million; in 1997 that figure was $2.6 million. The company's cash contributions for 1995 were equivalent to 0.14 percent of its earnings before taxes. In 1997, the company donated $15 million worth of products to food banks across the country and $4.5 million for school equipment through its Labels for Education.

In 1995, Campbell donated $500,000 to the Camden Development Collaborative in their headquarter city of Camden, New Jersey. The Campbell's Foundation's grants are focused primarily in places where the company has operations, including both plant locations and its world headquarters. In 1994, more than $1.6 million was given to causes in the communities surrounding the headquarters.

Family Benefits: In 1983, Campbell established an on-site day care center for employees' children at its Camden headquarters; the company provided startup funds and continues to subsidize its operation. Campbell also offers companywide flextime and alternate job arrangements, and flexible spending accounts that include dependent care. Campbell offers reimbursement up to $2000 for eligible adoption expenses and scholarships up to $3000 for employees whose children are seniors in high school and will be entering an accredited college or university.

Workplace Information: According to OSHA records, Campbell Soup was inspected six times from 1994 to 1996. Violations included one classified as "willful" or "repeat" and 20 classified as "serious" for a total of $10,385 in fines, averaging $1,731 per inspection. In comparison, the median amount of fines per inspection for other companies in the food, beverage, and household products industries was $1,515. From 1993 to 1997, Campbell reports that is/has seen a 36 percent decrease in lost time incidents at their facilities.

A new 3 year agreement gives 12,000 hourly workers at the Campbell Soup Co.'s Sacramento plant wage increases of 3 percent each year and early retirement incentives for employees as young as age fifty-five. The wage increase is the result of the compression of 21 wage brackets into seven. Such compression is also intended to give the company more flexibility in operating the plant. However, Campbell claims that this information is inaccurate.

46

Carolina Power & Light Company

STOCK SYMBOL: CPL

STOCK EXCHANGES: NY, B, C, CH, PH, P

Environment	REV
Women's Advancement	C?
Minority Advancement	C?
Charitable Giving	B
Community Outreach	B
Family Benefits	N
Workplace Issues	D?
Social Disclosure	C

Founded in 1908, Carolina Power and Light Company (CP&L) generates, transmits and sells electricity in North and South Carolina, a service area that has a population of 3.5 million. The Raleigh, North Carolina-based utility has 16 power plants that produce approximately 40 million megawatt-hours of electricity annually. During 1997, the company's revenues amounted to $3 billion and it employed 6,300 persons.

Environment: CP&L derives approximately two-thirds of its energy from coal with the balance largely nuclear-generated. Among the utilities CEP evaluated, the company ranked below average in terms of its projected percent increase in carbon dioxide emissions. In regard to sulfur dioxide and nitrogen oxides, however, the company performed slightly better than average. Natural gas turbines will comprise virtually all of the utility's anticipated capacity increase during the next 15 years. In March 1993, CP&L purchased 57 percent of the available emissions credits for sulfur dioxide (SO2) at the first auction by the U.S. EPA. The company paid $11.5 million for permission to emit 85,000 tons of SO2. The purchases will allow the company to defer installing scrubbers until 2005. CP&L burns low-sulfur coal, meeting requirements of Phase 1 of the Clean Air Act. In order to meet the requirements of the Act, CP&L is implementing nitrous oxide reductions at its larger coal-fired units and averaging reductions over its whole system. Between 1995 and 1999, the company will spend $82 million on low NO_x burners and over-fire-air technology on ten units; the cumulative cost of the Clean Air Act compliance through 2000 is projected at about $181 million. New EPA ozone and particulate limits may require additional controls at some of CP&L's units, and could create substantial costs.

In 1991, CP&L began an Adopt State Parks program in North Carolina to help protect and preserve the parks through education, volunteer programs and challenge grants. The company received the Edison Electric Institute's Common Goals Award in recognition of the program. Over the last eight years, more than 1,400 CP&L employees have completed over 200 projects in U.S. state parks, valued at over $600,000.

CP&L began voluntarily removing its 260-foot Quaker Neck Dam from the Neuse River. Secretary of Interior Bruce Babbitt described it as the nation's first dam to be removed both voluntarily and for environmental benefit. The company's urban forestry program, TreeSmart, puts over 5,000 seedlings in the hands of school children and civic groups annually.

The company was honored with the N.C. Wildlife Federation's Water Conservationist of the Year award.

EEO: Carolina Power & Light turned in an average overall performance in workforce diversity for S&P 500 companies in 1996. The company's 11-member board included one woman and one minority. Three women and no minorities served among the company's 27 corporate officers. In 1997, those numbers increased to one minority and four women of a total of 28 corporate officers.

Community Outreach: In 1996, Carolina Power & Light's charitable giving totaled $3.5 million in cash, or 0.57 percent of the company's pretax earnings for that year. The company's in-kind giving—the donation of products or services—came to a total of $500,000 in 1996. CP&L donated $5.1 million in cash in 1997.

The company is primarily interested in supporting adult education, economic development, and the environment.

Volunteers at CP&L participate in many programs including Habitat for Humanity, State Parks Improvement, and Cities in Schools, in which employees meet with students one hour each week while school is in session. CP&L's employees contribute one million volunteer hours annually.

Workplace Information: OSHA records indicate that CP&L underwent four health and safety inspections from 1994 to 1996. Violations included 11 classified as "serious" for a total of $24,000 in fines, $6,000 per inspection. In comparison, the median amount of fines per inspection for other companies in the utilities industry was $2,625.

Case Corporation

STOCK SYMBOL: CSE
STOCK EXCHANGES: NY, PH, P

Environment	B
Women's Advancement	D
Minority Advancement	B
Charitable Giving	N
Community Outreach	N
Family Benefits	N
Workplace Issues	F?
Social Disclosure	C

B ased in Racine, Wisconsin, Case Corporation is a leading manufacturer of agricultural and construction equipment, including large tractors, combines, loader/backhoes, crawler dozers, wheel loaders, and excavators. In 1996, the company had 17,500 employees and sales of $5.1 billion. Case was a subsidiary of Tenneco from 1970 until 1994, at which time the company was publicly offered.

Environment: Case has an environmental policy and environmental progress report available to the public. The company has established general environmental principles which all employees are required to follow. Case conducts annual environmental audits at all North American facilities. The company is not a participant in EPA's WasteWi$e waste reduction program or Green Lights energy conservation program, but was a participant in EPA's 33/50 toxics reduction program. Through this program, Case reduced tracked chemicals by 51 percent as of December 1994, using a 1990 baseline. The company has also reduced both hazardous and non-hazardous waste by over 50 percent since 1992.

Case has initiated a Pollution Prevention Program to reduce industrial waste, air emissions, and water usage by incorporating adjustments in business activity, recycling efforts and hazard assessments of raw materials. As part of this program, Case has developed an overall corporate pollution measurement which is tabulated using monthly data from all North American manufacturing facilities. The company has set a goal to reduce this score (and hence company pollution) by 5 percent each year, for a total reduction of 25 percent by the year 2000. In 1994, the company adopted the International Chamber of Commerce Principles of Environmental Management.

The company had the third highest toxic releases in its industry, both real and adjusted for size. Case also had the highest amount of spilled hazardous materials in the industry, from 1990 to 1994.

EEO: In 1996, Case Corporation's nine-member board of directors included one woman and one minority. Of 21 corporate officers at the company, one was a woman and one was a minority. One woman and one minority also ranked among the 25 highest paid employees at the company.

Community Outreach: The company provided no information about corporate giving and community outreach to CEP or other tracking sources.

Workplace Information: The records of the Occupational Safety and Health Administration indicate that Case underwent four health and safety inspections from 1994 to 1996. The violations reported by OSHA as a result of the inspections include two classified as "serious." The company was required to pay $5,350 as a result of its violations, or $1,338 per inspection. In comparison, the median amount of fines per inspection for other companies in the extractive business was $2,941.

Case has established an employee stock purchase plan, which allows employees to purchase stock at a 15 percent discount. In 1995, Case signed a three-year contract with UAW.

Caterpillar, Inc.

STOCK SYMBOL: CAT
STOCK EXCHANGES: NY, B, C, CH, P, PH

Environment	F
Women's Advancement	D?
Minority Advancement	N
Charitable Giving	D
Community Outreach	N
Family Benefits	N
Workplace Issues	F?
Social Disclosure	D

Based in Peoria, Illinois, Caterpillar is the world's largest manufacturer of crawler-tractors and of earthmoving and off-highway construction machinery. The company also produces agricultural machinery and engines, and offers services to finance and insure its products. In 1996, Caterpillar had $16.5 billion in total sales and 54,352 employees.

Environment: Caterpillar has no environmental report available to the public. The company participates only in EPA's 33/50 program. In 1994, Caterpillar spent $125 million on environmental compliance. The company, however, has few established environmental programs. Caterpillar recycles engine oil used in testing engines and participates in a federal program to develop a low-emission diesel engine. Recently, Caterpillar registered a large portion of a 700-acre tractor test site as a wildlife sanctuary.

EPA proposed a $32,000 fine against Caterpillar for failing to use PCB equipment properly and not maintaining adequate records. In September 1994, the UAW and Citizens for a Better Environment filed a complaint alleging that the company stored contaminated soil in its Peoria, Illinois, plant. The company has the highest toxic releases in the industry, the second worst spills record, and the highest hazardous waste generation total, all adjusted for sales. Caterpillar has been named a potentially responsible party at 17 Superfund sites.

EEO: In 1996, Caterpillar Inc.'s board totaled 11 directors, including one woman and no minorities, while three of a total of 33 corporate officers were women, and none were minorities.

Community Involvement: Caterpillar Inc.'s charitable contributions totaled $10 million in cash in 1996. The $10 million cash-giving figure was identical to the company's 1995 cash contributions.

While Caterpillar Inc. Foundation gave $10 million in 1996, the company's giving program contributed $2.5 million for capital grants for community development, and trade and public policy organizations. Cash contributions in 1996 were equivalent to 0.6 percent of company pretax earnings for the same year. Under the giving category of education, the majority of money is donated through Excellence Funds, which support scholarships, curriculum and faculty development, and capital improvements.

Workplace Information: According to the Occupational Safety and Health Administration's records, Caterpillar Inc. was inspected 46 times from 1994 to 1996. The OSHA inspectors' citations included 17 violations classified as "willful" or "repeat" and 177 violations classified as "serious." A total of $380,775 in fines was assessed to the company following the inspections, or an average of $8,278 per inspection. In comparison, the median amount of fines per inspection for other companies in similar manufacturing industries was $2,412.

Caterpillar has a long history of disputes with its union workers, dating back to a seven month strike in 1982-3 of 17,000 workers. A 17 month strike ended in December of 1995, during which the NLRB filed over 100 unfair labor practice charges against the company. Cases that arose in 1997 include the following: In one June of 1997 case, Caterpillar was ordered to post a notice "for 60 days indicating it will not threaten employees with loss of benefits for engaging in protected activity, will not refuse to post notices of union meetings, and will not interfere with the exercise of guaranteed rights," according to the *Peoria Star Journal*. In a separate ruling from July, Caterpillar was told to "stop singling out union officials and to stop making workers take down union materials inside plants" according to the Associated Press.

International: In April, 1995, Caterpillar's Asia Division opened an office of Myanmar Tractors and Trading in Bahan, Myanmar (Burma).

Weapons Contracts: In 1994, the company had $49 million in contracts with the Department of Defense. None of these contracts were weapons related.

CBS Corporation

STOCK SYMBOL: CBS
STOCK EXCHANGES: NY, B, CH, P, PH

Environment	C?
Women's Advancement	F?
Minority Advancement	A?
Charitable Giving	A
Community Outreach	C
Family Benefits	N
Workplace Issues	F?
Social Disclosure	B

Based in New York City, CBS (formerly known as Westinghouse Electric) is primarily a television and radio broadcaster today, having dramatically redefined its business portfolio during recent years. It acquired CBS Inc. in 1995 and Infinity Broadcasting in 1996, and divested a number of its industrial businesses. In 1996, CBS employed approximately 59,275 people and had $8.6 billion in revenues.

Environment: The company has an environmental policy and a corporate environmental report. The company has implemented an integrated environmental management system and provides environmental health and safety (EH&S) training to employees. It also considers contribution towards EH&S goals in the job performance reviews of executives and managers. CBS has a written pollution prevention policy and has initiated a company-wide pollution prevention program. The company also has a corporate policy on community involvement relating to local environmental concerns; however, it does not have any community advisory panels. The company has a written policy on product stewardship and evaluates its products with the objective of reducing their life-cycle impacts on the environment.

Westinghouse Electric's average toxic releases and transfers during the years 1993–1994 were among the highest compared to the industry sample. However, although its emissions decreased by a seventh during those years, its performance was still below average within the industry sample.

In November 1996, the company was fined $5.4 million, the largest fine assessed by the state Environmental Hearing Board, for releases of degreasers that are alleged to have contaminated wells near its former Gettysburg, Pennsylvania elevator manufacturing plant. The state Department of Environmental Protection characterized the company's conduct as negligent.

EEO: In 1996, the company's 11-member board of directors included one woman, an African American, and an Asian American.

In April 1993, 388 former employees filed a class-action age discrimination lawsuit against Westinghouse. Many older workers are among the 12,000 employees who have lost their jobs as a result of scaling down Westinghouse's business sector. One of the largest cases against Westinghouse was a class-action suit filed by the EEOC on behalf of 250 employees, aged 40 and older, who were laid off by a former Westinghouse defense unit. This case was settled jointly by Westinghouse and the purchaser of its defense unit.

Community Involvement: Due to declines in profits, the Westinghouse Foundation's giving decreased by almost half from 1989 to 1996. The company donated $6.5 million in cash and $2 million in products and services in 1996, even though Westinghouse posted negative earnings. The foundation provides annual grants to the Westinghouse High School of Science and Mathematics, where employees also volunteer as mentors. The school's program is designed to encourage women and minority students to pursue careers in science.

Workplace Information: OSHA records indicate that the company underwent 12 health and safety inspections from 1994 to 1996. Violations include four classified as "willful" or "repeat" and 47 classified as "serious" for a total of $86,650 in fines.

Weapons Contracts: The company sold its defense electronics operations to Northrop Grumman for $3.6 billion in early 1996.

Nuclear Power: The company is the largest U.S. producer of nuclear power facilities, but is in the process of divesting these businesses.

Legal Proceedings: In December 1994, Westinghouse agreed to pay more than $1.8 million to the U.S. Air Force for not passing on savings it gained through mass production with other contracts. In August 1993, it was found liable for $3.3 million in damages in asbestos-related litigation.

Central & South West

STOCK SYMBOL: CSR
STOCK EXCHANGES: NY, B, C, CH, P, PH

Central & South West is an electricity holding company, headquartered in Dallas, Texas. At the end of 1997, the company employed 11,000 persons and its revenues amounted to $5.3 billion.

Environment	N
Women's Advancement	D
Minority Advancement	B
Charitable Giving	N
Community Outreach	N
Family Benefits	C
Workplace Issues	B
Social Disclosure	A

Environment: Over the course of five years, Central & South West will spend $17 million to develop and manage a major solar and wind generating facility. If the project is successful the company hopes to integrate similar renewable resources on a broader scale in its fuel mix in the future. CSR is also exploring new ways to recycle coal combustion byproducts (CCB) like bottom and fly ash to replace cement in concrete and to replace gravel in highway construction.

Central & South West's units currently burn low-sulfur coal and remove sulfur dioxide from exhaust gases with scrubbers, but in the event that its emissions exceed Clean Air Act requirements, the company will purchase allowances. Central & South West has a number of demand-side management programs to promote energy efficiency among its customers and it educates its employees on the virtues of such environmentally sound practices as the use of public transportation or carpooling.

EEO: In 1996, Central & South West's nine-member board of directors included one woman and one minority; the numbers were the same as of February 1998. Of 11 corporate officers at the company in 1996, none were women and two were minorities; as of February, 1998, two women and one minority were among 16 officers. Two women and one minority also ranked among the 25 highest paid employees at the company in 1996 and 1997.

Also in 1997, Central & South West purchased over $27.5 million in goods and services from women- and minority-owned businesses.

Central & South West maintains diversity goals for both women and minorities, and offers mentoring programs for its female employees. The company also operates a recruitment program for women and minorities as a part of its diversity program.

Community Involvement: Central and South West reports that it is involved in its communities in many different ways—from employee volunteerism to charitable contributions. The Central and South West Foundation contributes mainly to colleges and universities through a matching-gifts program. Most of the giving from the corporation or its foundation goes to institutions or groups in the 735 communities where the company operates in Texas, Oklahoma, Louisiana, and Arkansas.

Family Benefits: Central & South West makes available a child care resource/referral service to its employees who have children, and offers a dependent-care spending account plan.

The company also offers such flexible scheduling options as a compressed work week, work-at-home arrangements, telecommuting/virtual office, flextime, and part-time return to work following leave.

Workplace Information: The records of the Occupational Safety and Health Administration indicate that Central & South West was not inspected from 1994 to 1997. Consequently no fines or violations were assessed to the company. In comparison, the median amount of fines per inspection for other companies in the utilities industry was $2,625.

51

Ceridian Corporation

STOCK SYMBOL: CEN
STOCK EXCHANGES: NY, To, B, C, CH, PH, P

Environment	N
Women's Advancement	A
Minority Advancement	B
Charitable Giving	N
Community Outreach	N
Family Benefits	N
Workplace Issues	B
Social Disclosure	C

Headquartered in Minneapolis, Minnesota, Ceridian Corporation is the information services and defense electronics company that emerged from the reshaping of Control Data in 1992. In 1997, the company spun off its defense business, which had constituted roughly 40 percent of Ceridian's revenues, to General Dynamics. Ceridian serves the human resources, electronic media, and transportation markets. Its information services segment includes payroll and tax filing, media research, employee advisory services, and transaction processing services. 1997 sales were $1.1 billion. The company has 8,000 employees.

Environment: Ceridian's U.S. defense electronics operations cut releases of toxic chemicals by about 20 percent in 1992, with similar reductions in subsequent years. The company generated roughly 180,000 pounds of hazardous waste in 1994, virtually all of which was shipped off-site for recycling. Ceridian does not participate in EPA's Green Lights or WasteWi$e programs.

EEO: Two women and one minority serve on Ceridian's ten-member board. There is one female officer among 11 corporate officials. In 1995, CEO Lawrence Perlman was one of four recipients of the Breaking the Glass Ceiling award given by Women Executives in State Government.

In 1993, Ceridian's Computing Devices subsidiary was one of four firms to receive Department of Defense recognition for minority subcontracting. That year the company awarded $5 million in contracts to minority vendors (an impressive 6.8 percent of total purchases).

Ceridian was sued by 419 former employees who claimed the company discriminated on the basis of age during its restructuring. In late 1993, the company settled 92 of these claims for $600,000. Ceridian maintains that the plaintiffs were simply among those to be cut during downsizing.

Community Involvement: Control Data had one of the most aggressive corporate community outreach programs from the 1960s through the 70s and 80s. The company initiated substantial programs to assist prison inmates and people on welfare. Several facilities were

specifically sited in economically distressed areas such as Washington, DC, and rural Appalachia.

Whether such innovative programs continue today is unclear. Most of the facilities described above were sold off as the company restructured. The company does not disclose the total level of corporate giving. Through its Community Action Field Program, Ceridian gives $500 grants to organizations at which employees volunteer.

Workplace Information: Ceridian was cited in *Business Ethics: Profiles in Civic Virtue* (Fulcrum, 1990) as being the first major company in the U.S. to adopt flexible work schedules and to establish an employee assistance program. In 1996, Ceridian was awarded a Department of Labor Corporate Citizen Award for "dedication to employees and the community." Several of Ceridian's businesses offer work-at-home programs, job-sharing, and flexible benefits for part-time employees.

Thousands of Ceridian employees lost their jobs in restructurings during the 1980's. The company offers generous severance assistance, but certain benefits have been scaled back. As of January 1995, for example, new hires were placed in a 401(k) savings program rather than Ceridian's traditional defined benefit plan.

Weapons Contracts: Once the 76th largest supplier to the U.S. Department of Defense (1993), Ceridian no longer has any defense or military contracts.

Additional Information: Ceridian spun off its lottery operations in 1992 to Video Lottery Technologies. The company spun off its Comdata subsidiary, which provided funds transfer and data processing services to the gambling industry, in 1998.

Champion International

STOCK SYMBOL: CHA
STOCK EXCHANGES: NY, B, C, CH, P, PH

Environment	B
Women's Advancement	A
Minority Advancement	B
Charitable Giving	A
Community Outreach	B
Family Benefits	D
Workplace Issues	D
Social Disclosure	A

Based in Stamford, Connecticut, Champion International is one of the leading producers of paper products, including newsprint and business communications materials and other wood products. The company owns more than five million acres of domestic forestland over eighteen states, and timber properties in Canada and Brazil. 1996 revenues for Champion totaled $5.9 billion, and the company has 25,250 employees.

Environment: Champion International has an environmental policy and a corporate environmental report. Champion International has not implemented an integrated environmental management system, but does have an environmental, health and safety (EH&S) training program. It also considers contribution towards EH&S goals in the job performance reviews of EH&S staff and facility staff. Champion International has a pollution prevention policy and program. The company also has a corporate policy on community involvement relating to local environmental concerns. Champion International is in compliance with the American Forest & Paper Association's Sustainable Forestry Initiative.

Champion International's average total toxic releases and transfers during the years 1993–1994 were less than the industry sample average. However, its emissions increased by about a fifth during those years, a below average performance.

In September 1997, Champion was sued by two Pigeon River, Tennessee residents who claim to represent 200 landowners who own property on the river. The plaintiffs seek class action status and compensatory damages and punitive damages. Plaintiffs purport to limit their damages to $74,000 per claimant. The plaintiffs argue that Champion's operations in Canton, North Carolina, have diminished the quality of the water in the river, created a nuisance, and reduced their property values. An earlier class action lawsuit concerning this matter was settled in 1992; however, the company intends to vigorously contest the current suit.

EEO: In 1996, Champion International achieved a higher than average rating in both diversity categories, placing them easily in the top third of S&P 500 companies. Two women and one minority served on Champion International's 11-member board. Of 13 corporate officers at the company, none were women and none were minorities.

Community Involvement: Champion International's 1996 charitable contributions totaled $8.2 million in cash, and $100,000 in in-kind donations. The $8.2 million cash-giving figure represented 4 percent of the company's pretax earnings for the same year, partially the result of a dip in earnings from 1995. In 1995, the company contributed 0.66 percent of its pretax earnings for that year to charity.

Through its Middle School Partnership program, Champion will help to restructure middle schools in participating school districts through staff development. The program uses the recommendations of the Carnegie report on adolescent development. Champion contributes $1.7 million annually to the Carnegie efforts. In its Guidelines for Giving, Champion encourages "all employees to take an active part in the affairs of their communities," and states that it believes that "through these volunteer efforts, along with donated funds, both the interests of our company and our various constituencies can best be met."

Family Benefits: Most of Champion's family benefits are offered only to employees at its headquarters.

Workplace Information: OSHA records indicate that Champion was inspected 23 times from 1994 to 1996. Violations included four classified as "willful" or "repeat" and 128 classified as "serious" for a total of $134,018 in fines, or $5,837 per inspection. In comparison, the median amount of fines per inspection for other companies in the extractive business was $2,941.

Approximately 80 percent of Champion's payroll is unionized, and the relationship between management and unions has been good. The company was an industry leader in the establishment of worker/management safety teams, peer hiring programs, and conflict resolution procedures.

53

Chase Manhattan

STOCK SYMBOL: CMB
STOCK EXCHANGES: NY, B, C, CH, P

Environment	N
Women's Advancement	B
Minority Advancement	D?
Charitable Giving	N
Community Outreach	C
Family Benefits	C
Workplace Issues	B
Social Disclosure	C

Headquartered in New York City, Chase Manhattan is the sixth largest bank in the U.S. The company's diverse operations include consumer products, regional banking, private banking, corporate finance, and risk management and information services. The bank has total assets of more than $100 billion and approximately 34,400 full-time employees. Chase operates over 400 branches, one-quarter of which are outside the U.S. in such places as Brazil, Hong Kong, and Saudi Arabia.

EEO: In 1996, Chase Manhattan Corp.'s 16-member board of directors included three women and one minority. Of 12 corporate officers at the company, one was a woman and none were minorities.

In 1994, Chase Manhattan instituted leadership training programs and a performance management policy through which women employees may develop their skills.

In 1993, Chase administered the leveraged buyout of what became the largest minority employee-owned company in the U.S., Advanced Technical Solutions in Brooklyn, N.Y. Chase has a policy that prohibits discrimination on the basis of sexual orientation.

Chase Manhattan Corp. offers mentoring programs and apprenticeship programs for its female employees.

Community Involvement: Chase Manhattan, through its Foundation and the Corporate Social Responsibility department, supports community development, precollegiate education, art and nonprofits mainly in the tri-state region and Texas, but also in the rest of the U.S. and internationally.

Chase offers community development loans, partnerships, programs, grants and investments primarily to low- and moderate-income communities, their residents and small businesses, with a special focus on women and minority entrepreneurs and nonprofits. Chase was rated "outstanding" by the Federal Reserve Bank of New York for complying with the Community Reinvestment Act. It also won the Bank Enterprise Award given by the U.S. Department of the Treasury for investments in community financial institutions. Chase assists disadvantaged, unemployed adults through a $3 million initiative to support various skills training programs.

The Chase Community Development Corporation (CCDC) is a residential real estate, small business and community development lender to low- and moderate-income neighborhoods in the greater New York area. Through CCDC, Chase keeps in contact with developers in the profit and non-profit sectors who are forming public/private partnerships in neighborhoods. In 1993, Chase and three other New York banks invested $12 million in the New York Equity Fund's multi-family developments, to create 543 affordable family units. The company also established two revolving lines of credit for $20 million for the Community Preservation Corporation, to provide construction and permanent financing of housing. In the boroughs of Brooklyn, Queens and Staten Island, Chase has given $19 million to three projects through the city's Turnkey program. Two of these are for construction and rehabilitation of 371 low-income rental units, and one is for a day-treatment facility for mentally-handicapped persons.

Family Benefits: Chase Manhattan Corp. makes available on-site or near-site child care and a subsidy for child care to employees with children. The company also offers such flexible scheduling options as a compressed work week, work-at-home arrangements, flextime, and job sharing.

Workplace Information: The records of the Occupational Safety and Health Administration indicate that Chase Manhattan underwent one health and safety inspection from 1994 to 1996. The only violations reported by OSHA were classified as "other," the least serious kind of violation. The company was not required to pay any fines as a result of its violations. In comparison, the median amount of fines per inspection for other companies in the service industry, such as banks and communications companies, was $573.

54

⚜ Chevron Corporation

STOCK SYMBOL: CHV
STOCK EXCHANGES: NY, B, C, CH, PH, P, VC

Environment	A
Women's Advancement	B
Minority Advancement	A
Charitable Giving	D
Community Outreach	C
Family Benefits	A
Workplace Issues	A
Social Disclosure	A

San Francisco, California-based Chevron, once known as Standard Oil of California (Socal), is the fourth largest U.S. petroleum company and is the biggest corporation based in California. In 1996, Chevron had sales of $37.5 billion and 40,820 employees.

Environment: Chevron Corporation has an environmental policy and publishes a corporate environmental report, which is updated biennially and is available on the Internet. Chevron has implemented an integrated environmental management system as part of its "Protecting People and the Environment" program. The company has a written pollution prevention policy, and has initiated a company-wide pollution prevention program, which establishes annual reduction goals for point sources, secondary emissions, fugitive emissions, and solid waste. The company also has a corporate policy on community involvement relating to local environmental concerns, and currently has community advisory panels at 12 of its facilities. Chevron has a written policy on product stewardship and evaluates its products with the objective of reducing their life-cycle impacts on the environment.

Chevron made history by making the first ever donation of water rights to protect a river and its wildlife at Gunnison River Gorge. Chevron contributed more than $100,000 to study the habitat of the endangered Great Gray Owl of Yosemite National Park. The company supports National Coastal Cleanup Day each year and other beach cleanup efforts around the country. Chevron partnered with World Wildlife Fund in Papua New Guinea with the Kutubu Project. It also participated in EPA's 33/50 and Natural Gas Star programs.

Chevron Corporation's average toxic releases and transfers during the years 1994–1995 were less than the industry sample average. However, its emissions increased by about a half during those years, the worst performance within the industry sample. The company ranked third out of 15 for CEP's Campaign for Cleaner Corporations' (C-3) 1997 Petroleum Refining Report. It was also identified as one of the "best" performers for refining operations.

Chevron has paid nearly $700,000 after exceeding pollution limits for a decade at its Perth Amboy facility. The facility has been brought into compliance with emission standards; Chevron denies any wrongdoing.

Communities for a Better Environment filed suits in 1997 against Tosco Corp, Chevron Corp, Unocal Corp, GATX Corp, and Ultramar Corp., saying they are taking advantage of a pollution credit program to continue polluting in poor neighborhoods. Chevron claims this really targets the rulemaking actions of the regulatory agencies involved and their associated administrative procedures for rule approval. Chevron also claims that its loading facilities are actually closer to higher priced real estate property.

EEO: In 1996, Chevron Corporation achieved a higher than average rating in both diversity categories. Two women and two minorities served on Chevron Corporation's 13-member board. Of 14 corporate officers at the company, one was a woman and none were minorities.

Chevron agreed to pay $8.5 million in November, 1996 to settle a class-action discrimination suit brought by 777 current and former female employees at the Chevron Information Technology Corporation (CITC), a San Ramon-based operating unit of Chevron Corporation. The lawsuit claimed that qualified women were routinely passed over for promotions, and that male colleagues were paid salaries as much as $80,000 higher. Chevron agreed to a formula payment based on salary level and years of service amounting to a total of $7 million, with an additional $1 million fund which would supply supplemental payments of $5,000 to $50,000 for the emotional distress experienced by the employees. Chevron could have to pay considerably more if a number of the plaintiffs are not satisfied by the offer and opt for arbitration. In a January 1997 racial

Continued on next page

discrimination case, a judge ordered Chevron USA Inc. to pay $368,000 to two African-American employees who had been denied promotions in 1985.

Charles Walker, executive director of the National Society of Blacks in Engineering, stated that Chevron is among the oil industry leaders in minority recruitment.

Community Involvement: In 1996, Chevron Corporation's charitable giving totaled $18.3 million in cash, which was equal to 0.4 percent of the company's pretax earnings for that year. In terms of the actual dollar amount donated by the company, the level of cash contributions in 1996 represented a decrease of 0.6 percent from that of 1995, which was 1 percent of the company's earnings for that year.

Chevron gave more money to environmental affairs in 1995 than any other corporation according to the April, 1997 issue of *Corporate Giving Watch*. The company primarily supports conservation and habitat and wildlife preservation in California, but also gives grants to educational and research institutions with emphasis on environmental affairs. Chevron has given over $50 million towards education in the last decade, and has matched an additional $15 million in employee gifts to higher education in the same period. The company has been recognized by the Council for Aid to Education for its support of the Accelerated Schools Program. The program assists at-risk youth who often start school far behind their peers.

Chevron Canada created a program in 1995 entitled Employees in Action. Through the program, employees are permitted to take eight to ten hours a year off with pay to work with a local community organization. Currently, Chevron Corporation does not have such a policy.

Workplace Information: OSHA records indicate that Chevron Corporation was inspected 57 times from 1994 to 1996. Violations include two classified as "willful" or "repeat" and 124 classified as "serious" for a total of $135,102 in fines, or $2,370 per inspection. In comparison, the median amount of fines per inspection for other companies in the extractive business was $2,941.

Legal Proceedings: A suit brought by a Houston neighborhood claims that Gulf Oil, acquired by Chevron in 1984, covered up toxic hazards when the area was marketed to African Americans beginning in 1967. Residents complain of a collection of illnesses they attribute to past pollution by the company. A federal judge declared a mistrial in 1997, citing the previous judge's racially insensitive remarks. The neighborhood, which contends it is the victim of environmental racism, has garnered the support of Jesse Jackson and NAACP head Kweisi Mfume in its charges against Chevron.

56

Chrysler Corporation

STOCK SYMBOL: C
STOCK EXCHANGES: NY, TO, B, C, CH, P, PH, MO

Environment	C
Women's Advancement	F?
Minority Advancement	D?
Charitable Giving	D
Community Outreach	C
Family Benefits	N
Workplace Issues	D?
Social Disclosure	C

The Chrysler Corporation, based in Highland Park, Michigan, manufactures cars, minivans, sport utility vehicles, and trucks for customers throughout the world. In North America, its vehicles are marketed under the Chrysler/Plymouth, Dodge, and Jeep/Eagle divisions. The corporation also includes the Chrysler Financial Corporation, the Chrysler Technologies Corporation, and the Pentastar Transportation Group, Inc. In 1996, the company had worldwide revenues of $61.4 billion and approximately 126,000 employees.

Environment: Chrysler does not have an environmental policy available to the public or publish an annual report. The company's brochure "Chrysler Corporation Environmental Programs" outlines its commitment to reducing emissions and improving air quality. Chrysler strongly supports the use of reformulated gasoline in its vehicles and has an active Natural Gas Vehicle program. The company is also developing flexible fuel vehicle technology, which will operate on alcohol, gasoline, or any combination of these two fuels. Chrysler is also a founding member of the U.S. Advanced Battery Consortium, a group working on battery technology for electric vehicles.

The company is a participant in the Auto/Oil Air Quality Improvement Research Program, a joint undertaking of the big three automakers and 14 oil companies. As part of its pollution prevention strategy, Chrysler works with its suppliers to identify materials of concern, to eliminate/reduce volumes, or to make substitution with less hazardous materials. Each Chrysler plant has a conservation committee, and more than 75 percent of Chrysler's fuel use is natural gas.

EEO: Chrysler had one woman and one minority on its 14-member board in 1996. The company's 31 corporate officers included one woman and no minorities.

In 1997, Franklin Research withdrew a shareholder resolution proposing that Chrysler report on its sexual orientation policies which generally indicates that an agreement has been reached with management. In April 1997, workers went on strike at a Detroit Chrysler plant for reasons that included allegations of discrimination against minority workers.

Community Involvement: Chrysler Corporation's charitable contributions totaled $22.7 million in cash in 1996. The $22.7 million cash-giving figure represented the equivalent of 0.4 percent of the company's pretax earnings for the same year, and a decrease of 11.9 percent from the company's cash contributions in 1995. In 1995, the company contributed 0.7 percent of its pretax earnings for that year to charity.

Employees volunteer through the company's "Involve to Solve" Program to make improvements on buildings in the communities where plants are located. More than 2,000 employees and retirees participated in the company's World of Work program in 1996, a volunteer effort that connects classroom and workplace learning.

Workplace Information: 1996 Osha violations included seven classified as "willful" or "repeat" and 108 classified as "serious." The company was fined $49,334, slightly below average for the industry.

Chrysler reported in July, 1997, that its profit that quarter had dropped 53 percent due largely to the Mound Road engine plant strike in April, the longest in company history, that shut down seven plants temporarily, idling over 23,000 workers. The strike ended with an agreement that included Chrysler's pledge to install a new machining line and to upgrade the prop-shaft division of the plant, while in the meantime that work will be outsourced. In spite of the agreement, the *Los Angeles Times* reported that Chrysler intends to make the outsourcing permanent.

Weapons Contracts: In 1994, Chrysler had approximately $251 million in contracts with the Department of Defense. Of this amount, $409,000 was for nuclear weapons systems.

57

CINergy Corp.

STOCK SYMBOL: CIN
STOCK EXCHANGES: NY, B, C, CH, PH, P

Environment	REV
Women's Advancement	B?
Minority Advancement	D?
Charitable Giving	A
Community Outreach	C
Family Benefits	N
Workplace Issues	N
Social Disclosure	D

CINergy Corp., based in Cincinnati, Ohio, is the parent company of the Cincinnati Gas & Electric Company and PSI Energy, Inc., utilities that serve a combined 1.4 million electric customers and 440,000 gas customers in a 25,000-square-mile area of Ohio, Indiana, and Kentucky. CINergy has several subsidiaries that are engaged in energy-related businesses, and a 50 percent ownership of Midlands Electricity plc, a Regional Electric Company serving 2.2 million customers in the United Kingdom. In 1996, CINergy had revenues of $3 billion and employed 7,973 people.

Environment: CINergy does not currently publish a corporate environmental report. As mandated by the Clean Air Act Amendments of 1990 to decrease sulfur dioxide and nitrogen oxide emissions from utility sources, the company is in the process of switching to lower-sulfur coal blends and utilizing an emission allowance banking strategy. CINergy is also active in the global climate change arena, and addresses this problem by reducing its greenhouse gas emissions, encouraging the use of alternative fuels for transportation vehicles, funding research for electricity generating technologies, and engaging in discussion of global climate change issues. The company also joined the U.S. Department of Energy Climate Challenge Program in 1995.

In December 1997, the U.S. Environmental Protection Agency awarded PSI Energy and five other utilities bonus acid rain allowances for undertaking energy efficiency and renewable energy measures. These measures were designed to reduce emissions of sulfur dioxide and nitrogen oxide, the main precursors of acid rain, and carbon dioxide, the principal greenhouse gas.

In November 1997, CINergy and other utilities and manufacturing organizations in the Midwest Ozone Group sued the Environmental Protection Agency, saying new agency plans to cut smog in Northeast states overstep its authority. CINergy estimates that it will incur costs of $540 million over five years to install additional anti-pollution equipment to comply with the proposed EPA nitrogen-oxide emissions standards. The agency wants to reduce nitrogen-oxide emission levels 85 percent by 2002. CINergy's most recent integrated resource plan outlines the company's intent to install up to 1,400 MW of fuel cell capacity from 2009 to 2015 and switch several of its existing high-sulfur coal-fired generating units to medium or low-sulfur coal to comply with Phase Two of the federal acid rain rules.

In September 1997, CINergy had also stated its intention to spend up to $204 million to voluntarily reduce nitrogen oxide emissions to one-third of 1990 levels.

EEO: Two women have attained corporate officer positions at CINergy, up from one in 1995 (the company has 14 such positions). However, none of the company's 16 board members was a woman or a minority as of December 31, 1996.

Community Involvement: CINergy Community Partners, the company's volunteer program, offers employee volunteer assistance for corporate-wide group projects in the communities it serves. About eight percent of the company's employees are involved in the two-year-old program. The volunteer program makes use of an internal community needs assignment program to define and identify corporate-wide projects. Major projects have included a clothing drive for youth and the Grant-a-School Wish Project.

The company works to create partnerships with certain school systems to create educational reform, and supports projects which foster creativity, innovation, and motivation in schools. Support for community development places special emphasis on programs that lead to community self-sufficiency.

Workplace Information: OSHA records indicate that CINergy was not inspected from 1994 to 1996. Consequently, no fines or violations were assessed to the company.

# Citicorp

STOCK SYMBOL: CCI
STOCK EXCHANGES: NY, B, C, CH, PH, P

Environment	N
Women's Advancement	B
Minority Advancement	A
Charitable Giving	B
Community Outreach	C
Family Benefits	A
Workplace Issues	A
Social Disclosure	A

New York City–based Citicorp is a global financial services organization. Citicorp's activities are conducted primarily within the two franchises of the consumer business which includes branch banking, credit and charge cards, and private banking. The bank has affiliates and subsidiaries in 98 countries and territories throughout the world. In 1996, Citicorp had total revenues of $21.5 billion. Citicorp employs 89,400 persons worldwide.

Environment: Citicorp has provided funding to the Smithsonian Institute, for land use studies in Kenya and Brazil; the American University of Cairo, for its environmental studies program; and the World Wildlife Fund, for a biodiversity community project in India. In 1989, the bank announced it would cease funding energy projects in developing countries; the projects frequently resulted in environmental degradation. Citicorp is a member of the EPA's Green Lights program.

EEO: In 1996, Citicorp achieved a higher than average rating in both diversity categories, placing them easily in the top third of S&P 500 companies. One woman and three minorities served on Citicorp's 14-member board. Of 12 corporate officers at the company, two were women and three were minorities.

A group of African-American employees recently sued Citicorp, charging racial discrimination. Separately, a woman formerly employed at the company brought a sexual harassment suit against the company. The corporation denied the allegations contained in both suits.

Citicorp offers mentoring and recruitment programs, maintains diversity goals, and offers developmental training to both women and minorities. Citicorp also provides various support networks for employees who belong to minority groups.

Community Involvement: In 1996, Citicorp's charitable giving totaled $31 million in cash, which was equal to 0.5 percent of the company's pretax earnings for that year. In terms of the actual dollar amount donated by the company, the level of cash contributions in 1996 represented an increase of $5.9 million over 1995 contributions, which were 0.6 percent of the company's earnings for that year.

Through a corporate giving program administered by its subsidiaries and through its foundation, contributions from Citicorp are directed to not-for-profit organizations and other programs that the company supports for charitable and educational purposes. Priorities are community development and education, with more than 70 percent of grants reserved for these purposes. Other interests are arts and culture, health and human services and the environment. The community development grant program supports institutions with initiatives for affordable housing and small businesses, as well as those seeking to expand job creation and child care opportunities.

Workplace Information: The records of the Occupational Safety and Health Administration indicate that Citicorp underwent one health and safety inspection from 1994 to 1996. The violations reported by OSHA as a result of the inspection include one classified as "serious." The company was not required to pay any fines as a result of its violations. In comparison, the median amount of fines per inspection for other companies in the service industry, such as banks and communications companies, was $573.

In 1997, Citicorp realized an $889 million restructuring charge to improve operational efficiency and productivity. This will result in a net reduction of 7,500 positions.

Clorox Company

STOCK SYMBOL: CLX
STOCK EXCHANGES: NY, B, C, CH, P, PH

Environment	A
Women's Advancement	D?
Minority Advancement	C?
Charitable Giving	B
Community Outreach	B?
Family Benefits	N
Workplace Issues	A?
Social Disclosure	C

Founded in 1913, Clorox has dominated the market for bleach, but reports that it is much more than a bleach company. Since its 1993 divestiture of its frozen food and bottled water operations, the company has returned to its core business of household cleaning products, which continues to grow. The company still maintains its Kingsford products (charcoal, cat litters, and insecticide) and food products (dressings and sauces) businesses. The company also manufactures and markets Brita water filtration systems. In 1997, Clorox had 5,500 employees and sales of $2.5 billion, 16 percent of which were from international markets. The company is headquartered in Oakland, California.

Environment: Concerned for the environment, Clorox works to prevent accidents during the production of bleach. Company safety programs include state-of-the-art automatic safety controls, electronic chlorine gas detection devices, fail-safe tank-car valve actuators, and completely enclosed unloading facilities at all bleach manufacturing plants. For 14 consecutive years, the company has not had a reportable chlorine release. Toxic emissions (TRI) directly to the environment decreased nearly 40 percent between 1992 and 1993, to a level well below the industry average. From 1992 to 1994, the company reduced the amount of spilled hazardous wastes by about half (121,000 pounds). The company reduced packaging materials by 35 million pounds the past 10 years; 34 percent of packaging consists of post-consumer recycled materials.

Clorox upgraded its charcoal plant in Missouri, which resulted in a 60 percent reduction in overall emissions. The company reduced packaging materials by 30 million pounds between 1988 and 1994. Now 27 percent of Clorox's packaging consists of post-consumer recycled materials.

EEO: In 1996, Clorox Co.'s board totaled 13 directors, including one woman and one minority, while two of a total of 22 corporate officers were women. As of February, 1998, two women and one minority were among Clorox's 17 directors, and a minority was added to the company's now 23 corporate officers.

Clorox established an Affirmative Action compliance program to broaden recruitment efforts to attract the best possible men and women from all groups. The company created a "Workforce Diversity Specialist" position to oversee implementation of its EEO policy.

Community Involvement: Clorox Co.'s charitable contributions totaled $2.8 million in cash in 1996, and $3.1 million in 1997. The $2.8 million cash-giving figure was equal to 0.76 percent of the company's pretax earnings for the same year, and was identical to the company's cash contributions in 1995.

Clorox Chairman and CEO Craig Sullivan was given the "1996 Spirit of Achievement Award" by Junior Achievement for his impact on the lives of minority and low-income youth and the company's commitment to JA's Elementary School Program in Oakland and Pleasanton public schools. The Clorox Employee Volunteer Program engages over one-third of all employees in volunteer work annually, logging some 63,000 hours in 1996. Clorox has received several awards for its community efforts, including CEP's 1993 Corporate Conscience Award for Community Involvement.

Workplace Information: OSHA records indicate that Clorox was inspected three times from 1994 to 1996, receiving just one "serious" violation and $1,250 in fines, less than one third of the median average for similar companies. Ten percent of Clorox's workforce is unionized. In the last five years, there has been one two-week strike.

Animal Testing: Between 1995 and 1997, Clorox reduced the numbers of animals used in testing by 40 percent, from 945 to 563, despite increased product introductions and acquisitions. Clorox spent about $30,000 on alternative efforts in 1997, and started two alternative test programs which evaluate replacement tests for the Draize eye irritation test and the rabbit-based skin irritation test. The company also provides financial support to The Institute for In Vitro Sciences, the Center for Alternatives to Animal Testing, and the Scientist Center for Animal Welfare.

The Coca-Cola Company

STOCK SYMBOL: KO

STOCK EXCHANGES: NY, B, C, CH, P, PH

Environment	B
Women's Advancement	C
Minority Advancement	A
Charitable Giving	B
Community Outreach	A
Family Benefits	A
Workplace Issues	B
Social Disclosure	A

The Coca-Cola Company is the world's largest manufacturer, marketer, and distributor of soft drink concentrates and syrups, and the world's largest marketer and distributor of juice and juice-drink products, including those produced under the Minute Maid and Hi-C brand names. Most of Coca-Cola's bottlers are independently owned, though the company owns minority shares in many of them, including a 45 percent interest in Coca-Cola Enterprises, the world's largest bottler of Coca-Cola beverages. Coca-Cola's net operating revenues for 1996 were $18.5 billion, while employees numbered 32,000. The company is based in Atlanta, Georgia.

Environment: Coca-Cola has a well-developed environmental program, which the company describes in its publicly available environmental report. In early 1998, the company endorsed the CERES principles. Each Coca-Cola operating group and division has an environmental coordinator, and all company-owned production facilities are audited every three years. CEP found little evidence of noncompliance at Coca-Cola facilities, though a Puerto Rico plant sold in 1994 was discharging wastewater without a permit in 1993. The company's toxic releases were at the industry's average level in 1994.

Coca-Cola's main environmental concerns are solid waste and water quality. In 1991, the company introduced the world's first plastic drink container made with recycled materials. Coca-Cola's goal is to use recycled materials in all soft drink packaging, and it is now working on eliminating the base cups of plastic bottles, reducing the aluminum used in cans, and printing labels without heavy-metal inks. Between 1992 and 1995, the company spent over $100 million on its wastewater quality policy, which requires that all wastewater discharged into natural bodies of water be capable of sustaining fish life.

EEO: In 1996, Coca-Cola Company's 14-member board of directors included two women and two minorities. Of 43 corporate officers at the company, five were women and six were minorities. Three minorities also ranked among the 25 highest paid employees at the company.

From 1992 to 1996, the Coca-Cola business system purchased nearly $1.1 billion worth of goods and services from business owned by minorities and women.

Community Involvement: In 1994, Coca-Cola Company made over $31.8 million in cash contributions to charitable institutions, the equivalent of 0.85 percent of the company's earnings before taxes that year. The company also made in-kind donations of products and services totaling over $1.1 million in the same year.

In 1989, the Coca-Cola Foundation made a ten-year, $50 million pledge to support over 400 schools and associations. That endowment goal was achieved four years early, in 1995. The foundation has since doubled the endowment goal to $100 million to be reached by 1999. The foundation gives exclusively to educational interests. Recipients include programs to help keep children in school, minority scholarships, teacher development, and programs to increase international understanding and arts education.

Coca-Cola's volunteer program, "Reaching Out," has over 1200 participants who have tallied over 60,000 hours in local community service projects.

Workplace Information: OSHA's records indicate that Coca-Cola Company underwent three inspections from 1994 to 1996. The violations reported by OSHA as a result of the inspections include three classified as "serious." The company was required to pay $5,265 as a result of its violations.

⚙️ Colgate-Palmolive

STOCK SYMBOL: CL
STOCK EXCHANGES: NY, B, C, CH, P, PH

Environment	B
Women's Advancement	A
Minority Advancement	A
Charitable Giving	B
Community Outreach	A
Family Benefits	B
Workplace Issues	A
Social Disclosure	A

Colgate-Palmolive, based in New York City, is a leading oral and personal care products company with manufacturing and sales operations in more than 80 countries worldwide. Among its best-known products are Colgate toothpaste, Palmolive soap and dishwashing products, Ajax household cleaners, Fab laundry detergent, Murphy Oil Soap, and Hill's pet products. In 1996, total revenues reached $8.7 billion, and the company had 37,300 employees.

Environment: Colgate has a comprehensive environmental policy but does not publish an environmental report. The company has made significant efforts to reduce toxic emissions and hazardous waste. Colgate TRI emissions directly to the environment declined by more than 50 percent from 1991 to 1993; the household products industry average was 1.3 million pounds in 1993, while Colgate emitted 28,827 pounds. From 1991 to 1994, there was a total toxic release reduction of 43.6 percent.

The company also uses super-concentrated soap formulas, which reduce chemicals, energy, and packaging materials used in manufacturing and marketing. Some products are now packaged in post-consumer recycled PET and HDPE containers, resulting in less waste generation and reduced emissions.

Although Colgate's compliance record has been good, the company was fined $110,000 for violations of the wastewater permit at its Jeffersonville, Indiana, plant.

EEO: Two women and one minority served on Colgate's ten-member board. Of 25 corporate officers at the company, two were women and two were minorities, while two of the top 25 paid employees were women, and two were minorities.

Colgate-Palmolive received the Exemplary Voluntary Efforts Award (EVE) from the Secretary of Labor in 1996 for its work in creating greater workforce diversity. Colgate's multi-functional training programs continue to provide employees, including women and minorities, a wide range of experiences in various business activities throughout the company. Training, education and on-the-job skill-building are provided to increase opportunities for personal and career advancement of Colgate employees with an emphasis on mentoring, partnerships and support networks.

Colgate's senior management stands behind the company's efforts to increase diversity; any employee who is absent from a mandatory two-day diversity seminar must personally explain his/her absence to the vice president in charge of the company's North American and European operations.

Community Involvement: Colgate-Palmolive's charitable contributions totaled $10.8 million in cash in 1996, and $627,000 in in-kind donations. The $10.8 million cash-giving figure represented the equivalent of 1.13 percent of the company's pretax earnings for the same year, and a decrease of 5.6 percent from the company's cash contributions in 1995. In 1995, the company contributed 3 percent of its pretax earnings for that year to charity.

The "Everybody Wins" program, sponsored by the company, encourages employee mentoring of local school children on extended lunch hours.

CEO Reuben Mark chairs the New York City Partnership's Education and Youth Employment Committee, which provides summer jobs, trains teachers to better teach employability skills, and lobbies for educational reform.

Workplace Information: According to the Occupational Safety and Health Administration's records, Colgate-Palmolive was inspected four times from 1994 to 1996. Violations included three classified as "serious." A total of $5,200 in fines was assessed to the company following the inspections.

Animal Testing: Colgate stopped in-house animal testing in 1989. The company contracts for such testing with outside laboratories. However, Colgate has worked for 15 years to develop non-animal research and testing methods. Between 1994 and 1995, it reduced animal testing by 45 percent (and a total of 93 percent since 1982).

Compaq Computer

STOCK SYMBOL: CPQ
STOCK EXCHANGES: NY, B, CH, P

Environment	A
Women's Advancement	D
Minority Advancement	C
Charitable Giving	F
Community Outreach	C
Family Benefits	B
Workplace Issues	A
Social Disclosure	A

In 1994, Compaq became the world's largest personal computer manufacturer, with sales totaling $10.9 billion. In 1996, revenues reached $18.1 billion. The company's manufacturing operations consist of assembling finished products that are acquired from a wide range of vendors. Located worldwide—with recent facilities in Brazil and China—Compaq employed 23,884 people in 1996. The company is based in Houston, Texas.

Environment: Compaq has an environmental policy and a corporate environmental report, which is updated biennially and is available on the internet. Compaq has implemented an integrated environmental management system and provides Environmental Health and Safety (EH&S) training to all employees. The company also considers contribution towards EH&S goals in the job performance reviews of EH&S staff, facility staff, and executives, presenting awards to employees for their contribution to environmental issues. Compaq has a written pollution prevention policy and a companywide pollution prevention program, which establishes goals for point sources, fugitive emissions, secondary emissions, and solid waste. Compaq also has a corporate policy on community involvement relating to environmental concerns. Internationally, the company monitors SARA Title III emissions of non-U.S. operations and follows worldwide standards regardless of locations.

Compaq's average toxic releases and transfers during the years 1995–1996 were the lowest compared to an industry sample. However, although its emissions decreased by about a sixth during those years, its performance was still below average within the sample.

Compaq Computer received the 1997 World Environment Center (WEC) Gold Medal for International Corporate Environmental Achievement. The WEC Gold Medal Jury based its decision on Compaq's dynamic application of Design for Environment principals. Compaq is also a recipient of the EPA's WasteWi$e Comprehensive Program Recognition Award, in recognition of the company's solid waste reduction efforts.

EEO: In 1996, Compaq's ten-member board of directors included one woman and no minorities. Of 12 corporate officers at the company, none were women and one was a minority. Three women and two minorities also ranked among the 25 highest paid employees at the company. Also in 1996, Compaq created the position of Director of Corporate Diversity and Compliance, reporting directly to the Sr. Vice President of Human Resources, responsible for worldwide diversity programs and U.S. Affirmative Action. The company reports that it is partnering with various diversity organizations to recruit a diverse candidate pool for open positions and to implement its diversity commitment.

A Compaq executive apologized to Packard Bell in 1995 for offensive remarks about Mexicans and Chinese. According to Compaq, the comments, which were construed as racist, were actually criticism of Packard Bell's practice of using outside contractors for design and manufacturing. Compaq was one of 15 of the nation's 100 largest companies that did not have any minorities directors in 1996.

Community Involvement: In 1996, Compaq's cash and in-kind giving totaled $7 million, which was equal to 0.4 percent of the company's pretax earnings. While records are not available of fair market value of each computer, Compaq bases its charitable giving on cash value and fair market value of computers donated.

Family Benefits: Compaq makes on-site or near-site child care and a resource/referral service for child care available to employees with children. The company also offers such flexible scheduling options as a compressed work week, work-at-home arrangements, flextime, and part-time return to work following leave.

Workplace Information: OSHA records indicate that Compaq was not inspected from 1994 to 1996; thus the company received no fines or violations. All corporate manufacturing sites have safety committees and safety training for all new employees. Compaq's work-related injury rates are approximately 50 percent below the industry average.

63

ConAgra, Inc.

STOCK SYMBOL: CAG
STOCK EXCHANGES: NY, B, CH, P, PH

Environment	D
Women's Advancement	B
Minority Advancement	C
Charitable Giving	B
Community Outreach	C
Family Benefits	N
Workplace Issues	F
Social Disclosure	A

ConAgra, Inc., headquartered in Omaha, Nebraska, is a diversified international food company headquartered in Omaha, Nebraska. The company's food products range from prepared foods to agricultural supplies. In 1996, ConAgra had sales of $24.8 billion and 83,123 employees in 27 countries. ConAgra owns 21 popular food brands (each with annual retail sales exceeding $100 million), including La Choy, Wesson, Healthy Choice, Orville Redenbacher's, and Hunt's.

Environment: ConAgra promotes improved environmental performance through its Sustainable Development Council and its awards program. For example, its wastewater treatment facility in Quincy, Washington, uses native plants to transform damp solid waste into humus, a soil nutrient. Packaging materials were reduced by 800,000 pounds at a frozen food company, and the Armour Swift-Eckrich plant in Hastings, Nebraska, reduced water consumption by 50,000 gallons per day. Ecochem, a joint venture with DuPont, developed a technology to use waste products in lactic acid, which in turn are used in the production of fully biodegradable packaging material.

As one of the country's largest farming and livestock companies, much of ConAgra's environmental impact stems from pesticides and land use issues. ConAgra's TRI releases were the highest in the food industry and almost 10 times worse than the industry average. The company released 5.4 million pounds in 1994, an increase of over 20 percent from 1993. ConAgra's hazardous waste generation and accidental spill record were also worse than the industry average.

EEO: In 1996, ConAgra's 16-member board of directors included two women and no minorities. Of 23 corporate officers at the company, four were women and none were minorities. No women or minorities ranked among the 25 highest paid employees at the company. The Interfaith Center on Corporate Responsibility (ICCR) reports that it sponsored a 1997 shareholders' resolution proposing that ConAgra disclose diversity data.

Community Involvement: ConAgra's charitable contributions totaled $8 million in cash in 1996. The

$8 million cash-giving figure represented the equivalent of 2.0 percent of the company's pretax earnings for the same year, and an increase of 10.5 percent from the company's cash contributions in 1995. In 1995, the company contributed 1.0 percent of its pretax earnings for that year to charity.

ConAgra's giving to education focuses on higher education, with about three-quarters given directly to colleges and universities. ConAgra also initiated and has funded a school-to-work education program in Omaha aimed at young people ages 16-22 who do not plan to go on to college.

Workplace Information: The records of the Occupational Safety and Health Administration indicate that ConAgra underwent 26 health and safety inspections from 1994 to 1996. The violations reported by OSHA as a result of the inspections include nine classified as "willful" or "repeat" and 114 classified as "serious." The company was required to pay $264,575 as a result of its violations or an average of $10,176 per inspection. In comparison, the median amount of fines per inspection for other companies in the food, beverage, and household products industries was $1,515.

ConAgra closed 9 plants and businesses in 22 states in 1996, resulting in the loss of 6,300 jobs, or seven percent of the company's workforce (the company reports that 5,346 jobs were added over the following year). The restructuring was undertaken to improve the company's efficiency, and targeted what the company described as older and less productive facilities. In the largest plant closing, 1,322 workers lost their jobs at a Monfort beef plant in Des Moines, Iowa.

Consolidated Natural Gas

STOCK SYMBOL: CNG
STOCK EXCHANGES: NY, TO, B, C, CH, P

Consolidated Natural Gas, headquartered in Pittsburgh, Pennsylvania, operates in all phases of the natural gas business, explores for and produces oil, and provides a variety of energy marketing services. In 1996, the company formed a new subsidiary, CNG International Corp. to engage in energy related activities outside the U.S. At the end of 1996, CNG International and El Paso Energy corp. entered into a joint venture to own and operate the Australian pipeline assets formerly held by Tenneco Energy. In 1996, the company had revenues of $3.8 billion and employed 6,426 people.

Environment: Consolidated Natural Gas Company (CNG) has an environmental policy, signed by the Chairman and CEO, that is committed to assuming responsible stewardship for natural resources and conducting its businesses responsibly by employing sound environmental practices in designing, constructing, and operating its facilities. The company has taken on the responsibility of monitoring its facilities to resolve potential environmental matters as a part of its normal business operations, and conducts general environmental surveys continuously in order to monitor compliance at its facilities. CNG also promotes natural gas vehicles (NGV), which emit less carbon monoxide, nitrogen oxides, and non-methane hydrocarbons, compared to gasoline-driven vehicles.

EEO: In 1996, Consolidated Natural Gas's board totaled ten directors, including two women and one minority, while one of a total of seven corporate officers was a woman, and none were minorities. Additionally, one woman and no minorities were among the 25 employees with the highest salaries at the company. Five women were among the 50 highest paid CNG employees. At the end of 1997, 16.1 percent of CNG executives were women or minorities, up from 8.5 percent in 1994. The company reports that the increase can be attributed to CNG's efforts in the areas of diversity and the recruitment and development of women and minorities.

Consolidated Natural Gas offers mentoring programs, recruitment programs, and maintains diversity goals for both women and minorities.

Environment	REV
Women's Advancement	B
Minority Advancement	C
Charitable Giving	C
Community Outreach	C
Family Benefits	N
Workplace Issues	B
Social Disclosure	A

Community Involvement: In 1996, Consolidated Natural Gas's charitable giving totaled $2.8 million in cash, which was equal to 0.5 percent of the company's pretax earnings for that year. In terms of the actual dollar amount donated by the company, the level of cash contributions in 1996 was identical to that of 1995, which was 1.9 percent of the company's earnings for that year.

The CNG Foundation's largest area of giving in 1996 was education. One foundation grant will fund the study of environmental issues in 19 economically distressed Western Pennsylvania school districts. Other areas of support include health and human services, culture and the arts, community and economic development, and the environment. The majority of the Foundation's contributions are made through the various CNG companies and are based on individual needs and priorities of particular service areas as determined by those companies.

In the late 1980s, the CNG Foundation and WQED, Pittsburgh's public broadcasting station, established the Volunteer in the Arts (VITA) Award, which honors volunteers monthly and annually.

Workplace Information: The records of the Occupational Safety and Health Administration indicate that Consolidated Natural Gas was not inspected from 1994 to 1996. Consequently no fines or violations were assessed to the company.

CNG established a formalized audit program in 1997, through which at least one fifth of each company's operations will receive a comprehensive safety and health review annually.

Cooper Industries

Environment	B
Women's Advancement	C
Minority Advancement	F
Charitable Giving	B
Community Outreach	B
Family Benefits	D
Workplace Issues	F
Social Disclosure	A

Houston-based Cooper Industries, headquartered in Houston, Texas, is a major manufacturer of electrical products, electrical power equipment, tools and hardware, and automotive products. In 1995, the company spun off its petroleum equipment operations, Cooper Cameron, for a $313 million write-off. The company had 40,400 employees and sales of $5.3 billion in 1996.

Environment: The company has a general environmental policy and publishes an annual environmental issue in its newsletter. All facilities are audited every three years. Cooper does not follow U.S. environmental standards abroad but in the past three years audited all the company's manufacturing plants in Mexico. A participant in EPA's 33/50 toxics reduction program, the company reduced targeted chemicals by 75 percent by 1995. In 1994, Cooper was named Green Lights Manufacturing Ally of the Year by the EPA. The company produces energy-efficient lighting fixtures and trains customers in energy-efficient lighting. Cooper participates in EPA's Energy Star program to produce high-efficiency transformers for the electric utilities industry. The company is not a member of EPA's WasteWi$e waste management program, but it does recycle paper and metal. Cooper sponsors employees' annual Environmental Excellence Awards.

Cooper has the third highest toxic releases in the industry but is below the industry average for releases adjusted for size. The company had the second highest hazardous waste generation in the industry for 1993.

EEO: In 1996, Cooper Industries' board totaled ten directors, including one woman and one minority, while two of a total of 14 corporate officers were women, and none were minorities. Additionally, two women and no minorities were among the 25 employees with the highest salaries at the company.

Community Involvement: In 1996, Cooper Industries' charitable giving totaled $3.9 million in cash, which was equal to 0.7 percent of the company's pretax earnings for that year. In terms of the actual dollar amount donated by the company, the level of cash contributions in 1996 represented a decrease of 12.7 percent from that of 1995, which was 0.8 percent of the company's earnings for that year. The company's

in-kind giving—the donation of products or services—came to a total of $20,000 in 1996.

Cooper Industries' company-wide programs focus on protecting and preserving the environment, rewarding safety efforts in the workplace, improving vocational education and encouraging employee volunteer efforts. The Environmental Excellence Awards program recognizes individual Cooper operations for their efforts to go beyond basic environmental standards. Winning facilities direct Foundation grants to local organizations that are working to improve or protect the environment. Project PACE (Partnership to Aid Career Education) provides financial incentives to participating schools to improve the curriculum of vocational students and create a relationship between the schools and the local industry. Schools participating in the program receive an unrestricted annual grant of $10,000.

Workplace Information: The records of the Occupational Safety and Health Administration indicate that Cooper Industries underwent two health and safety inspections from 1994 to 1996. The violations reported by OSHA as a result of the inspections include nine classified as "serious." The company was required to pay an average of $2,400 per inspection. In comparison, the median amount of fines per inspection for other companies in similar manufacturing industries was $2,412.

Animal Testing: Although the company does not conduct in-house animal testing, it uses Wagner's brake fluid, an animal-tested product. The company maintains that these tests are required by federal laws.

Weapons Contracts: In 1994, Cooper had $4.7 million in Defense Department contracts — $1.6 million of which was weapons related and $1.3 million nuclear related.

Cooper Tire & Rubber

STOCK SYMBOL: CTB

STOCK EXCHANGES: NY, CH, PH, P

Environment	C
Women's Advancement	C?
Minority Advancement	F?
Charitable Giving	C
Community Outreach	N
Family Benefits	N
Workplace Issues	F?
Social Disclosure	D

In 1991, the trade magazine *Modern Tire Dealer* described Cooper Tire and Rubber as "the best-run and far-and-away the most successful tire company in the world." Indeed, while the U.S. tire industry experienced a loss of 40 plants in the 1980s, Cooper nearly doubled its workforce. The company's marketing strategy has been to focus on higher margin replacement tires, while also selling automotive products such as hoses, sealing systems and seating components. At year-end 1996, the Findlay, Ohio–based company had 8,932 employees and net sales of $1.6 billion.

Environment: CEP's review of EPA databases found no instances of material noncompliance. All Cooper plants use natural gas as a primary or secondary energy source. The company states that it seeks to utilize recyclable materials for internal shipments.

EEO: In 1996, Cooper Tire & Rubber's nine-member board of directors included one woman and no minorities.

In 1996, a shareholder resolution, asking that Cooper Tire & Rubber diversify its board of directors, was sponsored by the Interfaith Center on Corporate Responsibility. The resolution was withdrawn prior to the annual shareholders meeting, which usually indicates that some type of agreement was reached with the company's management

Community Involvement: Cooper Tire & Rubber's charitable contributions totaled $500,000 in cash in 1996. The $500,000 cash-giving figure represented the equivalent of 0.3 percent of the company's pretax earnings for the same year, and a decrease of 20 percent from the company's cash contributions in 1995. In 1995, the company contributed 0.3 percent of its pretax earnings for that year to charity.

Workplace Information: According to the Occupational Safety and Health Administration's records, Cooper Tire & Rubber was inspected three times from 1994 to 1996. The OSHA inspectors' citations included 18 violations classified as "serious." A total of $12,950 in fines was assessed to the company following the inspections, or an average of $4,316 per inspection. In comparison, the median amount of fines per inspection for other companies in similar manufacturing industries was $2,412.

In an industry recently characterized by bitter disputes between labor and management, Cooper maintains a positive relationship with its employees. Tire builders stamp their names inside the tires they produce and retirees are invited back each year for a special dinner. Altogether, employees own a 13 percent stake in the company from stock they receive through the plan.

International: Cooper produces all its domestically sold tires in the U.S. and touts the American-Made theme in its advertisements. It serves the Latin American market with a facility in Piedras, Mexico. Employees there are unionized.

⬡ Adolph Coors Company

STOCK SYMBOL: ACCOB
STOCK EXCHANGE: NNM

Environment	B
Women's Advancement	C
Minority Advancement	A
Charitable Giving	A
Community Outreach	B
Family Benefits	C
Workplace Issues	A
Social Disclosure	A

Coors, based in Golden, Colorado, is engaged almost exclusively in the brewing, packaging, and distribution of malt-based beverages. Its other businesses serve its brewing facilities. In 1996, the company employed 6,200 people and generated $1.7 billion in total sales.

Environment: Coors' major environmental concerns involve water quality, solid waste, and air emissions. The company keeps annual progress reports and audits all facilities on a three-year cycle. Coor's toxic release inventory (TRI) emissions are less than half the industry average, but its spill record is twice the average.

In 1995, the company received an award from the Coalition of Northeastern Governors and in September 1996 another from the EPA's WasteWi$e program for its leadership in reducing solid waste.

A 1993 company environmental audit revealed that beer-brewing facilities emitted a very large quantity of volatile organic compounds, prompting the Colorado Department of Health to propose $1 million in fines. Coors maintains that it undertook the audit voluntarily and was punished for being proactive. The company's complaints led to a controversial Colorado bill, often called the Polluter Protection Act, that keeps information gathered in such audits secret from the public as long as companies promptly take corrective action.

EEO: In 1996, Adolph Coors Company's board totaled seven directors, including one woman and two minorities, while three of a total of 26 corporate officers were women, and three were minorities. Additionally, three women and three minorities were among the 25 employees with the highest salaries at the company.

The company received a 1996 award from the Hispanic Association on Corporate Responsibility. In May 1995, the board of directors voted unanimously to extend health care coverage to the domestic partners of homosexual employees and has stood by the decision despite protests from conservative organizations.

In 1996, an age discrimination suit filed by seven former security guards against Coors was dismissed when the judge found that the plaintiffs, who allege that they were forced to retire and were then replaced by younger employees, had signed away their right to

sue when they accepted severance packages. Coors recognizes eight employee councils which consult with management and educate employees on group-specific issues, according to company publications.

Adolph Coors Company offers mentoring programs, support networks, and maintains diversity goals for both women and minorities.

Community Involvement: Adolph Coors Company's charitable contributions totaled $2.3 million in cash in 1996. The $2.3 million cash-giving figure represented the equivalent of 3.1 percent of the company's pretax earnings for the same year, and a decrease of 3.4 percent from the company's cash contributions in 1995. In 1995, the company contributed 3.2 percent of its pretax earnings for that year to charity.

Coors was one of the founding members of the "Two Percent Club," a group of companies that pledge to give a minimum of two percent of pretax profits back to the community. In 1996, the company was ranked second overall in the rating done by Business Ethics Magazine for the 100 Best Corporate Citizens. Coors seeks to support programs that empower minorities and women and programs that address issues affecting consumers, distributors, and retailers in the hospitality and foodservice industry.

Workplace Information: The records of the Occupational Safety and Health Administration indicate that Adolph Coors Company was not inspected from 1994 to 1996. Consequently no fines or violations were assessed to the company.

Weapons Contracts: Coors sold $1,700 worth of stainless steel drums to the Department of Defense in 1994 for use in a nuclear waste containment project.

CoreStates Financial

STOCK SYMBOL: CFL
STOCK EXCHANGES: NY, PH, P

Environment	N
Women's Advancement	A
Minority Advancement	B
Charitable Giving	A
Community Outreach	B
Family Benefits	N
Workplace Issues	N
Social Disclosure	B

CoreStates Financial, based in Philadelphia, Pennsylvania, assumed its current name after the May 1983 merger between Philadelphia National Central and National Central Financial. The holding company provides financial services in such areas as corporate and institutional banking, community and international banking, and other personal financial services. CoreStates is ranked 32nd in the United States with assets of nearly $24 billion. As of December 1996, the firm employed 15,835 workers.

Environment: CoreStates has a six-point environmental policy and a management task force that meets periodically to assess progress and consider new ideas. The company has joined the EPA's Green Lights initiative to improve lighting efficiency and educates employees through its internal magazine.

EEO: In 1996, CoreStates Financial Corp. achieved a higher than average rating in both diversity categories, placing them easily in the top third of S&P 500 companies. Five women and two minorities served on CoreStates Financial Corp.'s 34-member board.

CoreStates Financial Group of Philadelphia reserved $1 million for loans to women-owned businesses in 1994. In May 1996, Rosemarie Greco was named President of the holding company, becoming one of the highest ranking women in commercial banking.

Community Involvement: CoreStates Financial Corp.'s charitable contributions totaled $17.8 million in cash in 1996, and $3 million in in-kind donations. The company made cash contributions equivalent to 2 percent of its pretax earnings in both 1995 and 1996.

Company initiatives are numerous. CoreStates' Affordable Lending Unit has provided $46 million in financing to nearly 2,900 first-time homeowners, most of whom are minorities. The bank supports the City of Philadelphia's Homestart program, which provides funds for renovation and purchase of properties in low-income neighborhoods. Its Community Business Lending and Community Real Estate Lending departments reach out to disinvested communities with small business and development loans. Earlier this year, CoreStates' community banking division created a $1 million loan pool to provide start-up financing to women-owned businesses.

CoreStates' direct giving program and its foundation are focused mainly on neighborhood economic development but also support education, art, historic preservation and youth. The giving takes place in the states of Pennsylvania, New Jersey and Delaware. CoreStates has formed a partnership with the Greater Philadelphia Urban Affairs Coalition, a nonprofit, to find jobs for homeless people. Bank employees act as mentors to the homeless, and job training is provided by another organization, the Women's Alliance for Job Equity. These programs have placed 43 homeless people in full-time jobs.

Workplace Information: According to the Occupational Safety and Health Administration's records, CoreStates Financial Corp. was not inspected from 1994 to 1996. Consequently no violations or fines were assessed to the company

Additional Information: CoreStates has a detailed code of ethics statement covering such items as discrimination, conflicts of interest and advertising integrity.

Darden Restaurants

STOCK SYMBOL: DRI
STOCK EXCHANGE: NY

Environment	N
Women's Advancement	C?
Minority Advancement	A
Charitable Giving	N
Community Outreach	N
Family Benefits	N
Workplace Issues	A?
Social Disclosure	B

Spun off from General Mills in 1995, the Orlando, Florida–based Darden Restaurants is the world's largest casual dining restaurant company, operating more than 1,200 Red Lobster, Olive Garden, and Bahama Breeze restaurants in North America. In 1996, the company employed nearly 115,000 people and had sales of $3.2 billion.

Environment: A company-initiated "Partnership in Preservation" (PIP) program runs a year-round program that has so far completed hundreds of public area cleanups. Since PIP started in 1991, more than 500 Red Lobster restaurants have organized a PIP program. In four years, some 25,000 volunteers have cleared away more than 850 tons of debris.

EEO: In 1996, Darden Restaurants' nine-member board of directors included one woman and no minorities. Of 11 corporate officers at the company, none were women and two were minorities.

Darden Restaurants reports that in 1996 it established a Diversity Management Department and maintains a Diversity Advisory Council. The Diversity Management Department is "committed to continuing to build on [the company's] diversity initiatives," according to Darden, while the Advisory Council's function is to ensure that the company's "efforts reflect the needs and concerns" of its workforce and customer base. Darden supports and works with the LEAD, INROADS, and National MBA Association Recruitment programs. The company also retains an independent firm to conduct a "comprehensive cultural assessment" and advise the company on ways it can enhance its performance on diversity.

Community Involvement: Darden Restaurants gave $2.7 million to local organizations in Florida in the first five months after spinning off from General Mills in 1995.

Workplace Information: Darden takes pride in its flexible management style, which allows its employees to get experience in different aspects of the restaurant business. Nearly one-third of restaurant managers began as entry-level employees. Many have risen to be officers or directors. For example, Valerie Collins, who now is vice president and controller of The Olive Garden, joined the company as a computer systems specialist. "An important aspect of this company is that they're willing to move people into new roles that allow them to grow," states Collins.

Darden also has a low turnover rate for the industry. Sixty percent of Red Lobster's restaurant management teams have six or more years of experience; thirty percent have been on their jobs ten or more years. Nearly a quarter of The Olive Garden's management teams have been with the chain six or more years.

The Red Lobster chain recently set up a peer review process that communicates to its employees the company's commitment to resolve disputes equitably. Though it had an open-door policy already, it was felt that peer review—still a rarity in the restaurant industry—would strengthen that commitment.

In August, 1995, Darden decided to close its China Coast chain, but noted that many of the 3,000 employees would find employment at its Olive Garden and Red Lobster restaurants. Still, according to company documents, Darden shed more than 5,700 workers from 1995 to 1996. None of its employees are covered by collective bargaining agreements.

Additional Information: Darden has historically been recognized as one of the leading proponents of quality control in the restaurant industry. Company-operated food laboratories are the foundation for a far-reaching quality assurance program. Laboratories include a Microbiology Laboratory in Orlando—a state-certified facility opened in 1976 where microbiologists continually perform analysis on samples of seafood and commodity products. Company policy mandates that no food can be served without a guarantee of safety and freshness. Over the years, Darden labs have acted as consultants to other foodservice companies, helping them establish their own quality control labs and test kitchens.

Data General Corporation

STOCK SYMBOL: DGN
STOCK EXCHANGES: NY, B, CH, P, PH

Environment	F
Women's Advancement	F
Minority Advancement	F
Charitable Giving	N
Community Outreach	D?
Family Benefits	F
Workplace Issues	C
Social Disclosure	B

Data General, based in Westboro, Massachusetts, has evolved from a minicomputer and closed systems manufacturer and supplier to a company providing open systems and computer services. The company's products range from database services to mass storage devices. Data General's revenues totaled $1.3 billion in 1996. Operating in more than 70 countries, the company has consolidated its total workforce to 4,900 employees.

Environment: Data General has a written environmental policy, but does not currently publish a corporate environmental report. The company has not implemented an integrated environmental management system. Data General states that it "may have a written resource use policy." It does not have a written pollution prevention policy, nor does it have any company-wide pollution prevention programs in place. Although Data General does not have a written commitment to product stewardship, it does evaluate its products with the objective of reducing their life-cycle impacts on the environment. The company has an environmental audit program with worldwide standards/applicability. In 1996, 100 percent of U.S. facilities and 50 percent of international facilities were audited. Internationally, the company monitors SARA Title III Emissions in non-U.S. operations and follows U.S. regulations in the U.S. and abroad, unless local regulations are stricter.

EEO: Data General turned in a below average performance in the area of diversity in 1996, compared to other S&P 500 companies. Among the companies surveyed by CEP, the average representation of women and minorities on S&P corporate boards was 10.8 percent and 7.5 percent, respectively. In comparison, Data General had no women and minorities on its seven-member board. Additionally, the company's total of 26 corporate officers included no women or minorities, while the company counted one woman and no minorities among the 25 highest paid employees.

In 1995, Data General was disqualified from a $569,198 contract with California's State University at San Marcos because the company failed to make "good faith efforts" to find minority subcontractors. DGN bypassed state requirements to advertise contracts

in minority-targeted publications. The company claims that "the minority trade journal publication date would have been subsequent to the bid due date."

Community Involvement: In 1994, Data General made $200,000 in cash contributions to charitable institutions.

Data General's community support includes a two-year-old relationship with Worcester North High School in Worcester, Massachusetts. The company has donated $400,000 in equipment and employees have logged over 1,000 hours in volunteer time with the school. Volunteers at the school are allowed to submit the hours spent working there as regular work time.

Family Benefits: The company offers part-time work for working mothers and flextime and job-sharing at certain locations. Child/elder care resource and referral services are provided as part of an Employee Assistance Program.

Workplace Information: According to the Occupational Safety and Health Administration's records, Data General was not inspected from 1994 to 1996. Consequently no violations or fines were assessed to the company. In the last 10 years, Data General has reduced its workforce from a peak of 17,700 employees in 1985 to its present level.

Data General currently faces a pending civil case filed by a former employee who charged the company with wrongful discharge. The employee accused the company of intentional and/or negligent infliction of emotional distress.

Weapons Contracts: In 1994, Data General had $8.1 million in contracts with the U.S. Department of Defense — $659,000 of which had military applications, and just $40,000 weapons related.

Dayton Hudson Corporation

STOCK SYMBOL: DH

STOCK EXCHANGES: NY, B, CH, P, PH

Environment	N
Women's Advancement	A
Minority Advancement	B
Charitable Giving	A
Community Outreach	B
Family Benefits	C
Workplace Issues	D
Social Disclosure	A

America's fourth largest general merchandise retailer, Dayton Hudson's operations include the discount chain store Target and four department store chains: Mervyn's, Dayton's, Hudson's, and Marshall Field's. In 1996, with 21,400 employees, the Minneapolis, Minnesota–based company had $23.5 billion in sales.

Environment: All of Dayton Hudson's divisions made energy conservation and recycling a priority. A participant in EPA's Energy Star, WasteWi$e and Green Lights programs, the company received multiple awards including the U.N.'s United Earth program award. In 1995, Dayton Hudson saved 16.3 million kilowatt hours through improved lighting efficiency. In 1995, its Target division recycled 75 percent of its waste and received EPA's WasteWi$e Award.

EEO: In 1996, Dayton Hudson achieved a higher than average rating in both diversity categories, placing them easily in the top third of S&P 500 companies. Three women and two minorities served on Dayton Hudson's 14-member board. Of 22 corporate officers at the company, seven were women and one was a minority.

In 1996, over 10 percent of shares held were voted in favor of an ICCR sponsored shareholder resolution, proposing that Dayton Hudson distribute an EEO report. Now, Dayton Hudson has a written policy stating its commitment to diversity and equal opportunity employment. The company also publishes an annual EEO report documenting the percentages of women and minorities employed in each job category. The company implemented its program for purchasing from minority-owned businesses, and so did not report its purchasing amounts for 1996.

Community Involvement: In 1996, Dayton Hudson's charitable giving totaled over $23.2 million in cash.

Dayton Hudson has donated 5 percent of its pretax profits to charity every year since 1946. The company contributes to the causes of high school drop-out prevention, women's education, quality child care, adult literacy, and artistic expression in underserved communities. Target stores have entered into a three-year partnership with the Points of Light Foundation and the Conference Board in order to develop volunteer projects for employees and their families. 60 percent of Target employees are involved in the volunteer program. The employees of Target stores alone volunteer 14,000 hours per month.

Workplace Information: The company is commended for its hassle-free environment where individuality is respected. In 1994, however, investigations by the U.S. Department of Labor found that Dayton Hudson had purchased garments from Texas home-work mills that were violating fair wage and safety laws. The company stated it was unaware of the illegally manufactured goods.

International: Dayton Hudson does not have any international operations, but it has adopted sourcing guidelines for its vendors, which cover basic workers' rights, child labor, working hours, wages, and monitoring. The company explicitly states its rights to carry out "on-site inspection of production facilities in order to implement and monitor these standards."

Deere & Company

STOCK SYMBOL: DE
STOCK EXCHANGES: NY, B, CH, P

Environment	A
Women's Advancement	N
Minority Advancement	N
Charitable Giving	B
Community Outreach	D
Family Benefits	N
Workplace Issues	D?
Social Disclosure	C

Deere & Company, based in Moline, Illinois, is the world's largest agricultural equipment manufacturer. The company is also a major producer of lawn care, industrial, and power equipment, and offers credit, insurance, and health care services. In 1996, the company had sales of $11 billion and 33,900 employees.

Environment: The company has a general environmental policy covering compliance, elimination of environmental risks, and the implementation of pollution control programs. Deere publishes a general environmental report, as well as an annual update on hazardous waste, recycling, and compliance progress available to the public. Its Green Company Steering Committee, founded in 1992, coordinates company environmental programs. Deere audits all manufacturing and marketing units. As part of a program to formalize environmental management systems, using Total Quality Management, in 1995 the company developed a manual with over 50 environmental guidelines, distributed to manufacturing and marketing units worldwide. Deere uses the new R134a refrigerant in its products' air conditioning systems and has introduced biodegradable oils for use in its products.

The company has reduced hazardous waste generation by 60 percent. In one five-year period, the use of returnable containers for incoming parts shipments at several facilities reduced the amount of waste sent to landfills by more than 50 percent. Deere is a signatory to the International Chamber of Commerce Business Charter for Sustainable Development and a participant in EPA's Green Lights energy conservation program.

EEO: In 1996, one minority sat on Deere & Co.'s board of directors.

Deere first addressed diversity in the early 1960s as one of the original signers of Plans for Progress, an affirmative action effort to recruit major employers to agree to ban discrimination based on race, gender, religion, age, nationality, and disability. Deere won the 1995 Work Force Diversity Award, presented by Equal Opportunity Publications, as one of 12 firms honored for expanding employment opportunities for people with disabilities.

Community Involvement: Deere & Co.'s charitable contributions totaled $8.1 million in cash in 1996, and $1 million in in-kind donations. The $8.1 million cash-giving figure represented the equivalent of 0.7 percent of the company's pretax earnings for the same year, and a decrease of 25.9 percent from the company's cash contributions in 1995. In 1995, the company contributed 0.6 percent of its pretax earnings for that year to charity.

Workplace Information: The records of the Occupational Safety and Health Administration indicate that Deere & Co. underwent six health and safety inspections from 1994 to 1996. The violations reported by OSHA as a result of the inspections include 30 classified as "serious." The company was required to pay $14,546 as a result of its violations, or $2,424 per inspection. In comparison, the median amount of fines per inspection for other companies in similar manufacturing industries was $2,412.

Because of a downturn in the farm equipment business, during the 1980's Deere cut its workforce by almost half. Despite the company's financial difficulties during this time, Deere was able to keep all of its factories open. In 1988, UAW negotiated a contract that secured the first wage increase since 1981 and a guarantee that none of the factory workers would be laid off. Now business is booming, relations with the United Auto Workers are relatively strong, and the company is experimenting with participatory management programs.

Weapons Contracts: In 1994, Deere had $4.6 million in contracts with the Department of Defense. None of these contracts were weapons related.

Dell Computer Corporation

STOCK SYMBOL: DELL
STOCK EXCHANGE: NNM

Environment	D
Women's Advancement	C
Minority Advancement	B?
Charitable Giving	N
Community Outreach	N
Family Benefits	B
Workplace Issues	C
Social Disclosure	C

Founded in 1984, Austin, Texas–based Dell Computer is now third among the world's largest computer companies. Dell had revenues reaching $7.8 billion and approximately 11,000 employees in fiscal 1997. Dell develops, manufactures, and sells a complete range of computer systems from desktop computers to network servers and workstations. In 1987, the company expanded its operations with the addition of international sales offices. Dell currently manufactures in the U.S. and Ireland, and currently maintains sales offices in 32 countries around the world.

Environment: Dell Computer has an environmental policy, but does not publish a corporate environmental report. Dell Computer has not implemented an integrated environmental management system, but does provide environmental health and safety (EH&S) training to EH&S, and facility staff. Dell Computer has a written pollution prevention policy and has initiated a companywide pollution prevention program, which establishes annual reduction goals for non-hazardous solid waste. Because Dell does not emit hazardous wastes, the company has been able to focus on reducing non-hazardous solid waste, including corregated cardboard, plastics and foam. Currently, Dell has achieved 60 percent landfill avoidance, company wide, through reduction, recycling, and reuse. Dell Computer has a written policy on product stewardship and evaluates its products with the objective of reducing their life-cycle impacts on the environment. The company does not have an environmental audit program. Internationally, Dell Computer monitors SARA Title III, or equivalent emissions and follows U.S. regulations in the U.S. and abroad unless local regulations are stricter.

EEO: In 1996, Dell Computer's nine-member board of directors included one woman and no minorities. Of 13 corporate officers at the company, none were minorities and two were women (one of 16 in 1997).

Community Outreach: In 1995, Dell Computer established a foundation to direct its corporate giving.

The company's direct donations, in-kind giving, executive involvement, and employee volunteerism focus on preventative health programs for children in Austin, Texas. The foundation has contributed to more than 100 youth-oriented organizations in Central Texas. Additionally, the company has funded major sponsorships with the City of Austin's Austin Project, which provides computer labs to children in East Austin and to the Austin Museum.

Workplace Information: The records of the Occupational Safety and Health Administration indicate that Dell Computer underwent four health and safety inspections from 1994 to 1996. The violations reported by OSHA as a result of the inspections include 24 classified as "serious." The company was required to pay $19,300 as a result of its violations.

Legal Proceedings: In November, 1994, Dell announced that it had reached a settlement with plaintiffs charging the company with the failure to disclose adverse material information about the company's business. The plaintiff claimed that this induced shareholders to buy company common stock at artificially high prices. Neither the company nor Dell admitted liability or obligation. The court approved the settlement and entered a final judgment of dismissal on February 24, 1995. The settlement did not have a material effect on the company.

Weapons Contracts: In 1994, Dell had $3.4 million in contracts with the U.S. Department of Defense. The contracts were for computer systems and services which were not weapons related.

Delta Air Lines

STOCK SYMBOL: DAL
STOCK EXCHANGES: NY, B, C, CH, P, PH

Environment	C
Women's Advancement	D?
Minority Advancement	N
Charitable Giving	D
Community Outreach	D
Family Benefits	N
Workplace Issues	C?
Social Disclosure	B

Delta Air Lines is a major passenger airline based in Atlanta, Georgia. In 1991, Delta's acquisitions — including Pan Am's New York-to-Boston shuttle—made Delta the world's largest airline, but these moves also incurred debt that, along with other conditions, caused a series of annual losses. In 1996, Delta had 60,289 employees and $12.5 billion in sales.

Environment: Delta recycles aluminum and paper, and purchases some recycled paper. The Airport Noise and Capacity Act (1990) required the phase-out of all Stage 2 (noisier) aircraft by year-end 1999. More than half of Delta's fleet is now made up of the quieter Stage 3 jets, but the company will spend $3.5 billion to bring the rest of its fleet into compliance by the deadline.

Delta is a potentially responsible party for two Superfund sites. However, the company has developed an extensive hazardous waste program to remove older underground storage tanks that may leak, and to replace ozone-harming solvents and toxic de-icers. Delta is negotiating an agreement with the state of Georgia whereby the company will pay more than $315,000 for violations of the Clean Air Act.

Delta reduced its generation of hazardous waste by 45 percent from 1992 to 1994.

EEO: In 1996, Delta Air Lines' board totaled 12 directors, including one woman and no minorities. Delta Airlines is currently the defendant of certain legal actions relating to alleged employment discrimination practices and other matters, concerning past and present employees.

Community Outreach: Delta Air Lines donated over 500 Paralympic Games tickets to organizations working with disabled and disadvantaged children in the Atlanta area. Delta's charitable contributions support organizations that work to strengthen communities, promote families or improve cultural understanding. The Delta Air Lines Foundation matches employee gifts to universities.

Workplace Information: Although Delta is mostly non-union, leaders of the Transport Workers Union are running a campaign to organize workers at Delta in order to address issues of outsourcing of work, part-time employees working long hours receiving few benefits, improved retirement, and retiree medical benefits. Delta officials stated that they respect workers' rights to be unionized, yet are not particularly anxious about unionization since good pay and benefits have inhibited unionization in the past, despite the initiation of cost-cutting programs in 1993.

The records of the Occupational Safety and Health Administration indicate that Delta Air Lines underwent six health and safety inspections from 1994 to 1996. Violations include six classified as "serious" and a total of $11,525 in fines.

Legal Proceedings: In 1992, Pan Am and a group of its creditors filed a $2.5 billion breach-of-contract suit against Delta for backing away from an agreement to help rescue it from bankruptcy. In December 1994, the suit was ruled in Delta's favor.

Eight airlines, including Delta, in 1992 settled a class-action lawsuit accusing them of price-fixing. The companies agreed to pay $44 million in cash and issue $368.5 million in ticket vouchers, but admitted no liability.

Additional Information: In 1985, Delta excluded passengers with AIDS, but hastily dropped the clause when lawsuits were threatened. The company has since had several discriminatory incidents involving gay men and people with AIDS. Each time the incidents are publicized, Delta apologizes and promises to educate its employees about AIDS, but as late as 1993, a Delta spokesperson told *Business Week*, "We haven't seen a need for a specific program." The book *Cracking the Corporate Closet* (Harper Business, 1995) ranked Delta as one of the ten worst places in America for gays and lesbians to work because of its ongoing mistreatment of both gay employees and passengers.

Digital Equipment Corporation

STOCK SYMBOL: DEC
STOCK EXCHANGES: NY, B, C, CH, P, PH

Environment	B
Women's Advancement	B
Minority Advancement	F
Charitable Giving	N
Community Outreach	D?
Family Benefits	C
Workplace Issues	B
Social Disclosure	A

Digital Equipment Corp. (DEC), based in Maynard, Massachusetts, is the world's largest supplier of network computer systems and services. In 1996, it had $14.6 billion in revenues and 59,100 employees.

Environment: Digital Equipment has an environmental policy and a corporate environmental report, which is updated annually and is available on the Internet. Digital provides Environmental Health and Safety (EH&S) training to EH&S staff and facility staff. The company considers contribution towards EH&S goals in the job performance reviews of all employees. In the selection of suppliers, Digital conducts or reviews environmental audits on suppliers' facilities. Digital also has a corporate policy on community involvement relating to environmental concerns. All facilities have community advisory panels. Digital has an environmental audit program with worldwide standards/applicability. Internationally, the company monitors SARA Title III or equivalent emissions in non-U.S. operations and follows U.S. regulations in the U.S. and abroad, unless local regulations are stricter.

Digital Equipment Corp.'s average toxic releases and transfers during the years 1994–1996 were among the lowest compared to an industry sample. However, its emissions increased by an average of about four–fifths annually during those years, the worst performance within the industry sample.

EEO: In 1996, Digital Equipment Corp.'s board totaled nine directors, including one woman and no minorities, while one of nine corporate officers was a woman, and none were minorities.

Digital Equipment assesses the effectiveness of its diversity training program by asking the employees for feedback. Internal surveys show that employees feel that the company respects and values diversity. The company has assigned a staff member specifically responsible for overseeing diversity programs. In 1988, DEC was the first company in the world to establish an office to deal exclusively with the issue of AIDS.

Community Involvement: In 1994, Digital Equipment Corp. made $3.1 million in cash contributions to charitable institutions.

Digital Equipment Corp. places special emphasis on youth-related issues throughout its giving. Gifts towards education emphasize programs that connect schools with communities and enhance learning, especially those involving math, science, and access to technology. International funding focuses on relief organizations and education for K-12. One of the company's top three priorities is the development of leadership and excellence programs in academic achievement and youth community service.

Workplace Information: OSHA records indicate that Digital was inspected once from 1994 to 1996. The only violations reported by OSHA were classified as "other," the least serious kind of violation. The company was not required to pay any fines as a result of its violations. In comparison, the median amount of fines per inspection for other companies in the electronic manufacturing industries was $1,347.

Digital Equipment Corp. will eliminate 7,000 jobs resulting in a $475 million loss, adding to its problems of losses in its personal computer business and sales problems in Europe. Although several restructuring efforts resulted in profitable quarters, Digital has been plagued by low profits and high costs. Digital halved its 125,000 workforce in the early 1990s, but the additional 12 percent reduction seems to convey the sense that its employment target of 60,000 employees is no longer the optimal workforce size.

Weapons Contracts: DEC ranked 75th in the top one hundred defense companies worldwide in 1995. Its defense revenue of $385 million represented 2.8% of its overall revenue.

Dillard Department Stores

STOCK SYMBOL: DDS

STOCK EXCHANGES: NY, CH

Environment	N
Women's Advancement	F?
Minority Advancement	D?
Charitable Giving	N
Community Outreach	N
Family Benefits	N
Workplace Issues	A?
Social Disclosure	F

Dillard Department Stores encompasses a regional group of 238 department stores in 23 states, primarily focusing on fashion apparel and home furnishings. Dillard is based in Little Rock, Arkansas, and in 1996, had $6.2 billion in sales. The company employs about 35,000 people.

EEO: Dillard Department Stores turned in a below average performance in the area of diversity in 1996, compared to other S&P 500 companies. Among the companies surveyed by CEP, the average representation of women and minorities on S&P corporate boards was 10.8 percent and 7.5 percent, respectively. In comparison, Dillard Department Stores had one woman and one minority on its 14-member board. Additionally, the company's total of 47 corporate officers included two women and no minorities.

In 1994, the Fair Share Program of the National Association for the Advancement of Colored People removed Dillard from its rolls because a review of company performance showed little or no cooperation in meeting program requirements.

In 1995, Dillard Department Stores settled a religious discrimination suit filed by the EEOC on behalf of a dozen plaintiffs who were allegedly denied employment at Dillard because they did not want to work on Sundays. The company agreed to pay the plaintiffs up to $30,000 in back pay, and not to ask job applicants whether they can work on weekends or refuse to hire those who prefer not to work on a particular day because it is their sabbath.

In 1996, 13.9 percent of the shares of Dillard Department Stores were voted for a proposal to publish a company EEO Report. In that proxy statement, the resolution to publish a "Glass Ceiling" report was omitted by the company with the permission of the Securities and Exchange Commission. A proposal for board inclusiveness was reported as not having been filed. The proposal to prepare an updated diversity report, with a summary in the annual report, including the EEO-1 report was presented at the company's annual meeting on May 17, 1997.

Workplace Information: According to the Occupational Safety and Health Administration's records, Dillard Department Stores was inspected three times from 1994 to 1996. OSHA inspectors cited the company only for violations classified as "other," the least egregious type of violation. The company was not required to pay any fines as a result of its violations. In comparison, the median amount of fines per inspection for other companies in similar retail industries was $694.

In February 1995, the United Food and Commercial Workers attempted to organize Dillard stores in the St. Louis area. When an earlier vote rejected the union, it filed charges with the NLRB alleging unfair labor practices. The company, the union, and the NLRB then made an agreement that the union would drop its unfair labor practice charge in exchange for a new round of voting. The union hoped to win representation and negotiate company-paid health insurance for the two-thirds of employees who were part-timers and not entitled to medical coverage.

Legal Procedures: Early in 1996, the Federal Trade Commission dropped a 1994 lawsuit that charged Dillard Department Stores with violating the Truth in Lending Act. The suit alleged that Dillard made it unreasonably difficult for consumers to have unauthorized charges removed from their Dillard charge accounts by putting the burden of proof on the consumer. The act had required issuers to investigate all disputed charges, whether or not customers participated in the investigation.

The decision to dismiss the complaint was based on the Federal Reserve Board's issuance of new standards for investigating claims made under the Truth in Lending Act. Under the new interpretation, a customer's refusal to participate can halt an investigation if the issuer has no other way to get the information.

The Walt Disney Company

STOCK SYMBOL: DIS
STOCK EXCHANGES: NY, B, C, CH, P, PH

Environment	C
Women's Advancement	F?
Minority Advancement	C?
Charitable Giving	F?
Community Outreach	B
Family Benefits	N
Workplace Issues	D?
Social Disclosure	C

Started as an animation film business in 1923, the Walt Disney Company has grown to include theme parks, hotels, music recordings, a cable TV network, a hockey team, and the production and marketing of Disney merchandise. Disney World has made Orlando, Florida, the world's most popular tourist destination. In 1995, the company acquired Capital Cities/ABC, making Disney the largest entertainment production and distribution company in the world. In 1996, the Burbank, California–based company had revenues of $18.7 billion and 62,000 employees.

Environment: Recently, a company-wide program called Environmentality was implemented and a position of Vice President, Environmental Policy, was created. Disney World in Florida opened a 30,000 square foot recycling and composting facility, which recycles an average of 135 tons of waste a week. Disney was the first studio in Hollywood to join EPA's Green Lights Program.

In 1994, although state lawmakers supported Disney's plan for an America theme park in the historic Shenandoah Valley region of Virginia, the federal EPA (along with environmentalists, historians and farmers' groups) defeated the project.

EEO: In 1996, The Walt Disney Co.'s board totaled 17 directors, including one woman and one minority, while none of seven corporate officers were women or minorities.

Disney began offering benefits to the domestic partners of gay and lesbian employees in 1997. The Southern Baptist Convention voted in June of that year to boycott Disney as a result. Disney has stood by its decision, stating that extending domestic partner benefits follows from its nondiscrimination policy.

Walt Disney is the defendant in several sexual harrassment suits connected to the actions of David Humdy, an employee. An L.A. district court found in favor of the company and Humdy in one case, though the plaintiff, who charges Disney with responding with hostility to her complaints of sexual harrassment, intends to appeal. African-American hotel workers filed a class-action suit for an unspecified number of claimants in 1997 alleging that Disney discriminated in hiring, promotion, and compensation.

The National Hispanic Media Coalition has called for a boycott of Disney for what it calls a poor record of hiring Latinos. The company states that it has good working relations with Hispanic groups including La Raza and Imagen.

Community Involvement: Disney's main giving objectives include the environment and preventative programs on substance abuse for children. The Walt Disney Company pledged to contribute one million hours of volunteering by the year 2000. Disney collaborates with and supports groups like the Boys and Girls Clubs of America and Wonderful Outdoor World through volunteerism.

Workplace Information: According to OSHA records, The Walt Disney Co. was inspected two times from 1994 to 1996. Violations included one classified as "willful" or "repeat" and seven classified as "serious" for a total of $400 in fines. In comparison, the median amount of fines per inspection for other companies in the service industry, such as banks, was $573.

A one-year contract was narrowly ratified by a multi-union craft maintenance council giving up to 900 workers at Disneyland a three percent wage increase, but at the expense of retirement health benefits.

International: Disney previously suffered negative publicity for sourcing toys in China and has encountered damaging publicity on wages in Haiti and Vietnam. Citing human rights abuse endured by Chinese workers, the AFL-CIO's youth arm, Frontlash, called for a boycott of toys made in China in 1992. More recently, in 1996, the National Labor Committee and Global Exchange launched an international grassroots campiagn against Disney calling for improved wages and working conditions in Haiti and Vietnam.

Product: The company's theme parks have won praise for their people-oriented design and accommodations for people with disabilities.

🏅 Dole Food Company

STOCK SYMBOL: DOL
STOCK EXCHANGES: NY, B, CH, P

Environment	B
Women's Advancement	A
Minority Advancement	A
Charitable Giving	A
Community Outreach	B
Family Benefits	B
Workplace Issues	REV
Social Disclosure	A

Dole Food produces fresh fruit and vegetables, packaged foods, and dried fruit and nuts. Dole sources fruit from the U.S. as well as countries in Latin America, Asia, Europe, and the Caribbean. The California-based company had $3.8 billion in sales in 1996, a 14 percent increase over 1994, and 46,000 employees.

Environment: Since 1991, Dole has been implementing and refining a companywide environmental management system involving senior executives, scientists, engineers, managers, and attorneys from inside and outside the company. Primary objectives include determination of environmental impacts, establishment of objectives to implement environmental policy, pollution prevention, waste minimization, compliance with relevant laws, and effectiveness of operational controls. Dole reports that it seeks to conform to emerging international environmental management standards. It has made use of integrated pest management technology since the 1960's.

EEO: Dole has one woman and one minority on its seven-member board of directors. Among 17 corporate officers and division heads, there are two women and three minorities.

Community Involvement: In 1995, Dole Food gave $2.1 million in cash (or 2 percent of average worldwide pretax earnings) to charity and made substantial in-kind donations including free medical treatment to needy children, reforestation and soil erosion projects, and emergency relief to flood victims in Asia and Latin America. Dole reports that it has been one of the largest and most consistent donors to food banks in the nation. The company's expanded CD-ROM package on nutrition education, "5-a-Day Adventures," is distributed free of charge to 24,000 schools nationwide. Dole remains one of the largest and most consistent donors to national food banks.

Workplace Information: Dole claims that it is among the highest paying agricultural employers in the countries where it operates and that it provides comprehensive medical, wellness, and retirement benefits to its employees. Over 50 percent of the Company's workforce worldwide is covered by union collective bargaining agreements. Beginning in 1991, Dole began retooling its occupational safety program to improve the company's performance in the areas of safety and health.

International: Dole reports that it has a clear policy and mission statement for protection of health and the environment that applies to all countries in which it operates.

Dole's European sales grew 20 percent from 1994 to over $900 million in 1995. That year, Dole acquired companies in Italy and Spain, and strengthened alliances with regional distributors in France, the U.K., and South Africa. In Asia, Dole has a presence in Japan, the Philippines, China, East Russia, and New Zealand. Sales in Asia were over $700 million in 1995.

Legal Proceedings: Dole, like other major banana producers, has been drawn into litigation initiated more than a decade ago against former DBCP manufacturers, Dow Chemical Co., Shell Oil Co., and Occidental Chemical Corp. While some settlements have recently occurred, cases pertaining to crop protection and worker safety practices that were allegedly in effect 20 to 30 years ago have been pending for years. Allegations of certain plaintiff's counsel to the effect that Dole used the pesticide after it should have known that it had harmful effects to agricultural workers and after the pesticide was banned have never been proven or accepted in any court of law.

79

Dominion Resources

STOCK SYMBOL: D
STOCK EXCHANGES: NY, B, C, CH, PH, P

Environment	REV
Women's Advancement	C
Minority Advancement	C
Charitable Giving	N
Community Outreach	B
Family Benefits	C
Workplace Issues	B
Social Disclosure	A

Dominion Resources, based in Richmond, Virginia, is a holding company for its primary business, Virginia Power, which generates, transmits, and sells electricity to nearly 1.8 million customers. Dominion Resources also owns independent power production companies, natural gas companies, financial services, and real estate. In 1996, Dominion had revenues of $4.8 billion and employed about 11,174 people.

Environment: Dominion Resources is not actively utilizing solar, geothermal, or wind energy resources in its fuel mix. Virginia Power operates several hydro-electric power stations in its service area. Dominion Energy, an independent power subsidiary of Dominion Resources, has one solar, two geothermal and several hydroelectric plants in the U.S. and South America. Dominion has been able to delay creation of new coal-powered units by increasing conservation efforts including demand-side management programs (to promote wise energy use) and advanced electro-technologies.

EEO: Dominion Resources' 18-member board included two women and two minorities in 1996 (three minorities in 1998). Also in 1996, three women and one minority served among the company's 32 corporate officers, and the company's 25 highest paid employees included one woman and no minorities.

Dominion reports that it is "recognized as having one of the strongest [minority advancement] records in Virginia," and cites its minority scholarship program, a cooperative agreement with the National Association for the Advancement of Colored People, and a diversity program in its fossil fuel and hydroelectric unit.

Dominion Resources' Equal Employment Opportunity policy outlines general responsibilities for the company's supervisors. The policy states that the supervisors' responsibilities include "creating and maintaining a work environment free from racial or sexual harassment… taking appropriate steps to prevent sexual harassment from occurring… taking immediate and appropriate corrective action when necessary."

Workplace Information: According to the Occupational Safety and Health Administration's records, Dominion Resources was not inspected from 1994 to 1996. Consequently no violations or fines were assessed to the company.

The International Brotherhood of Electrical Workers has accused Virginia Power of unfair labor practices in putting the company's restructuring plan into effect in early 1996. The restructuring resulted in a 30 percent reduction in the company's fossil and hydro business unit's workforce, or 537 jobs. Workers had recently ratified an agreement that IBEW negotiated with Virginia power which did not include severance packages for any hourly workers laid-off during the restructuring. Virginia Power had originally made an offer which included severance benefits of up to 18 months pay and other benefits, with the stipulation that the company could use "pooling" to determine which hourly workers would be laid off. Pooling is a grouping of employees based on ability and performance rather than seniority. The IBEW rejected the offer, arguing pooling was unfair.

As a result of the contract agreement, over 200 hourly workers were cut who received just one-month's pay as severance, but were given the opportunity to bump less senior workers. Virginia Power maintained offers of severance packages in return for other concessions regarding seniority, bumping, and pay protection for employees moved into lower-paying positions. The union filed unfair labor practice charges with the NLRB, accusing Virginia Power of bypassing the union in attempts to convince employees to accept the pooling process in return for greater severance packages, of withholding information regarding hourly worker layoffs, of extending hourly employees' duties without compensating them, and of outsourcing work reserved for hourly employees. The charges were settled between the company and the IBEW in August 1997 without any involvement by the NLRB. Dominion reports that the settlement included a severance package.

Dow Chemical Company

STOCK SYMBOL: DOW

STOCK EXCHANGES: NY, TO, B, C, CH, P, PH

Environment	B
Women's Advancement	D
Minority Advancement	A
Charitable Giving	D
Community Outreach	A
Family Benefits	C
Workplace Issues	A
Social Disclosure	A

Headquartered in Midland, Michigan, Dow Chemical is a leading manufacturer of chemical, agricultural, pharmaceutical, and plastic products. In 1997, Dow had 40,900 employees and sales of $20 billion.

Environment: Dow has an environmental policy and a Corporate Environmental Report, which is updated as needed and is available on the Internet. The company has implemented an integrated Environmental Management System. Dow has a written pollution prevention policy and has initiated a company-wide pollution prevention program, which establishes annual reduction goals for point sources, secondary emissions, fugitive emissions, and solid waste. Dow also has a corporate policy on community involvement relating to local environmental concerns and has established community advisory panels at its largest manufacturing sites around the world. Dow has a written policy on product stewardship and a product stewardship review board; it evaluates all products with the objective of reducing their life-cycle impacts on the environment.

Dow Chemical's average total toxic releases and transfers during the years 1994–1996 were less than the industry average. On average, emissions showed a slight annual increase during those years, a below average performance.

In May 1997, Dow and other pesticide manufacturers reached a multimillion-dollar settlement with Costa Rican banana workers who claimed they became sterile or were afflicted with other ailments because of exposure to a U.S.-made pesticide, dibromochloropropane (DBCP). The companies argue they weren't at fault and stated that any sterility resulting from exposure to the pesticide was the result of improper handling by those who purchased it.

Also in May 1997, Dow was named as the defendant in a $20 million suit by San Francisco BayKeeper, an environmental group. BayKeeper claimed that Dow's Pittsburg, California, plant has been illegally discharging cancer-causing chemicals in violation of the state's Safe Drinking Water and Toxic Enforcement Act of 1986. Dow maintains that its Pittsburg facility remains in full compliance with each of its discharge permits and site clean-up requirements, and notes that BayKeeper's interpretation of the Toxic Enforcement Act has not been adopted by the State of California.

EEO: In 1996, Dow Chemical's board totaled 18 directors, including two women and three minorities, while one of 18 corporate officers was a woman, and five were minorities. Additionally, four minorities were among the 25 highest paid employees. Dow first introduced a policy on purchasing from minority- and women-owned businesses in 1980. An updated policy implemented in March, 1995, requires all Dow locations to work with recognized minority purchasing organizations to improve their purchasing programs.

Community Involvement: In 1997, Dow Chemical's charitable giving totaled $20 million in cash, which was equal to 0.5 percent of the company's pretax earnings for that year, up from 0.5 percent in 1995. Dow's in-kind giving came to a total of $2 million in 1996.

Workplace Issues: OSHA records indicate that Dow was inspected ten times from 1994 to 1996. Violations included one classified as "willful" or "repeat" and 13 classified as "serious" for a total of $19,335 in fines.

Product Issues: In an out-of-court settlement of a class-action lawsuit, Dow paid 19.5 percent of the $180 million relief fund established in 1984 for Vietnam veterans exposed to Agent Orange.

In late 1995, a jury found in favor of a plaintiff who sued Dow, claiming illnesses caused by silicone breast implants made by Dow Corning Corp. Dow owns 50 percent of Dow Corning, the leading maker of breast implants. All litigation against Dow Corning was frozen when it filed for bankruptcy in May 1995. Dow Chemical has appealed the decision.

Dow Jones & Company, Inc.

STOCK SYMBOL: DJ
STOCK EXCHANGES: NY. B, CH, P, PH

Dow Jones & Company, based in New York City, is a leading publisher of business news, information services, and community newspapers. Its flagship publication, the *Wall Street Journal*, has a combined worldwide circulation of more than 1.9 million. Other major publications are *Barron's, Far Eastern Economic Review, SmartMoney,* and *American Demographics*. In 1996, the company had revenues of $2.5 billion and 11,800 employees.

Environment	N
Women's Advancement	B
Minority Advancement	B
Charitable Giving	D
Community Outreach	N
Family Benefits	B
Workplace Issues	D
Social Disclosure	C

EEO: There are three women and three minorities, including former Urban League president Vernon Jordan Jr., on the 17-member board of directors. Of 23 officers, two are women.

In February 1993, a statement banning discrimination against employees based on their sexual orientation appeared for the first time in print in the Independent Association of Publishers' Employees (IAPE) contract.

Community Involvement: In 1995, Dow Jones contributed about $2.3 million (including foundation, direct, and nonmonetary giving), or 0.8 percent of average pretax earnings, to charitable causes. Between 55 and 60 percent of the company's donations goes to education, and another 25 percent aids united funds.

Family Benefits: The company was listed in *Working Mother*'s "100 Best Companies for Mothers in 1994." New mothers may take six months unpaid family leave and return to work part-time over the next three months. There is a sick child subsidy of up to $400 per year. The company has signed on to the ABC coalition to support child care.

Workplace Information: In September 1995, IAPE, which represents 2,300 employees at Dow Jones, announced a National Labor Relations Board finding that the company had violated federal labor law by prohibiting union meetings at its facilities, while other groups were allowed to meet.

In September 1993, IAPE filed two shareholder resolutions attempting to limit the compensation package of

CEO Peter R. Kann to 20 times the average compensation of his employees. Kann's 1992 compensation was about $1 million, or 63.5 times the amount earned by the lowest-paid IAPE member at Dow Jones (who made $20,000 less than the least experienced reporters at news organizations like Reuters, *Consumer Reports,* and the *New York Times*). The Securities and Exchange Commission (SEC) barred the resolutions from the 1994 ballot. A similar 1995 proposal to limit Kann's compensation received about 6 percent of total votes cast.

International: In addition to the *Asian Wall Street Journal* and the *Wall Street Journal Europe,* in 1994, Dow Jones began supplying foreign-language inserts to newspapers in South Korea, Poland, and Latin America. It also started broadcasting its European Business News network from London. Nikkei, Japan's leading business publisher, was added to Dow's online database in 1995. In May 1994, the government of Singapore eased its restriction on the circulation of the *Asian Wall Street Journal* to 7,000 copies a day from 5,000. Authorities had accused the newspaper of interfering in domestic political matters.

Additional Information: In 1995, Dow Jones joined with ITT Corporation to buy public television station WNYC, which became WBIS, a business and sports channel.

DTE Energy

STOCK SYMBOL: DTE
STOCK EXCHANGES: NY, N, C, CH, PH

Environment	REV
Women's Advancement	C
Minority Advancement	A
Charitable Giving	C
Community Outreach	C
Family Benefits	D
Workplace Issues	D
Social Disclosure	A

DTE Energy is a Detroit-based diversified energy company involved in the development and management of energy-related businesses and services nationwide. Its principal subsidiary is Detroit Edison, an electric utility that generates, transmits, and sells electricity to over 2 million customers in the Southeastern Michigan area. In 1996, company revenues totaled $3.64 billion. DTE had approximately 8,400 employees.

Environment: Detroit Edison states that a major strategy of carbon dioxide reduction is to offset its emissions through the planting of 10 million trees through the year 2000. The company is also involved in a multi-electric utility project with The Nature Conservancy and the government of Belize for international joint CO_2 sequestration. Detroit Edison joined the Department of Energy's Climate Challenge program in 1995.

DTE saved more than one-half million tons of CO_2 in 1996 through DTE Biomass projects, and achieved new levels of energy efficiency through energy partnerships with major industrial customers. Over the past three years, Detroit Edison has led a project under the DOE's Team Up program to increase the use of photovoltaics in the U.S., where customers may elect to purchase units of energy from a solar power facility. The company also sponsors a Soar School program—a solar energy curriculum for schools—and has been chosen by the Maryland Energy Administration to implement a similar program in that state.

EEO: In 1996, Detroit Edison Co.'s 13-member board of directors included two women and one minority (two minorities in 1997). Of 16 corporate officers at the company, one was a woman and two were minorities. Three minorities also ranked among the 25 highest paid employees at the company.

On February 10, 1998, Detroit Edison announced a settlement agreement in three class action lawsuits involving allegations of age, race, and national origin discrimination. The lawsuits arose out of departmental reorganizations conducted between 1991 and 1995 as the company began preparing for industry restructuring and competition. The agreement calls for: creation of long-term programs focused on career development and job opportunities, including work reentry and job movement opportunities for qualified individuals; binding arbitration to determine lump sum monetary relief for those current and former employees who can demonstrate economic or non-economic injury; an appointment of an independent monitoring committee, led by a former circuit court judge who has decision making authority involving the five-year monitoring program. The total lump sum monetary relief to be determined by the arbitrator will range from a minimum of $17.5 million to a maximum of $65 million. DTE reports that the agreement is viewed by all involved as the start of the healing process for the utility, permitting a concentrated focus on the challenges of a changing marketplace.

Community Involvement: Detroit Edison Co.'s charitable contributions totaled $3.9 million in cash in 1996. This figure represented the equivalent of 0.7 percent of the company's pretax earnings for the same year. In 1997, Detroit Edison and the Detroit Edison Foundation's contributions totaled $3.3 million.

The Detroit Edison Foundation has been placing more emphasis on efforts to improve precollege public education, and raising the academic achievement of elementary and secondary students, with a focus on math and science. Detroit Edison also offers awards to employees for volunteer service, which are matched by grants to the organizations with which they were involved.

Workplace Information: According to OSHA records, DTE was inspected 28 times from 1994 to 1996. Violations included 13 violations classified as "willful" or "repeat" and 164 violations classified as "serious." A total of $80,981 in fines was assessed to the company following the inspections.

83

Duke Energy Corporation

STOCK SYMBOL: DUK
STOCK EXCHANGES: NY, B, C, CH, P, PH

Environment	REV
Women's Advancement	D?
Minority Advancement	C?
Charitable Giving	C
Community Outreach	C
Family Benefits	N
Workplace Issues	C?
Social Disclosure	B

In June, 1997, Duke Power merged with Houston-based PanEnergy Corp. to create the Charlotte, North Carolina–based Duke Energy Corporation. Duke Energy is a global energy company with more than $22 billion in assets. Duke Energy companies provide electric service to approximately two million customers; operate pipelines that deliver 12 percent of the natural gas consumed in the U.S.; and are leading marketers of electricity, natural gas, and natural gas liquids. Globally, the companies develop, own, and operate energy facilities and provide engineering, management, operating, and environmental services. Duke Energy employs 22,000 people worldwide.

Environment: Duke Energy reports that it created a new Corporate Environment, Health and Safety Department. Corporate EHS is responsible (among other things) for developing environmental policy for the corporation as well as for assessing the corporation's performance related to that policy. The company has also established an Environmental Committee and a Safety Committee, each comprised of senior management from across the corporation. These committees report to executive management and are charged with assisting the corporation in implementing and monitoring Duke's progress on compliance with its environmental policy and with regulatory requirements.

Due to Clean Air Act regulations, Duke is working to reduce its emissions of nitrogen oxide, sulfur dioxide, and carbon dioxide. The company expects to be below the industry average based on electricity delivered for those chemicals through the year 2000.

Duke is a member of one of three company consortiums to receive funding from the Department of Energy's Clean Coal Technology program.

EEO: In 1996, Duke's board totaled 13 directors, including one minority and no women while nine of 42 corporate officers were women, and none were minorities. At the beginning of 1998, Duke's 16-member board included one minority and one woman; 12 women and three minorities ranked among Duke's 77 corporate officers.

Community Involvement: In 1996, Duke Energy's charitable giving totaled $7.1 million in cash, which was equal to 0.6 percent of the company's pretax earnings for that year. In terms of the actual dollar amount donated by the company, the level of cash contributions in 1996 represented a decrease of 4.2 percent from that of 1995, which was 0.6 percent of the company's earnings for that year. The company's in-kind giving — the donation of products or services — came to a total of $126,000 in 1996.

Family Benefits: In 1987, at then-CEO Bill Lee's urging, Charlotte's largest employers raised nearly $7 million for a community fund to develop child care resources in the area. Corporate benefits include child care support, flexible work scheduling, dependent care spending accounts, part-time benefit coverage, and the LifeBalance referral service for information in areas such as dependent care, children's doctors, and financial and legal assistance.

Workplace Information: OSHA records indicate that Duke was inspected 11 times from 1994 to 1996. Violations included 16 classified as "serious" for a total of $24,500 in fines, or $2,227 per inspection. In comparison, the median amount of fines per inspection for other companies in the utilities industry was $2,625.

Eleven percent of Duke's employees are represented by the various unions. Duke reports that due to the effects of the merger and of changes in company activity, almost 900 employees were laid off in 1997; these employees received severance pay, continued benefit coverage for six months, and outplacement.

Nuclear Power: Three nuclear power facilities provide more than half of Duke's generation mix in its North and South Carolina service areas. Approximately 20 million customers in a 20,000 square mile area are served by these facilities.

DuPont

STOCK SYMBOL: DD
STOCK EXCHANGES: NY, B, C, CH, P, PH

Environment	A
Women's Advancement	B
Minority Advancement	A
Charitable Giving	D
Community Outreach	C
Family Benefits	A
Workplace Issues	B
Social Disclosure	A

DuPont, based in Wilmington, Delaware, is the largest producer of chemicals in the U.S., and operates globally. In 1996, the company had 105,000 employees and sales of over $43 billion.

Environment: DuPont has an environmental policy and a Corporate Environmental Report (CER), which is updated annually and is available on the internet, and has implemented an integrated Environmental Management System. The company has a written pollution prevention policy and has initiated a company-wide pollution prevention program, which establishes annual reduction goals for point sources, secondary emissions, fugitive emissions, and solid waste. The company also has a corporate policy on community involvement relating to local environmental concerns. All U.S. sites and 25 sites outside of the U.S. have community advisory panels. DuPont has a written policy on product stewardship, a product stewardship review board, and evaluates its products with the objective of reducing their life-cycle impacts on the environment.

DuPont's average total toxic releases and transfers during the years 1994–1996 were higher than the industry sample average. Emissions decreased by an average of about a third annually during those years, a better than average performance.

In September 1997, the Department of Justice filed a lawsuit against DuPont alleging the company did not properly contain a 1995 leak of sulfuric acid that prompted the evacuation of 1,000 nearby residents. The Department also charges that DuPont did not promptly notify authorities of the leak and failed to design and maintain a safe facility for handling hazardous substances. DuPont is contesting the charges, arguing it has paid $140,000 to state agencies and invested $460,000 in environmental improvements following the incident.

In April 1997, DuPont received Tennessee's Excellence in Hazardous Waste Management award after it had installed a cyanide recovery system in its Memphis plant. In March 1997, the US EPA overrode Colorado authorities, who had fined Conoco $33,000, and levied a fine of $666,771 for 78 hazardous waste violations at the DuPont subsidiary's Denver refinery. Conoco planned to appeal.

EEO: In 1996, two women and two minorities served on DuPont's 13-member board. Of 61 corporate officers at the company, four were women and eight were minorities, while one of the top 29 paid employees was a woman, and three were minorities.

Community Involvement: Du Pont's charitable contributions totaled $28 million in cash in 1996, or 0.47 percent of the company's pretax earnings.

Workplace Information: According to OSHA's records, DuPont was inspected 23 times from 1994 to 1996. Violations included two classified as "willful" or "repeat" and 72 classified as "serious" for a total of $154,343 in fines. A major review of safety practices between 1994 and 1995 resulted in a 40 percent reduction of injury and illness at the company.

In March, 1996, union employees at two DuPont plants filed charges with the NLRB over the company's employee-management teams. The Niagara Plant Employees union charges that such teams violate federal labor law. The teams were organized to address issues such as safety and morale, which the union argues are employment conditions and thus interfere with the union's purpose.

DuPont is a defendant in a lawsuit brought by former IBM employees who were exposed to chemicals DuPont and other companies supplied and installed in IBM plants in Fishkill, NY and Burlington, VT. The chemicals were alleged to have caused cancer and other sicknesses among the workers.

Animal Testing: DuPont has reduced the number of animals used in certain tests by 60 percent.

Legal Proceedings: DuPont is a defendant in about 100 lawsuits claiming property damage from leaks in polybutylene plumbing systems. Shell and Hoechst-Celanese are codefendants. DuPont has already paid $34 million for thousands of claims settled out of court.

85

Eastern Enterprises

STOCK SYMBOL: EFU
STOCK EXCHANGES: NY, B, C, CH,PH, P

Environment	N
Women's Advancement	C
Minority Advancement	F
Charitable Giving	B
Community Outreach	C?
Family Benefits	N
Workplace Issues	D?
Social Disclosure	C

Eastern Enterprises, based in Weston, Massachusetts, is an unincorporated voluntary association whose principle subsidiaries are Boston Gas Co., Midland Enterprises and WaterPro. Boston Gas Co. furnishes natural gas services to 74 communities in Massachusetts. Midland Enterprises Inc., is primarily engaged in the operation of a fleet of barges and towboats on the Mississippi and Ohio rivers. WaterPro is a wholesale distributor of water and wastewater system components to contractors and municipal customers in 23 states. At the end of 1996 the trust had 3,000 employees and its operating revenues were $1 billion.

EEO: In 1996, Eastern Enterprises' board totaled eight directors, including one woman and one minority, while two of a total of nine corporate officers were women, and none were minorities. Additionally, two women and no minorities were among the 25 employees with the highest salaries at the company.

Community Involvement: Eastern Enterprises' charitable contributions totaled $1 million in cash in 1996. The $1 million cash-giving figure represented the equivalent of 1.0 percent of the company's pretax earnings for the same year, and was identical to the company's cash contributions in 1995. In 1995, the company contributed 1.2 percent of its pretax earnings for that year to charity.

Eastern Enterprises Foundation matches employee gifts to organizations at which the employee is actively involved at a three-to-one ratio. In 1991, the foundation expanded its matching gift program to include all 501(c)(3) organizations, and increased the annual maximum per family from $1,000 to $2,000 in 1992.

In 1994, the foundation created a Neighborhood Matching Fund to help schools and organizations in certain parts of Massachusetts institute youth aspiration programs. Eastern Enterprises makes booklets and brochures of organizations in need of volunteers available to employees, and gives consideration to funding organizations at which employees actively participate.

Foundation giving to education places emphasis on educational programs for youth and supports youth programs that "offer lasting solutions to problems."

When making funding decisions, the foundation gives special consideration to organizations at which employees volunteer.

Workplace Information: The records of the Occupational Safety and Health Administration indicate that Eastern Enterprises underwent one health and safety inspection from 1994 to 1996. The violations reported by OSHA as a result of the inspection include five classified as "serious." The company was required to pay $600 as a result of its violations. In comparison, the median amount of fines per inspection for other utilities was $2,625.

Eastman Chemical

STOCK SYMBOL: EMN
STOCK EXCHANGES: NY, PH, P

Environment	B
Women's Advancement	D?
Minority Advancement	B?
Charitable Giving	F?
Community Outreach	C
Family Benefits	N
Workplace Issues	N
Social Disclosure	B

Headquartered in Kingsport, Tennessee, Eastman Chemical Company produces plastics, chemicals, and fibers. It is the world leader in polyester plastics used for packaging. Eastman also makes food ingredients, such as antioxidants and emulsifiers that extend the shelf life of foods. Formerly owned by Eastman Kodak, Eastman Chemical was spun off and became an independent, public company on December 31, 1993. In 1996, Eastman Chemical employed 17,500 and had sales of $4.8 billion.

Environment: Eastman Chemical publishes a Responsible Care Progress Report, which is available on the internet. The company provides environmental health and safety (EH&S) training to operating personnel through its Environmental Operations Specialist Apprenticeship Program. Eastman Chemical has a written pollution prevention policy and has initiated a company-wide pollution prevention program, which establishes annual reduction goals for point sources, fugitive emissions, and solid waste. The company also reports an open communication with neighbors, surrounding communities, and government officials and has community advisory panels at all of its four major U.S. facilities. Eastman Chemical has a written policy on product stewardship and evaluates its products with the objective of reducing their life-cycle impacts on the environment. Eastman Chemical's HSE guiding principles and HSE performance standards apply equally to all facilities worldwide.

Eastman Chemical's average total toxic releases and transfers during the years 1993–1994 were higher than the industry sample average. Emissions decreased by about two-thirds during those years, a better than average performance.

Eastman Chemical was among 10 companies nationwide receiving awards for energy efficiency from the Chemical Manufacturers Association in 1997. The company received two awards for its Tennessee division for its significant improvement in manufacturing. In 1997, the division also received its fourth consecutive Operational Excellence Award from the Kentucky-Tennessee Water Environment Association, for the efficient operation of its wastewater treatment facility. In the last four years, Eastman's wastewater treatment plant, the fourth largest in the U.S. chemical industry, only had one exceedance of their National Pollutant Discharge Elimination System permit.

Eastman Chemical was fined $50,000 for illegal emissions at the Arkansas chemical plant, due to a defective smokestack scrubber. After smell was reported coming from the stairwell at the plant, Eastman fixed the problem and reported it to the state.

In 1997, Eastman was one of 19 companies presented with the Chemical Transportation Safety Pinnacle Award from Union Pacific Railroad. The award recognizes companies that have done an outstanding job in performing safe loading techniques and preventing non-accidental chemical releases. Eastman was among five companies that shipped more than 3,000 cars in 1995 to win the honor.

EEO: In 1996, Eastman Chemical's board totaled ten directors, including one woman and two minorities, while one of a total of 12 corporate officers was a woman, and none were minorities.

Community Involvement: In 1994, Eastman Chemical made $2.5 million in cash contributions to charitable institutions, the equivalent of 0.5 percent of the company's earnings before taxes that year. The main areas of giving were higher education, health associations, and united funds.

Workplace Information: The records of the Occupational Safety and Health Administration indicate that Eastman Chemical was not inspected from 1994 to 1996. Consequently no fines or violations were assessed to the company.

Under the spin-off agreement with Kodak, Eastman assumed obligation for pension benefits of active U.S. Eastman employees, and Kodak retained responsibility for pensions of Eastman retirees. None of Eastman's U.S. employees are covered by collective bargaining, and only one percent of workers elsewhere are unionized.

Eastman Kodak

STOCK SYMBOL: EK
STOCK EXCHANGES: NY, B, C, CH, P, PH

Environment	C
Women's Advancement	A
Minority Advancement	C?
Charitable Giving	C
Community Outreach	B?
Family Benefits	B
Workplace Issues	B
Social Disclosure	A

Based in Rochester, New York, Eastman Kodak is the largest supplier of photography products in the U.S. In the past two years the company has liquidated nearly all nonimaging businesses. In 1997, the company had sales of approximately $14.5 billion and about 97,500 employees, approximately 43 percent of whom are based outside the U.S.

Environment: Kodak has an annual environmental report and a comprehensive environmental policy available to the public. The company requires compliance with corporate environmental standards at all facilities worldwide. A member of EPA's 33/50 toxics reduction program, the company cut tracked toxic releases by 71 percent from 1988 to 1994. However, Kodak is still New York state's largest emitter of toxic chemicals. Kodak was responsible for 300,000 pounds of spilled hazardous materials from 1991 to 1994. In 1994, Kodak agreed to pay a $5 million fine and spend tens of millions on environmental improvements to settle charges of ground water contamination at its facility in Rochester. Kodak has joined 23 other manufacturers in a voluntary partnership with the EPA to reduce the emissions of perfluoro and hydrofluoro compunds.

The company is also a member of EPA's WasteWi$e program, and has invested $15 million in new "air scrubbing" technology in one of the buildings at its key manufacturing site in Rochester. With the new scrubbers, Kodak reports that it "expects to exceed the level of performance required by EPA regulations. Recently, Kodak constructed a full-scale office paper recycling and pulp production facility at its headquarters. The company is also incorporating environmental criteria into its worldwide supplier rating system. Kodak accomplished its goal of completely eliminating CFCs in manufacturing by the end of 1995.

EEO: In 1996, Eastman Kodak's board totaled 11 directors, including three women and one minority. In 1997, four women and three minorities were among 44 corporate officers, though no minorities sat on the 12-member board.

In 1996, The Interfaith Center for Corporate Responsibility submitted a shareholder resolution proposing that Eastman Kodak distribute an EEO report. It then withdrew the resolution, which generally indicates that an agreement has been reached with management. Eastman Kodak is now a member of the Working Women Count Honor Roll and is recognized for its HIV/AIDS Awareness Program.

Community Involvement: In 1997, Eastman Kodak's contributions to various charitable institutions included cash donations totaling $10.7 million, including the largest corporate donation to a single United Way in the U.S. Cash contributions in 1995 were equivalent to 0.6 percent of pretax earnings.

Kodak reports that "in addition to its released time policy for volunteerism, [the company] facilitates ongoing requests for volunteerism and in 1997 sponsored thousands of employees in Make a Difference Day (in 16 countries)." Other organizations receiving support and participation from Kodak and its employees include Junior Achievement, National Urban League, World Wildlife Fund, and Habitat for Humanity.

Family Benefits: Kodak offers various alternative work arrangements, including part-time, job-sharing, flextime, work-at-home, benefits for part-time employees and compressed work week. Kodak provides resource and referral services for elder and child care and care of disabled dependents, as well as subsidizing emergency in-home backup care.

Workplace Information: According to the Occupational Safety and Health Administration's records, Eastman Kodak was not inspected from 1994 to 1996. Consequently no violations or fines were assessed to the company.

Under competitive pressures from Japanese film producers such as Fuji, Eastman Kodak Co. cut 10,000 employees from its ranks.

Weapons Contracts: In 1994, the company had $138 million in military contracts, of which $106 million was weapons related.

Ecolab, Inc.

STOCK SYMBOL: ECL
STOCK EXCHANGES: NY, CH, PH

Environment	C
Women's Advancement	B
Minority Advancement	N
Charitable Giving	B
Community Outreach	B
Family Benefits	B
Workplace Issues	B
Social Disclosure	B

Ecolab, based in St. Paul, Minnesota, provides specialty services including cleaning, pest elimination, and maintenance for clients in hospitality, institutional, and industrial markets. The company has a 50-50 joint venture with the German chemical firm Henkel to provide industrial cleaning services in Europe. In 1997, Ecolab had over 10,000 employees and sales of $1.5 billion.

Environment: Ecolab has an environmental policy but does not publish an environmental report. The company offers some environmentally improved products such as non-caustic, non chlorine soaps, enzyme-based detergents (which reduce the amount of hypochlorite bleach in laundering), and nonchlorinated sanitizers. Ecolab's Food and Beverage Division started a nationwide recycling program for 55-gallon polyethylene drums used to distribute sanitation chemicals. Ecolab reports that it achieves substantial savings of packaging and transportation resources. The company's patented Turbo-Rev industrial laundry product line provides customers a 50 percent energy savings and a 20 percent water savings; the technology has been endorsed by the EPA's Design for the Environment Program.

Ecolab's operations have minimal toxic emissions. The company does not participate in EPA's voluntary programs—33/50, WasteWi$e or Green Lights. Ecolab is a potentially responsible party at 12 federal Superfund sites.

EEO: One woman serves on Ecolab's 13-member board, and two women are among 24 corporate officers. Information on minority representation was not available.

Community Involvement: In 1996, Ecolab gave an estimated $1.3 million (or approximately 0.9 percent of its average pretax earnings); in 1997 that figure was $2 million, or 1.3 percent of pretax earnings. About 25 percent of Ecolab's donations go through plant-based giving. Employee volunteerism is encouraged through a cash award program.

In addition to cash contributions, Ecolab donates surplus products both in the U.S. and abroad. For example, in 1996 Ecolab donated six truckloads of cleaning and sanitizing supplies and over $275,000 in cash to support relief efforts in Grand Forks, North Dakota. Ecolab has received national recognition for its partnership with St. Paul's Humboldt school, which has a predominantly minority student body.

Family Benefits: Ecolab has offered flextime for about a decade and maintains job sharing on an informal basis. It has contracted with a child care agency to provide resource and referral services for employees. The company operates a day care center near its plant in Puerto Rico.

Workplace Information: Ecolab offers a defined benefit pension plan, a 401(k) savings program, and stock purchase programs. The company celebrated strong financial results in early 1997 by distributing five shares of stock to each of its approximately 9,000 nonmanagement employees. Ecolab offers counseling services through an employee assistance program, and comprehensive medical insurance, which includes preventative care. The company is not known to have any significant safety concerns.

International: Ecolab's international manufacturing locations include Santa Cruz, Brazil; Singapore; Seoul, Korea; Mexico City; Shanghai; and Chile. Additional operations are planned for Indonesia.

Weapons Contracts: In 1994, Ecolab had $491,000 in nonweapons contracts with the Department of Defense.

Eli Lilly

Environment	C
Women's Advancement	D
Minority Advancement	B?
Charitable Giving	A?
Community Outreach	B
Family Benefits	A
Workplace Issues	D
Social Disclosure	B

Indianapolis-based Eli Lilly is one of the largest research pharmaceutical companies, marketing products in 106 countries worldwide. The company, best known for developing the antidepressant drug Prozac, also makes diagnostic products and medical devices. In 1996, Lilly had revenues of $7.3 billion and 26,800 employees.

Environment: Eli Lilly has an environmental policy and a corporate environmental report, which is updated annually. The company has implemented an integrated environmental management system. The company considers contribution towards environment, health & safety goals in the job performance reviews of all employees. Lilly has a pollution prevention policy and has initiated company-wide program strategies for source reduction, reuse, recycling, and treatment. The company has a corporate policy on community involvement relating to local environmental concerns, and currently has two community advisory panels. Lilly has a written commitment to product stewardship and a product stewardship review board.

Eli Lilly's average total toxic releases and transfers during the years 1993–1994 were above the industry sample average. Emissions decreased by more than one-half annually during those years, an above average performance.

EEO: In 1996, Eli Lilly's 13-member board of directors included two women and two minorities. Of 17 corporate officers at the company, one was a woman; none were minorities. Women hold four of the 25 highest-paid positions. The company provides all employees with diversity training and has a written policy banning discrimination based on sexual orientation.

Community Involvement: In 1995, Eli Lilly's contributions to various charitable institutions included cash donations totaling $23 million, and a total of $46 million in in-kind giving, which is the donation of products or services by the company. The company's cash contributions for 1995 were equivalent to 1.3 percent of its earnings before taxes for the same year.

In 1995, Eli Lilly & Company was among the top ten corporate contributors to international and health issues according to the Corporate Giving Watch. Eli Lilly donated medical products in 90 countries in 1994 and has pledged 80,000 volunteer hours by the year 2000.

A November 1996 *Wall Street Journal* article reported that Eli Lilly has used homeless alcoholics in the initial safety testing of experimental drugs. The company's Indianapolis-based clinical research center was mentioned for its lenient policies (e.g., not confirming home addresses) that enables the homeless to volunteer as paid patients. Eli Lilly was admonished in 1994 by the FDA for using alcoholics in a drug study that resulted in one death and a hospitalization that went unreported at the time.

Family Benefits: In 1996, Eli Lilly was praised by *Working Mother* magazine for outstanding family-friendly policies and programs. The company's CEO, Randall Tobais, was also honored by the magazine for his dedication to making Eli Lilly a family-friendly model. Exemplary benefits include 24-month maternal leave, adoption aid up to $10,000, and on-site/near-site day care.

Workplace Information: OSHA records indicate that Eli Lilly was inspected twice from 1994 to 1996. Violations included one violation classified as "serious" for an average of $2,450 per inspection. In comparison, the median amount of fines per inspection for medical and cosmetic companies was $2,266.

International: Eli Lilly states that it follows U.S. environmental regulations and maintains occupational and health and safety standards in the U.S. and abroad, unless local regulations are stricter. However, the company does not have a code of conduct that addresses the use of child labor, forced labor, bonded labor and minimum wage.

Additional Information: In 1995, Lilly ended its community programs intended to educate people about depression after the FDA began examining whether the program was also deceptive advertising.

Englehard Corporation

STOCK SYMBOL: EC
STOCK EXCHANGES: NY, B

Environment	N
Women's Advancement	A?
Minority Advancement	B?
Charitable Giving	N
Community Outreach	N
Family Benefits	N
Workplace Issues	N
Social Disclosure	F

Based in Iselin, New Jersey, Englehard Corporation is a leading provider of specialty chemical products, engineered materials, and precious metals management services. In 1996, Englehard Corp. employed approximately 6,300 people and had sales of $3.2 billion.

Environment: Englehard does not have an environmental policy or a corporate environmental report.

Englehard's average total toxic releases and transfers during the years 1993–1994 were slightly below the industry sample average. Emissions decreased by almost two-thirds during those years, a better than average performance.

A main thrust of Englehard's business has been to reduce auto emissions through catalytic converters and to supply cost-effective catalytic systems to control carbon monoxide and volatile organic compound emissions, thus helping manufacturers to comply with environmental regulations. Ford Motor is a major customer. Englehard sometimes works with Ford to develop new pollution control systems: in June 1995, they began joint research on a new technology that could allow ordinary car radiators to become "smog-eating" filtration systems, literally reducing pollution as they drive.

In 1994, Englehard entered into a joint venture (Englehard/ICC) to produce and market a new type of air conditioner. The new design eliminates or greatly cuts down on the need for chemical refrigerants that harm the ozone layer. To be run by gas or electricity, the pioneering technology uses a dessicant (air-drying agent) which will help reduce the fungal/microbial growth in moist ductwork that can cause health problems.

Englehard is currently involved with environmental investigations for cleanup at four sites it owns and/or operates: Plainville, Massachusetts; Salt Lake City, Utah; Attapulgus, Georgia; and Newark, New Jersey. In addition, it is a potentially responsible party, with others, of 16 waste sites. Cash payments for environmentally-related cleanup were expected to be about $10 million for 1995.

EEO: In 1996, Englehard Corp.'s board totaled 11 directors, including three women and one minority, while none of a total of nine corporate officers were women, and none were minorities.

Community Involvement: CEP researchers were unable to find any information on the charitable or community involvement practices of Englehard.

Workplace Information: According to the Occupational Safety and Health Administration's records, Englehard Corp. was not inspected in 1996. Consequently no violations or fines were assessed to the company.

Englehard unveiled some new employee benefits in 1995 and wanted to make sure employees understood how to take advantage of them. It commissioned a new benefit guidebook, which was used for the company's open enrollment period. It helped employees to organize their benefit choices before using a toll-free telephone number to select their benefits.

International: The company recently bought Kali-Chemie GmbH, an auto catalyst maker in Nienburg, Germany. It has now built a $25 million factory to meet the growing demand for diesel engine catalytic converters in the European Community. This facility was instrumental in developing new technology allowing European auto manufacturers to simplify emission control systems and meet stringent "Euro II" standards. BMW now uses Englehard's new Trimax catalysts in several of its models and recently awarded the company its Outstanding Supplier Award.

Englehard has developed a fluid catalytic cracking (FCC) catalyst, used to change oil into gasoline and other fuels. The company hopes to expand its presence in Asia over the next few years, where a huge market for this type of product should open up. In 1995, the French subsidiary of Engelhard and Rhone-Poulenc were hoping to form a joint venture — Cycleon — to recycle precious metals from used automotive catalytic converters, if approved by the European Commission.

Enron Corporation

STOCK SYMBOL: ENE
STOCK EXCHANGES: NY, To, B, C, CH,
P, PH

Environment	B
Women's Advancement	C
Minority Advancement	B
Charitable Giving	C
Community Outreach	B
Family Benefits	B
Workplace Issues	D
Social Disclosure	A

Enron reports that it is the "world's leading integrated natural gas and electricity company." The company, based in Houston, Texas, manages 38,000 miles of gas pipelines and 4,800 megawatts of gas-fired power plants. It is aggressively pursuing power contracts overseas, particularly in central Asia and Latin America. In 1996, revenues were $20.3 billion, and the company had 16,000 employees.

Environment: Natural gas is an environmentally preferred fuel because of its cleaner burning properties, which result in significantly lower emissions of sulfur dioxide, nitrogen oxide, and carbon dioxide.

Enron Wind Corp. was awarded contracts for the world's three largest wind power generation projects; financing and construction is underway on the first, a 100-megawatt wind farm in Minnesota. In a joint venture with Amoco, Enron is building the world's first utility-scale solar power plant in southern Nevada and is pursuing potential projects in Japan, Greece, and China.

Enron conducts environmental audits company-wide and participates in EPA's Green Lights program. Its recycling education committee received Clean Houston's Proud Partners award in 1994 for supplying four schools with recycling bins and educational materials. In 1997, Enron received the U.S. EPA Natural Gas Star Program Partner award.

EEO: In 1996, Enron Corp.'s 13-member board of directors included one woman and two minorities; the board had 17 members in 1997. Of 25 corporate officers at the company, five were women and two were minorities; in 1997, the 28 corporate officers included eight women and three minorities. Two women and two minorities also ranked among the 36 highest paid employees at the company in 1996. In 1997, three women and four minorities ranked among the 50 highest paid employees at Enron. As head of the Greater Houston Partnership, CEO Ken Lay oversaw the formation of the Minority Partnership Program, an initiative designed to foster ties between heads of minority firms and other corporate CEOs.

Community Involvement: In 1996, Enron Corp.'s charitable giving totaled $5.7 million in cash, which was equal to 0.5 percent of the company's pretax earnings for that year. Cash contributions in 1997 totaled $6.5 million, 0.9 percent of pretax earnings.

Enron merged with Portland General Corp. in July, 1997. The two entities committed $20 million to the creation of the Enron/Portland General Foundation.

Family Benefits: Work/family programs are well rounded and include a $100,000 commitment to assist in construction and operation of a child care facility in downtown Houston.

Workplace Information: Enron Methanol was fined $369,000 in 1996 as a result of a 1994 accident, for four violations classified as "willful" and 39 classified as "serious." Aristech Chemical, which operates a plant adjacent to the site of the 1994 explosion, filed a lawsuit charging that numerous safety problems at the methanol plant were not sufficiently addressed before or after the explosion. The suit was withdrawn after Enron agreed to have a third-party inspection of the plant.

In 1997, the American Gas Association presented three safety awards to Enron for outstanding performance in the pipeline industry.

Employees currently own about 7.5 percent of the company. Less than 1 percent of Enron's domestic workforce is unionized. The company has grievance procedures for nonrepresented employees.

Entergy Corporation

STOCK SYMBOL: ETR
STOCK EXCHANGES: NY, B, C, CH, P

Environment	C
Women's Advancement	F?
Minority Advancement	C?
Charitable Giving	N
Community Outreach	N
Family Benefits	N
Workplace Issues	F?
Social Disclosure	C

Entergy, based in New Orleans, Louisiana, is a global energy company with power production, distribution operations, and related diversified services on five continents. Entergy distributes energy to 4.8 million customers, about half of whom reside in the U.S. (portions of Arkansas, Louisiana, Mississippi, and Texas) and half in international markets (London, England; Melbourne, Australia; and Buenos Aires, Argentina). Entergy also owns, manages, or invests in power plants generating nearly 30,000 megawatts, provides power marketing services, sells electricity wholesale, and offers a range of energy management, security monitoring, and telecommunications services.

Environment: During the period from 1989 through 1992, Entergy performed better than the industry average on emissions of carbon dioxide (CO_2), sulfur dioxide, and nitrous oxides. The company has taken voluntary action to reduce its emissions still further, for example, by joining the Department of Energy's Climate Challenge initiative to reduce and sequester greenhouse gases. The agreement would reduce CO_2 emissions by over 27 million tons through the year 2000. Entergy has a moderate demand-side management program to promote energy efficiency among its customers.

Entergy is working to reduce hazardous waste such as parts washer solvent and paint waste through product substitution and/or source reduction. Many of its facilities are testing alternative solvents that — after use — may be filtered, blended with waste oil, and sold for recycle. Paints are selected that reduce the volume of waste generated; a solvent recovery system allows recycling of used thinners.

Entergy reported paying $61,000 from 1992 to early 1995 for environmental citations. The company has spent $10 million since 1989 for five Superfund site cleanups throughout its operating system. Its subsidiaries have recently been involved in lawsuits alleging that the company was negligent in avoiding exposure to asbestos and hazardous waste at its sites.

EEO: In 1996, Entergy Corp.'s board totaled 14 directors, including one woman and one minority, while no women or minorities were among 14 corporate officers; as of 1998, one woman was a corporate officer.

Entergy Corporation, along with four of its subsidiaries, is a defendant in numerous lawsuits that have been filed by former employees who claim that they were wrongfully terminated or discriminated against due to their age, race, or sex, two of which seek class certification. Entergy denies any liability to the plaintiffs. An age discrimination suit against Entergy is scheduled to be heard by the Supreme Court in 1998.

Community Involvement: Entergy was the "premier underwriter" of the United Way Day of Caring in the New Orleans area, in which over 1,300 volunteers participated. As a part of its concentration on education and economic development programs, Entergy supports literacy and workplace training programs, teacher education programs, and services that help low-income families find affordable housing.

Workplace Information: OSHA records indicate that Entergy Corp. underwent one health and safety inspection from 1994 to 1996. Violations include five classified as "serious" for a total of $100,500 in fines. In comparison, the median amount of fines per inspection for other utilities was $2,625.

Exxon Corporation

STOCK SYMBOL: XON
STOCK EXCHANGES: NY, B, C, CH, PH, P

Exxon, based in Irving, Texas, is the largest oil company in the U.S., and the second largest industrial company. In 1996, revenue was $134.2 billion and Exxon employed 79,000 people.

Environment	A
Women's Advancement	D
Minority Advancement	B
Charitable Giving	D
Community Outreach	C?
Family Benefits	D
Workplace Issues	D
Social Disclosure	A

Environment: Exxon Corporation has an environmental policy and publishes a corporate environmental report, which is available on the internet. Exxon has implemented an integrated environmental management system. Exxon has a written pollution prevention policy, and has initiated a company-wide pollution prevention program which establishes annual reduction goals for solid waste. The company employs a tiered approach to reducing hazardous waste. First, when cost-effective, the company reduces waste at its source. Secondly, Exxon recycles or reuses waste "to the extent feasible." Remaining waste is treated to a nonhazardous classification or disposed of at a secure site. The company also has a corporate policy on community involvement relating to local environmental concerns, and currently has community advisory panels at all of its facilities. Though Exxon has a written policy on product stewardship, it does not evaluate its products with the objective of reducing their life-cycle impacts on the environment. Most of Exxon's products are fuels and lubricants which are consumed in their use; product evaluations include a range of health, safety, and environmental considerations. Exxon sponsors a study of Piracicaba River, which protects drinking water supply; protects the American jaguar in Argentina; sponsors the Royal Society for Nature Conservation; and runs a campaign called "Save the Tiger," to save endangered tigers in the wild, which involves a commitment of $5 million over 5 years. The company participated in EPA's 33/50 and WasteWi$e programs.

Exxon Corporation's average toxic releases and transfers during the years 1994–1996 were among the lowest compared to an industry sample. However, its emissions increased by an average of about a sixth annually during those years, one of the worst performances within the industry sample. The company ranked second out of 15 for CEP's Campaign for Cleaner Corporations' (C-3) 1997 Petroleum Refining Report. It was also identified as one of the "best" performers for refining operations.

An attorney representing a group of Alaska natives stated that "It is impossible to overstate the depth of Exxon's insensitivity to the Alaskan natives," in response to the company's request that the *Valdez*, renamed the *Mediterranean*, be permitted to enter Prince William Sound. Exxon reports that "SeaRiver Maritime, which owns the vessel, believes the federal law in question is discriminatory, unconstitutional, and should be overturned."

In 1996, a Texas citizens group and a public interest law firm claimed Exxon had illegally dumped more than 2 billion gallons of untreated wastewater from its Baytown facility over the past five years. Four of the five claims in the suit have been dismissed. Exxon states the claims are unfounded, and that the refinery operated within the parameters set by its permit.

A federal judge ruled in 1996 that Exxon crafted an arrangement through which it attempted to redirect back to the company hundreds of millions of dollars from the $5 billion of punitive damages awarded victims of the 1989 *Exxon Valdez* oil spill . Exxon agreed to pay $70 million to settle the processors' oil-spill claims with certain fish processors if they returned most of any punitive damages from any later spill-related cases. Exxon reports that it disagreed with this ruling and that the matter is being appealed.

In his speech to the 15th World Petroleum Congress, Lee R. Raymond, chairman of Exxon, stated "the most pressing environmental problems of the developing nations are related to poverty which is itself the worst polluter, not climate change."

EEO: In 1996, one woman sat on Exxon Corp.'s board of directors; in 1997, the number increased to two.

In June of 1995, the EEOC brought a discrimination suit against Exxon on behalf of two employees,

Comtinued on next page

94

claiming a company policy was in violation of the Americans With Disabilities Act. Exxon's 1989 policy excludes all employees with incidents of substance abuse in their past from holding jobs designated as safety sensitive positions. One plaintiff had undergone treatment for drug abuse more than 25 years ago when he was 18, and the second had participated in an outpatient program for alcoholism in 1985; both were excepted from the application of the policy until 1994, when Exxon decided to apply the policy without exceptions.

In 1994, Exxon Production Research Co. settled a complaint brought by some Asian applicants and employees of the Exxon affiliate. The company said it chose to settle the case in order to avoid lengthy and costly legal proceedings. An undisclosed amount of compensation was paid to one applicant and several current and former Exxon employees.

Two shareholder resolutions, one proposing a report of progress to the Glass Ceiling Commission and one proposing that the company adopt a policy barring discrimination on the basis of sexual orientation, were omitted from the company's 1997 proxy with the SEC's permission.

Exxon Research & Engineering was cited by the Glass Ceiling Commission as one of 83 companies that have implemented "employment practices that help break the glass ceiling," specifically for its Internship and Mentoring Program. The program provides female and minority high school students with professional-level mentors and work experience in engineering.

According to a survey of oil companies conducted by *The Oil Daily* in December 1996, Exxon is one of several companies that "employ relatively large numbers of minorities." Charles Walker, executive director of the National Society of Blacks in Engineering, has noted that Exxon is among the companies that lead the industry in minority recruitment.

Community Involvement: In 1996, Exxon Corp.'s charitable giving totaled $54.8 million in cash, which was equal to 1.13 percent of the company's domestic pretax earnings for that year. In terms of the actual dollar amount donated by the company, the level of cash contributions in 1996 represented an increase of 0.10 percent from that of 1995, which was 0.52 percent of the company's earnings for that year.

The Exxon Education Foundation's three-to-one matching gift program for employee donations to educational institutions is the largest educational matching gift program in the country, awarding $12.6 million in 1996 grants.

Workplace Information: OSHA records indicate that Exxon Corp. was inspected 24 times from 1994 to 1996. Violations included two classified as "willful" or "repeat" and 57 classified as "serious" for a total of $471,988 in fines, or an average of $19,666 per inspection. In comparison, the median amount of fines per inspection for other companies in the extractive business was $2,941.

Fannie Mae

STOCK SYMBOL: FNM
STOCK EXCHANGES: NY, B, C, CH, P, PH

Environment	N
Women's Advancement	A
Minority Advancement	A
Charitable Giving	N
Community Outreach	A
Family Benefits	A
Workplace Issues	N
Social Disclosure	A

The Federal National Mortgage Association (Fannie Mae), based in Washington, D.C., started out as a U.S. government agency in 1938. Thirty years later, it became a privately managed corporation, but with the same mission: to purchase mortgages from lending institutions and provide a constant source of mortgage funds for low- and middle-income buyers. Fannie Mae is the nation's largest investor in American home mortgages. In 1996, it had revenues of $25 billion and 2,500 employees.

EEO: Four women and one Hispanic man serve on the 16-member board. Of 135 corporate officers, 49 are women. A special career development program has helped encourage the advancement of women. Fannie Mae reports that minorities account for over 21 percent of the company's managment ranks, that 48 of 114 vice presidents are women, as are seven of 28 senior vice presidents.

Community Involvement: A decade ago, Fannie Mae announced a $1 million 10-year commitment to its Woodson Senior High School Incentive Scholarship Program, which awards students who earn B or above $4,000 toward their post–high school education. Many employees act as mentors and career guidance counselors. The students participate in a Futures 500 Club, attend extracurricular activities, and have opportunities for summer employment at Fannie Mae.

Each year, the company holds a Help the Homeless Week, which includes an educational fair, fund-raising for selected organizations serving the homeless, and a collection of toilet essentials for homeless men, women, and children. Employee giving is matched by the foundation.

Fannie Mae donates full funding for the Fannie Mae Foundation, a seperate and distinct entity since April 1996. At that time, Fannie Mae made a $350 million stock contribution to the Foundation. The company's giving program is relatively small, with donations in 1995 of an estimated $14 million (or 0.4 percent of average pretax profits). The Foundation directs about half of its grants to neighborhood housing and development. Another 40 percent is divided between social service organizations and arts, health, and education groups.

Having invested over $1.2 billion over the past ten years, Fannie Mae is the largest corporate investor in Low Income Housing Tax Credits in the U.S.

New Initiatives: By the year 2000, Fannie Mae will provide an unprecedented $1 trillion in housing loans for those most in need: low-income individuals, minorities, new immigrants, and central city residents. Rejected mortgage applications will get another look, and the supply of multifamily rental housing will increase.

In June 1994, Fannie Mae entered an agreement with Freddie Mac and the Department of Housing and Urban Development to spread the risk among them for financing rental housing units for low- and middle-income families. Loans may be for acquisition, rehabilitation, construction, or refinancing of an estimated 12,500 housing units.

Family Benefits: The company offers all employees flextime and allows part-time schedules for managers. The maximum length of family leave allowed is 22 weeks, 10 weeks above the legal minimum. An emergency child care center for children from 6 months to 12 years old is available on-site for Washington, DC, headquarters employees. Reimbursement for overnight child care is provided to employees called away on business trips. The company also offers a variety of onsite screenings.

Mothers may take up to 16 weeks for maternity; fathers and adoptive parents are allowed an unusual two weeks of paid leave.

Workplace Information: One unusual benefit offered by Fannie Mae is its Employer Assisted Housing program, which provides a forgivable loan to eligible employees to use for the downpayment and closing costs on a home. The company also offers financial assistance to employees seeking undergraduate or graduate degrees.

Federated Department Stores

STOCK SYMBOL: FD
STOCK EXCHANGES: NY, PH, P

Environment	N
Women's Advancement	C?
Minority Advancement	C?
Charitable Giving	A
Community Outreach	C
Family Benefits	N
Workplace Issues	B?
Social Disclosure	B

Federated Department Stores, based in Cincinatti, Ohio, is the nation's largest operator of department stores. The company runs 411 department stores and 150 specialty stores in 36 states. Store names include Bloomingdale's, Burdines, The Bon Marche, Macy's, Lazarus, Rich's, and Stern's. In 1996, sales were $15 billion, and the company had 119,100 employees.

Environment: Federated's corporate publications are printed on recycled paper with soy-based inks "whenever possible." All paper contains recycled fiber, and all cardboard containers received at distribution centers are sent to local recycling centers. Rich's is operating an in-house recycling program, and Macy's uses recycled packaging and wrapping materials.

EEO: Federated Department Stores turned in an average overall performance in workforce diversity for S&P 500 companies in 1996. The company's 11-member board included one woman and one minority, as compared with the average of 10.8 percent women and 7.6 percent minorities for other S&P 500 companies. Two women and no minorities served among the company's 15 corporate officers.

Community Involvement: In 1996, Federated Department Stores' charitable giving totaled $9.6 million in cash, which was equal to 2.2 percent of the company's pretax earnings for that year. In terms of the actual dollar amount donated by the company, the level of cash contributions in 1996 represented a decrease of 18.7 percent from that of 1995, which was 4.8 percent of the company's earnings for that year. The company matches employee contributions to education, arts & culture and to the areas of breast cancer research, domestic violence and abuse programs, and HIV/AIDS research and support.

Between 25 percent and 50 percent of the Federated Department Stores employees are involved in the corporate volunteer program, Partners in Time, which received the 1991 President's Volunteer Action Award. The major projects undertaken through the program concern education, AIDS, women's issues, shelter, the Special Olympics, and holiday events. Federated also was selected to participate in the President's Summit on Volunteerism in April of 1997, on the basis of its new Earning for Learning employee education volunteer grant program.

Workplace Information: According to the Occupational Safety and Health Administration's records, Federated Department Stores was inspected two times from 1994 to 1996. The OSHA inspectors' citations included one violation classified as "serious." A total of $375 in fines was assessed to the company following the inspections. In comparison, the median amount of fines per inspection for other companies in the retail industry was $694.

Federated Department Stores is among seven major retailer chains that the Sweatshop Watch coalition accused in early 1996 of ignoring evidence that some of their goods were manufactured in sweatshop conditions. Federated had been named by federal labor investigators as a possible recipient of garments produced by a sweatshop in El Monte, California, that had been raided six months earlier. All the retailers bought goods from contractors that purchased garments from the El Monte sweatshop. Federated denied any wrongdoing, and said that it pulled any goods suspected of being produced in El Monte from its shelves. The El Monte facility housed 72 Thai workers, and eight of its operators pleaded guilty to federal civil rights violations and other charges.

International: Federated has both a standard Code of Good Business Conduct (shared with all Federated associates, and reviewed annually by all management associates) and a Statement of Corporate Policy (sent with every purchase order to all vendors). Together, the documents address basic workers' rights such as harassment, worker safety, and child and forced labor.

First Union Corporation

STOCK SYMBOL: FTU
STOCK EXCHANGES: NY, PH, P

Environment	N
Women's Advancement	D
Minority Advancement	D?
Charitable Giving	D
Community Outreach	C?
Family Benefits	B
Workplace Issues	B
Social Disclosure	C

First Union, based in Charlotte, North Carolina, is the sixth largest bank holding company in the U.S., offering full financial services through offices along the East Coast in 12 states. In addition to offering traditional banking services at 1,900 financial centers (the second largest branch network in the U.S.), First Union reports that it offers mutual funds and annuities for individuals, plus financial expertise in cash management, capital management, access to the capital markets and international banking for business customers. First Union ended the 1996 fiscal year with almost $12 billion in income and assets of $71 billion. The company has approximately 44,300 employees.

EEO: First Union Corp. turned in a below average performance in the area of diversity in 1996, compared to other S&P 500 companies. Among the companies surveyed by CEP, the average representation of women and minorities on S&P corporate boards was 10.8 percent and 7.5 percent, respectively. In comparison, First Union Corp. had one woman and one minority on its 29-member board. Additionally, the company's total of six corporate officers included no women or minorities.

Following First Union's mid-1993 acquisition of First American Metro Corp., over 100 former employees charged the bank with discriminating against older and minority workers in postmerger layoffs. The plaintiffs maintain that First Union reneged on its promise to give laid-off workers preference in filling vacancies that later developed, instead offering those positions to younger, white workers. The case is pending in U.S. District Court in Washington, D.C., where the plaintiffs seek reinstatement and back pay.

First Union has established a grant to fund a diversity program to improve race relations in the District.

Community Involvement: In 1996, First Union Corp. made $11.8 million in cash contributions to charitable institutions.

In April, 1997, First Union joined with two other companies and the local Urban League in a coalition to support pro-tolerance, pro-diversity leadership in the Charlotte, North Carolina, political arena. With the creation of a coalition which will function as a civic organization or a political action committee, NationsBank, Duke Power, First Union, and the Charlotte-Mecklenburg Urban League, which promotes economic self-sufficiency among African Americans, took a public stance in response to what they considered to be intolerance on the part of local officials. County commissioners had recently voted to end funding for the Charlotte-Mecklenburg Arts & Science Council after the Council had sponsored plays that portrayed gays and lesbians. The commissioners had created an atmosphere of "divisiveness and intolerance for very specific groups," according to Henry Doss, a senior Vice President at First Union. The corporate group plans to begin its efforts in the summer of 1997 with a series of community forums.

First Union sponsors programs for providing affordable housing, economic development and environmental protection and conservation. There is special consideration for minorities, children, youth and the disadvantaged. Charitable giving is limited geographically to: District of Columbia, Florida, Georgia, Maryland, North Carolina, South Carolina, Tennessee, Virginia.

Workplace Information: According to the Occupational Safety and Health Administration's records, First Union Corp. was inspected two times from 1994 to 1996. OSHA inspectors cited the company only for violations classified as "other," the least egregious type of violation, and First Union was not fined. In comparison, the median amount of fines per inspection for other companies in the service industry, such as banks and communications companies, was $573.

Fleet Financial

STOCK SYMBOL: FLT

STOCK EXCHANGES: NY, B, CH, PH, P

Environment	N
Women's Advancement	C?
Minority Advancement	D?
Charitable Giving	B?
Community Outreach	A
Family Benefits	N
Workplace Issues	N
Social Disclosure	C

Fleet, based in Providence, Rhode Island, is engaged in general commercial banking and trust business throughout the states of Rhode Island, New York, Connecticut, Massachusetts, New Jersey, Maine, and New Hampshire. Fleet provides a variety of financial services including mortgage banking, asset-backed lending, equipment leasing, real estate financing, securities brokerage services, investment banking, investment advice and management, data processing, and student loan servicing. At year-end 1996, Fleet had income of $8 billion and assets totaling $ 85.5 billion. The corporation has approximately 36,000 employees.

Environment: Fleet was at the center of regulatory and legal deliberations of whether banks could be held liable for environmental remediation of sites owned or operated by their clients. In response, Fleet became the first major firm to require borrowers to secure environmental-liability insurance.

EEO: A $1.8 billion law suit accusing Fleet Financial Group of racial discrimination was filed in March, 1996. As of June of that year, the case was still pending. The plaintiffs in the case are seven current and former African-American employees who allege that Fleet participated in racially abusive practices and job discrimination. The company denied any wrongdoing. In the past several years, Fleet spent over $100 million settling suits with several states for using allegedly biased lending practices. Recently Fleet has made an effort to increase its diversity efforts. It has created a diversity council and implemented diversity training for its top managers. The managers' bonuses have been linked to the plans. The group will send all 35,000 employees to diversity training sessions and foster a mentoring program for women and minorities to retain diverse candidates.

Community Involvement: In 1995, Fleet Financial Group's contributions to various charitable institutions included cash donations totaling $10 million. The company's cash contributions for 1995 were equivalent to one percent of its earnings before taxes for the same year.

Fleet's Corporate Charitable Contributions Program provides resources for community and economic development, education, healthcare, human services, art and humanities. Support is given to programs such as affordable housing, educational, health, child care and human service purposes, and job training. Fleet supports partnership initiatives throughout the Northeast. Through partnerships, Fleet helps low- and moderate-income neighborhoods. Women- and minority-owned businesses are also a priority for Fleet financial. Fleet sponsors seminars for women starting their own businesses, managing personal finances and saving for retirement. Fleet joined a partnership with the National Association for Teaching Entrepreneurship. From 1994 through 1997, Fleet operated an $8 billion lending program for home buyers and businesses in low- and moderate-income neighborhoods. Fleet allows its employees to volunteer for two paid days a year.

Workplace Information: According to the Occupational Safety and Health Administration's records, Fleet Financial Group was not inspected from 1994 to 1996. Consequently no violations or fines were assessed to the company. As inspections are often called in response to a complaint regarding the health or safety conditions at a company's facility, a lack of inspections can frequently indicate a well-run workplace in terms of safety and health issues.

FMC Corporation

STOCK SYMBOL: FMC

STOCK EXCHANGES: NY, B, C, CH, PH, P

Environment	D
Women's Advancement	F?
Minority Advancement	D?
Charitable Giving	C?
Community Outreach	D?
Family Benefits	N
Workplace Issues	F?
Social Disclosure	C

FMC Corporation, headquartered in Chicago, Illinois, is the world leader in natural soda ash production. Its industrial and agricultural chemical plants and gold, silver, and soda ash mining facilities are located across the nation and in 20 other countries. The company's defense division manufactures the Bradley fighting vehicle. Sales in 1996 were over $5 billion and there were 22,048 employees.

Environment: FMC Corp. has an environmental policy and a corporate environmental report. FMC's policy states that employees are to be involved in assuming responsibility for understanding and complying with the company's worldwide environmental policy. FMC Corp. has a corporate policy on community involvement relating to local environmental concerns; however, it does not have any community advisory panels.

FMC Corp.'s average total toxic releases and transfers during the years 1993–1994 were less than the industry sample average. Emissions decreased slightly during those years, a below average performance.

In 1996, West Virginia environmental protection officials charged that FMC violated the state Air Pollution Control Act after highly toxic phosphorous trichloride was leaked from an FMC facility. Rainfall combined with the spilled chemical to form a toxic cloud of hydrochloric acid. A state air quality official noted that between 1994-1995, 30 separate accidental releases of air pollutants were recorded by FMC, but only one incident was reported to authorities. FMC is also facing a class action suit filed on behalf of residents claiming harm from the leak.

In 1995, decomposing chemicals at an FMC warehouse in Tonawanda, New York, caused an explosion and fire that killed one man, seriously injured another, and led to the evacuation of nearby residents.

FMC makes Furadan, said to be the largest selling insecticide in the world, and listed by the EPA as an extremely hazardous substance linked with birth defects.

FMC Corp. has agreed to pay $209,600 in civil penalties to settle an Environmental Protection Agency complaint that the company's phosphorus plant in Pocatello, Idaho, underreported the quantities of wastes it released into the environment in violation of the federal right-to-know law.

EEO: In 1996, FMC had one woman and no minorities on its 13-member board. Additionally, the company's total of 24 corporate officers included one woman.

FMC Corp. was listed by the Chicago Area Partnerships, an organization which includes community, government, and corporate representatives, in its report on Corporate Best Practices to Shatter the Glass Ceiling. A Network Symposium in 1996 was established to induce communication between various networking and support groups.

Community Involvement: In 1995, FMC Corp.'s contributions to various charitable institutions included cash donations totaling $1.5 million. The company's cash contributions for 1995 were equivalent to 0.47 percent of its earnings before taxes for the same year.

Workplace Information: OSHA records indicate that FMC Corp. underwent seven inspections from 1994 to 1996. Violations included 32 classified as "serious" for a total of $541,745 in fines. In comparison, the median amount of fines per inspection for other companies in the extractive business was $2,941.

International: In February 1995, FMC Corp. sold a minority interest in its soda ash business, FMC Wyoming Corp., to Japan's Nippon Sheet Glass and Sumitomo Corp. for $150 million. The companies now hold a combined 20 percent interest in FMC's soda ash business.

Weapons Contracts: FMC ranked 39th on the list of worldwide defense manufacturers in 1995 with $968 million in defense revenue. This represented 21.5 percent of overall revenue. FMC manufactures armored vehicles and artillery, is involved in defense electronics and builds communications and ordnance systems.

Food Lion, Inc.

STOCK SYMBOL: FDLNA
STOCK EXCHANGE: NNM

Environment	N
Women's Advancement	B
Minority Advancement	C
Charitable Giving	F
Community Outreach	D
Family Benefits	D
Workplace Issues	D
Social Disclosure	D

Based in Salisbury, North Carolina, Food Lion operates approximately 1,100 supermarkets, primarily in the Southeast and Middle Atlantic regions. The company experienced explosive growth throughout the 1970s and 1980s, though the pace of expansion has slowed in recent years. In 1997, Food Lion had sales of $10.2 billion and 80,000 employees. The Belgian company Delhaize controls half of its voting stock.

Environment: Through office and retail recycling programs, in 1995 Food Lion recycled 13,700 tons of cardboard and 1,200 tons of plastic. The company boasts of having one of the most efficient trucking fleets in the industry and has had an award-winning energy management system since the late 1970s.

EEO: By 1995, Food Lion had named two women to its board of directors and promoted three women to the position of vice president. An African-American man also serves on the ten-member board. Recent information on diversity among store managers is not available, though a survey conducted several years ago by the United Food and Commercial Workers (UFCW) found sparse representation of women and African Americans. The company, however, has been more willing to locate stores in inner-city communities than its competitors.

In 1995, Food Lion was recognized for its ten-year participation in the NAACP's Fair Share program. The company was honored again by the NAACP in 1997, for its participation in the organization's minority vendor program. The company recently established a Diversity Planning Department.

Food Lion faces litigation brought by five employees alleging age discrimination.

Community Involvement: Food Lion is the largest supermarket supporter of Children's Miracle Network, having donated $2.2 million during the past five years. Much of this amount, however, has been raised from customers and employees. Corporate contributions appear to be limited. In 1995, Food Lion donated a modest $95,000 worth of food and products to the Food Industry Crusade Against Hunger, which supports Second Harvest food banks and other hunger relief efforts.

Workplace Information: Food Lion is aggressively opposed to organized labor and has long had a confrontational relationship with the UFCW, the industry's primary union. In 1990, the UFCW filed a complaint against Food Lion charging it with systematically terminating employees before their pension benefits were vested. While the case remains pending, initial rulings have not supported the union's position.

In August 1995, Food Lion filed a multimillion-dollar suit against the UFCW, charging that for more than a decade the union had engaged in "a conspiracy to cause massive injury" to the company's business and reputation.

In 1993, Food Lion settled the largest overtime and child labor case ever brought by the Department of Labor by agreeing to pay $16.2 million in fines and back pay. The company admitted no wrongdoing.

Product Safety: In 1992, ABC-TV's *Prime Time Live* reported on unsanitary practices at some of the company's stores. Two ABC correspondents gained employment at different Food Lion stores and with hidden cameras recorded that meat that had passed its "sell by" date was repackaged as fresh; aged ground beef, mixed with new shipments was resold, and meat-cutting equipment was improperly maintained.

Food Lion sued ABC, alleging fraud and misrepresentation. In December 1996, the jury found that the producers had defrauded the company, and ABC was asked to pay $5.5 million in punitive damages. ABC has filed an appeal.

Recent inspections have resulted in positive reviews. The union and consumer organizations maintain that the company has had prior knowledge of inspection schedules, but an FDA review of the matter refuted those claims.

Ford Motor Company

STOCK SYMBOL: F
STOCK EXCHANGES: NY, TO, B, C, CH, P, PH, MO

Environment	C
Women's Advancement	A
Minority Advancement	A
Charitable Giving	C?
Community Outreach	C
Family Benefits	A
Workplace Issues	C
Social Disclosure	B

Ford, headquartered in Dearborn, Michigan, is the world's largest producer of trucks, the second largest producer of cars and trucks combined, and one of the largest financial services providers in the world. In 1996, Ford had revenues of $147 billion and 371,700 employees in 200 countries.

Environment: Ford has a vice president for environmental and safety engineering and an audit committee that reviews environmental compliance. Every U.S. facility is audited annually, and half of the international facilities are audited at least biennially. Audit information is not publicly available. Ford's suppliers are not subject to environmental guidelines as a contract condition.

The company is a cofounder of the Great Lakes Pollution Prevention Agreement. Ford plans to have all its global manufacturing facilities independently certified to the ISO 14000 environmental management standards. The company offers a range of alternative-fueled vehicles.

A member of EPA's 33/50 program, Ford has cut emissions of targeted chemicals by 37 percent. However, it owns five of the top ten TRI-releasing auto/auto parts facilities. Its TRI releases adjusted for sales are above the industry average. Between 1991 and 1995, the total toxic releases dropped by 5.7 percent. Ford is a corporate sponsor of the Heartland Institute, which promotes environmental deregulation and free-market environmentalism.

EEO: In 1996, two women and two minorities served on Ford Motor Co.'s 13-member board. Of 46 corporate officers at the company, three were women and five were minorities.

In early 1997, eight African-American and Asian production workers alleged that they had been denied jobs at the Ford plant in Essex because its recruitment policy was racially discriminatory; the workers were compensated for "hurt feelings." Ford then developed a training procedure in compliance with the company's EEO policy.

Ford was accused by the DOL of discrimination against female job applicants at the Louisville, Kentucky, plant. In 1993, Ford hired 800 people to work on its assembly line, 200 of whom were women. Ford was surprised at the allegations, stating that it

had designed a program to interview and hire a greater percentage of women prior to the hirings. Ford further cited the fact that in the Louisville area, women held 23.8 percent of durable goods manufacturing jobs, and Ford's new hires included over 26 percent women. However, women made up 37 percent of the 1600-person applicant pool, and the Department of Labor charged that the percentage of women among the new hires should have been the same.

Allegations of racial discrimination have been made against Associates First Capital Corp., a consumer and commercial lending company, principally owned by Ford. Associates is said to have taken advantage of borrowers who were poorly educated or from low-income or minority groups. A review will be conducted to decide whether any action is warranted.

Community Involvement: In 1995, Ford Motor Co.'s contributions to various charitable institutions included cash donations totaling $35.3 million. The company's cash contributions for 1995 were equivalent to 0.5 percent of its earnings before taxes for the same year. Ford Motor Co. was ranked among the top five corporate contributors in 1995 in the areas of arts & humanities, civic & public affairs, and international issues by awarding $8.4 million, $7.6 million, and $7.5 million, respectively. It was also ranked among the top ten contributors in the areas of education and health. The company contributed $2 million through the employee matching gifts program. Over five percent of Ford's employees are involved in the company's volunteer program.

Workplace Information: OSHA records indicate that Ford was inspected 58 times from 1994 to 1996. Violations included 11 classified as "willful" or "repeat" and 303 classified as "serious" for a total of

Continued on next page

102

$318,355 in fines, or an average of $5,488 per inspection. In comparison, the median amount of fines per inspection for other companies in similar manufacturing industries was $2,412.

An early 1997 strike at Johnson Controls, the company that manufactures seats for Ford's high-selling Expedition and other light trucks, cut into Ford's production. Johnson Controls recognized the UAW at two of its plants at the prompting of Ford (for whom the two facilities were established). Ford also recognized the UAW as the certified bargaining agent at the unionized Johnson Controls plants as well as at Ford. Johnson Controls had planned on manufacturing seats during the strike using manage-ment and temporary workers. However, Ford refused to accept any seats manufactured by Johnson Controls while the UAW strike continued.

Ford's contract with the UAW, established in 1996, guarantees that the company keep its UAW hourly worker employment level at a minimum of 95 percent of the level at the time of the agreement through the duration of the three-year agreement. Ford's workforce was not considered to be likely to decline beyond the 95 percent figure, an expectation bolstered by the prospect of increasing parts work. The company also obtained some escape clauses in the event of an industry downturn. Dale Brickner, a Michigan State University Labor professor, stated that "It's a huge breakthrough for any union to have a core labor force defined in a collective-bargaining agreement," noting

that the only other industry where this occurs is professional sports.

Ford was reported to have agreed to pay all workers a $2,000 signing bonus, to increase wages by three percent in 1997 and 1998, and to increase pensions by 11 percent. The company won the right to shed some unproductive parts businesses, and to pay new parts workers a lower rate. Workers hired in the first two years will be given health care coverage through an HMO or other low-cost provider. The company also obtained more expansive permission to assign skilled-trade workers to additional tasks outside the employee's main job.

International: Ford has business operations in Europe, North America, Latin America, and Asia. In 1996, a report by a nongovernment organization in Brazil implicated Ford, among others, in the purchasing of raw materials produced by child labor. Ford Brasil sent a formal letter to all local suppliers; however, this was not a worldwide effort. A complete code of conduct is unavailable.

Legal Proceedings: Several class action suits were brought against Ford in 1996, alleging faulty ignition switches on certain vehicles.

103

Product Safety: In September 1996, complaints were received about 1997 F-150 truck seat belts not being securely bolted to the floor. The company has added more inspections of this operation.

Fort Howard Corporation

STOCK SYMBOL: FORT

STOCK EXCHANGE: NNM

Environment	B
Women's Advancement	C
Minority Advancement	N
Charitable Giving	C
Community Outreach	B
Family Benefits	N
Workplace Issues	B
Social Disclosure	C

Fort Howard is the world's largest manufacturer of tissue products made from recycled fiber. The company owns plants in Georgia, Oklahoma, Wisconsin, England, and China. In 1996, sales were $1.6 billion, and the company employed 7,000 people. In August, 1997, Fort Howard merged with James River Corporation to become Fort James (stock symbol FJ). This profile reflects information about Fort Howard prior to the merger.

Environment: Fort Howard does not harvest trees, but makes 99 percent of its products from recycled paper, 36 percent of which is postconsumer waste. For this reason, the company has said, "We don't own forests. The cities are our forests." In 1991, Fort Howard was one of the first companies to win the EPA Administrator's Award for excellence in recycling. It was the first American company to introduce a full line of commercial tissue products — Envision — that meets or exceeds EPA guidelines for postconsumer wastepaper content. The company recycled 1.4 million tons of wastepaper in 1996.

104

All of the company's electricity and steam demands are met through energy-saving cogeneration. Fort Howard is the first and only company in the tissue industry to have all of its mills ISO 9002 certified. ISO registration is an international standard ensuring customers of high-quality products, processes, and services. In 1996, the company was one of 20 organizations to receive the U.S. EPA's WasteWi$e award for successful waste reduction programs.

The company is one of seven paper companies named as potentially responsible parties for contamination of the Fox River in Wisconsin caused by alleged discharges of PCB's from the companies' de-inking facilities. In January 1997, the seven companies agreed with Wisconsin state authorities to pursue a negotiated settlement and to pay $10 million toward damage assessment and exploration of remedial actions. In February 1997, the U.S. Department of Interior, Fish and Wildlife Service notified the companies it would file suit to recover natural resource damages.

EEO: Kathleen Hempel serves as vice-chairman and chief financial officer and is the only woman on the board and among top executives.

Community Involvement: Over the past 10 years, Fort Howard has contributed more than $1 million annually to support educational, human service, cultural, and environmental organizations. The latter include the Georgia Conservancy and the National Recycling Coalition. Executives are involved in a wide variety of national and community organizations that promote recycling and environmental awareness.

Workplace Information: The company's U.S. plants are not unionized but have a reputation for paying competitive wages and offering good benefits. The latter include a "goodwill bonus" and profit-sharing programs. The company has had low turnover, and its tissue operations have not had any layoffs for more than 40 years.

FPL Group

STOCK SYMBOL: FPL
STOCK EXCHANGES: NY, B, C, CH, PH, P

Environment	B
Women's Advancement	F?
Minority Advancement	A?
Charitable Giving	F
Community Outreach	N
Family Benefits	C
Workplace Issues	D
Social Disclosure	C

FPL Group, based in Juno Beach, FL, is a holding company for Florida Power & Light (FP&L), an electric utility serving more than 7 million people in southern and eastern Florida. Other subsidiaries include FPL Energy, consisting of domestic independent power and international power projects, and Turner Foods, a Florida citrus producer. In 1997, FPL Group's revenues amounted to $6.4 billion and had about 10,100 employees.

Environment: While FP&L performed above the industry average related to projected increases in carbon dioxide emissions, its present emissions of sulfur dioxide and nitrogen oxide are below the industry average. In addition, by 2002 FP&L aims to reduce peak demand by 30 percent through demand-side management (DSM) programs. FPL's ESI Energy subsidiary focuses on alternative energy including solar, wind and geothermal. ESI's efforts earned FPL 109 SO_2 emission allowances through an EPA program that awards bonuses to companies that incorporate efficiency and renewable energy into their Clean Air Act compliance plans. FPL has also created a Solar Energy Test Facility to evaluate the potential of solar power to contribute to its business.

FPL Energy is the largest wind and solar power producer in the world, and among the largest geothermal generators. With the acquisition of Central Maine Power's nonnuclear generating assets, FPL Group will have more than 12,000 megawatts of environmentally-favored generating capacity, including natural gas, hydro, wind, solar, biomass, and geothermal plants.

FPL is a significant contributor to statewide wildlife management and protection activities and produces a variety of pamphlets focusing on the wildlife indigenous to Florida.

FPL was one of the early members of the Global Environmental Management Initiative (GEMI). Shareholders have asked the company to endorse the CERES Principles.

EEO: In 1996, FPL Group's board totaled 14 directors, including one woman and two minorities. None of 14 corporate officers were women (two in 1998), and none were minorities.

Community Involvement: FPL Group's charitable contributions totaled $2.2 million in cash in 1996 (about the same in 1997). The $2.2 million cash-giving figure represented the equivalent of 0.25 percent of the company's pretax earnings for the same year, and a decrease of 4.7 percent from the company's cash contributions in 1995. In 1995, the company contributed 0.25 percent of its pretax earnings for that year to charity.

FPL reports that it focuses its giving on selected community issues that are periodically reviewed and updated to match business and community needs. Areas of concentration include the environment, educational institutions that provide industry recruitment, research and development; training opportunities or social service programs that support the needs of FPL's customer base; and community development projects and activities in FPL's service area. FPL's volunteer assistance program provides T-shirts, refreshments, and recognition items to support employees who volunteer on group community projects.

Workplace Information: The records of the Occupational Safety and Health Administration indicate that FPL Group underwent four health and safety inspections from 1994 to 1996. The violations reported by OSHA as a result of the inspections include 14 classified as "serious." The company was required to pay $13,500 as a result of its violations. In comparison, the median amount of fines per inspection for other utilities was $2,625.

Frontier Corporation

STOCK SYMBOL: FRO
STOCK EXCHANGES: NY, B, CH, PH, P

Environment	N
Women's Advancement	B
Minority Advancement	B
Charitable Giving	D
Community Outreach	B
Family Benefits	N
Workplace Issues	B?
Social Disclosure	B

Frontier is a telecommunications company, based in Rochester, N.Y., offering integrated long distance, local and wireless services. The Long Distance Communication services segment provides telecommunications Services to customers throughout the U.S., Canada and Great Britain. The Local Communications Services segment consists of 34 local telephone companies which serve approximately 976,000 access lines in thirteen states. In 1996, Frontier had sales of $2.6 billion and employed 7,900 people.

EEO: In 1996, Frontier Corp. achieved a higher than average rating in both diversity categories, placing them easily in the top third of S&P 500 companies. Two women and two minorities served on Frontier Corp.'s 12-member board. Of ten corporate officers at the company, two were women and none were minorities.

Though Frontier does not have any special programs for banking with minority-owned banks, it does utilize minority-owned banks as part of normal business operations. However, the company has not provided information to CEP regarding the amounts involved.

Community Involvement: Frontier Corp.'s charitable contributions totaled $1.5 million in cash in 1996. The $1.5 million cash-giving figure represented the equivalent of 0.4 percent of the company's pretax earnings for the same year, and an increase of 5 percent from the company's cash contributions in 1995. In 1995, the company contributed 0.6 percent of its pretax earnings for that year to charity.

Frontier Corporation gives primarily to programs concerned with educational opportunities for children, especially those at risk of becoming high school dropouts. In 1996, Frontier and the Rochester City School District collaborated on a program called "How Was School Today?" The program was intended to encourage parental involvement, in hopes of enhancing educational results and students' social growth. Frontier also donates resources to the United Way, in areas where Frontier has major operations. Arts and cultural organizations receive contributions from Frontier, especially those that serve impoverished children.

The Frontier volunteer service group, the "Frontier Pioneers," has over 1,200 employee and retiree members.

Workplace Information: The records of the Occupational Safety and Health Administration indicate that Frontier Corp. underwent three health and safety inspections from 1994 to 1996. The violations reported by OSHA as a result of the inspections include three classified as "serious." The company was required to pay $1,720 as a result of its violations. In comparison, the median amount of fines per inspection for other companies in the service industry, which include businesses such as banks and communications companies, was $573.

106

Fruit of the Loom

STOCK SYMBOL: FTL
STOCK EXCHANGES: NY, CH, P, PH

Environment	N
Women's Advancement	F
Minority Advancement	B
Charitable Giving	N
Community Outreach	N
Family Benefits	N
Workplace Issues	C?
Social Disclosure	B

Chicago-based Fruit of the Loom is the top underwear manufacturer in America. During the past decade, it has diversified into other areas including casual wear, infants wear, and hosiery. CEO William Farley's holding company, Farley, Inc., once owned the controlling interest in the company. This body's voting power has since fallen below 16 percent, though Farley himself retains 33 percent of the vote and the right to select one-quarter of the board. Sales in 1996 were $2.4 billion and there were 33,000 employees.

Environment: In April 1995, Fruit of the Loom became a member of the American Textile Manufacturers Institute's "Encouraging Environmental Excellence" program. It joined 53 other companies that already meet 10 criteria, including top management commitment to environmental excellence, environmental preservation, and the minimization of waste.

EEO: In 1996, Fruit of the Loom's board totaled nine directors, including no women and two minorities. One of 18 corporate officers was a woman, and none were minorities. Additionally, one woman and no minorities were among the 25 employees with the highest salaries at the company.

Community Involvement: Fruit of the Loom's "Quality of Life" program seeks to improve the living environments of individuals by providing resources to support education, youth leadership, health and social services, culture and the arts. By creating public awareness on issues like AIDS, substance abuse, and domestic violence, Fruit of the Loom strengthens the quality of life by removing barriers that would otherwise prevent people from fully participating in society.

Workplace Information: OSHA records indicate that Fruit of the Loom underwent seven inspections from 1994 to 1996. Violations included 18 classified as "serious" for a total of $20,855 in fines. In comparison, the median amount of fines per inspection for other companies in similar manufacturing industries was $2,412.

Fruit of the Loom Inc. plans to eliminate 2,900 jobs in Kentucky and Lousiana, over 17 percent of its domestic workforce, and move those jobs to offshore manufacturing sites with cheaper labor. The announcement follows the elimination of 4,800 jobs in August, 1997. Almost all of Fruit of the Loom's sewing units are now offshore. Textile production for clothing, a more capital-intensive process, will remain in the United States, adding over 700 employees to that sector. Although competitive pressures were cited as reasons for moving offshore, Fruit of the Loom has been beset by transportation complications.

International: Fruit of the Loom is the largest manufacturer of underwear and sports clothing in the U.S., with international locations in Canada, Mexico, Morocco, Puerto Rico, Japan, Central America, Europe and the West Indies. Three years ago, a July 25, 1995, *New York Daily News* article reported that FTL was linked to sweatshop conditions and child labor; FTL states that the article had unfairly included FTL, and that the company was not actually linked to such conditions. Presently, FTL has a "Contractor Code of Conduct" which is signed by contractors (or their suppliers) before execution of a purchase order. These guidelines address child labor (defining *child* as 15 years old and under or the locally stipulated school age), wages, and disciplinary practices among other things. Notably, the code is very explicit on provisions for termination in case of violation, and clearly specifies provisions for sharing the code with all subcontractors. The company has not been subject to any media attacks in 1997 regarding labor rights issues.

H.B. Fuller

STOCK SYMBOL: FULL
STOCK EXCHANGE: NNM

Environment	B
Women's Advancement	C
Minority Advancement	B
Charitable Giving	A
Community Outreach	B
Family Benefits	C
Workplace Issues	A
Social Disclosure	A

H.B. Fuller, based in St. Paul, Minnesota, is a worldwide manufacturer and marketer of adhesives, sealants, coatings, paints, and waxes. The company has manufacturing and sales operations in 44 countries. In 1997, the company had sales of $1.3 billion and 6,000 employees.

Environment: Fuller was the first specialty chemical manufacturer and the second Fortune 500 company to sign the CERES (Coalition for Environmentally Responsible Economies) Principles. The company publishes an environmental progress report and has a Vice President of Environment, Health, and Safety, who reports to the CEO. Fuller uses only six of the 17 toxic chemicals in the EPA's 33/50 program, but it reduced these chemicals by 72 percent in 1993, surpassing its 1995 goal. By the end of 1994, the company also eliminated the use of methyl chloroform, and it expects to reduce by half all facility waste by the year 2000. A participant in the Green Lights program, Fuller will upgrade its lighting equipment to be more energy-efficient by the end of 1998.

EEO: Two women serve on Fuller's 12-member board, one of whom is an African American; an Hispanic man also serves on the board. Of the 20 corporate officers in the U.S., one is a woman and three are minorities. One of the two U.S. group presidents is a woman. Fuller provides diversity awareness training and bans discrimination based on factors other than performance. Fuller reports that it has several programs used to identify, recruit, retain, and develop minorities and women. The company has no programs for banking with, or purchasing from, minority- or women-owned firms, but reports that "an aggressive supplier diversity program has contributed to a signficant sourcing of products/services from these companies."

Community Involvement: In 1992, H.B. Fuller's board set its charitable contributions at 3.5 percent of global pretax earnings. More than half of the employees in 43 countries participate in H.B. Fuller's community involvement program.

Product: For almost a decade, activists have targeted a toluene-based adhesive produced by Fuller's Central American subsidiaries as being among several substances commonly abused by the region's street children. A civil suit was refiled in 1996 under Minnesota's wrongful death statute, accusing Fuller of responsibility for the death of a Guatemalan teenager; the suit was dismissed in September of that year.

In 1992, after Fuller's board passed a resolution to discontinue sale of this adhesive or to reformulate it in order to minimize or eliminate its abuse, over-the-counter sales were stopped in Honduras and Guatemala. Throughout the rest of Central America, the product was reformulated with toluene being replaced by cyclohexane, a less attractive but still toxic ingredient. The company's subsidiaries made the same change in their industrial rubber cement product, even though apparently it has never been illegitimately distributed or abused.

Fuller argues that societal conditions are responsible for substance abuse by children. Critics counter that the company has researched water-based adhesives since 1980 but has not brought them to market. The company reports that it has developed water-based products for the footwear industry and is in the process of launching them.

At the 1996 annual meeting of the company, shareholders represented by the Interfaith Center for Corporate Responsibility asked Fuller to halt sales of adhesives to the tobacco industry. The company had previously denied involvement in this industry sector, though it advertised its adhesives in tobacco trade publications. The resolution received 10.8 percent of shareholders' votes. At the 1997 meeting, a proposal that the board of directors make available a report addressing the company's involvement in the tobacco industry did not pass; 84 percent voted against the proposal. A 16 percent vote for it is, however, considered signifiant.

Gannett, Inc.

STOCK SYMBOL: GCI
STOCK EXCHANGES: NY, B, CH, P, PH

Environment	N
Women's Advancement	A
Minority Advancement	A
Charitable Giving	A
Community Outreach	B
Family Benefits	A
Workplace Issues	F
Social Disclosure	A

Gannett is a diversified news and information company that publishes newspapers and operates broadcasting stations and outdoor advertising businesses. It is the nation's largest newspaper group, with 88 daily newspapers, including *USA Today*. Total paid daily circulation of its newspapers in 1997 exceeded 6.7 million, more than any other newspaper group. The 1995 acquisition of Multimedia Inc. for $1.7 billion added 10 daily newspapers, numerous non-daily publications, and more TV stations, many of which are in states without a Gannett presence. Revenues in 1997 totaled $4.7 billion and the company employed 37,200 people.

Environment: Gannett instructs its newspapers to handle and dispose hazardous inks and solvents properly. It also encourages its units to use alternative materials, like soy- and water-based inks and solvents. Gannett is committed to increasing the use of recycled paper in its newspapers, and it has a company wide waste reduction/recycling program.

EEO: Diversity seems to thrive among the top leadership. In 1996, there were four women (one of whom is African-American), one Asian man, and two African-American men on the 13-member board. Nine of 33 corporate officers are women and two are African-American men. Six of the women, and the latter two men are among the 25 highest paid. Women were nearly 37 percent and minorities were almost 15 percent of officials and managers.

However, a 1989 study by a Rochester unit of the Newspaper Guild found that in the past, men, on average, made 13 percent more than women, and whites, on average, made 16 percent more than minorities. Now, each division has a diversity committee with specific goals to foster advancement.

Community Involvement: In 1996, Gannett's Communities Fund donated about $5.7 million, primarily to health and human services organizations in Gannett-served communities. Also in 1996, Gannett contributed $26.5 million in nonmonetary support (in-kind advertising and public service announcements).

Family Benefits: Gannett has been on *Working Mother* magazine's "Best" list for 11 years. It provides flexible scheduling through job-sharing, flextime, work-at-home, and compressed work week arrangements. Gannett funds community child care, and maintains an on-site center at the *Louisville Courier-Journal*.

Workplace Information: A July 1995 strike of 2,600 employees over staffing and pay issues at the *Detroit News*, owned by Gannett, and the *Detroit Free Press*, owned by Knight-Ridder, remained unresolved in 1997. A representative of the Newspaper Guild reported that most of the workers were still locked out despite an unconditional offer to return to work in February 1998. Gannett reports that its offers of raises totaling 10.3 percent and a no lay-off guarantee have been turned down by the unions. It also reports that 200 workers were discharged for strike violence; 80 discharges were contested. Unions have filed charges with the National Labor Relations Board, which are now in litigation. Other unions involved are the Teamsters and Graphic Communications International.

Several refusal-to-bargain cases have been upheld by the NLRB against Gannett. For example, employees at Cincinnati and Burlington voted to unionize but were stonewalled in trying to negotiate a contract with Gannett. When dissatisfied workers left, they were replaced by employees not interested in union representation. In 1993, the U.S. Trust Company of Boston decided that it could no longer include Gannett securities in the portfolios of clients concerned about corporate labor relations.

The Gap

STOCK SYMBOL: GPS
STOCK EXCHANGES: NY, B, CH, P, PH

Environment	N
Women's Advancement	A
Minority Advancement	C
Charitable Giving	C
Community Outreach	A
Family Benefits	B
Workplace Issues	B
Social Disclosure	A

The Gap, based in San Francisco, California, operates more than 1,500 clothing retail stores under the names Gap, GapKids, Banana Republic, and Old Navy. The San Francisco–based company had net sales of $3.7 million in fiscal 1996 and 60,000 employees. Founders Donald and Doris Fisher retain a 23 percent stake in the company.

Environment: Gap was featured in the February 1996 edition of *The Green Business Letter* as a model for retailers on minimizing environmental impact.

The company has cut energy use by 30 percent in new stores, eliminated volatile organic compounds (VOCs) from paints in new stores, and runs extensive recycling programs. Gap encourages business partners to adopt energy conservation, waste reduction, and recycling policies.

Gap is exploring the use of organically grown cotton and recycled denim. The company is also involved in a UCLA program to find preferred alternatives to dry cleaning. Gap is the largest purchaser of tagua nut buttons, made from sustainable rainforest materials by Conservation International.

EEO: In 1996, The Gap's 11-member board of directors included two women. Of 42 corporate officers at the company, 11 were women and one was a minority. Seven women and one minority also ranked among the 26 highest paid employees at the company.

The Gap distributes a written discrimination policy, detailing the areas of concern and methods of enforcement. The company reports it has formal and informal recruitment, support and mentoring programs for minorities. Gap prohibits sexual orientation discrimination, offers benefits to same-sex partners, and supports lesbian and gay philanthropic programs.

Community Involvement: In 1996, The Gap's charitable giving totaled $4 million in cash, which was equal to 0.5 percent of the company's pretax earnings for that year. In terms of the actual dollar amount donated by the company, the level of cash contributions in 1996 represented a decrease of 15.33 percent from that of 1995, which was 0.7 percent of the company's earnings for that year. The company's in-kind giving — the donation of products or services — came to a total of about $3.5 million in 1996.

The Gap reports that its divisions (Gap/GapKids, Banana Republic and Old Navy) all carry out charitable activity through the Community Relations Program, which consists of three major components: divisional components, which focus on communities where stores are located; a sourcing component, which seeks to benefit garment workers and their communities; and a corporate component, which focuses on the company's headquarters region around San Francisco.

Workplace Information: OSHA records indicate that The Gap was not inspected from 1994 to 1996. Consequently no violations or fines were assessed to the company. Several years ago, it redesigned its work-stations to help avoid injuries, and in 1991, it instituted an injury and illness prevention program. An open-door policy exists for employee grievances.

International: In December 1995, Gap reached an agreement with the National Labor Committee, a New York–based advocacy group that had launched a protest campaign against the work conditions at Central American producers of Gap clothing. An unprecedented provision of the accord allows independent entities to monitor the operating practices of these producers. The Department of Labor added Gap to its Fair Labor Fashion Trendsetter list for combating sweatshop conditions.

Gap has a Code of Vendor Conduct that covers environment, discrimination, forced labor, child labor, wages and hours, working conditions, and freedom of association. The company conducts an initial evaluation of new vendors to ensure compliance and may terminate relations if policy violations are subsequently discovered.

🏅 General Electric

STOCK SYMBOL: GE
STOCK EXCHANGES: NY, B, C, CH, P, PH

Environment	B
Women's Advancement	A
Minority Advancement	A
Charitable Giving	D
Community Outreach	A
Family Benefits	A
Workplace Issues	C
Social Disclosure	A

GE, based in Fairfield, Connecticut, has operations in aerospace, broadcasting (NBC), electrical equipment, financial services, and lighting products. In 1996, the company had revenues of 79.2 billion and 222,000 employees.

Environment: GE has an environmental policy and a corporate environmental report. GE's environmental policy, which is available in more than 20 languages, has been distributed worldwide to all employees as part of an extensive policy education program. GE has implemented an integrated environmental management system. GE has a written pollution prevention policy and has initiated a companywide pollution prevention program in 1990 (the POWER Program), which establishes annual reduction goals for solid waste and TRI emissions. GE does not have a corporate policy on community involvement relating to local environmental concerns; however, it does have community advisory panels at some facilities. GE has a written policy on product stewardship and evaluates products with the goal of reducing life-cycle impacts on the environment.

GE's average toxic releases and transfers from 1993 to 1994 were below the industry sample average. Emissions decreased by about a seventh during those years, a below average performance for the sample.

GE has received criticism for its involvement in several international projects that have potential environmental significance. The company was awarded a contract to supply turbines and generators to the Three Gorges dam project in China. In addition, GE had won a bid to provide two reactors and related equipment to Taiwan for the construction of its fourth nuclear power plant. Opponents claim the plant is unnecessary and threatens the environment of northern Taiwan.

EEO: In 1996, two women and two minorities served on GE's 14-member board. Seven women and three minorities served among 143 corporate officers that year. A GE employee who lost his job during 1995 layoffs filed an age discrimination suit alleging the layoff had a "disparate affect" on employees over 40. The case has gained class certification.

Community Involvement: In 1996, General Electric's charitable giving totaled $47.5 million in cash, or 0.4 percent of its pretax earnings for that year. In 1995 the company contributed 0.5 percent in cash. GE's in-kind giving totaled $2.1 million in 1996.

GE's volunteer group has pledged to have GE give one million hours of volunteer time annually by the year 2000. The *Corporate Giving Watch* lists GE as one of the top ten corporate givers to five of nine areas, such as education and the arts. GE's $20 million "College Bound" program aims to double the students going to college from chosen inner-city schools by 2000.

Workplace Information: OSHA records indicate that GE was inspected 53 times from 1994 to 1996. Violations included one classified as "willful" or "repeat" and 200 classified as "serious" for an average of $3,501 in fines per inspection. In comparison, the median amount of fines per inspection for other electronic manufacturing companies was $1,347. GE has cut over 100,000 positions since 1986.

International: In February 1994, the United Electrical Workers accused GE of firing Mexican employees for attempting to organize. A DOL review panel found that because employees accepted severance benefits, authorities could not investigate.

Weapons Contracts: GE ranked 23rd among worldwide defense contractors with $1.7 billion in revenue generated through defense in 1996, or 2.1 percent of its total revenue. In 1996, GE was the tenth-largest contractor to the U.S. Department of Defense with $1.5 billion in prime contracts.

Nuclear Power: GE designed about one-third of U.S. nuclear power plants. The company maintains that in spite of recent problems with shroud cracking, its reactors perform comparably well.

Legal Proceedings: In 1995, GE paid $7.1 million to settle allegations that its aerospace division sold thousands of jet engines to the military that did not comply with military testing requirements.

General Mills

STOCK SYMBOL: GIS
STOCK EXCHANGES: NY, B, C, CH, P, PH

Environment	C
Women's Advancement	A
Minority Advancement	B
Charitable Giving	A
Community Outreach	A
Family Benefits	C
Workplace Issues	C
Social Disclosure	A

Founded in 1866, General Mills is the world's second largest cereal producer (after Kellogg). The company, based in in Minneapolis, Minnesota, markets such popular brands as Betty Crocker, Cheerios, Hamburger Helper, and Yoplait yogurt. In 1995, the company spun off its restaurant operations, which include the Red Lobster, Olive Garden, and China Coast chains, into a separate company, Darden Restaurants. In 1997, General Mills had sales of $5.4 billion and 10,200 employees.

Environment: General Mills does not publish an environmental report but appears to have a very good environmental record. Its environmental programs are directed primarily to solid waste reduction and recycling. The company has been recognized as a "Sustained Leader" in EPA's WasteWi$e voluntary program. It averages 52 percent postconsumer waste in overall packaging. The paperboard used is 90 percent postconsumer waste. Product stewardship programs focus on further development of recyclable packaging.

EEO: In 1996, General Mills achieved a higher than average rating in both diversity categories, placing them easily in the top third of S&P 500 companies. Two women and one minority served on General Mills' 12-member board. Of 23 corporate officers at the company, four were women and one was a minority, while four of the 23 top-paid employees were women, and one was a minority.

General Mills received CEP's 1992 America's Corporate Conscience Award for Equal Employment Opportunity for its long-standing commitment to diversity. General Mills encourages diversity in the workforce by supporting and sponsoring a variety of programs, networks, and training sessions. Their efforts are visible in the company's Corporate Policy Statement on Employment and Job Opportunities, LEAD program, Supplier Diversity Program, and employee diversity training. The company reports it is committed to minority and women's advancement both inside and outside the company.

Community Involvement: General Mills' charitable contributions totaled $16 million in cash in 1997,

and $12 million in in-kind donations. The $16 million cash-giving figure represented the equivalent of 2 percent of the company's pretax earnings for the same year. In 1996, the company contributed 2.2 percent of its pretax earnings for that year to charity. Twenty million pounds of food were donated in 1996 to food distribution programs and banks.

An estimated 75 percent of employees, past and present, volunteer at least once a year through General Mills' Volunteer Connection and Retirement PLUS programs, and use the assistance of the company's Volunteer Advisory Board. The Management Assistance Project, sponsored by General Mills, provides managerial and technical assistance to nonprofit organizations.

Family Benefits: General Mills offers job sharing, dependent care as an option in flexible spending accounts, and resource and referral services for child/elder care companywide. The company will also reimburse $1,500 in eligible adoption expenses and 85 percent of sick-child care costs. On-site day care, part-time return to work after parental leave, flextime, and work-at-home arrangements are available at some locations.

Workplace Information: OSHA records indicate that General Mills underwent seven health and safety inspections from 1994 to 1996. Violations included 31 classified as "serious" for a total of $74,150 in fines.

Approximately 30 percent of the workforce is unionized. General Mills has a grievance procedure for nonunionized workers.

112

General Motors Corporation

STOCK SYMBOL: GM

STOCK EXCHANGES: NY, To, B, C, CH, P, PH, MO

Environment	B
Women's Advancement	B
Minority Advancement	A
Charitable Giving	C
Community Outreach	C
Family Benefits	B
Workplace Issues	REV
Social Disclosure	A

The General Motors Corporation, based in Detroit, Michigan, is the world's largest full-line vehicle manufacturer. In 1996, the company had revenues of $164 billion and 647,000 employees.

Environment: GM adopted its environmental principles in 1991. The company joined CERES in 1994 and is currently the only major auto manufacturer participating in this initiative. Since 1994, the company has published an annual environmental report based on the CERES reporting standard. GM's supplier program PICOs assists its suppliers to implement environmental improvements. GM also has Waste Elimination and Cost Awareness Rewards Everyone pollution prevention programs. GM was awarded the eighth annual *Business Ethics* Award for Environmental Excellence in 1996. In 1996, GM became the first major automobile manufacturer to market an electric vehicle, which is available for lease in four Western cities.

GM remains the top TRI emitter for the auto industry when adjusted for sales; the company, however, has reduced TRI emissions by 40 percent since 1988. GM is a corporate sponsor of the Heartland Institute, which promotes environmental deregulation and free-market environmentalism. GM committed $5 million over five years when it entered into a partnership with The Nature Conservancy in 1995 to help preserve land and water ecosystems.

EEO: In 1996, two women and one minority served on GM's 16-member board. Of 70 corporate officers at the company, four were women and seven were minorities. GM was one of the first companies to include "sexual orientation" in its anti-discrimination policy.

Community Involvement: GM proved to be one of the biggest charitable givers in 1995 by making five of the *Corporate Giving Watch*'s nine lists of the ten largest corporate contributors to different giving areas.

Workplace Information: OSHA records indicate that GM was inspected 150 times from 1994 to 1996. Violations included 37 classified as "willful" or "repeat" and 770 classified as "serious" for a total of more than $1.1 million in fines, or an average of $7,333 per inspection. In comparison, the median amount of fines per inspection for other manufacturing companies was $2,412.

GM was subject to six strikes in 1997, an effect of its attempts to reduce its workforce to match the efficiency of companies like Ford and the consequent job security concerns. Strikes at plants in Michigan and Oklahoma cost the company approximately $490 million after taxes; lost production is estimated at 96,000 cars and trucks. The cost of the strikes is one the company says it is willing to take in its effort to cut its workforce. The *Wall Street Journal* reports that the "average GM assembly-plant worker is paid about $1,000 a week, before overtime and taxes."

The company has made efforts to reduce its workforce by not replacing retirees or other employees who have left the company's plant staffs. The UAW has charged that these efforts have led to unsafe working conditions and an overburdening of workers with overtime hours.

International: A report released in December 1995 by a nongovernmental organization in Brazil (Abrinq Foundation) implicated GM, among other U.S. and European automakers, in the purchasing of raw materials produced by child labor in that country. According to a formal April 1996 letter to Abrinq, GM Brasil has a contractual agreement for purchasing raw materials from child labor-free suppliers. In September 1996, GM Brasil signed an agreement with the Brasilian Foundation for the Rights of Children. GM does not have a general code of conduct available for review.

Legal Proceedings: The Federal EEOC sued GM in April 1996, alleging violations of the Americans With Disabilities Act (ADA). GM terminated an employee in 1995 who tested positive for the HIV virus. In July 1996, GM reached agreement with U.S. owners of five million 1973–1987 C/K pickup trucks with side-mounted fuel tanks that were allegedly dangerous in certain collisions.

Georgia-Pacific

STOCK SYMBOL: GP
STOCK EXCHANGES: NY, B, C, CH, P, PH

Environment	A
Women's Advancement	D
Minority Advancement	B
Charitable Giving	C
Community Outreach	C
Family Benefits	D
Workplace Issues	B
Social Disclosure	A

Georgia-Pacific, based in Atlanta, Georgia, is the world's second largest forest products company, with $13 billion in sales and 47,500 employees worldwide in 1996.

Environment: Georgia-Pacific has an environmental policy and a corporate environmental report, which is updated biennially, and is available on the internet. Georgia-Pacific has not implemented an integrated environmental management system, but has many elements of an EMS in place. All locations follow company environmental principles. Georgia-Pacific is in compliance with the American Forest & Paper Association's Sustainable Forestry Initiative.

Georgia-Pacific has a written pollution prevention policy and has initiated a company-wide pollution prevention program, which establishes annual reduction goals for point sources and solid waste. The company also has a corporate policy on community involvement relating to local environmental concerns and has community advisory panels at some facilities. Georgia-Pacific has a written policy on product stewardship and evaluates some of its products with the objective of reducing their life-cycle impacts on the environment.

Georgia Pacific's average total toxic releases and transfers during the years 1994–1996 were lower than the industry sample average. Furthermore, its emissions decreased by an average of more than five percent annually during those years, an above average performance.

In September 1997, Georgia-Pacific agreed to pay $320,000 to the Georgia Environmental Protection Division to settle violations of the federal Clean Air Act at the company's Brunswick plant. Georgia-Pacific also agreed to spend about $200,000 more on projects to further reduce emissions from the plant.

In December 1997, the Puget Soundkeeper Alliance filed a Clean Water Act lawsuit in federal court against a Georgia-Pacific facility in Bellingham, Washington. The complaint alleges that Georgia-Pacific improperly monitors and reports mercury releases to the public, and refuses to complete a report on mercury sources and control measures as ordered by the state. The company states that the mill is operating in compliance with its state permits. The Department of Ecology agrees that the mill is in compliance, although the Alliance claims that the agency is not doing its job.

EEO: In 1996, Georgia-Pacific's board totaled 12 directors, including one woman and one minority, while two of a total of 50 corporate officers were women (four as of February, 1998), and one was a minority. Additionally, one minority was among the 25 highest paid employees.

Community Involvement: Georgia-Pacific's charitable contributions totaled $4 million in cash in 1996 (1.3 percent of that year's pretax earnings), and $1 million in in-kind donations.

The Georgia-Pacific Foundation announced in 1996 that it would double its annual giving from $1.5 to $3 million, and that the company's overall corporate giving was also expected to increase. The increased giving is part of a commitment by Georgia-Pacific to invest more in the communities in which the company does business. By the end of 1995, approximately 28 percent of the company's manufacturing facilities had community involvement plans in place. The plans differ from site to site, and may involve charitable giving, presentations to community and school groups, and working with the local media.

Georgia-Pacific was honored with the National Arbor Day Foundation's 1996 Education Award for the company's Tree Wishes program.

Workplace Information: OSHA records indicate that Georgia-Pacific underwent 77 inspections from 1994 to 1996. Violations included 284 classified as "serious" for a total of $236,412 in fines. Georgia-Pacific reports that it was the safest large company in the forest products industry for the fifth year in a row in 1997, with an incidence rate of 2.7.

Giant Food Inc.

STOCK SYMBOL: GFSA
STOCK EXCHANGES: AS, B, CH, P, PH

Environment	N
Women's Advancement	B
Minority Advancement	A
Charitable Giving	A
Community Outreach	B
Family Benefits	D
Workplace Issues	B
Social Disclosure	A

Founded in 1936, Giant Food operates about 180 supermarkets in Maryland, Virginia, Pennsylvania, New Jersey, Delaware, and the District of Columbia. Unlike many of its competitors, Giant is highly vertically integrated, with company units involved in all aspects of operations from construction of stores to production of private-label goods. For 1997, Giant's revenues were over $4 billion. The company, based in Landover, Michigan, has about 28,500 employees. In November 1995, Giant chairman and company icon Israel Cohen died, passing his voting stock to senior management. J. Sainsbury PLC, Britain's top grocer, has a 20 percent stake in Giant and controls four board seats.

Environment: Though Giant has not joined EPA's Green Lights and WasteWi$e programs, it has been in many respects an industry leader on environmental matters. The company has recycled cardboard since 1965, and added plastic bags, film wrap, aluminum cans, office paper, truck oil, and photographic chemicals to its recycling program. The company buys parking stops made from recycled plastics and uses natural gas for some of its delivery fleet.

Giant offers a number of environmentally preferred products, such as cloth diapers and eggs produced by free-range hens. Shoppers can carry their groceries home in reusable mesh bags made by a local company employing the visually impaired. They also get a three-cent discount if they reuse their regular shopping bags.

EEO: In 1996, two women and one minority served on Giant Food's nine-member board. Of 23 corporate officers at the company, one was a woman and one was a minority.

In September, 1996, ten African-American employees of Giant Food filed a discrimination suit seeking $280 million a few days after the announcement of the results of the company's internal investigation into allegations of discrimination. The company fired one supervisor and two others were disciplined as a result of the investigation, which found that white employees had placed nooses in the warehouse, told racist jokes, and written the names of black co-workers on pictures of monkeys that were placed on a bulletin board. In addition to these incidents, the suit claims that the plaintiffs were frequently given demerits for infractions that were overlooked when committed by white employees. The attorney for the plaintiffs alleges that the incidents are not isolated, but that discrimination is "pervasive and institutionalized." Some African-American employees claimed that racist remarks are ignored and that they are held to more rigorous standards of behavior than their white co-workers. Tom McNutt, president of the United Food and Commercial Workers Union Local 400, which represents about 12,00 Giant workers, said that "of all the companies that we work with, Giant probably does the most to avoid race problems," and that "they have always responded immediately to any complaints that have come up." Harry Silva, a regional chairman of the Southern Christian Leadership Conference, led a protest against Giant stores in 1988 when a woman filed a discrimination suit that was eventually thrown out of court. Giant officials met repeatedly with black leaders at Silva's request, and Silva relates that they complied with the leaders' recommendations and generally "bent over backwards to make sure they were being fair to all minorities."

Giant was criticized by Democratic Representative Elijah Cummings for the fact that only one of 18 executives is African-American at the time of the suit. Giant defended its record of promoting by pointing out that at the director and management levels there are many African-Americans in supervisory and management positions. At its 1996 shareholders meeting, the company announced the creation of a new position, vice president of community development, to enhance the company's relationship with minorities.

Community Involvement: Through "Apples for the Students PLUS" program, Giant Food has donated over 100,000 free computers and educational tools to community elementary and high schools since 1989.

115

Continued on next page

Giant Food Inc. (continued)

Giant Foods' charitable contributions totaled $1.1 million in cash in 1996, and $4.5 million in in-kind donations. The $1.1 million cash-giving figure represented the equivalent of 0.7 percent of the company's pretax earnings for the same year, and a decrease of 6.4 percent from the company's cash contributions in 1995. In 1995, the company contributed 0.7 percent of its pretax earnings for that year to charity.

Family Benefits: Noteworthy among Giant's work/family programs is a directory that lists child care service providers with whom the company has negotiated a discounted fee structure.

Workplace Information: OSHA records indicate that Giant Food underwent four health and safety inspections from 1994 to 1996. Violations included two classified as "serious" for a total of $625 in fines, $312 per inspection. In comparison, the median amount of fines per inspection for other companies in the food, beverage, and household products industries was $1,515.

Teamsters at Giant Food held a one-month strike starting in mid-December 1996 against the food retailer that had long prided itself on strong worker relations. The *Washington Post* described the walkout by union drivers as the "first major strike against Giant in 20 years" at a company with 28,500 union employees and over 50 separate contracts. The newspaper reports that competitive pressures were likely a major influence on the strike—in contract negotiations, Giant wanted the freedom to outsource distribution functions for its new stores. The Teamsters wanted restrictions on deliveries conducted by outside contractors to the new stores,

which Giant believed would adversely affect its ability to compete with other chains that already outsource much or all of their delivery work. Roger Olson, senior vice president for labor relations at Giant, noted that such practices could save the company up to 50 percent in delivery expenses. The Teamsters were concerned that the initial moves towards contracting out delivery work would ultimately jeopardize the jobs of their 320 members.

The contract agreed to following the strike guarantees the members of Local 639 that they will retain their jobs for life, rather than the initial five-year contract offered by Giant. Giant also made a pledge that the Teamsters local's drivers will retain control over Washington-Baltimore area distribution. To compensate for the higher costs, Giant will be able to cut the starting wage for newly hired drivers. Giant has one of the highest-paid workforces among supermarkets; Teamsters drivers are paid $19.07 an hour in addition to receiving benefits.

All other unions represented at Giant, including the United Food and Commercial Workers union, which counts over 10,000 Giant employees among its ranks, did not sanction the Teamsters strike, allowing the stores to stay open over the course of the strike.

Legal Proceedings: In June 1996, Giant was sued by managed care company Merck-Medco for allegedly conspiring with Rite Aid to boycott a prescription plan run by Merck-Medco for Maryland state employees. Court documents filed by Giant state that Merck had submitted a bid to the state including terms to which Giant had never agreed and subsequently rejected.

The Gillette Company

STOCK SYMBOL: G
STOCK EXCHANGES: NY, B, C, CH, P, PH

Environment	A
Women's Advancement	F
Minority Advancement	F
Charitable Giving	B
Community Outreach	D
Family Benefits	B
Workplace Issues	D
Social Disclosure	A

Based in Boston, Massachusetts, the Gillette Company (Gillette) is the world leader in several consumer products: men's razors and blades, shaving preparations, and electric shavers; women's wet shaving products and hair epilation devices; writing instruments and correction products; and toothbrushes and oral care appliances. In 1996, the company had sales of $9.7 billion and 44,100 employees, and manufacturing operations in 64 facilities in 27 countries.

Environment: Gillette has an environmental policy and a corporate environmental report, which is updated biennially, is verified by a third party, and follows the Public Environmental Reporting Initiative (PERI) reporting guidelines. Gillette has implemented an integrated environmental management system. Gillette has a written pollution prevention policy and has initiated a company-wide pollution prevention program, which establishes annual reduction goals for point sources, secondary emissions, fugitive emissions, and solid waste. The company also has a corporate policy on community involvement relating to local environmental concerns; however, it does not have any community advisory panels. Gillette has a written policy on product stewardship and evaluates its products with the objective of reducing their life-cycle impacts on the environment.

Gillette's average total toxic releases and transfers during the years 1994–1996 were less than the industry sample average. Emissions decreased by an average of about two fifths annually during those years, a better than average performance.

Gillette was among 12 private- and public-sector participants in the year-long pilot phase of the EPA's Environmental Leadership Program (ELP) that ended this fall. Gillette piloted the project at three of its facilities, evaluating EMS and compliance audits. Gillette's ELP program focuses on the development of a monitoring system that uses independent, third-party auditors to verify the company's efforts to maintain and improve its environmental performance. Gillette is a participant in EPA's WasteWi$e Program, Green Lights, and 33/50 program.

EEO: In 1996, Gillette had one woman and one minority on its 12-member board. Additionally, the company's total of 39 corporate officers included two women and

no minorities. Gillette evaluates achievement of affirmative action goals in management job reviews and sponsors support networks for women and minorities, has a program for purchasing from minority- and women-owned businesses, and has a written policy banning discrimination based on sexual orientation.

Community Involvement: In 1996, Gillette's charitable giving totaled $9.1 million in cash, or 0.6 percent of its pretax earnings for that year, and in-kind giving totaled $6.6 million. Also in 1996, Gillette promised a $5 million contribution over five years to the Women's Cancer Program.

Workplace Information: OSHA records indicate that Gillette was inspected twice from 1994 to 1996. Violations included 21 classified as "serious" for a total of $14,475 in fines.

International: Gillette's mission statement makes reference to compliance with "applicable laws and regulations" at all levels of government, but does not explicitly address health and safety, child labor, forced and bonded labor, or minimum wage issues. However, several news reports state that Gillette frequently offers minimum wages well above legal minimums — in Indonesia, for example, Gillette was reported to pay an average of three or four times the required minimum, and provides U.S.-style health and retirement benefits.

Animal Testing: In November 1996, Gillette announced that it had conducted no animal testing for personal care or other consumer products or ingredients during the 1996 reporting period, and that for the third consecutive year, no animals were used to test cosmetic products or ingredients. As a result, PETA ended its campaign against the company. In 1996, Gillette invested over $1 million in alternative testing research, and maintains its own Gillette In Vitro Testing and Research Laboratory.

Golden West Financial

STOCK SYMBOL: GDW
STOCK EXCHANGES: NY, B, CH, P

Environment	N
Women's Advancement	A?
Minority Advancement	A?
Charitable Giving	N
Community Outreach	B
Family Benefits	N
Workplace Issues	N
Social Disclosure	F

Based in Oakland, California, Golden West Financial is a holding company whose operations are carried out primarily by its World Savings and Loan Association subsidiary. The company also provides investment advisory services and manages a series of mutual funds through Atlas Advisers, Inc. The corporation operates 120 savings branch offices and 214 loan origination offices in California, Colorado, Florida, Texas, Arizona, New Jersey and Kansas. At year-end 1996, Golden West Financial had income of $2.65 billion and assets of $37.7 billion. There are approximately 4,000 people employed.

EEO: In 1996, Golden West Financial Corp. achieved a higher than average rating in both diversity categories, placing them easily in the top third of S&P 500 companies. Four women and four minorities served on Golden West Financial Corp.'s ten-member board. Of 15 corporate officers at the company, five were women and none were minorities.

Ms. Marion Sandler, Co-CEO and Co-Chair of Golden West Financial, is one of the ten highest paid executive women in the US.

Community Involvement: Golden West's subsidiary, World Savings Bank, has created several programs and initiatives to fund and develop affordable housing. The Community Outreach Committee ensures senior management commitment to fair lending and equal housing opportunities. In 1995, World won the National Outstanding Community Investment Award, the Outstanding Leadership Award (given by the Social Compact) and the Community Partnership Award (given by the Federal Housing Finance Board and the Federal Home Loan Bank) for exceptional affordable housing or community investment initiatives that benefit low-income people, neighborhoods and communities. The Community Service Center of World Savings serves borrowers with affordable housing loan programs.

Many of Golden West's community investment activities are conducted through third-party organizations. For example, in 1980 the company established the Urban Housing Institute (UHI), a non-profit organization that could draw on both company and philanthropic funds to develop creative inner-city housing solutions. World Savings also provided $15 million in seed money for an innovative affordable housing collaborative effort involving California Public Employees' Retirement System/California State Teachers' Retirement System (CalPERS/CalSTRS), The Ford Foundation, major California banks and the BRIDGE Housing Corporation. Other partnerships include working with ACORN and Habitat for Humanity to develop housing for those at the lowest end of the economic ladder.

Golden West also has various internal programs to enhance its impact. Loan requests receive multiple reviews to ensure fair treatment and a dedicated staff reviews affordable housing loan applicants. Also, a Telefinancing Program helps serve customers with disabilities and areas where branches are scarce. (Over 30 percent of these loan applicants are in low-income and/or minority delineated areas.) An annual Chairman's Award honors employees who have been particularly active in outreach efforts. In 1993, World Savings opened a branch in the Crenshaw area of South Central Los Angeles.

World Savings employees participate in volunteer programs rehabilitating homes of low income households.

Workplace Information: The records of the Occupational Safety and Health Administration indicate that Golden West Financial Corp. was not inspected from 1994 to 1996. Consequently no fines or violations were assessed to the company. As inspections are often called in response to complaints regarding the health and safety conditions at a company, a lack of inspections may reflect a relatively safe and healthy workplace.

118

B.F. Goodrich

STOCK SYMBOL: GR
STOCK EXCHANGES: NY, B, C, CH, P, PH

Environment	C
Women's Advancement	D?
Minority Advancement	N
Charitable Giving	B
Community Outreach	N
Family Benefits	N
Workplace Issues	D?
Social Disclosure	C

Based in Richfield, Ohio, B.F. Goodrich manufactures and supplies the aerospace industry with a variety of component parts for commercial aircraft. Also a manufacturer of specialty chemicals, the company is North America's largest producer of polyvinyl chloride. In 1996, the company's worldwide operations employed 14,160 workers and generated revenues of $2.2 billion.

Environment: Goodrich was the recipient of a 1995 Good Neighbor Award from Citizen Action for reducing emissions from its Akron facility by 90 percent within two years. The company has a vice president of Environment, Health and Safety Management Systems and a Responsible Care Oversight Committee. A participant in EPA's 33/50 program, the company surpassed the 50 percent reduction goal set for 1995. Goodrich also participates in EPA's WasteWi$e program for reducing solid waste, increasing recycling, and purchasing products with recycled content. The company has not, however, joined the EPA's Green Lights program for energy-efficient lighting.

EEO: In 1996, B.F. Goodrich's 14-member board of directors included one woman and no minorities. Of 18 corporate officers at the company, two were women and none were minorities.

Community Involvement: In 1996, B.F. Goodrich's charitable giving totaled over $2.3 million in cash, which was equal to 1.30 percent of the company's pretax earnings for that year. In terms of the actual dollar amount donated by the company, the level of cash contributions in 1996 represented a decrease of 3.8 percent from that of 1995, which was 1.3 percent of the company's earnings for that year.

B.F. Goodrich's CEO, John Ong, is the chairman of the Cleveland Foundation's Civic Study Commission on the Performing Arts and has been made the chairman of the Cleveland Orchestra's campaign steering committee. The committee was formed to orchestrate a campaign to raise $100 million by the end of 2000.

The B.F. Goodrich Foundation emphasizes giving to educational institutions located near its major operating facilities and those that conduct research in areas of company interests or that graduate significant numbers of future employees.

Workplace Information: OSHA records indicate that B.F. Goodrich was inspected seven times from 1994 to 1996. Violations included 32 classified as "serious" for a total of $19,380 in fines, $2,768 per inspection. In comparison, the median amount of fines per inspection for other companies in the extractive business was $2,941.

With fewer than 1,000 people overseas, the majority of the company's employees are based in the U.S. Approximately 6,900 hourly employees are covered by collective bargaining agreements. The company has not experienced any significant strikes in recent years.

Weapons Contracts: In 1994, Goodrich had $73.3 million (or 3 percent of total revenues) in contracts with the Department of Defense. Of this amount, $29.7 million was for nuclear weapons systems.

Legal Proceedings: In July 1995, Goodrich agreed to pay $552,500 to settle government allegations that the company had knowingly sold the U.S. Army defective rubber rafts from 1986 to 1988. Goodrich has denied the allegations but claims it settled to avoid the cost of further litigation.

Additional Information: In 1995, Goodrich announced that it will amend its compensation for outside directors after a shareholder proposal to eliminate director pensions received 48 percent of the votes.

W.R. Grace

STOCK SYMBOL: GRA
STOCK EXCHANGES: NY, B, C, CH, P, PH

Environment	B
Women's Advancement	A
Minority Advancement	B
Charitable Giving	F
Community Outreach	B
Family Benefits	F
Workplace Issues	D
Social Disclosure	A

W.R. Grace is a leading global supplier of specialty chemicals, which account for about 45 percent of the company's total revenue. The company's products and services also includes packaging. W.R. Grace, based in Boca Raton, Florida, had 17,400 employees and sales of $3.5 billion in 1996.

Environment: W.R. Grace has an environmental policy and a Corporate Environmental Report (CER), which is updated biennially. W.R. Grace has implemented an integrated Environmental Management System (EMS) and provides training to employees tailored to job responsibilities. The company considers contribution towards EH&S goals in the job performance reviews of senior management. W.R. Grace has a written pollution prevention policy and has initiated a company-wide pollution prevention program. The company also has a corporate policy on community involvement relating to local environmental concerns. Two facilities have community advisory panels. W.R. Grace has a written policy on product stewardship and evaluates its products with the objective of reducing their life-cycle impacts on the environment.

W.R. Grace's average total toxic releases and transfers from 1994 to 1996 were less than the industry sample average. Emissions increased slightly on average annually during those years, a below average performance.

Since 1990, Grace has received three Toxic Substance Control Act violations that resulted in $33,600 in penalties. The company also received four water permit violation notifications, none of which resulted in penalties. These pale in comparison to its activities prior to 1990, during which Grace has had several environmental litigations and public issues. Problems included a guilty plea for making a false statement about its pollution at a hazardous waste site, and unrestored strip mine lands.

EEO: In 1996, W.R. Grace achieved a higher than average rating in both diversity categories. Two women and one minority served on W.R. Grace's 12-member board. Of 16 corporate officers at the company, three were women and none were minorities, while three of the top 25 paid employees were women, and one was a minority.

In 1996, ICCR withdrew its proposal that Grace produce a report on board inclusiveness. Such a withdrawal usually indicates that an agreement with managmeent was reached. In 1995, J. P. Bolduc, Grace's chief executive, was ousted amid charges of sexual harassment. He received a severance package of $43 million.

Community Involvement: In 1996, W.R. Grace's charitable giving totaled $3 million in cash, which was equal to 0.2 percent of the company's pretax earnings for that year. W.R. Grace's main focus is support of education; 36 percent of the foundation's support of education is in the form of matching gifts.

Workplace Information: OSHA records indicate that W. R. Grace was inspected seven times from 1994 to 1996. Violations included 15 classified as "serious" for a total of $13,187 in fines.

One of W.R. Grace and Co.'s largest shareholders, the California Public Employees' Retirement System, joined other shareholders in five suits alleging Grace made excessive payments to its former chairman and CEO. The former received $20 million in benefits and perquisites; the latter, $12 million.

Product Issues: Grace's National Medical Care unit agreed in 1994 to correct manufacturing problems at its five U.S. production facilities. According to the FDA, product safety and quality problems contributed to an elevated mortality level among dialysis patients. The company sold National Medical Care in 1996.

Legal Proceedings: Grace is a defendant in multiple lawsuits involving previously sold asbestos products. Some cases seek restitution for personal injuries, but the majority seek remuneration for the cost of removing asbestos from affected buildings. The company, in conjunction with the Department of Energy's Brookhaven National Laboratory, has recently developed a new product capable of destroying asbestos without diminishing the fire-resistance of the fireproofing.

120

W.W. Grainger

STOCK SYMBOL: GWW
STOCK EXCHANGES: NY, B, CH, PH, P

W.W. Grainger, based in Skokie, Illinois, is a leading nationwide distributor of maintenance, repair, and operating supplies (i.e. air conditioning and refrigeration equipment, computer supplies, electric motors, etc.). It serves commercial, industrial, contractor and institutional customers through its mail order catalog and branch sales outlets. In 1996, Grainger had $3.5 billion in sales and over 12,000 employees.

Environment	B
Women's Advancement	D?
Minority Advancement	D?
Charitable Giving	N
Community Outreach	C
Family Benefits	F
Workplace Issues	D
Social Disclosure	B

Environment: Grainger has an environmental policy but does not currently publish a corporate environmental report. Grainger has not implemented an integrated environmental management system, but does provide environmental health and safety (EH&S) training to all employees. It also considers contribution towards EH&S goals in the job performance reviews of all employees. Grainger has a written pollution prevention policy and establishes annual reduction goals for solid waste. The company also has a written policy on product stewardship and a product steward-ship review board. The company evaluates its products with the objective of reducing their life-cycle impacts on the environment.

In the selection of its suppliers, Grainger determines whether suppliers have necessary permits and requires suppliers to follow the company's environmental guidelines as a contract condition. Grainger has formal procurement guidelines for minimizing environmental impact associated with goods and services purchased by the company. The company has an environmental audit program, which has worldwide standards and applicability. In 1996, 100 percent of U.S. facilities were audited. Internationally, the company follows U.S. regulations in the U.S. and abroad unless local regulations are stricter.

W.W. Grainger's average toxic releases and transfers during the years 1993–1994 were the lowest compared to the industry sample. Furthermore, its emissions decreased by almost 80 percent during those years, one of the best performances within the industry sample.

EEO: W.W. Grainger turned in a below average performance in the area of diversity in 1996, com-pared to other S&P 500 companies. There is one woman on its 11-member board. Additionally, one of a total of 19 corporate officers was a woman.

Grainger distributes a "Supplier Diversity Catalog," listing the businesses from which it purchases and whether they are women- and/or minority-owned. A "company vision" statement in the annual report makes reference to fairness and nondiscrimination in hiring, but does not explicitly mention sexual orientation.

Community Involvement: The *Corporate Giving Directory* reports that Grainger "prefers to remain low key, and does not seek recognition for contributions beyond those organizations it supports." In 1995, Grainger did contribute 257 acres to the Lake County Forest Preserve District, valued by the District at over $15 million.

Workplace Information: OSHA records indicate that Grainger was inspected once from 1994 to 1996. Violations include one classified as "serious" for a total of $750 in fines.

Additional Information: After completing a 1986 market research study, Grainger began computerizing its operations and streamlining customer service. The company opened more branches because it found that customers wanted a supply outlet "within 20 minutes' drive." Realizing that half of its sales derived from phone orders, it put increased time and money into training its telephone operators, so they can answer knowledgeably about products and services available. For example, in 1994, Grainger's Parts Company of America increased phone center staffing by 20 percent, and stayed open 24 hours a day to maintain a high level of service for its growing business. In 1994, Grainger won a number of awards, including General Motors' Quality, Service, and Price Award, and the U.S. Postal Service's National Quality Award.

Great Atlantic & Pacific Tea Co.

STOCK SYMBOL: GAP
STOCK EXCHANGES: NY, B, C, CH, P, PH

Environment	N
Women's Advancement	A?
Minority Advancement	C?
Charitable Giving	A
Community Outreach	D
Family Benefits	N
Workplace Issues	C?
Social Disclosure	A

Great Atlantic & Pacific Tea Co. (A&P) was founded in 1859 as a dockside stand where two New York City businessmen sold discounted teas. Today, the Montvale, New Jersey, company is one of the largest food retailers in North America, with approximately 1,000 stores in eastern U.S. and Canada. In recent years, the company has closed several hundred older stores and increased the size of newer supercenters. In 1996, the company had 89,000 employees and revenues totaling $10.1 billion.

Environment: A&P has a formal environmental policy and requires suppliers to adhere to environmental guidelines. The company has produced an environmental education program called Project Earth. A&P offers a wide array of organically grown produce and does not sell milk from cows treated with bovine growth hormone (BGH). It has joined both EPA's Green Lights and WasteWi$e programs and has installed recycling programs in company stores.

EEO: In 1996, Great Atlantic & Pacific's 12-member board of directors included three women and one minority. Of 30 corporate officers at the company, two were women and one was a minority.

A&P offers diversity awareness training and makes a special effort to recruit minority candidates. However, programs such as mentoring, support networks, and minority-business purchasing have not been established. A&P has not adopted a policy to bar discrimination based on sexual orientation.

Community Involvement: In 1996, Great Atlantic & Pacific's charitable giving totaled $319,000 in cash, which was equal to 0.3 percent of the company's pre-tax earnings for that year. In terms of the actual dollar amount donated by the company, the level of cash contributions in 1996 represented a decrease of 23.2 percent from that of 1995, which was 0.4 percent of the company's earnings for that year. The company's in-kind giving—the donation of products or services—came to a total of $3.5 million in 1996.

Family Benefits: A&P offers a variety of flexible work arrangements and provides resource materials related to dependent care needs.

Workplace Information: According to the Occupational Safety and Health Administration's records, Great Atlantic & Pacific was inspected three times from 1994 to 1996. The OSHA inspectors' citations included eight violations classified as "serious." A total of $9,469 in fines was assessed to the company following the inspections, $3,156 per inspection. In comparison, the median amount of fines per inspection for other companies in the food, beverage, and household products industries was $1,515.

Approximately 90 percent of A&P's employees are unionized; the majority of them are represented by the United Food and Commercial Workers (UFCW). Unlike many of its competitors, the company has historically enjoyed amiable relations with its union employees. Most recent agreements have been negotiated without major dispute. The primary exception was a 14-week strike in 1994 in Ontario, where the company faces tough competition. In a September 1995 agreement covering workers in Detroit, the company pledged to open 15 additional stores and to keep open 15 outlets slated for closure.

In 1994, two Department of Labor lawsuits charged the company with unintentional violations of record-keeping and overtime-labor laws. A&P was ordered to pay a total of $5.3 million in back wages and damages to its Waldbaum subsidiary employees. Approximately 70 percent of A&P's workforce is part-time. These employees generally receive few benefits.

Product Information: In 1994, the Interfaith Center on Corporate Responsibility reported that A&P had agreed to remove Crazy Horse beverages from its stores. Native American groups object to the use of the spiritual leader's image for alcoholic products.

GTE Corporation

STOCK SYMBOL: GTE
STOCK EXCHANGES: NY, B, C, CH, PH, P

Environment	N
Women's Advancement	F
Minority Advancement	C?
Charitable Giving	D
Community Outreach	D?
Family Benefits	N
Workplace Issues	D?
Social Disclosure	C

With 1997 revenues of more than $23 billion, GTE is one of the world's largest telecommunications companies and a leading provider of integrated telecommunications services. In the United States, the Stamford, Connecticut, company provides local service in 28 states and wireless service in 17 states; nationwide long-distance and internet working services; as well as video service in selected markets. Outside the U.S., GTE serves over seven million telecommunications custumers; the company is also a leader in government and defense communications systems and equipment, directories and telecommunications-based information services, and aircraft-passenger telecommunications.

EEO: In 1996, GTE Corporation's board totaled 13 directors, including one woman and no minorities (a minority was added in 1997). One of a total of 11 corporate officers was a woman, and one was a minority, though there were no minority officers in 1997.

In April, 1997, a race-discrimination suit and allegations of fraud and document shredding were brought against GTE. In 1992, GTE stated that a unit created to market services to Spanish-speaking customers had billed customers for custom services that had not been ordered. The suit claims that GTE knew about the fraud two years before it made it known to California state regulators, and that an employee was instructed to destroy documents relevant to the investigation. An independent investigation conducted for GTE by former California Supreme Court Chief Justice Malcolm Lucas found just one case of document altering and no evidence of document shredding.

The suit also contends that only mid- and low-level employees associated with the fraud were disciplined while other senior white managers did not receive punishment. A manager involved in the suit reached an out-of-court settlement regarding his own discrimination claims. Two other plaintiffs have discrimination claims which are unrelated to the fraud issues. State regulators found that the marketing unit had added as much as $15 a month to the Spanish-speaking customers' bills in unordered services. In 1993 GTE was ordered to pay refunds of $2 million to customers and to make $3.2 million in contributions to educational programs. The company was also ordered to hire experts to revise its compensation, sales, and ethics standards for California managers and employees.

A 1996 proposal sponsored by ICCR, resolving that GTE produce an Equal Employment Opportunity report, was withdrawn by its proponents. Generally, the withdrawal of a resolution indicates that the sponsors have reached an agreement with management.

Community Involvement: GTE Corporation's charitable contributions totaled $24.5 million in cash in 1996, or 0.56 percent of the company's pretax earnings for the same year, down from 0.59 percent in 1995. In 1997, contributions were back at 0.59 percent with contributions of $26.5 million.

GTE's main giving priorites are math and science education, encouraging underrepresented minorities to continue their studies in these fields, and grants to math and science teachers through its GIFT program. One important aspect of the GTE education initiative is its research opportunities for United Negro College Fund professors and students.

Workplace Information: OSHA records indicate that GTE was inspected 29 times from 1994 to 1996. Violations included 23 classified as "serious" for a total of $20,015 in fines, or an average of $690 per inspection. In comparison, the median amount of fines per inspection for other communications companies and banks was $573.

Weapons Contracts: GTE ranked 51st on the list of worldwide defense companies in 1996 with $599 million in defense-related revenue, all from prime contracts with the U.S. government. This constituted 2.8 percent of its total business. GTE was the 19th-largest military contractor to the U.S. Department of Defense. GTE provides telecommunications,

123

Harnischfeger Industries

STOCK SYMBOL: HPH
STOCK EXCHANGES: NY, B, CH, P

Environment	C
Women's Advancement	F?
Minority Advancement	C?
Charitable Giving	C
Community Outreach	D
Family Benefits	N
Workplace Issues	B?
Social Disclosure	B

Based in Milwaukee, Wisconsin, Harnischfeger Industries specializes in the manufacture, distribution, and service of equipment for papermaking, mining, and material handling. In fiscal year ending in October 1997, the company had revenues of $3 billion and 17,200 employees.

Environment: Harnischfeger has a general environmental policy available to the public, but does not produce an environmental progress report. The company conducts regular environmental audits and includes progress toward environmental goals in performance evaluations. The company is not in the EPA's 33/50 toxics reduction, WasteWi$e waste reduction, or Green Lights energy conservation programs. Harnischfeger provided no information about any company pollution prevention programs. Company toxic releases have been declining steadily, to about average for the industry in both real amounts and adjusted for size. Harnischfeger's hazardous spills amount is also average for the industry.

The company's Beloit Corporation subsidiary designed and supplied Boise Cascade Corporation's $50 million newsprint-recycling mill in West Tacoma, Washington. Beloit is also the provider of recycling equipment in a number of other plants. In addition, Harnischfeger's board recently approved a new recycling pilot plant at Beloit's Research and Development center in Pittsfield, Massachusetts. The facility focuses on technologies and equipment for chemical pulping and bleaching, stock preparation, and recycling to support the fiber systems division and J & L fiber services division.

EEO: In 1996, Harnischfeger Industries's 14-member board of directors included one woman and one minority. Of six corporate officers at the company, none were women or minorities.

Community Involvement: The Harnischfeger Industries Foundation supports hospitals, medical research and social service agencies involved in the prevention and treatment of diseases, nutrition, hygiene, safety, and improvements of public health. The foundation also supports programs striving to better the community, the ecology, public safety, justice and the law, and public understanding of and participation in government activities.

Workplace Information: According to the Occupational Safety and Health Administration's records, Harnischfeger Industries was inspected two times from 1994 to 1996. The OSHA inspectors' citations included four violations classified as "serious." A total of $4,675 in fines was assessed to the company following the inspections, $2,337 per inspection. In comparison, the median amount of fines per inspection for other companies in similar manufacturing industries was $2,412.

Harnischfeger filed for judicial review of awards made by the Labor and Industry Relations Committee to three workers with pre-employment hearing loss who sustained occupational deafness. Although the LIRC awards were initially appealed, the Supreme Court of Wisconsin ultimately ruled in favor of the awards in 1995.

Weapons Contracts: In 1994, Harnischfeger had $639,000 in Department of Defense contracts, none of which were military related.

Hasbro Inc.

STOCK SYMBOL: HAS
STOCK EXCHANGES: AS, B, P

Environment	B
Women's Advancement	A?
Minority Advancement	N
Charitable Giving	B
Community Outreach	D
Family Benefits	N
Workplace Issues	N
Social Disclosure	B

Based in Pawtucket, Rhode Island, Hasbro is the world's number two toy company and is still run by descendants of the founding family. It markets such household names as G.I. Joe, Mr. Potato Head, Tonka trucks, Milton Bradley and Parker Brothers games and most recently, Barney. Hasbro has 13,000 employees worldwide and sales of $3 billion in 1996. It is a founding member of Businesses for Social Responsibility.

Environment: Hasbro's plastics recycling program takes waste from manufacturing and packaging and turns it into new products. Hasbro has agreed to upgrade to more energy-efficient lighting as part of the EPA's Green Lights program.

EEO: In 1996, Hasbro Inc.'s board totaled 16 directors, including four women and one minority, while two of a total of 13 corporate officers were women, and none were minorities.

Hasbro signed an agreement in 1991 to market ethnic dolls made by specialty toy-maker, Olmec Corporation. Olmec's dolls are unique in their use of authentic black and Hispanic features. In 1993, Hasbro asked Olmec to help develop a line of ethnic dolls dressed in African Kente cloth.

Community Involvement: Hasbro Inc.'s charitable contributions totaled $4 million in cash in 1996, and $750,000 in in-kind donations. The $4 million cash-giving figure represented the equivalent of 1.3 percent of the company's pretax earnings for the same year, and a decrease of 12.5 percent from the company's cash contributions in 1995. In 1995, the company contributed 1.6 percent of its pretax earnings for that year to charity.

The Hasbro Children's Foundation supports programs that improve the quality of life for disadvantaged children, from birth through age 12, their families, and their communities in the areas of health, education and societal needs. The Foundation also funds fully accessible play spaces for children. Some examples of organizations and institutions supported by Hasbro in 1996 include Very Special Arts in Boston, an early literacy intervention program; Pacific Oaks College, which provides services for children exposed to violence; Parent Leadership Training Institute, which helps parents communicate with their children; and Homes for the Homeless, which expanded the Together in Learning Family Literacy Program to ten shelters and transition housing organizations.

Workplace Information: Hasbro reports that recordable injury rates for the company have fallen nearly 50 percent since 1993. Its 1996 recordable injury rate of 6.19 compares favorably with the Bureau of Labor Statistics rate of 11.80 for similar manufacturing industries. A worldwide safety and health auditing system is in place at the company to ensure compliance with corporate policies and regulatory standards.

Hasbro's current leadership strives to maintain the family atmosphere cultivated by their predecessors. To foster open upward communication, envelopes labeled "Write to the Top" are distributed to enable employees to express their thoughts or concerns to senior management.

International: Hasbro's operations in China have made it one of the targets of the "Toycott" sponsored by Support Democracy in China to protest human rights violations.

H.J. Heinz Company

STOCK SYMBOL: HNZ

STOCK EXCHANGES: NY, B, CH, PH

Environment	C
Women's Advancement	F
Minority Advancement	F
Charitable Giving	C?
Community Outreach	C
Family Benefits	N
Workplace Issues	D?
Social Disclosure	B

Pittsburgh–based H.J. Heinz Company is a global provider of processed food products and nutritional services. Heinz offers more than 4,000 products and market brands, including 9-Lives, Ore-Ida, StarKist and Weight Watchers. The company had sales of $9.1 billion in 1996. Heinz employs approximately 43,300 people worldwide.

Environment: Heinz does not publish an environmental progress report or corporate policy. The company's StarKist brand of tuna is committed to reducing dolphin mortality and will not buy any fish caught with gill or drift nets. Heinz's toxic releases in 1994 were 224,147 pounds, a decrease from the previous year and below average for food companies researched by CEP. The hazardous waste generation in 1993, however, was above the industry average.

According to several environmental groups, pesticide residues in baby food from Heinz, Gerber, and Beech-Nut pose possible health risks to children. The pesticide levels are well below government limits and there is no cause for alarm, according to the companies. In 1996, Heinz acquired Earth's Best, a baby food company that uses organic ingredients.

A Puerto Rican environmental group has filed a lawsuit in a U.S. District Court against a Heinz subsidiary for allegedly failing to comply with its NPDES (effluent discharge) permit. The plaintiffs are seeking civil damages of approximately $100,000.

EEO: Heinz turned in a below average performance in the area of diversity in 1996, compared to other S&P 500 companies. Heinz had two women and no minorities on its 18-member board. Additionally, the company's total of 18 corporate officers included no women and one minority.

Heinz reports that it has affirmative action programs in place at all domestic locations. The goal of its programs is to increase representation of women and minorities in all categories. To achieve this goal, the company maintains a compliance/diversity department at Heinz world headquarters and routinely audits equal employment activities at all domestic affiliates. Heinz has also formed a corporate level department, the U.S. Management Development and Service Group to focus on issues surrounding diversity management.

Community Involvement: In 1995, Heinz's contributions to various charitable institutions included cash donations totaling $6 million, and a total of $780,000 in in-kind giving, which is the donation of products or services by the company. The company's cash contributions for 1995 were equivalent to 0.6 percent of its earnings before taxes for the same year.

Workplace Information: OSHA records indicate that Heinz was inspected 29 times from 1994 to 1996. Violations included two classified as "willful" or "repeat" and 74 classified as "serious" for an average of $5,622 per inspection. In comparison, the median amount of fines per inspection for other food, beverage, and household product companies was $1,515.

Through a restructuring plan announced early in 1997, Heinz closed 25 of its 111 worldwide manufacturing plants and reduced its workforce by an additional 2,500 workers, approximately six percent of its international workforce. Heinz planned to sell off Ore-Ida's food-service segments, while retaining its retail business.

International: In 1995 Heinz announced the formation of a joint venture (in which Heinz holds the majority share) with Sentraalwes Cooperative, a farmers' cooperative based in Klerksdrop, South Africa.

Animal Testing: About 500 animals participate in Heinz's in-house "food taste" and nutritional test annually. The company's Pet Products Animal Care Committee adheres to a code of ethics regulating testing activity.

Additional Information: Baby Milk Action (BMA)—a U.K. group that monitors compliance with the WHO/UNICEF Code for Marketing Breast Milk Substitutes—claims that Heinz's brand, Farley's, continues to violate the code in its labeling and product promotion internationally.

Hercules Inc.

STOCK SYMBOL: HPC
STOCK EXCHANGES: NY, B, CH, PH, P

Environment	F
Women's Advancement	C
Minority Advancement	B
Charitable Giving	F
Community Outreach	C
Family Benefits	N
Workplace Issues	F?
Social Disclosure	C

One of the largest producers of TNT in America, Hercules has moved to focus its core business on chemicals and pharmaceuticals. In 1996, Hercules employed 7,100 workers and reached sales of $2 billion. The companyy is headquartered in Wilmington, Delaware.

Environment: Hercules has an environmental policy, which is part of the Responsible Care principles; however, the company does not publish a corporate environmental report. Hercules considers contribution towards EH&S goals in the job performance reviews of senior management and operating personnel. The company does not conduct or review environmental audits on the facilities of potential suppliers. Hercules does have an environmental audit program. Internationally, Hercules follows U.S. regulations in the U.S. and local regulations abroad.

Hercules' average total toxic releases and transfers during the years 1993–1994 were the highest in the industry sample. Emissions increased by less than a fifth during those years, however—only a slightly below average performance.

EEO: In 1996, Hercules Inc.'s board totaled 12 directors, including two women and two minorities, while one of a total of 15 corporate officers was a woman, and one was a minority. Additionally, no women and one minority were among the 25 employees with the highest salaries at the company.

In 1995, Hercules Inc. settled an age discrimination suit filed in 1993 by Gary Dunn, who was 57 at the time. The terms of the settlement were not disclosed, but both parties confirmed that a monetary payment was made to Dunn.

Community Involvement: Hercules Inc.'s charitable contributions totaled $700,000 in cash in 1996. The $700,000 cash-giving figure represented the equivalent of 0.14 percent of the company's pretax earnings for the same year, and was identical to the company's cash contributions in 1995. In 1995, the company contributed 0.14 percent of its pretax earnings for that year to charity.

Hercules states that the company "fulfills its primary responsibility to its owners, employees, customers, and neighbors by providing a satisfactory return on investment, operating in a clean and safe manner, and supplying a reliable and quality product."

Workplace Information: The records of the Occupational Safety and Health Administration indicate that Hercules Inc. underwent six health and safety inspections from 1994 to 1996. The violations reported by OSHA as a result of the inspections include 42 classified as "serious." The company was required to pay $63,040 as a result of its violations, $10,506 per inspection. In comparison, the median amount of fines per inspection for other companies in the extractive business was $2,941.

In 1994, the Hercules Engine Inc. was ordered by a U.S. District Court to compensate disgruntled workers seeking lost benefits and vacation time. UAW represented the Hercules workers after the company sold its factory without giving workers a 60-day notice that the plant would close.

In 1993, Hercules was fined $6.3 million for "blatantly" disregarding federal safety requirements. The company's negligence had resulted in a large explosion and other serious safety violations.

Weapons Contracts: Prior to selling its aerospace division to Alliant Techsystems in March 1995, Hercules was a major weapons producer. The company produced everything from propellants for tactical and strategic missiles to rocket and submarine motors. Hercules retains 30 percent ownership of Alliant.

Hershey Foods Corporation

STOCK SYMBOL: HSY
STOCK EXCHANGES: NY, B, CH, P, PH

Environment	C
Women's Advancement	C
Minority Advancement	C
Charitable Giving	A
Community Outreach	C
Family Benefits	C
Workplace Issues	A
Social Disclosure	A

Hershey Foods Corporation is the leading North American manufacturer of quality chocolate, confectionery, and chocolate-related grocery products. Headquartered in Hershey, Pennsylvania, the company had sales close to $4 billion in 1996. Hershey manufactures five of the top ten chocolate brands in the United States. The company employs 15,300 people worldwide and has production facilities in the United States, Canada, Mexico, Italy, Germany, and Japan. Hershey's Pasta Group currently holds the number-one share position in the United States.

Environment: Hershey publishes an environmental brochure and a brief environmental policy, which is directed mainly toward compliance. There is no mention of environmental vision or proactivity. Although not a participant in EPA's voluntary WasteWi$e or Green Lights, Hershey has comparable solid waste and energy reduction programs. The company recycles 80 percent of its waste stream. It appears to have no significant environmental problems. The company endorses and encourages integrated pest management (IPM) and soil conservation in its supplier documents and its statement on pesticide use.

Hershey has reduced toxic releases by 75 percent since 1991. The company uses integrated pesticide management to reduce toxics use. It is also minimizing the use of methyl bromide, a suspected carcinogen on EPA's extremely hazardous substances list. Recycled-content material is utilized in nonfood packaging

EEO: In 1996, Hershey Foods Corporation had one woman and one minority on its 11-member board. Additionally, the company's total of ten corporate officers included one woman, while the company counted one woman among the 25 highest paid employees.

Hearing impaired employees have been part of the work force since the 1950's at the Hershey Pasta Louisville Plant. Hershey provides voluntary on-site training classes in sign language for all employees at the plant. Additionally, the Quality Assurance Manager at Louisville serves on the President's Council on Employment of People with Disabilities.

Community Involvement: In 1996, Hershey Foods Corporation's charitable giving totaled $2.5 million in cash, which was equal to 0.5 percent of the company's pretax earnings for that year. The dollar level of cash

128

contributions in 1996 was identical to that of 1995, which was 0.5 percent of the company's earnings. The company's in-kind giving came to a total of $18.2 million in 1996.

Family Benefits: Hershey offers flexible work arrangements including part-time return to work after parental leave, job-sharing, and flextime. At some Hershey locations, the company offers day care services.

Workplace Information: OSHA records indicate that Hershey Foods Corporation was not inspected from 1994 to 1996. Consequently no violations or fines were assessed to the company.

Twenty-nine percent of the company's domestic labor force is unionized. Grievance procedures exist for workers not covered by union contracts. The company recently implemented two new worker safety programs, "Safety Sense" and "No Lost Time Accident Record Award."

Workers recently picketed the annual stockholders' meeting over Hershey's 1995 decision to move the production of "Giant Kisses" to Mexico and concerns about low-wage foreign labor in general. The Bakery, Confectionery & Tobacco Workers International Union was defeated twice in its attempts to unionize at the company's HB Reese Candy Co. Union officials say that Hershey brought in an antiunion consultant, and removed union literature from the cafeteria and locker rooms. Wages at Reese roughly equal those of unionized Hershey workers.

International: Hershey has not yet adopted sourcing guidelines for international suppliers. However, the company does maintain worldwide occupational health and safety standards equivalent to the United States and minimum age standards for employees as set by national labor law.

Hewlett-Packard

STOCK SYMBOL: HWP
STOCK EXCHANGES: NY, B, C, CH, P, PH

Environment	B
Women's Advancement	A
Minority Advancement	A
Charitable Giving	B
Community Outreach	A
Family Benefits	B
Workplace Issues	A
Social Disclosure	A

Based in Palo Alto, California, Hewlett-Packard (HP) manufactures electronic equipment and systems primarily for measurement, computation, and communication. In 1997, the company had 122,000 employees and $42.9 billion in sales.

Environment: Hewlett-Packard has an environmental policy and an environmental report, which is produced for customers and is available on the internet. HP has implemented an integrated Environmental Management System (EMS) and provides Environmental Health and Safety (EH&S) training to all employees. HP has a written pollution prevention policy and a company-wide pollution prevention program, which establishes goals for solid waste. Although there is no formal policy on community involvement, the company has a citizen corporate objective and has employees at sites who are responsible for community relations.

Hewlett-Packard's average toxic releases and transfers during the years 1994–1996 were among the highest compared to an industry sample. Furthermore, its emissions increased by an average of about three-fifths annually during those years, one of the worst performances within the industry sample.

In July 1997, a former HP chemist sued the company for $57.5 million, claiming that HP officials demoted and later fired him after he brought environmental and safety violations to their attention. The employee claims that HP officials told him to ignore violations of the Toxic Substance Control Act, then fired him after accusing him of filing a false document with the EPA.

In March 1997, HP and AMD received the 1997 ENERGY STAR award for best technological innovation from the EPA.

EEO: In 1996, one woman served on HP's 13-member board. Of 34 corporate officers at the company, three were women and three were minorities. Hewlett-Packard is a past winner of the Catalyst award, and was one of 83 cited in the Glass Ceiling Commission's March 1995 report for implementing "employment practices that help break the glass ceiling." The Commission cited Hewlett-Packard specifically for its annual Technical Women's Conference.

Community Involvement: HP's charitable contributions totaled $15.4 million in cash in 1996, and $56.1 million in in-kind donations. The $15.4 million cash-giving figure represented the equivalent of 0.4 percent of the company's pretax earnings for the same year; the company also contributed 0.4 percent in 1995.

The *Corporate Giving Watch* lists Hewlett-Packard as the top-most giver to education and international efforts in 1995. Hewlett-Packard is also listed as giving more money to the environment and to social services than all but two companies in each category.

Workplace Information: OSHA records indicate that Hewlett-Packard underwent five health and safety inspections from 1994 to 1996. Violations included three classified as "serious" for a total of $5,995 in fines, $1,199 per inspection. In comparison, the median amount of fines per inspection for other companies in the industries manufacturing electronic equipment was $1,347.

In recent years, several thousand employees have been transferred. The company has never resorted to lay-offs; instead, employees whose jobs have been designated as "excess" are offered jobs elsewhere in the company or offered early retirement.

Military Contracts: For many years, HP sold electronic components used in various weapons systems. The company maintained that the components are strictly "off-the-shelf" products and recently stopped taking government orders for "high-reliability" components, which are generally the type purchased for military applications.

In 1992, the *New York Times* reported that HP products were exported to Iraqi military-related entities in the late 1980s. HP claims that the products were not licensed for weapons applications, and there is no evidence that any products were diverted for illegal use. HP also notes that Iraq was a U.S. ally at the time.

The Home Depot

STOCK SYMBOL: HD

STOCK EXCHANGES: NY, B, CH, P, PH

Environment	A
Women's Advancement	B?
Minority Advancement	B?
Charitable Giving	C
Community Outreach	B
Family Benefits	N
Workplace Issues	N
Social Disclosure	B

The Home Depot, based in Atlanta, Georgia, is the preeminent retailer of building and home improvement supplies in the U.S. The company has more than 600 stores in 42 states and 32 stores in Canada. In 1996, the company had sales of $19.5 billion and 106,000 employees. In 1997, for the fourth consecutive year, the company was named "Most Admired Retailer" by *Fortune* magazine.

Environment: The Home Depot is among a select number of retailers that have proactively addressed environmental issues. Its first companywide Environmental Principles were established in 1990.

The Home Depot screens suppliers to ensure that the products it sells are made and packaged in an environmentally responsible way. It offers only lead-free solders to help promote EPA's waterborne lead abatement program and in 1993 adopted a No Toxic Cement policy, refusing to sell cement and aggregate products made at plants that burn hazardous wastes.

In 1992, The Home Depot initiated the Environmental Greenprint program to educate customers and employees about alternative "green" products that are safer to use and easier on the environment. The Home Depot was the first home improvement retailer to become a partner in EPA's Green Lights energy-efficiency lighting program. Home Depot also uses forklifts powered by rechargeable batteries or propane, and computerized energy management systems that regulate its stores' heat, light, and air conditioning requirements.

The Home Depot aggressively recycles the waste stream in its stores. The company uses recycled materials in store supplies and advertising materials. In 1993, it opened a Recycling Depot prototype in Atlanta, in partnership with one of the largest recycling operations in the Southeast, to enable customers to recycle materials discarded from home improvement projects. In its first year, the center diverted more than one million pounds of recyclables from landfills.

EEO: In 1996, The Home Depot's 12-member board included two women and one minority. Four women and three minorities served among the company's 57 corporate officers.

The Home Depot, which won a 1995 award for its record of hiring individuals with disabilities, was named as a defendant in a class action gender discrimination suit. In September of 1997, the company settled the suit and three other gender discrimination suits for a total of approximately $100 million. The company admitted no wrongdoing and stands behind its hiring policies The four original plaintiffs had claimed that The Home Depot discriminated in promotions on the basis of sex.

In 1995, The Home Depot was recognized by The Association of Retarded Citizens of Long Beach, California, for its commitment toward recruiting and hiring workers who are physically and mentally challenged. That same year, Western Law Center for Disability Rights awarded The Home Depot with the Corporate Achievement Award.

Community Involvement: In 1996, The Home Depot's charitable giving totaled $8.5 million in cash, which was equal to 0.55 percent of the company's pretax earnings for that year ($10.3 million in 1997). In 1995, Team Depot, the company volunteer program, received the President's National Community Service award and *Business Ethics* magazine's award for community relations.

Workplace Information: OSHA records indicate that The Home Depot was inspected 39 times from 1994 to 1996. Violations included 31 classified as "serious" for a total of $55,982 in fines, $1,435 per inspection. In comparison, the median amount of fines per inspection for other companies in the retail industry was $694.

Honeywell Inc.

STOCK SYMBOL: HON
STOCK EXCHANGES: NY, B, C, CH, P, PH

Environment	B
Women's Advancement	C
Minority Advancement	A
Charitable Giving	A
Community Outreach	B
Family Benefits	A
Workplace Issues	B
Social Disclosure	A

Minneapolis-based Honeywell produces and markets automation and control systems and components. With $7.3 billion in revenues in 1996 and 53,000 employees worldwide, Honeywell continues to globalize by doubling its sales force in Eastern Europe and establishing a joint venture in China.

Environment: Honeywell has an environmental policy and publishes a corporate environmental report, which is updated every one to two years. Honeywell has implemented an integrated environmental management system. The company has a written pollution prevention policy and has initiated a company-wide pollution prevention program, which establishes annual reduction goals for solid waste. Honeywell also has a corporate policy on community involvement relating to local environmental concerns, but has no community advisory panels. Honeywell has a written policy on product stewardship and evaluates its products with the objective of reducing their life-cycle impacts on the environment.

Honeywell Inc.'s average toxic releases and transfers during the years 1994–1996 were among the lowest compared to an industry sample. Furthermore, its emissions decreased by an average of about a half annually during those years, a better than average performance.

EEO: In 1996, Honeywell Inc.'s board totaled 12 directors, including one woman and one minority, while two of 16 corporate officers were women. Three minorities were among the 25 highest paid employees.

In 1994, Honeywell agreed to invest $3 million in diversity programs following the settlement of a 17 year-old discrimination suit. Also in 1994, a former employee was awarded $486,000 in an age discrimination case. The company was cited in the Glass Ceiling Commission's 1995 report for its Women's Council, a group formed in 1978 to contribute to a working environment that would attract and retain quality female employees and support women working to advance.

Community Involvement: Honeywell Inc.'s charitable contributions totaled almost $9 million in cash in 1996, and over $1.1 million in in-kind donations. The cash-giving figure was equal to 1.5 percent of the company's pretax earnings for the same year; in 1995, Honeywell contributed 1.8 percent of its earnings.

The Honeywell Retiree Volunteer Project was started in 1979, and now involves over 1,100 former employees.

The Solid State Electronics Center, a Honeywell division, has incorporated volunteerism into management training for all employees. Michael Bonsignore, Honeywell's CEO, has volunteered in the construction of a Habitat for Humanity home, and announced an international partnership between Honeywell and the nonprofit organization.

Workplace Information: Honeywell had 21 state and federal OSHA inspections from 1994 to 1996. Violations included 33 classified as "serious" for a total of $70,735 in fines. Injury and illness rates are below comparable industry averages, and fell 25 percent during this time. Honeywell conducts compliance audits for health and safety on a global basis. The company's Employee Wellness program received the C. Everett Koop National Health Award in 1995.

International: Honeywell's Corporate Code of Ethics and Business Conduct avoids purchasing from companies that use forced or child labor.

In 1994, two unions accused Honeywell of firing Mexican employees for attempting to organize workers. Honeywell claimed that the workers were laid off "as part of an overall plan to downsize" the factory. A DOL review panel found that because the employees accepted severance benefits, Mexican labor authorities could not investigate. The company reports that very few employees were affected, and cites positive efforts on Honeywell's part—the company built a clinic in Tijuana for the community, and many employees volunteer in schools and agencies.

Weapons Contracts: Honeywell, which produces defense electronics, ranked 88th in the list of top defense companies worldwide in 1996. It generated $263.6 million in defense-related activities, 4.5 percent of its overall business, entirely from prime contracts with the U.S. Department of Defense.

Illinois Tool Works

STOCK SYMBOL: ITW
STOCK EXCHANGES: NY, B, CH

Environment	C
Women's Advancement	C?
Minority Advancement	A?
Charitable Giving	C
Community Outreach	B
Family Benefits	C
Workplace Issues	B
Social Disclosure	A

Founded in 1912, Illinois Tool Works (ITW) is a worldwide manufacturer of highly engineered components and industrial systems. Company products include fasteners, assemblies, packaging and construction materials, and precision tools and systems. ITW, based in Glenview, Illinois, has 24,400 employees and in 1996 had sales of $5 billion.

Environment: Illinois Tool Works has a brief written environmental policy and includes environmental regulations within its Principles of Conduct. However, the company does not publish an environmental report and has no environmental procedures manual. While its board has no committee assigned to overseeing corporate environmental concerns, an annual environmental report is given to the entire board. The company audits about 50 percent of its U.S. facilities, occasionally utilizing external auditors. ITW has tried to develop and sell environmentally compatible products.

A participant in EPA's 33/50 program, the company reduced targeted toxic chemicals by 35 percent. ITW has not joined EPA's Green Lights or WasteWi$e programs. The company has been identified as a potentially responsible party at one Superfund site under CERCLA.

EEO: ITW elected its first female director in 1994. Two African-American men are also on the board. No women or minorities are among the company's nine elected officers. Fifteen of ITW's officials and managers are women, a strong increase from 1993. Seven percent of this group are minorities. ITW prohibits discrimination based on sexual orientation.

Community Involvement: In 1996, ITW made direct and foundation gifts totaling $2.6 million, or about 0.5 percent of the company's average pretax earnings. ITW allocates half of its budget for a three-to-one employee, matching gift program.

The company is involved in several Junior Achievement programs, providing financial support and dozens of employee volunteers. Many of these participate through the company's Senior Outreach program, which links retirees with organizations needing assistance.

Family Benefits: A 1991 study by the Families and Work Institute found that ITW offered very few work/family benefits or programs. The company currently reports that it provides reimbursement for dependent care and adoption expenses through flexible spending accounts.

Workplace Information: Much of ITW's success has been attributed to its empowerment of line workers and devolvement of decision-making authority. Self-directed work teams are responsible for production and managing decisions. Employees are rewarded for cost-saving suggestions. ITW reimburses tuition costs for work-related courses and provides extensive on-site training.

Retirement funds are provided through a defined benefit plan, and employees may participate in a stock purchase program. The company has had no significant workplace safety concerns during the past five years.

International: ITW's operations are based primarily in developed countries in North America and Europe, though the company does have a presence in Malaysia.

Legal Proceedings: In 1994, ITW was found to have infringed on the patent for a fastener manufactured by Rawlplug Company and ordered to pay damages related to lost sales. In December 1990, ITW had to pay $900,000 in compensatory damages to a window subcontractor to which it supplied allegedly faulty screws. In a September 1988 ruling, ITW was assessed compensatory and punitive damages of $1.4 million for supplying faulty fasteners bought by a high-rise construction firm in 1984 and 1985.

132

Intel Corporation

STOCK SYMBOL: INTC
STOCK EXCHANGES: NNM

Environment	A
Women's Advancement	D
Minority Advancement	B
Charitable Giving	A
Community Outreach	A
Family Benefits	D
Workplace Issues	A
Social Disclosure	A

Intel is the world's largest semiconductor maker and is among the 10 "Most Admired" companies based on the latest *Fortune* survey. In 1997, the Santa Clara, California, company had $25.1 billion in revenues and 64,000 employees.

Environment: Intel has an environmental policy and a Corporate Environmental Report (CER), which is updated annually and is available on the internet. Intel has implemented an integrated Environmental Management System. Intel recognizes the environmental health & safety contributions made by employees. The company has a written pollution prevention policy and a company-wide pollution prevention. Intel also has a corporate policy on community involvement relating to local environmental concerns. Five facilities have Community Advisory Panels.

Intel's average toxic releases and transfers during the years 1993–1994 were less than the industry sample average. Furthermore, its emissions decreased by more than a fourth during those years, one of the best performances within the industry sample.

In November 1996, Intel became one of the first companies to participate in the pilot of the EPA's Project XL. All regulated air, water, and waste emissions, and other environmental goals were integrated into a single master plan. The agreement exempts Intel from having to update its permit every time it makes a small change in its manufacturing processes, and allows the company to file a single air, land, and water pollution report to the local county instead of filing separate reports to several agencies. Critics claim that in setting an overall ceiling on the plant's emissions, the government is allowing Intel to emit more of some pollutants as long as it curbs others.

EEO: In 1996, Intel Corp.'s 12-member board of directors included one woman and one minority. Of 29 corporate officers at the company, two were women and two were minorities. One woman and one minority ranked among Intel's 25 highest paid employees.

In 1996, an ICCR shareholder resolution proposing that Intel distribute an EEO report was withdrawn, which generally indicates that an agreement has been reached with management.

Community Involvement: In 1996, Intel Corp.'s charitable giving totaled $16.5 million in cash, which was equal to 0.2 percent of the company's pretax earnings for that year. The company's in-kind giving—the donation of products or services—came to a total of $39.1 million in 1996. Intel reports that it was one of the top ten givers in the U.S. in 1997.

In the fall of 1995, the company pledged to donate $30 million to the Rio Rancho Public Schools in Rio Rancho, New Mexico, to build a new high school. Intel has a major plant in the city. Each major Intel site has a volunteer program that focuses on elementary and secondary education.

Workplace Information: OSHA records indicate that Intel was inspected once from 1994 to 1996. Violations included five classified as "serious" for a total of $885 in fines.

Intel reported that it distributed $820 million in profit-sharing and retirement contributions to its 48,500 employees in 1996, and that stock options will be made available to all its employees. the *Wall Street Journal* reported that the offer represents "one of the more lucrative bonuses ever paid" to employees in light of the potential value of options on Intel stock.

Weapons Contracts: Intel has modest contracts with the Department of Defense. In 1995, the company was awarded a $45 million contract by the Department of Energy to develop a supercomputer to simulate nuclear weapons tests. Intel maintains that such a capability would "make it unnecessary for any country to stage live nuclear tests in the future."

Legal Proceedings: In 1995, Intel and AMD resolved several long-standing legal battles involving alleged patent infringement and breach of contract. Intel also settled patent infringement charges brought by Apple.

⊛ International Business Machines

STOCK SYMBOL: IBM
STOCK EXCHANGES: NY, TO, B, C, CH, P, PH

Environment	A
Women's Advancement	B
Minority Advancement	B
Charitable Giving	B
Community Outreach	A
Family Benefits	A
Workplace Issues	A
Social Disclosure	A

With 225,347 workers worldwide and revenues reaching $75.9 billion in 1996, IBM is the largest computer maker in the world.

Environment: IBM has an environmental policy and a corporate environmental report, which is updated annually, follows the Public Environmental Reporting Initiative (PERI) reporting guidelines, and is available on the Internet. IBM has implemented an integrated environmental management system and provides environmental health and safety (EH&S) training to its EH&S and facility staff and staff at certain locations where training is required. It also considers contribution towards EH&S goals in job performance reviews for its trained staff. IBM has a written pollution prevention policy and has initiated a companywide pollution prevention program, which establishes annual reduction goals for solid waste. The company also has a corporate policy on community involvement relating to local environmental concerns; however, it does not have any community advisory panels. IBM has a written policy on product stewardship and evaluates its products with the objective of reducing their life-cycle impacts on the environment. It utilizes the following criteria in selection of its suppliers: 1) conducting/reviewing environmental audits on suppliers' facilities, 2) evaluating environmental management systems of suppliers, 3) determining whether supplier has necessary permits, and 4) requiring suppliers to follow the company's environmental guidelines as a contract condition. The company has an environmental audit program, which has worldwide standards and applicability. In 1996, 100 percent of U.S. and international facilities were audited. IBM does not make the audit findings available to the public. IBM requirements are used worldwide if they are more stringent.

IBM's average toxic releases and transfers during the years 1994–1996 were among the highest compared to an industry sample. Furthermore, its emissions increased by an average of about 6 percent annually during those years, a below average performance.

IBM is a member of the Public Environmental Reporting Initiative and International Chamber of Commerce's Business Charter for Sustainable Development. In December 1997, IBM announced that it had received the first edition of a single worldwide ISO 14001 registration that will cover all of the company's global manufacturing and hardware development operations across all of its various business units. The company's Personal Systems Group division issues an environmental report, in addition to the companywide one published by IBM. The company's core environmental program is its Design For Environment (DFE) which includes materials reduction, use of recycled materials, coding plastics, initiating closed looped recycling, packaging reduction, recycling and reuse. IBM's DFE guidelines focus on 15 environmental attributes in total.

EEO: In 1996, two women and one minority served on International Business Machines's 12-member board. Of 15 corporate officers at the company, one was a woman and none were minorities.

IBM's record of purchasing from minority- and women-owned businesses through a program first implemented in the late 1960s has earned it numerous awards. In 1996, International Business Machines purchased over $508 million in goods and services from women- and minority-owned businesses; its total purchasing was $14 billion.

Community Involvement: In February, 1997, IBM announced that it will donate $10 million in products and services over the next three years to help modernize up to twelve school systems. The donation is in addition to the $25 million that the company reports it has donated to 10 schools since initiating its Reinventing Education Program in 1994. As a part of its education initiative and in collaboration with Apple Computer, Vanderbilt University, and Computers for Education, IBM will provide a free website for every K-12 school, teacher, and student in the U.S. IBM has denied that the program was created as a means to increase IBM sales to schools, stating that the company's interests would be served by a successfully educated pool of potential employees.

134

Continued on next page

International Business Machines (continued)

Corporate Giving Watch lists IBM as giving more money to social services than any other company, more money to the arts and humanities than all but two companies, more money to education and international efforts than all but one, and more money to the environment and health than all but three.

Approximately 45 percent of IBM employees participate in volunteer activities, which includes a program that provides paid leaves of absence for a limited number of employees to conduct volunteer work. The Fund for Community Service supports employees, retirees, and spouses in their volunteer efforts.

In 1996, International Business Machines' charitable giving totaled $36.5 million in cash, which was equal to 0.4 percent of the company's pretax earnings for that year. In terms of the actual dollar amount donated by the company, the level of cash contributions in 1996 represented a decrease of 21.6 percent from that of 1995, which was 0.5 percent of the company's earnings for that year. The company's in-kind giving—the donation of products or services—came to a total of $59.5 million in 1996.

Family Benefits: IBM funds or supports near-site centers in 54 locations and provides backup care to community child care programs. Employees are offered flexible work arrangements, alternative work schedules, and leaves of absence of up to three years after the birth of a child.

Workplace Information: OSHA records indicate that IBM was inspected once from 1994 to 1996, receiving only incidental violations and no fines. In comparison, the median amount of fines per inspection for other companies in the industries manufacturing electronic equipment was $1,347.

Over 60 former IBM employees filed suit in 1996 seeking over $1 billion in damages. The plaintiffs claimed they developed cancer and other illnesses as a result of being exposed to chemicals while working at IBM plants in Fishkill, N.Y. and Burlington, Vt. Other defendants in the suit include Union Carbide, Eastman Kodak, DuPont, and J.T. Baker Chemical Co., which was acquired by Mallinckrodt in 1995. The suit alleges the defendant companies were negligent in failing to test the potential danger of the chemicals in the event of exposure, failing to notify employees of the danger of the chemicals, and failing to maintain a safe working environment. Some plaintiffs have also alleged that their unborn children were affected by the chemicals. A May 17, 1996, memo from IBM stated that the company believes its plants are safe, and that its controls and programs against potential chemical exposures "generally are four times more stringent than government standards."

135

Weapons Contract: In 1994, IBM sold its Federal Systems, a defense-related unit, to Loral for $1.5 billion.

International Flavors & Fragrances

STOCK SYMBOL: IFF
STOCK EXCHANGES: NY, B, C, CH, PH, P

Environment	C?
Women's Advancement	D?
Minority Advancement	N
Charitable Giving	F
Community Outreach	N
Family Benefits	N
Workplace Issues	N
Social Disclosure	D

Based in New York City, New York, IFF is a leading international creator and manufacturer of flavors and fragrances used in consumer products. The company has foreign operations in Holland, France, Germany, Great Britain, Ireland, Spain, Switzerland, Argentina, Brazil, Mexico, Australia, China, Hong Kong, Indonesia, and Japan. In 1996, the company had 4,630 employees and revenues of $1.4 billion.

Environment: International Flavors & Fragrances did not respond to CEP's environment questionnaire in 1997. Though International Flavors and Fragrances does not produce an environmental report, it releases to the public both an environmental policy and a set of environmental principles. The policy emphasizes compliance, while the principles focus on environmentally sensitive design and operation. The company participates in none of EPA's pollution prevention programs and provided no information on any company waste reduction, emissions reduction, resource conservation, or environmental design programs. IFF does not have an environmental department or conduct environmental audits.

International Flavors and Fragrances' average total releases and transfers during the years 1993–1994 were less than the industry sample average. Emissions increased slightly during those years, a below average performance.

EEO: In 1996, International Flavors & Fragrances' board totaled 12 directors, including one woman and no minorities, while none of a total of 15 corporate officers were women, and none were minorities.

Community Involvement: International Flavors & Fragrances' charitable contributions totaled $450,000

in cash in 1996. The $450,000 cash-giving figure represented the equivalent of 0.15 percent of the company's pretax earnings for the same year, and was identical to the company's cash contributions in 1995. In 1995, the company contributed 0.11 percent of its pretax earnings for that year to charity.

The IFF Foundation's support of Arts and Humanities includes grants to ballets, operas, museums and libraries. As part of its commitment to health and science, the foundation supports hospitals, medical centers, and single-disease health associations. Social services, such as child welfare agencies and youth groups are also given funding by the IFF Foundation.

Workplace Information: The records of the Occupational Safety and Health Administration indicate that International Flavors & Fragrances was not inspected from 1994 to 1996. Consequently no fines or violations were assessed to the company.

Two thirds of IFF employees are based outside of the U.S. The company has never experienced a work stoppage or strike.

Animal Testing: The company does not disclose any information about animal testing.

136

International Paper

Environment	A
Women's Advancement	D
Minority Advancement	C
Charitable Giving	B
Community Outreach	A
Family Benefits	D
Workplace Issues	C
Social Disclosure	A

International Paper, based in Purchase, New York, produces and sells paper and wood products for consumer and industrial use worldwide. The company has manufacturing and distribution facilities throughout the United States, Canada, Europe, Asia, and Latin America. IP also owns and/or controls over six million acres of forestland in the U.S. through IP Timberlands, a limited partnership in which IP has a majority interest. IP's 1996 revenues totalled $20.1 billion, and the company employs 87,000 people.

Environment: International Paper has an environmental policy and a corporate environmental report, which is updated annually, is verified by a third party, and is available on the Internet. International Paper has implemented an integrated environmental management system and provides environmental health and safety (EH&S) training to EH&S staff and plant managers. It also considers contribution towards EH&S goals in the job performance reviews of EH&S staff and all employees above a certain pay level. International Paper has a written pollution prevention policy and has initiated a company-wide pollution prevention program, which establishes annual reduction goals for point sources, secondary emissions, fugitive emissions, and solid waste. The company also has a corporate policy on community involvement relating to local environmental concerns and has community advisory panels at all major facilities. International Paper does not have a written policy on product stewardship, but states that it does evaluate its products with the objective of reducing their life-cycle impacts on the environment. International Paper is in compliance with the American Forest & Paper Association's Sustainable Forestry Initiative.

International Paper's average total toxic releases and transfers during the years 1994–1996 were just less than the industry sample average. Furthermore, its emissions decreased by an average of about a seventh annually during those years, one of the best performances within the industry sample.

EEO: In 1996, International Paper's 14-member board of directors included one woman and one minority. Of 49 corporate officers, two were women and one was a minority.

Although International Paper does not currently bank with any minority-owned banks, it indicates that it is researching such banks and expects to do business with them by the end of 1997. The company also writes that it has implemented mentoring programs throughout the company, but they are not geared specifically towards minority and women. Further, International Paper makes a limited use of apprenticeship programs for women and minorities. The company's policy on harassment states that even if actions described as harassment in the policy "do not rise to the level of legally actionable harassment, they nonetheless are unacceptable in the workplace."

Community Involvement: In 1996, International Paper's charitable giving totaled $8.7 million in cash, which was equal to 1.1 percent of the company's pretax earnings for that year.

In June, 1996, International Paper pledged to donate any wood products needed to rebuild churches with predominantly African-American congregations that had been destroyed in racially-motivated incidents of arson. The company provided and delivered the material needed to rebuild the 30 churches qualified for aid by the National Council of Churches, without publicizing the act. IP arranged to have employee volunteers help with the construction at several sites.

One quarter of the International Paper Foundation's budget, approximately $750,000, is used to fund its Education and Community Resources (EDCORE) program. Implemented in 1981, EDCORE invites selected school districts to submit proposals addressing current educational issues, and has since received a "best in class" distinction from the Conference Board.

Workplace Information: OSHA records indicate that IP was inspected 38 times from 1994 to 1996. Violations included two classified as "willful" or "repeat" and 88 classified as "serious" for a total of $127,845 in fines.

137

James River Corporation

Environment	F
Women's Advancement	F
Minority Advancement	F
Charitable Giving	A
Community Outreach	N
Family Benefits	N
Workplace Issues	C?
Social Disclosure	C

James River Corporation is one of the leading manufacturers of consumer paper products under brand names such as Dixie, Vanity Fair, Brawny, and Quilted Northern. In August, 1997, James River and Fort Howard merged, becoming the Fort James Corporation (stock symbol FJ). This profile reflects information about James River prior to the merger. In 1996, James River's sales were $5.7 billion, and the company had 23,000 employees.

Environment: The company does not publish a corporate environmental report. James River considers contribution towards EH&S goals in the job performance reviews of executives and managers. In the selection of suppliers, James River conducts or reviews environmental audits on suppliers' facilities. The company has an environmental audit program, but does not make audit results publicly available.

Between 1994 and 1996, James River received 74 air quality violations at its Camas, OR mill. In addition, a January 1996 chlorine release forced the evacuation of 25 employees and the temporary closure of some downtown streets. In July 1997, a consent decree between the company and the Oregon Department of Ecology was finalized in which the company will pay an $82,357 fine and make emissions improvements in nine areas of the mill. James River will also provide the Camas Fire Department with $82,300 worth of radio equipment to improve emergency response for future accidents.

EEO: James River Corp. turned in a below average performance in the area of diversity in 1996, compared to other S&P 500 companies. Among the companies surveyed by CEP, the average representation of women and minorities on S&P corporate boards was 10.8 percent and 7.5 percent, respectively. In comparison, James River Corp. had one woman and no minorities on its ten-member board. Additionally, the company's total of 11 corporate officers included no women or minorities.

James River has published its first report on diversity, which has been made available to shareholders, on request, since May 15, 1997. The report was produced about a year after 10.8 percent of shares were voted in favor of a 1996 shareholder proposal asking that the company produce an EEO report. In 1997, James River appointed a woman who is a member of a minority group to its Board of Directors. According to correspondence from the company, James River also has a policy "supporting the employment of qualified individuals with AIDS."

Community Involvement: In 1996, James River Corp.'s charitable giving totaled $2 million in cash, which was equal to 0.7 percent of the company's pretax earnings for that year. In terms of the actual dollar amount donated by the company, the level of cash contributions in 1996 represented a decrease of 40 percent from that of 1995, which was 0.8 percent of the company's earnings for that year.

Workplace Information: OSHA records indicate that James River was inspected 32 times from 1994 to 1996. Violations included five classified as "willful" or "repeat" and 107 classified as "serious" for a total of $83,502 in fines, $2,609 per inspection. In comparison, the median amount of fines per inspection for other companies in the extractive business was $2,941.

Additional Information: In April 1995, for the fourth time in five years, the shareholders of James River voted against a proposal that would bind the company to the MacBride Principles. However, a significant 7.3 percent of votes cast did support it.

Johnson & Johnson

STOCK SYMBOL: JNJ
STOCK EXCHANGES: NY, To, B, C, CH, P, PH

Environment	B
Women's Advancement	B
Minority Advancement	C
Charitable Giving	A
Community Outreach	A
Family Benefits	A
Workplace Issues	A
Social Disclosure	A

Based in New Brunswick, New Jersey, Johnson & Johnson is the world's largest manufacturer of health care products. In 1997, the company had $22.6 billion in sales and 90,500 employees.

Environment: Johnson & Johnson has an environmental policy and a corporate environmental report, which is available on the Internet. The company has implemented an integrated environmental management system, and provides environmental health and safety (EH&S) training to EH&S staff, facility staff, and management. Johnson & Johnson also considers contribution towards EH&S goals in job performance reviews. It has a written pollution prevention policy and has initiated a companywide pollution prevention program, which established reduction goals for point sources and solid waste. The company has a written commitment on product stewardship, and evaluates its products with the objective of reducing their life-cycle impacts on the environment.

Johnson & Johnson's average total toxic releases and transfers during the years 1994–1996 were the lowest in the industry sample. Emissions decreased on average by about a half annually during those years, a better than average performance.

EEO: In 1996, Johnson & Johnson's board totaled 15 directors, including three women and one minority, while one of a total of 14 corporate officers was a woman and none were minorities. Additionally, one woman and no minorities were among the 25 employees with the highest salaries at the company.

J&J is a participant in the Inroads training program which hires minority high school seniors and college students for well-paying jobs leading to careers. The company has a written ethical business conduct statement which it distributes throughout the company. In 1996, Johnson & Johnson agreed to put into writing its policy banning discrimination on the basis of sexual orientation. In turn, Franklin Research withdrew a shareholder resolution, requesting the implementation of a set of equality principles on sexual orientation.

Community Involvement: J&J's charitable contributions totaled $44.5 million in cash in 1996, an increase of $2.3 million from 1995, and $44 million in in-kind donations, an increase of $14 million from 1995. The $44.5 million cash-giving figure represented the equivalent of 1.1 percent of the company's pretax earnings for the same year.

J&J was named the top contributor to the area of Health in 1995 by the Corporate Giving Watch; it is also among the top donors in the areas of Civic and Public Affairs, the Environment, and International Support. J&J has formed numerous partnerships to promote better health care throughout the world; these programs address issues such as child injury prevention, community health care, child survival in developing countries, and substance abuse. J&J also funds international programs and donates products around the world.

Workplace Information: OSHA records indicate that Johnson & Johnson underwent five health and safety inspections from 1994 to 1996. Violations included ten classified as "serious" for a total of $5,750 in fines. In comparison, the median amount of fines per inspection for other companies in the medical and cosmetics industries was $2,266.

International: J&J has purchasing terms that require suppliers to comply with international health, safety, and environmental laws, but does not monitor their implementation. The company has not developed a comprehensive code of conduct for suppliers.

Animal Testing: Each year the company spends more than $45 million in developing and using alternatives to animal testing. J&J does not disclose the annual numbers of animals used in testing.

Additional Information: After being charged with promoting bottle feeding in India by child welfare and nutrition organizations, J&J decided to withdraw from the country's infant feeding market in 1996.

139

🏅 Kellogg Company

STOCK SYMBOL: K
STOCK EXCHANGES: NY, B, C, CH, P, PH

Environment	A
Women's Advancement	B?
Minority Advancement	B
Charitable Giving	A
Community Outreach	A
Family Benefits	B
Workplace Issues	B
Social Disclosure	A

Based in Battle Creek, Michigan, Kellogg is the world's leading producer of ready-to-eat cereals, with 1996 sales of $6.7 billion and 14,500 employees worldwide. The company continues to expand overseas; it now has manufacturing facilities in 19 countries.

Environment: Kellogg established a worldwide environmental management program in 1990 (in North America, 1980). The program goes beyond compliance with federal and industry standards to addressing specific community concerns. All operating facilities must comply with such global policies as those dealing with new property assessment, waste management, hazardous materials management, packaging strategy, ozone-depleting chemicals, and environmental auditing.

Kellogg requires suppliers to adhere to company guidelines as a contract condition. The company has converted its printing to nontoxic water-based inks and is implementing a program to reduce or eliminate the use of phosphoric acid–based cleaning compounds. Wastes were reduced from 83,000 pounds in 1991 to 37,000 pounds in 1995. Kellogg is the lowest producer of toxic releases among companies in the food industry researched by CEP.

EEO: In 1996, Kellogg Company's board totaled 13 directors, including two women and two minorities, while three of a total of 29 corporate officers were women, and three were minorities. Kellogg provides diversity awareness training and bans discrimination based on sexual orientation. The company has programs for banking and purchasing from businesses owned by women and minorities.

Community Involvement: Kellogg Company's charitable contributions totaled $10.5 million in cash in 1996 and over $14.2 million in in-kind donations. The $10.5 million cash-giving figure represented the equivalent of 1.22 percent of the company's pretax earnings for the same year. In 1995, the company contributed 1.32 percent of its pretax earnings for that year to charity.

Since 1992, the W. K. Kellogg Foundation, a separate legal entity, has invested $11.6 million in a long-term effort called the African-American Men and Boys Initiative. The initiative plans to launch a National Dialogue on Race through a partnership with Fisk University and the Center for Living Democracy.

In June 1996, Kellogg Company announced its investment of $1 million in the initiative. The foundation and the company jointly won a 1997 Corporate Conscience Award for Community Involvement.

Family Benefits: Kellogg works with community leaders to support and improve the quality and accessibility of child care for all. It provides employees with referral and workbooks on child and elder care, and spouse relocation assistance.

Workplace Information: OSHA records indicate that Kellogg was inspected six times from 1994 to 1996. Violations included 17 classified as "serious" for a total of $19,245 in fines, an average of $3,414 per inspection. In comparison, the median amount of fines per inspection for other companies in the food, beverage, and household products industries was $1,515.

CEO Arnold Langbo was one of 17 company executives recently invited to President Clinton's panel discussions on social responsibility in the workplace. In an agreement with the American Federation of Grain Millers, the company instituted a pioneering large-scale hourly workers transfer program, which helped ease the impact of downsizing. Workers considering transfer visited new job sites and transferees received orientation, retraining, and relocation assistance. More than 150 hourly workers chose to transfer to Kellogg jobs in other areas. The company's workplace benefits include an unusual broad-based stock option plan covering nearly every employee in North America and in 21 other countries.

Kellogg received CEP's 1991 Corporate Conscience Award for Responsiveness to Employees. Union Label & Service Trades Department (UL&STD) of the AFL-CIO nominated the company for this award, and AFGM cited it for its "commitment to union labor and union products."

Kerr-McGee Corporation

STOCK SYMBOL: KMG
STOCK EXCHANGES: NY, TO, B, C, CH, PH, P

Environment	F?
Women's Advancement	C?
Minority Advancement	C?
Charitable Giving	D
Community Outreach	C
Family Benefits	N
Workplace Issues	C?
Social Disclosure	B

Kerr-McGee was founded in 1929 as the Anderson & Kerr Drilling Company in Ada, Oklahoma. Today, corporate activities are focused on three principle businesses: oil and gas exploration and production, production of specialty chemicals, and coal and mineral mining. The company announced in June it hoped to raise $400 million from the sale of its petroleum refining and marketing operations. The Oklahoma City–based company had revenues of $1.9 billion in 1996 and employs about 3,851 people.

Environment: Kerr-McGee did not respond to CEP's environmental questionnaire in 1997. The company does have a written environmental policy and publishes a corporate environmental report, which details facility specific programs. The company has a written pollution prevention policy and a corporate policy on community involvement relating to local environmental concerns. Kerr-McGee does not state that it has implemented a product stewardship program, but produces such products as "green" greases, which are developed with the objective of reducing their impact on the environment.

Kerr-McGee Corporation's average toxic releases and transfers during the years 1993–1994 were among the highest compared to an industry sample. Furthermore, its emissions increased by about 10 percent during those years, a below average performance.

The company is one of two under obligation to clean up perchlorate found in Southern Nevada's drinking water supply. State environmental officials are working to narrow an inquiry into where perchlorate is entering the Las Vegas Wash. Kerr-McGee will work through mid-June of 1998 to complete a field sampling plan that must be approved by the Nevada Environmental Protection's Remediation Branch. EPA is studying the health effects of perchlorate and has not, as of January, 1998, set a standard for consuming it in drinking water. Kerr-McGee is phasing out its ammonium perchlorate production but stores 5,000 tons of it at a facility 17 miles northeast of Las Vegas.

EEO: Kerr-McGee Corp. turned in an average overall performance in workforce diversity for S&P 500 companies in 1996. The company's 12-member board included one woman and no minorities, as compared with the average of 10.8 percent women and 7.6 percent minorities for other S&P 500 companies. Two women and one minority served among the company's 14 corporate officers.

Community Involvement: In 1996, Kerr-McGee Corp.'s charitable giving totaled $1.3 million in cash, which was equal to 0.40 percent of the company's pretax earnings for that year. The company's in-kind giving — the donation of products or services — came to a total of $52,000 in 1996. Kerr-McGee gives primarily in locations where it has operating facilities, including its corporate headquarters' state of Oklahoma.

Kerr-McGee faced considerable community opposition when it planned to build a permanent storage facility in residential West Chicago for the 13 million cubic feet of radioactive waste at its former processing plant. The company has since arranged to begin shipping material to a licensed facility in Utah. Kerr-McGee faces several personal injury lawsuits from West Chicago residents claiming to have acquired illnesses as a result of exposure to thorium wastes. One such case was settled in 1994 for an undisclosed sum.

Workplace Information: OSHA records indicate that Kerr-McGee was inspected once in 1996. Violations included three classified as "serious" for a total of $5,600 in fines. In comparison, the median amount of fines per inspection for other companies in the extractive business was $2,941.

Approximately 400 employees, seven percent of the workforce, are represented by collective bargaining agreements. In 1994, the company cut 250 jobs in Oklahoma City, or 20 percent of its headquarters staff.

KeyCorp

STOCK SYMBOL: KEY
STOCK EXCHANGE: NY

Environment	N
Women's Advancement	B
Minority Advancement	C
Charitable Giving	C
Community Outreach	B
Family Benefits	C
Workplace Issues	A
Social Disclosure	A

In March 1994, KeyCorp and Society Corporation merged to form a newly configured KeyCorp, providing banking services and now based in Cleveland, Ohio. Part of the company's mission statement is to "share talents and resources to improve the communities we serve." In 1996, the company had $6 billion in revenues and 29,963 employees.

EEO: In 1996, KeyCorp's board totaled 20 directors, including two women and one minority. None of eight corporate officers were women and none were minorities. Additionally, no women and no minorities were among the 25 employees with the highest salaries at the company.

In 1996, KeyCorp was one of eight employers given the Opportunity 2000 award in recognition of its efforts to promote diversity. Its diversity fund, which is subadvised by an African-American-owned, Cleveland-based institutional investment advisory firm, does not evaluate companies' historical records on diversity, but persuades the companies in which it invests to make diversity a top corporate priority. The corporation also received Cleveland's Regional Minority Purchasing Council's Business Consortium Fund Award of Excellence. Keycorp received the Exemplary Voluntary Efforts (EVE) Award from the U.S. Department of Labor in September of 1996. The award recognizes programs which promote equal employment opportunities.

KeyCorp offers mentoring programs, recruitment programs, and support networks, maintains diversity goals, and gives special consideration for management training to both women and minorities. In 1996, KeyCorp purchased almost $6.3 million in goods and services from women- and minority-owned businesses.

Community Involvement: Key Community Development Corporation (KCDC) offers loans and creates projects to provide affordable housing, helps create jobs, and stimulates investment in low- and moderate-income neighborhoods. Most of KeyCorp banks have earned an "outstanding" rating from their regulators, who evaluate compliance with the Community Reinvestment Act (CRA). Through

volunteer programs, KeyCorp's employees work on public-service projects in their communities.

Each fall, KeyCorp's entire workforce closes up shop and spends an afternoon volunteering at food banks, schools, day-care centers, and other community agencies. In Cleveland alone, 4,000 KeyCorp employees volunteered at 150 sites.

Family Benefits: KeyCorp offers such flexible scheduling options as a compressed work week, work-at-home arrangements, flextime, job sharing, and part-time return to work following leave.

Workplace Information: According to the Occupational Safety and Health Administration's records, KeyCorp was not inspected from 1994 to 1996. Consequently, no violations or fines were assessed to the company.

In late 1996, KeyCorp announced it would lay off 10 percent of its 28,337 employees and close or sell 23 percent of its branches. The layoffs and elimination of branches was part of a restructuring move through which the bank would focus on urban areas in an attempt to increase profitability.

Legal Proceedings: In April 1994, Electronic Payment Services Inc., owned jointly by KeyCorp and three other bank holding companies, was charged by the Justice Department with "monopolistic and exclusionary practices," which resulted in more than a thousand banks paying higher prices for ATM processing. The case was immediately settled through a consent agreement requiring Electronic Payment Services to open up its network on a nondiscriminatory basis.

Kimberly-Clark

STOCK SYMBOL: KMB

STOCK EXCHANGES: NY, B, C, CH, P, PH

Environment	C
Women's Advancement	B
Minority Advancement	B
Charitable Giving	C
Community Outreach	B
Family Benefits	B
Workplace Issues	A
Social Disclosure	A

Kimberly-Clark, based in Irving, Texas, is a pulp and paper company based in Dallas, Texas. Its products include newsprint, disposable diapers, and tissues. In December 1995, the company merged with Scott Paper. Earlier in the year, the company divested its commercial airlines and tobacco paper business. In 1996, KMB had 54,800 employees and $13.1 billion in sales.

Environment: Kimberly-Clark is in an industry with many environmental impacts, ranging from how it harvests timber to the chemicals released in converting it into products that often end up in landfills. The company states that it does not use fiber from old-growth forests or rain forests.

The chlorine bleaching process used in paper manufacturing creates dioxin as a byproduct. Three of KMB's mills are elementally chlorine free, two of them with no detectable dioxin levels. Two others recently acquired from Scott Paper are not, and one is totally chlorine free. The company has introduced diapers that are 50 percent thinner. It has a corporate goal to eliminate the use of landfills for all manufacturing waste worldwide by 2000. Kimberly-Clark does not participate in EPA's voluntary WasteWi$e program, but states that its waste reduction goals are more stringent than EPA's.

Toxic emissions directly to the environment (TRI) declined 41 percent between 1988 and 1994, to 2.54 million pounds, but are above the household products industry average. TRI adjusted for size show a decreasing trend, although the 0.39 pounds per $1,000 in sales was three times higher than the average among companies researched by CEP.

EEO: In 1996, two women and three minorities served on Kimberly-Clark's 12-member Board of Directors. Of 89 corporate officers at the company, 14 were women and four were minorities. One of the top 25 paid employees was a woman, and one was a minority. The company has multiple affirmative action programs and support groups for both women and minorities. In addition, Kimberly-Clark has special purchasing programs for women- and minority-owned businesses, and it banks with minority-owned institutions. Kimberly-Clark has a policy banning discrimination based on sexual orientation.

Community Involvement: Kimberly-Clark committed $100 million in 1996 to affordable housing for people with low and moderate incomes. In 1997, the company gave $545,500 to organizations where employees volunteered.

In 1996, Kimberly-Clark's charitable giving totaled $7.6 million in cash, which was equal to 0.38 percent of the company's pretax earnings for that year. In terms of the actual dollar amount donated by the company, the level of cash contributions in 1996 represented a decrease of 4 percent from that of 1995. The company experienced a sizable dip in earnings in 1995.

Workplace Information: OSHA records indicate that Kimberly-Clark was inspected seven times from 1994 to 1996. Violations included three classified as "serious" for a total of $3,600 in fines, an average of $514 per inspection. In comparison, the median amount of fines per inspection for other companies in the food, beverage, and househod products industries was $1,515.

In November, 1996, Kimberly-Clark canceled its contract with Protection Technology Inc. at the company's Mill in Winslow, ME and established a contract with a non-unionized security firm. The nine guards who lost their jobs, members of the International Union of United Plant Guard Workers, claim that their dismissal was the result of corporate greed and a "union-busting" mentality. The company maintains that the change in security companies was unrelated to union membership and was nothing more than an effort to cut costs.

Animal Testing: Kimberly-Clark tests its products on animals through outside contractors. From 1987 to 1992, the number of animals used in these tests decreased from 8,700 to 1,400, or 84 percent. In the last decade the number of tests decreased 90 percent. The company also donated $10,000 to fund research into alternatives to animal testing.

Kmart Corporation

STOCK SYMBOL: KM

STOCK EXCHANGES: NY, B, C, CH, P, PH

Kmart is one of the world's largest mass merchandise retailers, with more than 2,000 discount stores worldwide. The Troy, Michigan, company also operates Builders Square home improvement stores. With 300,000 employees, in 1995 the company reported a $100 million net loss. In 1996, Kmart had sales of $34.4 billion and 307,000 employees.

Environment	N
Women's Advancement	F?
Minority Advancement	D?
Charitable Giving	N
Community Outreach	C
Family Benefits	N
Workplace Issues	F?
Social Disclosure	C

Environment: California fined Kmart in 1991 and again in 1996 ($110,000) for violating state environmental laws relating to the sale of unlicensed pesticides.

Since establishing an environmental committee, Kmart has undertaken various programs, including battery and tire recycling. Environmental Management Concerns process the scrap tires into "crumb" rubber for use in new products.

EEO: In its 1996 Annual Report, Kmart claims that it has developed a practice of "regularly sharing key employment information with the NAACP" in order to gain "important insights in expanding economic opportunities for minorities." The Annual Report adds that the "Kmart Supplier Diversity Board continually reviews, creates and implements strategies to increase purchases from minority suppliers" and that "Kmart has an established process for minority vendors to obtain assistance in presenting their merchandise for consideration."

Community Involvement: The Kmart Family Foundation, which is committed to drug education and prevention programs, was created in response to a company survey which found drug abuse to be the most pressing concern of customers. The company's other philanthropic interests include children's needs and community-enhancing groups, especially in the areas surrounding Detroit. Kmart is one of the largest contributors to Gifts In-Kind America; in 1996 it donated $18 million worth of goods to this organization. Every organization that requests money from Kmart is asked how company volunteers can assist the cause with their time.

Workplace Information: According to the Occupational Safety and Health Administration's records, Kmart Corporation was inspected 156 times from 1994 to 1996. The OSHA inspectors' citations included 20 violations classified as "willful" or "repeat" and 357 violations classified as "serious." A total of $376,218 in fines was assessed to the company following the inspections, an average of $2,412 per inspection. In comparison, the median amount of fines per inspection for other companies in the retail industry was $694.

In recent years, Kmart has had several disputes with unions. Most recently, Kmart shareholders rejected two labor union proposals to seat a union representative on the company's board of directors. In 1996, the United Food and Commercial Workers International Union (UFCW) picketed Kmart for its low wages, especially for women. In 1995, AFL-CIO union workers urged consumers in the Midwest to boycott the company because of its substandard wages and benefits.

The Kmart Corp. doubled earnings through cost-cutting measures and plans to announce more cuts, including offering early retirement to 28,500 employees. Kmart expects about 60–70 percent of the employees offered to accept early retirement. These measures will allow Kmart to hire new workers at lower starting salaries.

Legal Proceedings: In March 1996, a former Kmart employee was awarded $750,000 from the company for being wrongfully fired 12 years earlier.

Knight-Ridder, Inc.

STOCK SYMBOL: KRI

STOCK EXCHANGES: NY, B, CH, P

Environment	N
Women's Advancement	A
Minority Advancement	A
Charitable Giving	REV
Community Outreach	B
Family Benefits	N
Workplace Issues	D
Social Disclosure	C

K night-Ridder is an international communications company involved in newspaper publishing, business news and information, and related services. Among the company's 31 daily papers are the *Miami Herald,* the *San Jose Mercury News*, the *Philadelphia Inquirer*, and the *Detroit Free Press*. Headquartered in Miami, Florida, the company in 1996 had revenues of $2.8 billion and 24,000 employees.

EEO: Of 14 board members, two are women and two men are African-American. One woman serves on the seven-member executive committee. There are three women and one minority among 13 corporate officers. Over the last few years, each operating unit has developed a five-year plan detailing affirmative action goals. Managers are evaluated on how much they increase the pool of women and minorities qualified to fill key positions. Training programs are offered on discrimination awareness and diversity for all employees. The company also maintains a minority hiring program, which attempts not only to recruit minority members into management offices but also to assist supervisors in developing minority talent.

Community Involvement: Knight-Ridder gives about $1.5 million annually, with another $50,000 in nonmonetary support. After Hurricane Andrew, Knight-Ridder joined with the *Miami Herald* to pledge $2.5 million over five years for the rebuilding of South Dade County. The company also supports local homeless shelters, the United Way, and education and minority development projects. KRI lends executives and has a matching gift program. Its various business units also operate their own giving programs locally.

Knight-Ridder in 1994 contributed nearly half the funds ($30,000) needed to keep alive the Southeastern Multicultural Newspaper Workshop at the University of South Carolina College of Journalism and Mass Communications. In a joint effort in 1994, Knight-Ridder's Information Design Lab introduced a student newspaper on the Internet, which covered a wide range of community issues. The Information Design Lab, created in 1992 as an experimental R&D unit, was closed down in 1995, and resources and efforts were diverted to the Knight-Ridder New Media Center

in San Jose, California, which is putting Knight-Ridder newspapers online.

Workplace Information: A July 1995 strike of 2,600 employees at the *Detroit Free Press* (Knight-Ridder) and the *Detroit News* (Gannett) ended in early 1997. No ruling had been made as of February 1998 as to whether the strike was over unfair labor practices on the part of management; the newspapers will be required to allow all striking workers to return to work if the strike is determined to have been prompted by such practices. If not, workers may return only as vacancies arise. In June, 1997, a non-binding decision did find that the strike was caused and prolonged by management's unfair labor practices; a binding decision had not been made as of early 1998. At that time, about 900 of the 2500 strikers remained on the company's call-back list, and 200 had been fired for misconduct. About 42 percent of KRI's employees are represented by unions, which include the Teamsters, Graphic Communications International, and the Newspaper Guild.

In February, 1998, a Detroit Newspapers Inc. suit accusing unions at the *Detroit News* and the *Detroit Free Press* of violating federal racketeering laws during the strike was allowed to go through; many instances of violence and property destruction on the part of strikers are permitted to be included in the suit. Unions had argued that these instances fell under the jurisdiction of the NLRB.

In late Fall 1995, KRI laid off 125 people, or 10 percent of the workforce, at its New York–based financial unit. The company cited a 40 percent hike in newsprint prices and the strike in Detroit, which was costing the company millions of dollars per week in lost advertising and circulation revenue.

145

Kroger Company

STOCK SYMBOL: KR

STOCK EXCHANGES: NY, B, C, CH, PH

Environment	N
Women's Advancement	A?
Minority Advancement	C?
Charitable Giving	B
Community Outreach	D
Family Benefits	N
Workplace Issues	B?
Social Disclosure	C

Founded in 1883, Kroger is the nation's largest food retailer in terms of sales. Headquarered in Cincinnati, Ohio, the company operates 1,392 supermarkets and 830 convenience stores in the South and Midwest. It also operates 37 food processing facilities that produce private-label goods. Kroger employs 220,000 persons, and its sales reached $26.6 billion in 1997. A committee of board members oversees corporate social responsibility issues.

Environment: Kroger recently discontinued reporting on environmental initiatives in its annual report. The company has been working to reduce packaging waste in its private-label lines and to promote recycling at its supermarkets. Kroger has requested that suppliers not use milk from cows treated with bovine growth hormone. In the early 1990s, however, the company was among many that successfully lobbied against "bottle-bill" legislation in Ohio.

Between 1996 and 1998, Kroger expects to spend approximately $35 million to eliminate CFCs from its refrigeration units and replace underground storage tanks.

EEO: In 1996, Kroger's board totaled 14 directors, including three women and one minority (two in 1997), while none of a total of 12 corporate officers were women (one in 1997).

Kroger is the defendant in a sexual harassment case filed by a meat plant employee. The Kroger employee, who had worked at the plant for nearly ten years, claims that he was sexually harassed by his co-workers because they thought he was gay. He also alleges he was discriminated against and forced to work in a hostile environment.

In 1996, the Cincinnati-Dayton division was honored as "Employer of the Year" by Arc, an agency that supports people with mental retardation, for its employment of store associates with physical and mental disabilities. *Hispanic Magazine* has listed Kroger among the 100 best firms for Hispanics, but dropped the company in 1997 when it narrowed the list to 75 companies.

Community Involvement: Kroger's charitable contributions totaled $5.5 million in cash in 1996, and $5.5 million in in-kind donations. The $5.5 million cash giving figure represented 0.97 percent of the company's

pretax earnings for the same year, a decrease of 3.6 percent from the company's cash contributions in 1995.

To celebrate its ninetieth anniversary, Kroger donated $90,000 to Columbus, OH charities. In 1996, the company participated in "Check-out Hunger" which raised money for food banks throughout Texas. Kroger also sought to aid children with disabilities by participating in the "Cash for Kids" campaign.

Workplace Information: OSHA records indicate that Kroger was inspected 42 times from 1994 to 1996. Violations included 68 classified as "serious" for a total of $40,507 in fines, an average of $964 per inspection. In comparison, the median amount of fines per inspection for other companies in the food, beverage, and household products industries was $1,515.

Approximately 90 percent of Kroger's retail store employees are unionized, many of them represented by the United Food and Commercial Workers (UFCW). Company representative Paul Bernish has described Kroger as "a tough, aggressive negotiator over pay, benefits, etc. … primarily because we compete in most markets with nonunion operators who can drastically undercut us on costs."

While most contracts are renegotiated without significant dispute, the company has experienced a few strikes in recent years. In the spring of 1996, workers in Colorado struck for six weeks before agreeing to a new contract. In 1992, workers in southeastern Michigan struck for 10 weeks when negotiations faltered. In November 1995, the National Labor Relations Board charged Kroger officials at a West Liberty, Ohio, plant with coercing workers to vote against unionization. In September 1996, an agreement was reached with the union in which it would withdraw all remaining unfair labor practice charges.

Liz Claiborne, Inc.

STOCK SYMBOL: LIZ
STOCK EXCHANGES: NY, PH

Environment	N
Women's Advancement	A
Minority Advancement	A
Charitable Giving	B
Community Outreach	C
Family Benefits	B
Workplace Issues	C
Social Disclosure	A

Liz Claiborne, based in New York City, is a leading designer of women's apparel that is marketed worldwide. The company also designs and markets various lines of men's clothing as well as fragrances, furnishings, and accessories. In 1996, the company had sales of $2.2 billion and 7,100 employees.

Environment: By the nature of its operations, the company has limited direct environmental impact. It has relatively few policies or programs related to environmental stewardship. Liz Claiborne has begun installing high-efficiency lighting, though it has not joined EPA's Green Lights program. Suppliers are required to follow environmental guidelines and company facilities are audited annually. Unlike some of its competitors, the company is not actively involved in producing clothing from more sustainable sources such as organic cotton.

EEO: In 1996, Liz Claiborne achieved a higher than average rating in both diversity categories, placing them easily in the top third of S&P 500 companies. Three women and one minority served on Liz Claiborne's 9-member board. Of 124 corporate officers at the company, 61 were women and six were minorities. Eleven of the top 25 paid employees were women and four were minorities.

Liz Claiborne was the first Fortune 1000 company to be founded by a woman. Its record on advancing women to senior ranks is matched by few. In 1995, Liz Claiborne received a Social Responsibility Award from Women Executives in Public Relations (WEPR) for its Women's Work Program, which aims to raise awareness about domestic violence. Liz Claiborne formally prohibits discrimination based on sexual orientation.

Community Involvement: In 1996, Liz Claiborne's charitable giving totaled $1.5 million in cash, which was equal to 0.60 percent of the company's pretax earnings for that year. The level of cash contributions in 1996 was identical to that of 1995, which was 0.74 percent of earnings for that year. The company's in-kind giving—the donation of products or services—came to a total of $2 million in 1996. Contributions in 1997 included $1.8 million in cash and $2 million in in-kind giving.

The Liz Claiborne Foundation works to improve opportunities for women and their families through programs addressing economic development and career growth, family violence, AIDS, and child development.

Workplace Information: OSHA records indicate that Liz Claiborne was inspected once from 1994 to 1996. Violations included two classified as "serious" for a total of $1,500 in fines. In comparison, the median amount of fines per inspection for other companies in similar manufacturing industries was $2412.

Approximately 27 percent of Liz Claiborne's domestic workforce is represented by the Union of Needletrades, Industrial and Textile Employees (UNITE). The company has experienced no strikes in the last few years.

International: Like most of the apparel industry, Liz Claiborne contracts extensively with international suppliers. The company has adopted the White House Apparel Industry Partnership workplace code of conduct covering wages, child and forced labor, worker safety, and the environment. Among other monitoring vehicles, the company visits suppliers to ensure compliance with the code. The two years it was released (1995 and 1996), the Department of Labor's Fair Labor Fashion Trendsetter list for combating sweatshop working conditions included Liz Claiborne. In 1997, the company was the first corporation to be awarded the Trumpeter Award from the National Consumers League.

In 1994, Liz Claiborne announced that it would cease sourcing clothing from Burmese subcontractors.

Lockheed Martin

STOCK SYMBOL: LMT
STOCK EXCHANGES: NY, P

Environment	N
Women's Advancement	D
Minority Advancement	N
Charitable Giving	N
Community Outreach	B?
Family Benefits	N
Workplace Issues	B?
Social Disclosure	B

Lockheed Martin Corporation is a highly diversified global enterprise principally engaged in the conception, research, design, development, manufacture and integration of advanced-technology products and services. In April 1996 Lockheed Martin merged with Loral Corp., acquiring its defense electronics and systems integration businesses. At year-end 1996, the Bethesda, Maryland, company had sales of $26.9 billion and 190,000 employees. In July, 1997, Lockheed Martin announced that it would acquire Northrop Grumman.

Environment: Lockheed Martin recently published its first environmental report, in the form of a special report brochure, entitled *Taking Care*. The company's strategy to prevent pollution and dominant theme is by "attacking waste at its source by reducing or eliminating those materials and processes that created the environmental hazard in the first place." This strategy has been in place for ten years during which the company participated in numerous EPA initiatives, including Environmental Leadership Program, 33/50 Program, Climate Wise, Green Lights, and WasteWi$e Program. Lockheed Martin has an environmental audit program that focuses on full compliance with government standards and regulations, and helps reduce risks to employees as well as the environment. To date, 31 facilities have been audited, and more than 100 are scheduled for completion by the end of 1997.

EEO: In 1996, Lockheed Martin's board totaled 19 directors, including two women and no minorities. Four of a total of 50 corporate officers were women and none were minorities. In 1998, two of 18 board members were minorities, as was one of the 50 corporate officers.

In November of 1996, Lockheed Martin agreed to pay an excess of $13 million to settle the claims of 2,000 workers who alleged that they had been unfairly terminated by Martin Marietta following the merger of the two companies. The settlement reached with the EEOC required that several hundred workers, aged 40 and older, be rehired. The company denies that it violated any laws or regulations and claimed that it reduced its workforce in response to "market conditions." The 2000 plaintiffs were awarded an average of $6,500 each. Lockheed Martin's recent effort to provide equal employment opportunity includes linking managers' compensation to their records of promoting minorities

and women. Lockheed Martin is also a member of the U.S. Department of Labor's Working Women Count Honor Roll for its Management through Growth Enhancement program.

Community Involvement: Lockheed Martin's primary educational interest is in K-16 math and science programs. The company's Employees' Con Trib Club gave $50,000 for the construction of the Parker County 4-H center in Weatherford, Texas in 1997. Over $570,000 of the foundation's $17 million contributions in 1996 went to organizations and programs in Central Florida alone. Norman R. Augustine, former chairman of Martin Marietta Corp., donated his $2.9 million merger bonus to charities in 1995 when Lockheed Corp. and Martin Marietta Corp. merged.

Workplace Information: OSHA records indicate that Lockheed Martin was inspected eight times from 1994 to 1996. The OSHA inspectors' citations included seven violations classified as "serious." A total of $30,755 in fines was assessed, an average of $3,732 per inspection. In comparison, the median amount of fines per inspection for other companies in similar manufacturing industries was $2,412.

Weapons Contracts: In 1996, Lockheed Martin was the number one defense manufacturer worldwide with $14.3 billion in defense revenue. The company derived 53.4 percent of its total revenue from defense. In 1996, Lockheed Martin was also the largest prime contractor to the U.S. Department of Defense, with nearly $12 billion in prime contract awards.

Lockheed Martin is the producer of aircraft such as the F-16 and F-4 fighter aircraft, the Trident missile, AEGIS missile systems, space systems, electronics and communications equipment, defense electronics and armored vehicles.

Louisiana Land & Exploration

STOCK SYMBOL: LLX
STOCK EXCHANGES: NY, TO, B, C, CH, P, PH

Environment	F
Women's Advancement	D?
Minority Advancement	D?
Charitable Giving	A?
Community Outreach	B
Family Benefits	N
Workplace Issues	N
Social Disclosure	D

Louisiana Land & Exploration (LLX), one of the largest independent oil and gas production companies, didn't actually begin exploration until the 1950s. Before then, the company leased out drilling rights on its large land holdings and is today rather unique in owning much of the land on which it drills. Exploration and production occurs primarily in the continental U.S., the Gulf of Mexico, the North Sea, Canada, Colombia, and Indonesia. Other sites include Algeria, Yemen, and Tunisia. LLX owns a single refinery, located near Mobile, Alabama. Revenues for 1996 were $863 million. The New Orleans, Louisiana–based company has 581 employees.

Environment: Louisiana Land did not respond to CEP's environmental questionnaire in 1997. The company published a report on preserving the natural environment of Louisiana, but does not publish a corporate environmental report or have a written environmental policy.

Louisiana Land & Exploration's average toxic releases and transfers during the years 1993–1994 were among the lowest compared to an industry sample. However, although its emissions decreased by about 6 percent during those years, its performance was still below average within its industry sample.

Environmentalists attempted to stop development of Louisiana Land & Exploration Co.'s new natural gas facility in central Wyoming in 1997. Their concerns were over further degradation of air quality in the Class 1 air sheds of the Big Horn Basin and the Cloud Peak Wilderness Area. The company predicts that production over the next 20 to 25 years will not cause any significant air quality impacts in the area. The Wyoming Outdoor Council says that it would only add to the pollution from other industrial developments.

EEO: Louisiana Land & Exploration turned in a below average performance in the area of diversity in 1996, compared to other S&P 500 companies. Among the companies surveyed by CEP, the average represen-tation of women and minorities on S&P corporate boards was 10.8 percent and 7.5 percent, respectively. In comparison, LLX had no women or minorities on its 11-member board. Additionally, the company's 14 corporate officers included one woman and no

minorities. The company has special recruitment and development programs to help diversify its management ranks. Discrimination based on sexual orientation is explicitly prohibited.

Community Involvement: LLX's top priority in its focus on education is support for colleges and universities in the form of unrestricted support, scholarships for dependents of company employees, and multi-year grants. The company matches employee donations only towards education; the matching gifts program accounted for approximately one third of Louisiana Land & Exploration's giving to education in 1995.

In 1995, LLX's contributions to various charitable institutions included cash donations totaling $796,000. The company's cash contributions for 1995 were equivalent to 2.76 percent of its earnings before taxes.

Workplace Information: According to the Occupational Safety and Health Administration's records, Louisiana Land & Exploration was not inspected from 1994 to 1996. Consequently no violations or fines were assessed to the company.

In 1995, the Mobile refinery received two awards from the National Petroleum Refiner's Association for reducing its accident incidence rate in 1994 by more than 25 percent and attaining a rate below 2.0 injuries per 200,000 work hours. LLX is not unionized.

International: LLX reports that it "generally implement[s] U.S. [environmental] standards used by the company's U.S. operations on a worldwide scale."

Legal Proceedings: LLX recently settled litigation with Texaco over royalty payments allegedly due to the company for production on LLX-owned land.

Louisiana-Pacific Corporation

STOCK SYMBOL: LPX
STOCK EXCHANGES: NY, B, CH, P, PH

Environment	B
Women's Advancement	C
Minority Advancement	C
Charitable Giving	N
Community Outreach	N
Family Benefits	D
Workplace Issues	D
Social Disclosure	A

Louisiana-Pacific, a major manufacturer of building products, had $2.4 billion in sales and 12,000 employees in 1997. The company is headquartered in Portland, Oregon. Internationally, the company operates three plants in Canada and one in Ireland.

Environment: Louisiana-Pacific has an environmental policy and an annual corporate environmental report. The company has developed and is implementing a corporate-wide environmental management system. Louisiana-Pacific is developing a policy on product stewardship and plans to evaluate life-cycle impacts of their products on the environment. Currently these activities are a function of the New Product Project Team and the capital Project Management Initiative. The company has an environmental audit program, which has worldwide standards and applicability.

Louisiana-Pacific's average total toxic releases and transfers during the years 1994–1996 were lower than the industry sample average. However, its emissions decreased by an average of about five percent annually during those years, an above average performance.

In August 1997 and January 1998, former managers at Louisiana-Pacific pleaded guilty to charges of violating air pollution laws and to federal charges that they repeatedly tampered with air-pollution monitoring equipment in the early 1990s. Louisiana-Pacific is scheduled to go to trial in April 1998 on 48 charges, including charges that it allegedly lied about air emissions from its Olathe, Colorado mill, and violations of the Clean Air Act. The lawsuit alleges the company engaged in "a scheme to defraud" customers and cheat on environmental laws. The company states that it has installed new pollution-control equipment at its mills, and changed management since the violations occurred. In August 1997, the EPA conducted an unscheduled audit of the Olathe mill. The company was commended for improvements in its environmental management system and employee environmental awareness.

EEO: Louisiana-Pacific's ten-member board included two women and two minorities. One woman served among the company's eight corporate officers.

In March, 1996, a settlement was reached in a sexual-harassment suit against Louisiana-Pacific involving the company's former chairman, Harry Merlo. The current CEO, Mark A. Suwyn, reports that L-P has undergone fundamental changes since he took over in January, 1996.

Community Involvement: Louisiana-Pacific's charitable contributions totaled over $2.4 million in cash in 1996, and $500,000 in in-kind donations. Virtually all of the money given went towards education. The company is currently re-evaluating its charitable giving policies, hoping to increase the positive impact on the community. Possible additions include an employee matching gift program in 1998 and a volunteer program.

Workplace Information: OSHA records indicated that Louisiana-Pacific was inspected 31 times from 1994 to 1996. Violations included 22 classified as "willful" or "repeat" and 254 classified as "serious" for a total of $960,575 in fines (stemming largely from $840,000 in fines following a 1994 accident), an average of $30,986 per inspection. In comparison, the median amount of fines per inspection for other companies in the extractive business was $2,941.

L-P was removed from the AFL-CIO "Don't Buy" list in January 1997.

In early 1997, Louisiana-Pacific shut down its pulp mill at Ward Cove in Alaska. The plant perennially lost money and needed $200 million in renovations to meet environmental standards. Further, the company cited Clinton Administration resistance to the restoration of the company's original contract as making future profitability extremely unlikely. Five hundred workers lost their jobs; severance pay topped a year's wages for some workers who had been long employed at the mill.

Mallinckrodt Inc.

Stock Symbol: MKG
Stock Exchanges: NY, B, C, Ch, Ph, P

Environment	D
Women's Advancement	C
Minority Advancement	B
Charitable Giving	B
Community Outreach	B
Family Benefits	N
Workplace Issues	C?
Social Disclosure	B

Mallinckrodt Inc., formerly IMCERA Group Inc., has narrowed its focus to healthcare products in three areas: respiratory care, medical imaging, and pharmaceutical specialties. In fiscal year ending June 1997, the company had $1.86 billion in sales and 7,800 employees. Foreign sales accounted for roughly 40 percent of Mallinckrodt's total revenues for the past three years. The company is based in St. Louis, Missouri.

Environment: Mallinckrodt has an environmental policy but does not currently publish a corporate environmental report. The company has implemented an integrated environmental management system and provides environmental health and safety (EH&S) training to its entire staff. It also considers contribution towards EH&S goals in job performance reviews for its EH&S and facility staff. Mallinckrodt has a written prevention policy and has initiated a companywide pollution prevention program, but does not establish annual reduction goals. The company also has a corporate policy on community involvement relating to local environmental concerns, and has three community advisory panels. It has a written policy on product stewardship and a product stewardship review board. It does not utilize a set of criteria in selection of its suppliers. Internationally, the company does not monitor SARA Title III or equivalent emissions, and states that it follows U.S. regulations in the U.S. and local regulations abroad.

Mallinkrodt emitted the highest quantity of toxic releases and transfers in both 1993 and 1994 compared to its industry sample. However, averaged from 1993 to 1996, emissions decreased by a small fraction, while the majority of other companies in the sample experienced increases.

EEO: In 1996, Mallinckrodt Group's 12-member board of directors included two women and two minorities. Of 21 corporate officers at the company, one was a woman and two were minorities. One woman and one minority also ranked among the 25 highest paid employees at the company.

Community Involvement: In 1996, Mallinckrodt Group's charitable giving totaled over $1.7 million in cash, equal to 0.58 percent of the company's pretax earnings. In terms of the actual dollar amount donated by the company, the level of cash contributions in 1996 represented a decrease of 12 percent from that of 1995, which was 0.67 percent of the company's earnings for that year.

Although the written giving philosophy provides guidelines for all corporate charitable contributions, the philanthropy of each plant is individualized. Generally, Mallinckrodt seeks to better the health of "at-risk" populations; some methods to meet this goal include funding initiatives that provide access to health care to uninsured and impoverished people and/or allocating resources to preventative health programs.

Workplace Information: OSHA records indicate that Mallinckrodt was inspected once from 1994 to 1996, and was cited for one "serious" violation for a total of $975 in fines. In comparison, the median amount of fines per inspection for other drugs, cosmetics, and medical supplies companies was $2266.

As of January, 1998, Mallinckrodt remained a defendant in a lawsuit brought by former IBM employees who were exposed to chemicals that J.T. Baker Chemical Co. (acquired by Mallinckrodt in 1995) and other companies supplied and installed in two IBM plants. The chemicals were alleged to have caused cancer and other sicknesses among the workers. The plaintiffs allege that Mallinckrodt and the other defendants of the suit were negligent in testing the potential health hazards of the chemicals and did not warn the employees of the dangers of exposure to the chemicals. The defendants, which include Union Carbide, Eastman Kodak, DuPont, and IBM, deny the charges and plan a vigorous defense.

Additional Information: Mallinckrodt's board has a Social Responsibility Committee which reviews company policies and procedures regarding environment protection, equal employment opportunities, community relations, occupational safety and health, regulatory compliance and product quality and safety.

Marriott International, Inc.

STOCK SYMBOL: MAR
STOCK EXCHANGE: NY

Environment	N
Women's Advancement	B
Minority Advancement	A
Charitable Giving	N
Community Outreach	C
Family Benefits	B
Workplace Issues	F
Social Disclosure	B

Marriott International, Inc., the world's leading hospitality company, became a public company in 1993, following the division of the former Marriott Corporation. It operates or franchises more than 850 hotels in 50 states and 25 countries. The Bethesda, Maryland–based company is also a major provider of food and services management to hospitals, businesses, and schools throughout the U.S. Sales in 1996 reached nearly $10.2 billion and there were 192,000 employees.

EEO: In 1996, one woman and one minority served on Marriott International's 8-member board. Of 39 corporate officers at the company, five were women and three were minorities.

Marriott has been graded by the NAACP for its hiring and promoting practices for African-Americans within the hotel industry. The company received a 'C', the highest grade given. Marriott supports the Hispanic Development Institute, an industry program which promotes awareness of hospitality careers within the Hispanic community and prepares Hispanics for managerial jobs in the industry. In 1996, Marriott was recognized by the National Organization on Disability as a business leader in support of the full participation of people with disabilities in employment and in all aspects of life. Marriott was recognized by Black Convention Magazine and the Black Convention Forum for its contribution to multicultural achievements in the hospitality industry.

Community Involvement: Marriott's support of education concentrates on higher education. Marriott states that it has a particular interest in supporting programs and organizations dedicated to promoting the participation of disabled and disadvantaged people in society and relieving hunger.

Family Benefits: Thousands of employees participate in Marriott's numerous flexible scheduling arrangements, such as job-sharing, flextime, work-at-home, compressed or reduced work weeks, and part-time return to work after parental leave. The company also provides a regularly updated directory of child care centers that are part of Marriott's Discount Program. These give a 10 percent tuition discount or waive enrollment fees. Other family-friendly benefits include an on-site child care center at headquarters, after-school and vacation programs, backup child care, resource/referral, pretax set-asides for child care, and a nursing mothers' room. In partnership with two other hotel companies, Marriott, in 1997, opened Atlanta's Inn for Children, a 24-hour subsidized child-care center. The company has a full-time work/family coordinator. In 1996, *BusinessWeek* named Marriott one of the top ten companies for work and family practices.

Workplace Information: OSHA records indicate that Marriott was inspected 49 times from 1994 to 1996. Violations included three classified as "willful" or "repeat" and 89 classified as "serious" for a total of $270,706 in fines, an average of $5,524 per inspection. In comparison, the median amount of fines per inspection for other companies in the service industry, such as banks and communications companies, was $573.

About 600 people have moved through Marriott's welfare-to-work program, which began in 1991 and by January 1997 had expanded to 15 cities. The government funds roughly half of the $5,000 cost of the program, and Marriott has saved money by retaining workers longer and increasing their productivity. The company has vigorously resisted unionization, offering benefits, programs, and training — but low wages ($7.40 an hour) — to roughly 134,000 hourly workers. Though criticized by unions and others, the hotel chain provides valuable models for assimilating a diverse group of employees who often pose major problems: foreign-born non-English-speakers, recently homeless, and many with serious personal/family difficulties.

International: The company is adding international hotels through management contracts and franchises. Over the next five years, more than 50 percent of its new, full-service rooms will be outside the U.S.

Mattel Inc.

STOCK SYMBOL: MAT
STOCK EXCHANGES: NY, B, CH, PH, P

Environment	B
Women's Advancement	B
Minority Advancement	N
Charitable Giving	C
Community Outreach	A
Family Benefits	A
Workplace Issues	D
Social Disclosure	C

Mattel became the world's largest toy company with its 1993 acquisition of Fisher-Price. The company's primary line is the Barbie doll (market research indicates that 95 percent of girls 3–11 years old own at least one Barbie). Other well-known toys include Hot Wheels cars and See 'N Say talking toys. Mattel, based in El Segundo, California, had sales of $3.78 billion in 1996 and employed 26,000 people.

Environment: Mattel's true environmental impact is difficult to assess because most of its operations are based overseas. The company states that it requires adherence to EPA standards "to the extent possible" when local guidelines are less stringent, though the effectiveness of its policy cannot be determined. Mattel's three U.S. plants reported no releases of toxic chemicals to the EPA. A significant portion of its packaging is made of recycled materials and the company has reduced its use of heavy metals. Mattel has joined the EPA's Green Lights program promoting energy efficient lighting systems and introduced various waste reduction initiatives.

EEO: In 1996, Mattel Inc.'s 13-member board of directors included one woman. Of 14 corporate officers at the company, three were women.

In 1997, the Interfaith Center on Corporate Responsibility sponsored a shareholder resolution proposing that Mattel make greater efforts to diversify its board of directors.

Community Involvement: In 1996, Mattel Inc.'s charitable giving totaled $4.3 million in cash, which was equal to 0.79 percent of the company's pretax earnings. The level of cash contributions in 1996 was identical to that of 1995.

Mattel operates five family learning centers and committed $250,000 in 1995 to the Children's' Wing at Puente Medical Center in Los Angeles, California.

The Mattel Volunteer Program involves over 45 percent of its employees in programs affecting children with AIDS, disadvantaged youth, homelessness, education, health issues for children, and arts and culture for children.

Workplace Information: OSHA records indicate that Mattel Inc. was inspected six times from 1994 to 1996. Violations included 26 classified as "serious" for a total of $12,161 in fines, an average of $2,080 per inspection. In comparison, the median amount of fines per inspection for other companies in similar manufacturing industries was $2,412.

Animal Testing: Mattel ceased its limited product safety testing involving animals in1989.

International: Virtually all of Mattel's manufacturing is done overseas at company-owned factories in China, Malaysia, Indonesia, and Mexico, and by independent contractors located throughout the Far East. There is growing concern regarding the working conditions for employees in many of these countries. The clearest example of worker neglect occurred on May 10, 1993, when a fire at Kader Enterprises' toy factory near Bangkok killed 188 people and injured 500. According to witnesses, fire escapes were locked. The building's fire alarm and sprinkler system were also grossly inadequate. Fisher-Price was among the firm's having merchandising arrangements with Kader.

In 1980, the Pacific Studies Center described Mattel's overseas dollmaking operations as the "archetype of a runaway industry. Assembly operations are expanded or reduced, or even closed, to minimize labor costs. Workers are reluctant to press demands for better pay and conditions, for fear that they would be laid off as production moved elsewhere." In 1988, for example, Mattel ceased its production in the Philippines following strikes by workers there. Two thousand employees were dismissed.

Along with other toy companies that manufacture in China, Mattel is the target of a boycott brought by a group called Supporting Democracy in China. The "toycott" protests human rights abuses by the Chinese government.

May Department Stores

STOCK SYMBOL: MAY
STOCK EXCHANGES: NY, B, C, CH, P, PH

Environment	N
Women's Advancement	D
Minority Advancement	C
Charitable Giving	A?
Community Outreach	N
Family Benefits	N
Workplace Issues	B?
Social Disclosure	C

May Department Stores is one of the nation's leading department store companies, operating 346 stores through eight divisions, some of which are quite well known: Lord & Taylor, Hecht's, Foley's, Robinsons-May, Kaufmann's, Filene's, Famous-Barr, and Meier & Frank. The company also operated 4,549 Payless ShoeSource stores, with 24,000 employees, until January 17, 1996, when it announced it would spin off this operation to shareowners. In 1996, the St. Louis, Missouri–based company had revenues of 12 billion, and 130,000 employees.

Environment: May has a fairly neutral environmental record. It has adopted the standard programs for a retail company (e.g., energy-efficient lighting, and recycling of paper, cardboard, and toner cartridges), and has had no regulatory violations.

EEO: In 1996, May Department Stores Company's board totaled 14 directors, including one woman and one minority, while four of a total of 40 corporate officers were women, and one was a minority. Also in 1996, May purchased over $29.8 million in goods and services from women- and minority-owned businesses. May operates recruitment programs and maintains diversity goals for minorities.

May Department Stores participates in INROADS; in 1996, 45 students interned at May Department Stores through the program. More than half of the senior merchandising executives and department store managers throughout the company are women. The company publishes its EEO-1 information in a publicly available document.

Community Involvement: In 1994, May made cash contributions totaling $13.8 million, or 1.1 percent of its average pre-tax earnings for the same year.

Family Benefits: The company reported that "since a large number of May's employees are part-time, the company has not worked to develop the kind of family-oriented benefits designed to attract and retain a dedicated full-time workforce." Little is offered outside of standard maternity leave.

Workplace Information: According to the Occupational Safety and Health Administration's records, May Department Stores Company was inspected ten times from 1994 to 1996. The OSHA inspectors' citations included ten violations classified as "serious."

A total of $3,301 in fines was assessed to the company following the inspections, an average of $330 per inspection.

UNITE and May Department Stores engaged in a conflict over resolutions UNITE wanted to be included in May's 1997 proxy statement. UNITE was in favor of a resolution against the company's "poison pill" anti-takeover policies, which the company describes as a "shareowner rights plan," and a resolution requiring May to monitor conditions at its subcontractors' facilities and to have the company's "Vendor Standards of Conduct" distributed to all its vendor employees. After UNITE distributed copies of a proxy containing the resolution to some shareholders, May sent a letter to shareholders stating that "UNITE's interests are not the same as yours," and that it is interested primarily in increasing union membership and garnering publicity.

International: May's sourcing guidelines for labor rights which reference prison/forced labor, health and safety, and child labor (it defines a child as however the country locally defines a child, whatever that age may be). All vendors are required to certify their compliance with the policies each time they accept a purchase order from May. The company has been the object of media and public attention for labor rights violation issues since UNITE released its report, Misery by Design, alleging that the company's subcontractor in Indonesia "not only pays its workers subminimum wages and robs them of retirement benefits, but also employs child workers under the legal minimum age of fifteen." Similar allegations were made about a facility in Honduras. The most recent allegations were from the National Labor Committee (NLC) in November 1997, accusing the company of doing business with a large contractor in Jakarta, Indonesia, who regularly violates both May's own code of conduct and local labor laws.

Maytag

STOCK SYMBOL: MYG
STOCK EXCHANGES: NY, B, CH, P

Environment	C
Women's Advancement	B?
Minority Advancement	D?
Charitable Giving	B
Community Outreach	N
Family Benefits	N
Workplace Issues	B?
Social Disclosure	B

Maytag, based in Newton, Iowa, is the fourth largest U.S. appliance manufacturer. The company employs 20,500 people, producing such brand names as Maytag, Hoover, Magic Chef, Jenn-Air, and Admiral. In 1995, Maytag divested certain European and Australian operations. 1996 sales from continuing operations were $3 billion.

Environment: Maytag has a formal environmental policy written in 1991, which covers compliance, energy and resources conservation, waste minimization, cooperation with government and public, and product stewardship. However, the company does not have an environmental progress report available to the public. The company's senior official with environmental responsibilities is the corporate vice-president of technology.

Maytag conducts environmental audits of its facilities. The company assesses supplier environmental performance in its supplier quality system survey. It has not joined EPA's 33/50 program, but participates in EPA's Green Lights program to retrofit 90 percent of its facilities, where economical, with energy-efficient lighting. Maytag has also joined EPA's WasteWi$e program to reduce solid waste, increase recycling, and promote purchase of products with recycled materials.

From 1990 to 1994, Maytag's spill record of 2,283 pounds of hazardous or oil-based material was significantly better than the industry average of over 16,000 pounds. Maytag has not been cited for any significant national environmental violation since 1990.

EEO: In 1996, Maytag Corp.'s board totaled 12 directors, including three women and no minorities. Out of a total of 22 corporate officers, none were women and one was a minority.

Community Involvement: Maytag Corp.'s charitable contributions totaled over $2.1 million in cash in 1996. The $2.1 million cash-giving figure represented 0.94 percent of the company's pretax earnings and a decrease of 11 percent from the company's cash contributions in 1995. Maytag experienced a sizable drop in earnings in 1995.

Maytag matches employee's gift to cultural organizations and higher education only, giving a total of $160,560 to those areas in 1995. The company has repeatedly awarded grants to Iowa College Foundation, the United Negro College Fund, and other selected national educational organizations. In 1994, the foundation awarded $200,000 to the University of Iowa Foundation for the Fellowship Fund for Writers' Workshop and for the Business Administration building campaign.

Workplace Information: OSHA records indicate that Maytag Corp. was inspected seven times from 1994 to 1996. Violations included nine classified as "serious" for a total of $9,750 in fines, an average of $1,391 per inspection. In comparison, the median amount of fines per inspection for other companies in similar manufacturing industries was $2,412.

Employees are covered by a defined benefits pension plan and may purchase company stock at a 10 percent discount through payroll deduction. Maytag was a pioneer in involving workers in decision-making and rewarding them for productivity-enhancing suggestions.

The company's workforce is 40 percent unionized and labor-management conflicts are uncommon. However, in August 1995, former employees of Dixie-Narco were awarded $16.5 million to settle claims that Maytag failed to adequately notify employees of its intention to close a West Virginia facility. In 1996, Maytag closed a cooking products plant in Indianapolis, transferring production to a plant in Cleveland, Tennessee. Some employees were offered transfers.

McCormick & Company, Inc.

STOCK SYMBOL: MCCRK
STOCK EXCHANGE: NNM

Environment	N
Women's Advancement	B
Minority Advancement	D
Charitable Giving	D
Community Outreach	B
Family Benefits	B
Workplace Issues	A
Social Disclosure	A

McCormick & Company, Inc. is the largest spice company in the world. It manufactures and sells spices, herbs, extracts, proprietary seasoning blends, sauces, and marinades. Headquartered in Sparks, Maryland, the company employed 7,600 people and had sales of $1.8 billion in 1997.

Environment: In January 1991, McCormick issued a statement that it does not irradiate any of its consumer products, has no plans to, and will not without full disclosure to the public. The company uses nonhazardous citrus-based cleaners and petroleum products for its maintenance parts.

McCormick has an environmental policy but does not publish an environmental progress report. It did not disclose to us any information about its environmental audit program, solid waste management measures, or environmental policy.

EEO: There is one woman on the 10-member board and two women among 18 corporate officers. Women constitute 26 percent of the company's managers. There is one minority on the board. Members of minority groups constitute 12 percent of the company's managers. McCormick has special purchasing programs for minority- and women-owned businesses and provides diversity awareness training.

Community Involvement: In 1995, McCormick donated $864,000 in cash gifts and $70,000 of in-kind giving (or 0.6 percent of its pretax income) to charitable organizations. Its giving priorities are social services, business education programs, professional and trade associations, and programs that promote economic development and free enterprise.

McCormick has an employee volunteer program, which includes loaned executives, work release for other employees, and grants to organizations at which employees volunteer. The company also recruits volunteers for school advisory boards and guest lecture programs.

McCormick supports Cultural Survival's marketing division in Indonesia, a project that discourages the expansion of farming operations into nearby standing forests by helping local cooperatives and farmers' organizations increase the yield and income from their land.

Family Benefits: Flexible work arrangements, including job-sharing, flextime, and work-at-home, are available at some company locations. Counseling and referral services for child care, elder care, and care of disabled dependents are also offered at some locations. Since 1954, McCormick has sponsored a scholarship program for the children of employees.

Workplace Information: For over 60 years, McCormick has operated a policy of "multiple management," promoting employee empowerment, participation at all levels, and sharing the company's success. Its extensive employee benefits package includes profit-sharing, stock ownership and purchase plans, tuition reimbursement, and employee assistance programs for all company employees.

Since 1993, McCormick has been cited for fourteen OSHA violations and paid penalties of approximately $8,000. The company's domestic labor force is not unionized, but an open-door policy exists to handle grievances.

The company was named one of the 100 best companies to work for in America by *Fortune*.

International: According to a company spokesperson, McCormick maintains worldwide occupational health and safety standards appropriate for each country, and minimum age standards for employees consistent with local practices. However, the company has not yet adopted international sourcing guidelines or a code of conduct for suppliers.

McDonald's

STOCK SYMBOL: MCD
STOCK EXCHANGES: NY, To, B, C, CH, PH, P

Environment	B
Women's Advancement	F
Minority Advancement	D?
Charitable Giving	N
Community Outreach	B
Family Benefits	N
Workplace Issues	C?
Social Disclosure	C

McDonald's is the world's largest food service retailer. The company, headquartered in Oak Brook, Illinois, restaurant managers, franchisees, and joint-venture partners operate over 18,000 restaurants in 89 countries. In 1996, sales reached $10.68 billion. There were approximately 237,000 employees worldwide.

Environment: Since 1990, in conjunction with the Environmental Defense Fund, McDonald's has worked to reduce solid waste generation, particularly with regard to packaging. It has switched from polystyrene foam to paper-based containers, which cut the volume of waste by as much as 80 percent. "McRecycle USA," purchasing recycled products, reached $328 million in 1995 for a cumulative total of $1.5 billion since the program began. In 1995, McDonald's was recognized by the EPA's WasteWi$e program. As a member of the EPA's Green Lights program, the company has ensured that all newly-built restaurants have energy-efficient lighting. Older restaurants will be converted to energy-saving lighting by 1998.

EEO: McDonald's turned in a below average performance in the area of diversity in 1996, compared to other S&P 500 companies. Among the companies surveyed by CEP, the average representation of women and minorities on S&P corporate boards was 10.8 percent and 7.5 percent, respectively. In comparison, McDonald's had one woman and one minority on its 19-member board.

McDonald's employs thousands of older workers in its nearly 12,000 U.S. restaurants. The company also actively recruits senior workers for management positions at the Chicago headquarters. McDonald's has trained approximately 7,000 people with disabilities to work in its restaurants, in conjunction with vocational rehabilitation services in several states. Twelve percent of McDonald's franchises are African-American-owned, according to *Black Enterprise* magazine. Workforce programs at McDonald's include Women's Career Development, Black Career Development, Hispanic Career Development, Managing Cultural Diversity, and Managing Diversity.

Community Involvement: Officials at McDonald's Corporation pledged in 1997 to increase their charitable spending from $12.4 million a year to an average of $20 million a year over the next five years. The McDonald's Corp. Charitable Foundation and the McDonald's Kids Charities generally support the activities of the Ronald McDonald House, which aids families of children with cancer. Ronald McDonald Children's Charities made a $5 million commitment in 1996 to Washington University in St. Louis and Children's Hospital in Philadelphia for medical research on neuroblastoma, a type of brain cancer. In 1996, McDonald's gave $7.5 million to Loyola University Medical Center. A Ronald McDonald Children's Hospital will be established in the medical center through a joint partnership.

In 1997, the fast-food chain paid $1 million to become the presenting sponsor of Nickelodeon's expanded Big Help program, which encourages kids age 6–14 to pledge volunteer activities. The company is putting together a national volunteer program and will begin donating to those organizations where employees volunteer.

Workplace Information: OSHA records indicate that McDonald's was inspected 85 times from 1994 to 1996. Violations included two classified as "willful" or "repeat" and 89 classified as "serious" for a total of $64,764 in fines, an average of $762 per inspection. In comparison, the median amount of fines per inspection for other companies in the food, beverage, and househod products industries was $1,515.

International: In 1995, international business represented 54 percent of consolidated operating income, compared with 37 percent in 1990. In 1995, alone, McDonald's introduced its restaurants to 11 new countries: Colombia, Estonia, Honduras, Jamaica, Jersey, Malta, Qatar, Romania, Slovakia, South Africa, and St. Maarten.

MCI Communications

STOCK SYMBOL: MCIC
STOCK EXCHANGE: NNM

Environment	N
Women's Advancement	B?
Minority Advancement	D?
Charitable Giving	D
Community Outreach	C
Family Benefits	N
Workplace Issues	N
Social Disclosure	D

The company, headquartered in Washington, D.C., is one of the largest long distance service providers in the U.S. and controls a good percent of the telecommunications market. MCI employs 55,000 persons and in 1996, the company's sales topped $18.5 billion.

Environment: MCI Communications did not respond to CEP's environmental questionnaire in 1997. The company does not have a written environmental policy, nor does it publish a corporate environmental report.

MCI Communications does not have any reported toxic emissions.

MCI allows new customers to donate five percent of their monthly phone bills to conservation groups (four percent for existing customers). In 1991, Environmental Action initiated a program to encourage the three major long distance carriers to bill customers using a two-way envelope that eliminates the need for a second envelope for replies. Earth Action estimates such envelopes could reduce paper use by 30 percent. While several utilities and mail order catalogue companies have adopted the practice, MCI stated that the system doesn't match its needs, noting, however, that its bills are printed on recycled paper. In a novel approach for high-volume users, MCI offers billing on CD-ROM — MCI's most active accounts can receive monthly bills of 10,000 pages or more.

EEO: In 1996, MCI Communications's 14-member board of directors included two women and one minority. Of 36 corporate officers at the company, five were women and none were minorities.

In 1997, the United States Trust Company sponsored a shareholder resolution proposing that MCI disclose equal opportunity information. With the permission of the SEC, the company planned to omit the resolution from the proxy.

Community Involvement: In 1996, MCI Communications's charitable giving totaled $5 million in cash, which was equal to 0.25 percent of the company's pretax earnings. In terms of the actual dollar amount donated by the company, the level of cash contributions in 1996 represented a decrease of 22 percent from that of 1995.

In 1997, MCI donated $2 million to Port Discovery, a children's museum in Baltimore. The foundation mainly contributes to organizations concerned with integrating information technology with educational tools and society, particularly in kindergarten through high school programs in financially disadvantaged communities. EducationMCI, MCI's commitment to education, pledged to provide recipients of the Milken Family Foundation National Educator Awards free Internet access for one year.

Since 1990, MCI has helped several schools set up evening homework and education assistance programs where students call in to discuss curricula items. MCI donates telephone lines and equipment and pays a small stipend to the teachers who answer the phones.

Workplace Information: According to the Occupational Safety and Health Administration's records, MCI Communications was not inspected from 1994 to 1996. Consequently no violations or fines were assessed to the company.

The Communications Workers of America describes MCI as intent on resisting efforts by workers to unionize at any of its facilities. The company maintains that a union isn't necessary because employees can take any grievances they might have to their supervisors, who will address them.

MCI offers a stock purchase plan that enables employees to buy shares in the company at a 15 percent discount.

Mead Corporation

STOCK SYMBOL: MEA

STOCK EXCHANGES: NY, B, C, CH, P, PH

Environment	C
Women's Advancement	A
Minority Advancement	C
Charitable Giving	B
Community Outreach	B
Family Benefits	C
Workplace Issues	B
Social Disclosure	B

One of the country's leaders in paper and packaging manufacturing, Mead is the nation's largest provider of school paper supplies and office stationery. In December 1994, one of Mead's largest divisions, electronic publisher (and Lexis/Nexis provider) Mead Data Central, was sold to Reed Elsevier for $1.5 billion. In 1997, Mead had revenues of $5.0 billion, and 16,600 employees.

Environment: Mead Corp. did not respond to CEP's environmental survey in 1997. The company publishes a corporate environmental report, which is available on the Internet, and has a written environmental policy. Mead Corp. has a written pollution prevention policy and a pollution prevention program, involving process recycling and materials substitution.

Mead Corp. was the second lightest emitter of toxic releases and transfers in 1993 and the third lightest in 1994, compared to a twelve company industry sample (in terms of emissions/$ sales). The company increased its emissions by 10 percent between the two years, the third best performance in the sample.

In February 1997, Mead's Rumford, Maine, mill announced a comprehensive environmental improvement program geared at eliminating the use of elemental chlorine, controlling odors, and adding natural gas to the mill's energy mix. The mill switched to an elemental chlorine free (ECF) process for pulp bleaching, planning to use chlorine dioxide instead. In addition, the mill outlined a $5 million capital project to remove and incinerate odorous compounds from the pulping process, a project that will allow the mill to recycle water generated from the steam-stripping process.

EEO: In 1996, Mead Corp.'s 12-member board of directors included one woman and one minority. Of 20 corporate officers at the company, five were women and one was a minority. Two women also ranked among the 25 highest paid employees at the company.

Community Involvement: The Mead Corporation Foundation primarily supports organizations at the community level. Unit managers at the company's locations review local applications for funding and are encouraged to adjust giving priorities to meet specific needs in the local community. The Taft Corporate Giving Directory of 1997 reports that the company "actively encourages employee volunteerism." In celebration of its 150th anniversary and Dayton, Ohio's 300th, Mead made a $150,000 contribution in 1996. An employee vote determined that $75,000 would go to the Dayton area's only shelter for runaway and homeless youth.

In 1996, Mead Corp.'s charitable giving totaled over $4 million in cash, equal to 1.38 percent of the company's pretax earnings for that year. The level of cash contributions in 1996 represented a decrease of 10 percent from that of 1995. The company's in-kind giving — the donation of products or services — came to a total of $376,000 in 1996.

Workplace Information: According to the Occupational Safety and Health Administration's records, Mead Corp. was inspected five times from 1994 to 1996. The OSHA inspectors' citations included one violation classified as "willful" or "repeat" and 20 violations classified as "serious." A total of $13,775 in fines was assessed to the company following the inspections, an average of $2,755 per inspection. In comparison, the median amount of fines per inspection for other companies in the extractive business was $2,941.

The company is a member of OSHA's Voluntary Protection Program and has developed its own Managing Employee Safety and Health program.

About 7,500 of Mead's workers are represented by unions; there have been no strikes at Mead facilities in recent years.

Medtronic, Inc.

STOCK SYMBOL: MDT
STOCK EXCHANGES: NY, B, CH, PH, P

Environment	C?
Women's Advancement	C
Minority Advancement	C
Charitable Giving	C
Community Outreach	B
Family Benefits	N
Workplace Issues	B?
Social Disclosure	C

Medtronic, based in Minneapolis, is a leading manufacturer of pacemakers, heart valves, angioplasty equipment, and other medical devices. Medtronic employs 13,700 people and does business in 80 countries. Sales in fiscal year 1997 were $2.43 billion.

Environment: Medtronic did not respond to CEP's environment questionnaire in 1997. Medtronic does not currently publish a corporate environmental report.

Medtronic's toxic releases and transfers were below the industry average for both 1993 and 1994 compared to its industry sample (in terms of emissions adjusted for the company's sales). The company decreased its emissions by 8 percent from 1993 to 1994, a better than average performance, and by over half from 1993 to 1995.

EEO: Medtronic Inc. turned in an average overall performance in workforce diversity for S&P 500 companies in 1996. The company's 14-member board included one woman and no minorities, as compared with the average of 10.8 percent women and 7.6 percent minorities for other S&P 500 companies. No women or minorities served among the company's three corporate officers. The company's 25 highest paid employees included two women and one minority.

Community Involvement: Medtronic Inc.'s charitable contributions totaled almost $5.2 million in cash in 1996, and about $1.4 million of in-kind donations. The $5.2 million cash-giving figure represented the equivalent of 0.78 percent of the company's pretax earnings, and an increase of 36.9 percent from the company's cash contributions in 1995, but a proportional decline from the 1.17 percent of its pretax earnings for 1995.

Over three years, Medtronic's STAR (Science and Technology Are Rewarding) program has donated over $2 million to schools located throughout the United States. In 1996, Medtronic made a four year commitment to financially support the renovation of Minneapolis school district science programs. A significant part of the Medtronic Foundation's contributions go to the economically disadvantaged, minorities, and the elderly. Medtronic also donates its products to the impoverished all over the world.

Workplace Information: According to the Occupational Safety and Health Administration's records, Medtronic Inc. was inspected four times from 1994 to 1996. The OSHA inspectors' citations included three violations classified as "serious." A total of $2,637 in fines was assessed to the company following the inspections, an average of $659 per inspection. In comparison, the median amount of fines per inspection for other companies in the drugs, cosmetics, and medical supplies industries was $2,266.

Animal Testing: Medtronic used 319 animals for testing purposes in 1993. This is a decline from 430 in 1988, despite a significant increase in research activity. The company reports that alternative methods such as cell culture testing and computer simulations increasingly substitute for animal testing in early stages of research.

Mellon Bank

STOCK SYMBOL: MEL
STOCK EXCHANGES: NY, B, CH, P

Environment	N
Women's Advancement	F?
Minority Advancement	D?
Charitable Giving	B
Community Outreach	B
Family Benefits	N
Workplace Issues	A?
Social Disclosure	B

Mellon Bank Corporation is a major financial services company headquartered in Pittsburgh, Pennsylvania. With balance sheet assets of approximately $43 billion, Mellon engages principally in two core businesses: Investment Services and Banking Services. While Mellon uses the brand name Mellon Bank for its banking activities in most markets, the brand name Mellon PSFS is used in Philadelphia, and Boston Safe Deposit and Trust Co. is used in Boston. Mellon uses Dreyfus and Mellon Trust as service marks for other investment products. In 1996, Mellon Bank's revenue was $4.76 billion and it employed 24,700 people.

EEO: Mellon Bank turned in a below average performance in the area of diversity in 1996, compared to other S&P 500 companies. Among the companies surveyed by CEP, the average representation of women and minorities on S&P corporate boards was 10.8 percent and 7.5 percent, respectively. In comparison, Mellon Bank had one woman and one minority on its 18-member board.

Mellon is a sponsor of the Black Expo, a two-day event in Monroeville, Pennsylvania that provides African-American awareness programs, conducts workshops and seminars and promotes business development and cultural diversity.

Community Involvement: In 1996, Mellon Bank's charitable giving totaled over $9.8 million in cash, which was equal to 0.86 percent of the company's pretax earnings for that year. In terms of the actual dollar amount donated by the company, the level of cash contributions in 1996 represented a decrease of 1.1 percent from that of 1995. The company's in-kind giving—the donation of products or services—came to a total of $10.6 million in 1996.

Mellon Bank's efforts for community outreach include support for affordable housing, job creation and workforce training, assistance to small business development, technical assistance and direct contributions, employees' community participation and leadership, and supporting art, promoting cultural diversity and addressing health and human service needs. Mellon's volunteer activities include food drives, walk-a-thons for charitable organizations, student tutoring programs and support for local arts and entertainment in western Pennsylvania. Mellon's philanthropic strategy focuses on economic development, offering grants through the Mellon Bank Community Fund. Through the Neighborhood Fund and Community Action programs, Mellon provides funds for community development, economic development and housing initiatives. The bank provides technical assistance in coordinating and preparing workshops and conferences for affordable housing. Mellon also sponsors public issues forums covering topics such as economic growth, poverty, women and juvenile violence. Mellon's Matching Gift Program matches employees' donations to educational and cultural organizations.

With its acquisition of Dreyfus, the company now has one of the most financially successful socially responsible mutual funds—Dreyfus's Third Century.

Workplace Information: According to the Occupational Safety and Health Administration's records, Mellon Bank was inspected once from 1994 to 1996. OSHA inspectors cited the company only for violations classified as "other," the least egregious type of violation. No fines were assessed to the company following the inspections. In comparison, the median amount of fines per inspection for other companies in the service industry, such as banks and communications companies, was $573.

⊙ Merck & Company, Inc.

STOCK SYMBOL: MRK
STOCK EXCHANGES: NY, B, C, CH, P, PH

Environment	B
Women's Advancement	A
Minority Advancement	A
Charitable Giving	A
Community Outreach	N
Family Benefits	A
Workplace Issues	B
Social Disclosure	A

Merck is the world's largest pharmaceutical company. The company, based in New Jersey, had sales of $19.8 billion and employed 49,100 people in 1996.

Environment: Merck & Company has an environmental policy and a corporate environmental report, which is updated biennially, follows the Public Environmental Reporting Initiative (PERI) guidelines, and is available on the Internet. The company has a written pollution prevention policy and has initiated a company-wide pollution prevention program, elements of which are source reduction, product redesign, treatment, process recycling, and reuse strategies. The company is active in community involvement relating to local environmental concerns, and currently has several community advisory panels. Merck has a written policy on product stewardship and evaluates its products with the goal of reducing their life-cycle impacts. Compared to other companies researched by CEP, Merck's toxic releases and transfers were below the industry average in both 1993 and 1994; emissions decreased by over a third during the same period. In 1997, Merck was named an Environmental Champion for the second time by the EPA for its leadership in voluntary initiatives, and is taking part in the EPA's Project XL program.

The Nuclear Regulatory Commission indicated that Merck faces up to $10,000 in fines for three June 1997 violations of radioactive material use rules. In September 1996, Merck has agreed to pay penalties of $1.8 million for air pollution from a San Diego kelp-processing plant, which the EPA has claimed was responsible for as much as 10 percent of San Diego's smog. The fine was the largest of its type in California history; Merck no longer owns the plant.

EEO: In 1996, two women and two minorities served on Merck's 13-member board. Of 17 corporate officers at the company, five were women and two were minorities. Five of the top 25 paid employees were women and one was a minority.

In 1995 a discrimination lawsuit was filed by three African-American employees in Tampa, Florida. Merck has created the African-American Coalition for Fairness and is a member of the Center for Women Policy Studies. In 1997, the Interfaith Center on Corporate Responsibility and Progressive Securities sponsored a shareholder resolution proposing that Merck disclose diversity data.

Community Involvement: In 1995, Merck's charitable contributions included cash donations totaling $21 million ($33 million in 1997), and a total of $100 million in in-kind giving. The company's cash contributions for 1995 were equivalent to 0.44 percent of its earnings before taxes. A 1997 *Corporate Giving Watch* report ranked Merck first in corporate giving.

Workplace Information: OSHA records indicate that Merck was inspected twice from 1994 to 1996. Violations included five classified as "serious" for a total of $8,650 in fines, an average of $4,325 per inspection

According to *Working Woman* magazine, Merck provides one of the ten healthiest workplaces for women. In 1995, Merck established an ethics office to investigate and resolve internal complaints, and operates a complaint hotline.

International: Merck has donated *Mectizan* to treat river blindness for ten years; in 1997, over 18 million people—mostly in Africa—received the medicine. In June of that year, Merck reaffirmed its commitment to donate the drug as long as necessary.

Merck has formed a ground-breaking partnership with a Costa Rican institution, the National Institute of Biodiversity (INBio). INBio supplies Merck with plant and insect samples that may become the basis for new medicines; in return, Merck funds conservation efforts to preserve the rain forest, and provides financial support for INBio's work. The agreement represents the first time provisions have been made for a developing country to receive royalties from drugs developed from its natural resources. In recognition of its international efforts, Merck was awarded with CEP's 1995 Corporate Conscience Award in Global Ethics.

Micron Technology

STOCK SYMBOL: MU

STOCK EXCHANGES: NY, CH, PH, P

Environment	N
Women's Advancement	B?
Minority Advancement	D?
Charitable Giving	N
Community Outreach	A
Family Benefits	N
Workplace Issues	D?
Social Disclosure	C

Micron Technology is a leading producer of semiconductors and in 1994 acquired computer maker ZEOS. Its sales have increased almost 10-fold since 1990, reaching nearly $3.5 billion in fiscal year ending in August 1997. With over 12,000 employees, the Boise-based company is Idaho's largest private sector employer.

Environment: Micron Technology does not currently publish a corporate environmental report.

Micron Technology's average toxic releases and transfers during the years 1993–1994 were just less than the industry sample average. However, its emissions decreased by more than a half during those years, one of the best performances within the industry sample.

In September 1997, the Environmental Protection Agency awarded Micron its Evergreen Award for Pollution Prevention for a series of pollution-control efforts undertaken over the past 10 years. The award is the highest pollution-control recognition a private company can receive from the EPA, and is the only Idaho -based company to have received it. (Micron has invested millions of dollars in pollution prevention in the past decade while at the same time realized an 80 percent annual increase in production of computer memory chips.) The company's efforts include eliminating the use of ozone-depleting chlorofluorocarbons, replacing its chemical-based process for cleaning silicon wafers with a more effective water-based process, investing more than $21 million in water reclamation and water-treatment projects; and installing the best available technology to reduce air emissions.

EEO: In 1996, Micron Technology's 7-member board of directors included no women or minorities. Of 15 corporate officers at the company, two were women and none were minorities.

The company offers English as a Second Language courses and incorporates diversity awareness into training.

Community Outreach: Since its founding in 1978, Micron has contributed over $7.8 million to educational programs in Idaho, including the Simplot/Micron Technology Center and the Micron Electronic Classroom at Boise State University. Micron established an employee matching gifts program in 1995 for both cash and equipment donations. Micron employees participate in various volunteer efforts; volunteer opportunities are posted on the company's electronic bulletin board.

Workplace Information: According to the Occupational Safety and Health Administration's records, Micron Technology was inspected five times from 1994 to 1996. The OSHA inspectors' citations included one violation classified as "willful" or "repeat" and 20 violations classified as "serious." A total of $7,475 in fines was assessed to the company, an average of $1,495 per inspection. In comparison, the median amount of fines per inspection for other companies in the industries manufacturing electronic equipment was $1,347.

Micron formerly offered a three month paid sabbatical for employees with seven years tenure. The company abandoned the policy in 1992 due to lack of usage. Most employees would simply cash out their vacation time. In an effort to help meet production demands, Micron offers additional compensation either in pay or alternate time off to employees that work holidays.

Weapons Contracts: In 1994, Micron received Department of Defense contracts worth $4.7 million. These contracts amount to less than 0.3 percent of total revenues for the year and did not involve weapons systems.

163

Minnesota Mining and Mfg. (3M)

STOCK SYMBOL: MMM
STOCK EXCHANGES: NY, B, C, CH, P, PH

3M, headquartered in Minneapolis, is a worldwide manufacturer of specialty chemicals, medical products, imaging, telecommunications, electrical equipment, and office supplies. In 1996, the company had revenues of $14.2 billion and employed 74,000 workers.

Environment	A
Women's Advancement	C
Minority Advancement	C
Charitable Giving	A
Community Outreach	C
Family Benefits	C
Workplace Issues	C
Social Disclosure	A

Environment: 3M received one of CEP's earliest Corporate Conscience Awards in 1988 for its Pollution Prevention Pays (3P) program. By the end of 1992, the 3P program had saved the company more than $570 million and cut 1.2 billion pounds of pollutants. The company aims to reduce total emissions by 90 percent by the year 2000, and monitors volatile organic compound emissions worldwide. 3M states that it maintains global environmental standards that meet or exceed U.S. regulations, and has a strong international environmental, health and safety policy. The company has joined EPA's Green Lights Program.

3M's spill record for 1990 through 1994 was below average, but hazardous waste generation was high. The company reports that it had no spills from 1994 to 1997.

EEO: In 1996, 3M's 12-member board included two women and two minorities. Two women (three in 1997) served among the company's 25 corporate officers, and the company's 25 highest paid employees included two women (three in 1997).

3M was one of 83 companies cited in the Glass Ceiling Commission's March 1995 report for implementing "employment practices that help break the glass ceiling," citing 3M's Women's Advisory Committee. The Committee focuses attention on promoting women's career and leadership development through identification of issues, communication of women's concerns, and recommendations for action. The Committee has contributed to the implementation of programs including supervisory and management development programs, internal programs on diversity, and an improved performance appraisal system.

Community Involvement: In 1996, 3M gave $7.5 million in cash grants ($8.2 million in 1997) to educational institutions that emphasized equal access to educational opportunities for minorities and women, particularly in technical and science education. Through a $2.18 million grant, 3M supported *Newton's Apple*, which is one of the longest running science shows on public television. The company also committed a $2.6 million gift to the Nature Conservancy's "Last Great Places." The Community Action Retired Employees Services program (CARES) helps over 800 retired employees annually find organizations at which to volunteer. The 3M Volunteer Program steers most of its participants into educational activities.

Workplace Information: OSHA records indicate that 3M was inspected five times from 1994 to 1996. Violations included five classified as "serious" for a total of $10,555 in fines, an average of $2,111 per inspection. In comparison, the median amount of fines per inspection for other companies in similar manufacturing industries was $2,412.

3M conducted a restructuring over 1995 and 1996 after an announcement in November 1995 that the company wanted to reduce its workforce by 6 percent, or 5,000 employees. The company reached that goal through regular retirements, early retirements, and separation plans which were all voluntary. Early retirements were offered to employees over 50, and voluntary separation agreements offered 1.5 weeks of pay for each year of service. The company also established an "unassigned pool" through which employees who lose their jobs can take up to six months to find work. The workforce reduction was partly in preparation for the spin-off of 3M's data storage, imaging, and publishing sectors as the Imation company in mid-1996.

Weapons Contracts: In 1997, 3M had $2 million in contracts with the Department of Defense; none of the contracts were for weapons-related or nuclear-related systems.

Animal Testing: 3M uses animals for testing product safety. It is a corporate sponsor of the Johns Hopkins Center for Alternatives to Animal Testing.

Product Issues: 3M has been named as a defendant in numerous cases citing allegedly defective breast implants.

Mobil Corporation

STOCK SYMBOL: MOB
STOCK EXCHANGES: NY, TO, B, C, CH, PH, P

Environment	B
Women's Advancement	B
Minority Advancement	B
Charitable Giving	C
Community Outreach	B
Family Benefits	C
Workplace Issues	D
Social Disclosure	A

Mobil, headquartered in Fairfax, Virginia, is the nation's second largest petroleum company and the sixth largest industrial company. In 1996, Mobil had 43,000 employees and $81.5 billion in sales.

Environment: Mobil Corporation has an environmental policy and publishes a corporate environmental report, updated annually and available on the Internet. Mobil has implemented an integrated environmental management system. Mobil has a written pollution prevention policy, and a company-wide pollution prevention program. The company also has community advisory panels at many of its facilities.

Mobil has a written policy on product stewardship and evaluates some of its products with the objective of reducing their life-cycle impacts on the environment. The company participated in EPA's 33/50, Energy Star, WasteWi$e, and Green Lights programs. Mobil is the 1998 Energy Star Buildings Partner of the Year.

Mobil Corporation's average toxic releases and transfers during the years 1994–1995 were less than the industry sample average. However, its emissions increased slightly during those years, indicating a below average performance. Mobil ranked 8th out of 15 for CEP's Campaign for Cleaner Corporations' (C-3) 1997 Petroleum Refining Report.

In February, 1997, a Texas Court of Appeals upheld a trial court's damage award in a wrongful death action brought against Mobil by the estate of a former contract worker. Mobil had been found grossly negligent in allowing the worker to be exposed to benzene, from which he developed terminal leukemia. The Texas Supreme Court recently agreed to decide Mobil's challenge to the verdict. In 1997 Mobil was ordered to pay Santa Monica $104,000 for the costs of replacing part of the city's ground water supply after leaky underground tanks allegedly tainted the drinking water.

In a *New York Times* advertisement, Mobil criticized EPA proposals to toughen the standards for smog and fine particles, claiming they were based on "shaky science."

EEO: In 1996, Mobil's 15-member board of directors included two women and one minority. Of 23 corporate officers at the company, two were women and one was a minority. Two women also ranked among the 25 highest paid employees at the company. Mobil ranked near the top of *The Oil Daily*'s December, 1996 survey, which ranked the nation's major oil companies on employment of minorities. Charles Walker, Executive Director of the National Society of Blacks in Engineering, has stated that Mobil is one of the industry leaders in minority recruitment.

Community Involvement: Mobil's charitable contributions totaled $28 million in cash in 1996, and in in-kind donations. The $28 million cash-giving figure represented the equivalent of 0.46 percent of the company's pretax earnings for 1996; in 1995, the company contributed 0.64 percent

For the past 16 years, Mobil has supported its Green Team Program, which provides local youth work initiatives during the summer months. Mobil's philanthropic interest in the arts includes multi-million dollar support of PBS's *Masterpiece Theater*. In 1995 the company donated the site of the only stable population of the endangered Attwater prairie chicken in Texas (over 2,000 acres) to the Nature Conservancy, along with mineral rights and $100,000 to help the Conservancy manage the reserve. Only 140 birds were still living at the time.

Workplace Information: Mobil reports that its "Joliet, Illinois, refinery won the OSHA 1996 'Impact Award' for its work in training OSHA compliance officers. Mobil is the only outside organization to receive this award."

The company did not disclose the amount it pays for employee medical coverage.

Monsanto

Environment	C
Women's Advancement	A
Minority Advancement	B
Charitable Giving	A
Community Outreach	C?
Family Benefits	N
Workplace Issues	B?
Social Disclosure	A

St. Louis–based Monsanto, America's fourth largest chemical company, has four major units, including an agricultural group, a chemical group, Searle pharmaceutical, and Nutrasweet. In September 1997, Monsanto spun off its chemical business (now Solutia Inc.) in order to focus on its agriculture, food and pharmaceuticals units. In 1996, Monsanto employed 28,000 people and had revenues of $9.3 billion.

Environment: CEO Robert Shapiro has been credited with transforming the company's mission by incorporating environmental and sustainability factors into overall business strategy. The company began selling genetically altered soybeans, potatoes and cotton in 1996. (Monsanto's first biotech product, Posilac, a hormone that increases cows' milk production, received relatively high public opposition.) One goal of genetic engineering is to render crops pest- and disease-resistant so farmers can eventually eliminate chemical spraying.

Greenpeace International led a multi-stakeholder group petitioning the EPA to reverse its approval of Bacillus Thuringiensis (BT) genetically engineered plants. Biotechnology critics warn of dangers such as pests developing resistance to BT, and argue that biotech products are being introduced into the environment too quickly without a full understanding of their impact.

Monsanto has an environmental policy and an annual corporate environmental report that is kept more current on the Internet. Adjusted for worldwide company sales, Monsanto's average total toxic releases and transfers from 1994 to 1996 were higher than the industry sample average. Emissions decreased slightly on average annually during those years, a below average performance.

Monsanto received EPA's 1996 Presidential Green Chemistry Challenge Award and was recognized as a 1997 Environmental Champion for an innovative "zero-waste'" chemical process to make di-sodium iminodiacetate, a key intermediate in the production of Monsanto's Roundup herbicide.

EEO: In 1996, two women and two minorities served on Monsanto's 13-member board. Of 27 corporate officers, four were women. Five of the top 25 paid employees were women, and one was a minority. In 1996, Monsanto settled a discrimination suit for $18.3 million, maintaining that it did not discriminate. The suit, joined by the EEOC, was brought by 43 employees at Ortho Consumer Products who were laid off following Monsanto's acquisition of Ortho from Chevron.

Community Involvement: Monsanto's charitable contributions totaled $13.4 million in cash in 1996, or 2.48 percent of its pretax earnings. Employees have worked to restore 1,000 acres of wetlands, and reintroduced grass and trees to mined land. Monsanto also provided $250,000 to help rebuild predominantly black churches that had been destroyed by arson in 1996.

Workplace Information: OSHA records indicate that Monsanto was inspected nine times from 1994 to 1996. Violations included 23 classified as "serious" for an average of $2,222 per inspection. The median amount of fines per inspection for other drugs, cosmetics, and medical supplies companies was $2,266.

An unusual incentive plan requires senior managers to buy a large number of shares ($6 million for Shapiro) with an interest-bearing loan from the company. If Monsanto is among the top 25 percent of S&P index over the next five years, the loans will be forgiven.

In June 1997, Western Growers Association filed unfair labor practice charges against Monsanto, Coastal Berry Corp, and the United Farm Workers. The Association claims that an agreement to conduct elections for the UFW between the union and Monsanto at its former Gargiulo subsidiary is illegal, and will intimidate strawberry workers into forming a union. Several California democratic lawmakers urged that the charges be dismissed, saying the agreement was a peaceful effort to allow workers to unionize.

Animal Testing: Monsanto conducts product-safety tests on animals; its Animal Use and Care Committee uses nonanimal computer tests when the company deems it possible.

Moore Corporation

STOCK SYMBOL: MCL
STOCK EXCHANGES: NY, TO, B, CH, MO, P

Environment	C
Women's Advancement	A
Minority Advancement	F
Charitable Giving	N
Community Outreach	N
Family Benefits	N
Workplace Issues	N
Social Disclosure	A

Moore Corporation Ltd., a multinational company based in Canada, provides business forms, labels, equipment, computer and office supplies, and information management services. The company operates in 53 countries with 155 manufacturing facilities (63 in the United States), and employs over 18,800 people worldwide. In 1996, Moore attained sales of $2.51 billion.

Environment: Moore Corp. has an environmental policy, but does not publicly publish a corporate environmental report. An environmental report is published internally every quarter to the Environmental Health and Safety (EH&S) committee made up of members of the board of directors. Moore has not implemented an integrated environmental management system, but does provide EH&S training to all employees. It also considers contribution towards EH&S goals in the job performance reviews of EH&S staff, facility staff, and senior staff.

Moore has a written pollution prevention policy and has initiated a company-wide pollution prevention program, which establishes annual reduction goals for point sources, fugitive emissions, and solid waste. The company also has a corporate policy on community involvement relating to local environmental concerns and has a community advisory panel at one facility. The company has an environmental audit program, which has worldwide standards and applicability. In 1996, 100 percent of U.S. facilities and 100 percent of international facilities were audited. Internationally, Moore monitors SARA Title III or equivalent emissions and states that it follows U.S. regulations in the U.S. and abroad unless local regulations are stricter.

Moore Corporation's average toxic releases and transfers during the years 1993–1994 were the highest compared to an industry sample. However, its emissions decreased by more than two-thirds during those years, an above average performance.

EEO: In 1996, Moore Corporation Ltd.'s 10-member board of directors included two women and no minorities.

Moore has a written policy banning discrimination based on sexual orientation. The company also has an affirmative action program to encourage the promotion of qualified women and minorities to upper management.

Community Involvement: The Moore Corporation reports that it is currently redefining its corporate contribution policies and procedures.

Family Benefits: Moore offers paid maternity disability leave for the length of time specified by a doctor, and also paternity leave. Additional unpaid leave may be taken for a maximum of six months. The company has child care and elder care resource and referral services.

Workplace Information: The records of the Occupational Safety and Health Administration indicate that Moore Corporation Ltd. was not inspected from 1994 to 1996. Consequently no fines or violations were assessed to the company.

Moore states, "the health and safety of every person is more important than any job objective." In 1994, Moore appointed a Corporate Health and Safety Manager to insure implementation of health and safety programs companywide. In addition, Moore produces a work safety newsletter and has introduced worker training programs concerning safety awareness, toxic substances handling, and back injury prevention.

Less than five percent of Moore's employees are unionized. In 1994, a restructuring program led to the reduction in the workforce by 2,642 persons.

Morton International

STOCK SYMBOL: MII
STOCK EXCHANGE: NY

Environment	C
Women's Advancement	C?
Minority Advancement	D?
Charitable Giving	F
Community Outreach	D?
Family Benefits	N
Workplace Issues	D?
Social Disclosure	D

Founded in 1848 as a distributor of salt products, Morton, headquartered in Chicago, Illinois, now derives approximately 50 percent of its revenues from specialty chemicals. Its Automotive Safety Products unit, developed under its Thiokol division (sold in 1989), is the world's leading producer of air bags. Morton's revenues in 1996 reached $3.6 billion, and the company had 14,100 employees.

Environment: Morton International has a corporate environmental report, which is available on the internet. The company has implemented an integrated environmental management system and considers contribution towards EH&S goals in the job performance reviews of executives and managers. Morton International has a written pollution prevention policy, a corporate policy on community involvement relating to local environmental concerns, and a written policy on product stewardship.

In the selection of suppliers, Morton International conducts or reviews environmental audits on suppliers' facilities. The company has an environmental audit program, through which 100 percent of U.S. facilities and 24 percent of international facilities were audited in 1996. Internationally, Morton International states that it monitors SARA Title III, or equivalent emissions and states that it follows U.S. regulations in the U.S. and abroad unless local regulations are stricter.

Morton International's average total toxic releases and transfers during the years 1993–1994 were less than the industry sample average. Emissions decreased by about a third during those years, a better than average performance.

EEO: In 1996, Morton International's 12-member board of directors included no women or minorities. Of 18 corporate officers at the company, two were women.

Community Involvement: In 1996, Morton International's charitable giving totaled $1.5 million in cash, which was equal to 0.3 percent of the company's pretax earnings for that year. In terms of the actual dollar amount donated by the company, the level of cash contributions in 1996 was identical to that of 1995.

Three to four company-sponsored volunteer projects are planned annually, including food and clothing drives, a Serve-a-thon program, and participation in Chicago Cares. Much of the company's arts funding comes through employee matching gifts.

Workplace Information: According to OSHA records, Morton International was inspected five times from 1994 to 1996. The OSHA inspectors' citations included 18 violations classified as "serious" for a total of $59,725 in fines, an average of $11,945 per inspection. In comparison, the median amount of fines per inspection for other companies in the extractive business was $2,941.

In May 1995, the Los Angeles District Attorney charged Morton, along with a plant manager and a foreman at the company's Long Beach salt processing plant, with involuntary manslaughter in connection with the death of a worker in 1994. The defendants were also charged with one count of violating the Corporate Criminal Liability Act for not informing plant employees of the danger inherent in cleaning a salt bin, and not training them in proper safety measures.

Weapons Contracts: In 1994, Morton had contracts totaling $142,000 with the Department of Defense (less than 0.1 percent of sales). These contracts were for products and services that are not considered weapons related.

Product Issues: Morton has received quality awards from each of the Big Three auto companies, and in 1993 was the only non-Japanese company to receive Honda's performance excellence award.

Motorola, Inc.

STOCK SYMBOL: MOT
STOCK EXCHANGES: NY, B, CH, P, PH

Environment	C
Women's Advancement	B
Minority Advancement	C?
Charitable Giving	F
Community Outreach	C
Family Benefits	A
Workplace Issues	D
Social Disclosure	C

Motorola, headquartered in Schaumburg, Illinois, is among the top makers of cellular phones, two-way radios, semiconductors, pagers, and navigational equipment. The company has a $1.7 billion stake in Nextel Communications. In 1996, it had $27.9 billion in revenues and 139,000 employees.

Environment: Motorola has no environmental materials available to the public. Motorola's average toxic releases and transfers during the years 1993–1994 were less than the industry sample average. Furthermore, its emissions decreased by about a half during those years, one of the best performances within the industry sample.

The company now faces some of the biggest environmental suits in history. One class action suit in Maricopa County Superior Court seeks medical monitoring for 700,000 current and former residents, as well as property damage for 54,000 homeowners. A separate suit in Federal Court in Phoenix seeks similar damages for 1,000 residents, as well as compensation for a variety of cancers and neurological illnesses. Motorola has spent tens of millions of dollars in legal fees.

EEO: In 1996, Motorola Inc.'s board totaled 17 directors, including two women and one minority. Of 59 total corporate officers, none were minorities or women.

Under a plan called the "Parity Initiative," Motorola has increased the number of women and minority vice presidents from two to 68 between 1989 and 1995. The company's CEO has set the goal of achieving a level of representation of women and minorities which reflects the availability of qualified women and minorities in the general population. Motorola was the 1993 winner of the Catalyst award, which recognizes companies for their efforts to promote women within the corporate structure.

Motorola is recognized by the Chicago Area Partnerships as being one of the eight companies with the "best practices" or effective company programs designed to eliminate the "glass ceiling."

Community Involvement: Motorola's Texas operations have conducted a volunteer program since 1994 in which approximately 10 percent of employees are involved. The company has donated radio equipment, systems, service, and support to the World Wildlife

Fund to enhance the group's conservation efforts. Motorola is conducting tests on equipment and systems in various habitats prior to making additional donations to WWF.

Motorola's charitable contributions totaled $7 million in cash in 1996. The $7 million cash-giving figure represented 0.4 percent of the company's pretax earnings for the same year, and was identical to the company's cash contributions in 1995.

Workplace Information: OSHA records indicate that Motorola was inspected five times from 1994 to 1996. Violations included three classified as "serious." The company was not fined. In comparison, the median amount of fines per inspection for other companies manufacturing electronic equipment was $1,347.

International: Motorola is one of the largest foreign investors in China. The company was cited in a recent *Asian Wall Street Journal* for strong employee relations in the Philippines.

Weapons Contracts: With $290 million in defense-related revenue, Motorola ranked 89th on the list of worldwide defense contractors in 1995, a significant drop from its position of 45th in 1994. Motorola was the 43rd-largest prime contractor to the U.S. Department of Defense in 1996 with all of its defense-related revenue derived from DOD contracts for communications and defense electronics systems.

In 1997, Motorola agreed to cease manufacturing of anti-personnel land mines in response to a study by Human Rights Watch.

Product Quality: Motorola was the first recipient of the Malcolm Baldrige National Quality Award in 1988 and was among the first electronics companies to achieve "Six Sigma" quality, or virtually defect-free products.

Nalco Chemical

STOCK SYMBOL: NLC
STOCK EXCHANGES: NY, B, CH, P

Environment	D
Women's Advancement	C?
Minority Advancement	D?
Charitable Giving	B
Community Outreach	C
Family Benefits	N
Workplace Issues	B
Social Disclosure	B

Nalco, headquartered in Naperville, Illinois, is the world's largest producer of specialty chemicals and services for water and waste treatment, pollution control, petroleum production, and other industrial processes. In 1994, Nalco and Exxon formed a joint venture partnership to provide specialty chemical products to petroleum and chemical industries. With 6,500 employees, the company revenues totaled $1.3 billion in 1996.

Environment: Although the company has a written environmental policy, it lacks substance, and scored below the industry average. Nalco distributes an environmental handbook to employees, which states that it is each employee's responsibility to become familiar with environmental laws and regulations and to be sure that the company's activities are in compliance with them. The company does not publish a corporate environmental report. Nalco's product line is designed to assist customers in economically meeting environmental discharge limits. In the selection of suppliers, Nalco conducts or reviews environmental audits on potential suppliers' facilities. The company has an environmental audit program, but it does not make findings available to the public. Its audit program also did not contain many of the more significant components compared to that of its sample industry.

Nalco Chemical's average total toxic releases and transfers during the years 1993–1994 were less than the industry sample average. Emissions decreased by almost three quarters during those years, the best performance in the sample.

Nalco Chemical's "Noxout" process offers cost-effective technology to reduce NO_x emissions by as much as 60 percent at many fuel burning sites. In 1991, the company received the Illinois Governor's Pollution Prevention Award as well as recognition from the National Environmental Development Association.

EEO: In 1996, Nalco Chemical's 10-member board of directors included no women or minorities. Of 21 corporate officers at the company, two were women and none were minorities.

Community Involvement: In 1996, Nalco Chemical's charitable giving totaled $2.4 million in cash, which was equal to one percent of the company's pretax earnings for that year. In terms of the actual dollar amount donated by the company, the level of cash contributions in 1996 represented an increase of 5.9 percent from that of 1995, which was 1.1 percent of the company's earnings for that year.

In April, 1997, Nalco was one of several companies to be recognized by the Volunteer and Information Agency, a United Way agency, for its efforts in Louisiana. Nalco sponsors a "Community Involvement" program, in which the company acts as an originator or organizer for employee participation in the community. The program includes the creation of Community Advisory Groups at company facilities. The company also reports that its company-sponsored volunteer programs include food, clothing, and toy drives, pledge-a-thons, and partnerships with educational institutions.

The company's matching gift program matches donations to colleges or universities at a rate of two-to-one up to $2,000, and matches gifts to not-for-profit hospitals and cultural institutions at one-to-one up to $500. The Nalco Foundation supports colleges and universities, with an emphasis on science-oriented projects, and interest in education of minorities.

Workplace Information: According to the Occupational Safety and Health Administration's records, Nalco Chemical was inspected once from 1994 to 1996. The OSHA inspectors' citations included two violations classified as "serious." A total of $2,475 in fines was assessed to the company following the inspections. In comparison, the median amount of fines per inspection for other companies in the extractive business was $2,941.

National Semiconductor

STOCK SYMBOL: NSM
STOCK EXCHANGES: NY, B, C, CH, P, PH

Environment	D
Women's Advancement	N
Minority Advancement	N
Charitable Giving	C
Community Outreach	A?
Family Benefits	N
Workplace Issues	N
Social Disclosure	B

Once the largest semiconductor manufacturer in the U.S., National Semiconductor, headquartered in Santa Clara, California, is gradually recovering from a string of losses that has plagued the company since 1986. Under the direction of CEO Gilbert Amelio, National underwent a massive restructuring that involved focusing resources on three core activities: personal systems, communications and analog. Sales for the fiscal year ending May 1997 were $2.5 billion. The company has approximately 12,400 employees.

Environment: National Semiconductor has an environmental policy and a corporate environmental report, which is available on the Internet. National Semiconductor has implemented an integrated environmental management system and provides environmental health and safety (EH&S) training to all employees. It also considers contribution towards EH&S goals in the job performance reviews of all employees and presents awards to employees for their contribution to environmental issues. The company also has a corporate policy on community involvement relating to local environmental concerns. In the selection of suppliers, National Semiconductor evaluates environmental management systems of suppliers. The company has an environmental audit program.

National Semiconductor's average toxic releases and transfers during the years 1993–1994 were less than the industry sample average. However, its emissions increased by more than threefold during those years, the worst performance within the industry sample.

In November 1996, National Semiconductor Corporation's facility in Greenock, Scotland, became the first UK semiconductor manufacturing site to achieve certification to two internationally recognized environmental quality standards: British standard BS7750 and international standard ISO 14001. The company, through its Environmental, Health and Safety Working Council and other internal teams, has developed a number of worldwide programs to facilitate continual improvement in environmental, health and safety performance.

EEO: In 1996, one minority but no women served on National Semiconductor's board of directors.

Community Involvement: In 1996, National Semiconductor's charitable giving totaled $1.6 million in cash, or .67 percent of the company's pretax earnings. In May, 1997, the company contributed the first part of a $100,000 donation to the Arlington Education Foundation, which awards grants to educators for innovative and creative learning programs.

Workplace Information: The records of the Occupational Safety and Health Administration indicate that National Semiconductor was not inspected from 1994 to 1996. Consequently no fines or violations were assessed to the company.

National increasingly relies on employee teams and ties profit sharing bonuses to group performance. A discount stock purchase plan is available for both domestic and international employees. The company employs a corporate ombudsman responsible for assisting in grievance resolution when traditional procedures are unsuccessful.

International: Two thirds of National's workforce is located outside the U.S. Most of these are employed at product assembly facilities in Southeast Asia. National also subcontracts certain manufacturing activities to third-party vendors. It is not known whether the company has taken steps to ensure such tasks do not involve child or forced labor. In January 1995, National entered into a majority-owned joint venture to manufacture circuit boards in Shanghai, China.

Weapons Contracts: In 1994, National received non-weapons-related Department of Defense contracts valued at $3.3 million, or 0.1 percent of revenues. However, the company reports that it is the second largest supplier of military and aerospace semiconductors in the world and appears to do most of its defense-related work as a subcontractor to such firms as Hughes and Loral.

NationsBank

Environment	N
Women's Advancement	C
Minority Advancement	D?
Charitable Giving	A?
Community Outreach	C?
Family Benefits	B
Workplace Issues	C?
Social Disclosure	D

NationsBank, headquartered in Charlotte, North Carolina, is the result of the 1991 merger of NCNB Corp. and C&S/Sovran. NationsBank provides a diversified range of banking and nonbanking financial services in the U.S. and in most global markets. Primary retail and commercial banking operations are located in 16 states and the District of Columbia. Upon the acquisition of Boatmen's Bancshares, Inc. on January 7, 1997, the corporation had approximately $227 billion in assets, making it the fourth largest banking company in the U.S. At year-end 1996, NationsBank had income of $17.5 billion and employed approximately 63,000 people.

Environment: In August 1993, a task force was organized by the Environmental Defense Fund, which aims to expand its members' use of "environmentally preferable" paper and paperboard, and to design a purchasing model applicable to a broad range of institutions. NationsBank is a founding member of the consortium.

EEO: In 1996, NationsBank's 28-member board of directors included two women and one minority. Of seven corporate officers at the company, none were women or minorities.

Three African-American business groups have accused NationsBank of "commercial redlining," refusing loans in certain neighborhoods, and have protested the merger of NationsBank on the basis of what they say are discriminatory practices against African-Americans. A civil rights group has also sued the bank over its lending records.

NationsBank is a "Platinum Sponsor" of Access 96, a trade fair held by one of the affiliates of the National Minority Supplier Development Council, designed to develop relationships between minority-owned businesses and corporate and public sector buyers, while identifying and exploring business opportunities. NationsBank's workforce includes about 17 percent people with disabilities.

In April, 1997, NationsBank joined with two other companies and the local Urban League in a coalition to support pro-tolerance, pro-diversity leadership in the Charlotte, North Carolina political arena. With the creation of a coalition which will function as a civic organization or a political action committee,

NationsBank, Duke Power, First Union, and the Charlotte-Mecklenburg Urban League, which promotes economic self-sufficiency among African-Americans, took a public stance in response to what they considered to be intolerance on the part of local officials. County commissioners had recently voted to end funding for the Charlotte-Mecklenburg Arts & Science Council after the Council had sponsored plays that portrayed gays and lesbians. The commissioners had created an atmosphere of "divisiveness and intolerance for very specific groups," according to Henry Doss, a senior Vice President at First Union. The corporate group plans to begin its efforts in the summer of 1997 with a series of community forums.

Community Involvement: NationsBank provides funding for community development groups like "Pulling America's Communities Together," which helps develop the leadership skills of citizens in Atlanta, Ga. In support of the President's national call for volunteerism, NationsBank pledged to open twenty-five after school centers for children between the ages of six and twelve; approximately 25,000 children nationwide will have access to the tutoring and activities available through these organizations.

Workplace Information: According to the Occupational Safety and Health Administration's records, Nationsbank was not inspected from 1994 to 1996. Consequently no violations or fines were assessed to the company. In comparison, the median amount of fines per inspection for other companies in the service industry, such as banks and communications companies, was $573.

The company paid roughly two thirds of employees' medical premium costs, one of the lowest levels among companies researched by CEP.

172

Niagara Mohawk

STOCK SYMBOL: NMK

STOCK EXCHANGES: NY, B, C, CH, PH, P

Environment	B
Women's Advancement	C
Minority Advancement	B
Charitable Giving	D
Community Outreach	C
Family Benefits	B
Workplace Issues	C
Social Disclosure	A

Niagara Mohawk, headquartered in Syracuse, New York, is the 12th largest investor-owned electric and gas utility with 1.5 million customers in a service territory that covers 24,000 square miles of upstate New York. In 1996, the company had revenues of almost $4 billion and 8,600 employees. Niagara recently announced plans to separate its power generation and distribution operations.

Environment: Niagara Mohawk has a mixed record on emissions. CEP estimates that its releases of carbon dioxide (CO_2) will remain at 1990 levels through the year 2000. CO_2 emissions are currently below industry averages. Niagara's sulfur dioxide emissions are above the industry average on a production-adjusted basis while its emissions of nitrous oxides are better than average. In November 1994, Niagara Mohawk traded excess carbon dioxide credits to Arizona Public Service in exchange for sulfur-dioxide credits. Niagara then donated the SO_2 credits to an environmental organization that will retire them.

Niagara Mohawk is one of the few major electric utilities to be actively researching wind power technology and photovoltaic cells. The utility aims to meet up to 25 percent of increased electricity needs through demand-side-management (DSM) programs. Niagara has developed an innovative methodology for gauging its overall environmental performance and has established an Investment Recovery Center that recycles and seeks markets for solid waste generated by company facilities.

Niagara has a fairly clean compliance record. The company has been cited mainly for minor oil spills at its facilities. In December 1991, Niagara paid a $100,000 penalty for discharging wastewater, used to cool its headquarters office building, into Lake Onondaga. The company ceased the 20-year practice upon notification from the New York Department of Environmental Conservation.

EEO: In 1996, Niagara Mowhawk's board totaled 13 directors, including two women, one of whom is a minority, while three of its 30 corporate officers were women and three were minorities. Additionally, two women and two minorities were among the 26 employees with the highest salaries at the company.

In February, 1997, the National Minority Business Council presented Niagara Mohawk with an award for supporting minority businesses. Niagara Mohawk received the award as a result of its track record as a large buyer of goods and services from minority- and women-owned businesses in New York state. The company purchased over $6 million in goods and services from women-owned businesses and almost $9 million from businesses owned by minorities.

Community Involvement: Niagara Mohawk's charitable contributions totaled about $1.4 million in cash in 1996, or 0.5 percent of its pretax earnings. The cash-giving figure represented an increase of 6.75 percent from the company's cash contributions in 1995.

The company supports community action teams in its different regions, whose activities include highway clean-up, painting school interiors, annual clean-up of downtown areas, and participation in fund-raising activities of groups such as Heart Walk and Habitat for Humanity.

Workplace Information: OSHA records indicate that Niagara Mohawk underwent two health and safety inspections from 1994 to 1996. Violations included three classified as "serious" for a total of $2,625 in fines, or $1,313 per inspection. In comparison, the median amount of fines per inspection for other utilities in 1996 was $2,625.

NICOR Inc.

STOCK SYMBOL: GAS
STOCK EXCHANGES: NY, B, C, CH, PH, P

Environment	N
Women's Advancement	B
Minority Advancement	A
Charitable Giving	D
Community Outreach	C
Family Benefits	F
Workplace Issues	D
Social Disclosure	B

NICOR, headquarted in Naperville, Illinois, is a holding company whose principal business, Northern Illinois Gas, delivers natural gas to 1.8 million customers in Illinois. While gas distribution accounted for most of its operating income, NICOR also owns Tropical Shipping which transports freight between the Port of Palm Beach, Florida, and 22 ports in the Caribbean, Central America and Mexico. At the end of 1996 the company's sales amounted to $1.85 billion, and at that time it employed 3,300 people.

Environment: NICOR has an environmental policy and publishes a corporate environmental report. The company recognizes the importance of standardizing environmental activities associated with providing service to its customers, and addressed the following specific issues: mercury handling, waste management, wetlands, and contaminated soil encountered during excavation. Ongoing goals for the company include waste minimization and recycling. Oil seals through which oil was pumped are recycled, along with paper, scrap metal, copper, and plastic. Furthermore, the company seeks to establish departmental accountability and responsibilities for its environmental performance. NICOR is a founding member of the DuPage River Coalition, formed to solve water resource problems. The company also became one of the Partners for Clean Air sponsored by the Illinois Environmental Protection Agency, which provides tips to minimize air pollution during peak ozone times.

EEO: In 1996, NICOR Inc. achieved a higher than average rating in both diversity categories, placing them easily in the top third of S&P 500 companies. One woman and one minority served on NICOR's 11-member board. Of 25 corporate officers at the company, four were women and two were minorities, while four of the top 25 paid employees were women, and two were minorities.

Community Involvement: In 1996, NICOR's charitable giving totaled over $1.2 million in cash, which was equal to 0.7 percent of the company's pretax earnings for that year. In terms of the actual dollar amount donated by the company, the level of cash contributions in 1996 represented an increase of 2.7 percent from 1995.

Northern Illinois Gas places emphasis on supporting precollegiate education, with priority given to organizations in the company's service area. Employee grants to human service organizations are matched up to $100.

Workplace Information: According to the Occupational Safety and Health Administration's records, NICOR Inc. was not inspected from 1994 to 1996. Consequently no violations or fines were assessed to the company. In comparison, the median amount of fines per inspection for other companies in the utility business in 1996 was $2,625.

Nike, Inc.

STOCK SYMBOL: NKE
STOCK EXCHANGES: NY, CH, P, PH

Environment	N
Women's Advancement	D
Minority Advancement	B
Charitable Giving	B
Community Outreach	B
Family Benefits	N
Workplace Issues	A?
Social Disclosure	B

Nike, headquartered in Beaverton, Oregon, designs, develops, and distributes footwear and apparel products. Most of its footwear production is done overseas, but the company has four dress shoe facilities in Maine and a plastics plant in Oregon. In 1996, Nike had $6.5 billion in revenues and 17,200 employees.

Environment: Using a process that pulverizes whole shoes into a material that can be used to make new soles, Nike is recycling many of the shoes it manufactures. The company has eliminated heavy metals from product packaging, has joined EPA's Green Lights program for lighting efficiency, and has stopped using CFCs in its manufacturing processes. Its program Bike, Run, Skate, Carpool offers incentives for employees who find alternative energy-efficient methods of getting to and from work.

EEO: In 1996, Nike, Inc.'s board totaled 11 directors, including one woman and two minorities. Two of its 15 corporate officers were women. Additionally, two women and one minority were among the 25 employees with the highest salaries.

In 1996, ICCR sponsored a shareholder resolution proposing that Nike distribute an EEO report. In 1997, ICCR sponsored another resolution proposing that Nike disclose diversity data.

Community Involvement: In 1994, Nike launched the Nike P.L.A.Y. (Participate in the Lives of American Youth) Foundation to provide under-served children access to inspirational coaches, organized activities, and safe places to play. Nike has made a $5 million commitment to the Boys & Girls Clubs of America. The five-year grant will fund the Nike P.L.A.Y. Sports program to train 40,000 volunteer coaches, and increase the overall youth participation at the Boys & Girls Clubs of America. Nike is funding a $3 million partnership with 100 Black Men of America that supports youth mentor programs. Also through the P.L.A.Y. program, Nike donated running tracks, playground padding, and tennis and basketball courts to organizations serving under-served kids, valued at $2 million since 1994.

Workplace Information: OSHA records indicate that Nike was inspected once from 1994 to 1996. Nike received only incidental violations, for a total of $300 in fines. In comparison, the median amount of fines per inspection for other companies in similar manufacturing industries was $2,412.

International: Nike shoes are manufactured in some 35 facilities across Asia. Over the last few years, the Asian-American Free Labor Institute, the AFL-CIO, Press for Change, and rights organizations have criticized Nike, alleging violations of national labor laws (pertaining to child labor, overtime, minimum wages, and dismissal for labor organizing) in Indonesia and Vietnam by Nike-licensed factories.

Nike states unequivocally that on the contrary, it is a leader in winning better pay and conditions for its workers. In Indonesia, for example, Nike maintains that independent audits by Ernst & Young confirm that average monthly salaries for factory employees are nearly twice the country's minimum wage. Subsidies are provided for meals, health care, and housing, and subcontractors have agreed since 1991 to Nike's guidelines on child labor, wages, and workplace conditions. Hundreds of Nike managers in Asia are charged with overseeing subcontractor operations and workplace conditions.

A 1995 survey funded by the U.S. Agency for International Development found that in West Java — where the majority of Nike shoes are made — over 80 percent of surveyed workers reported earning only the government-set minimum wage. Workers are subjected to forced overtime and punishment by local management for taking sick leave, humiliating treatment by supervisors, and lack of decent drinking water. According to rights groups, Nike's "average monthly wage" includes overtime earnings, making it seem higher than it really is.

Northern States Power

STOCK SYMBOL: NSP
STOCK EXCHANGES: NY, B, C, CH, P, PH

Environment	REV
Women's Advancement	A
Minority Advancement	B
Charitable Giving	B?
Community Outreach	N
Family Benefits	N
Workplace Issues	C?
Social Disclosure	B

Headquartered in Minneapolis, Northern States Power distributes electricity and natural gas to customers in Minnesota, Wisconsin, Michigan, and North and South Dakota. NSP's NRG Energy subsidiary is an independent power company with projects in the U.S., Australia, and Germany. In 1997, the company had revenues of $2.7 billion and 6,500 employees.

Environment: About half of the energy that Northern States generated in the early 1990s was from burning coal, but the company has integrated renewable resources into its fuel mix. The utility has increased the use of wind power and hydroelectric power. NSP is testing wet electrostatic precipitator technology, which, if implemented, would greatly reduce fine particulate emissions.

NSP participates in the EPA's Green Lights and WasteWi$e programs. Through its demand-side-management (DSM) programs, the company expects to offset future growth in demand by about 50 percent. In 1993, a natural gas explosion at NSP's distribution system in St. Paul cost $1 million in damages and prompted four lawsuits.

Nuclear Power: Nuclear power constitutes about 28 percent of NSP's fuel mix, and delays in federal site selection for permanent waste storage have caused problems for the company. Much of its renewable energy development commitment (see above) was made in an agreement with Minnesota legislators, who in exchange permitted the company to expand its on-site storage of nuclear waste. NSP is one of eight utilities involved in a consortium to license and build a private interim storage facility for spent nuclear fuel on the Skull Valley Band of Goshute Indian Reservation in Utah. A license application was submitted to the Nuclear Regulatory Commission in June 1997.

EEO: In 1996, Northern States Power achieved a higher than average rating in both diversity categories. Women and minorities each made up eight percent of Northern States Power's board. Ten percent of corporate officers at the company were women, but none were minorities. At the end of 1997, those numbers were eight percent for both categories. Three of the top 25 paid employees were women.

In March 1995, the utility agreed to pay $2.1 million to settle allegations of racial discrimination in its hiring practices. Approximately 600 plaintiffs benefited from the settlement.

Community Involvement: Northern States Power's main giving priority, Building Human Capacity, focuses on improving the ability of families and individuals to become more independent and self sufficient members of the community through support for programs that remove barriers for economically or socially disadvantaged groups. The company intends to mobilize the strengths and assets of communities, families, and individuals rather than focus on their problems or needs, and to take a preventive, long-term approach to community and individual development.

In 1995, Northern States Power's contributions to various charitable institutions included cash donations totaling $4.5 million ($4.9 million in 1997). The company's cash contributions for 1995 were equivalent to 1.07 percent of its pretax earnings for the same year.

Workplace Information: OSHA records indicate that Northern States Power was inspected 11 times from 1994 to 1996. Violations included 14 violations classified as "serious" for a total of $31,065 in fines, an average of $2,824 per inspection. In comparison, the median amount of fines per inspection for other utilities in 1996 was $2625.

Northern States Power Company and the International Brotherhood of Electrical Workers completed negotiations during 1997 that resulted in increased wages and continuation of the medical plan at the same cost-sharing level of 20 percent. The contract raises wages by six percent over three years. In the event of a staff reduction, the new contract will provide a laid off employee the equivalent of five months of pay plus one week for every year of employment. In return, NSP obtained more flexibility on subcontracting.

Northrop Grumman

STOCK SYMBOL: NOC
STOCK EXCHANGES: NY, B, CH, PH, P

Environment	N
Women's Advancement	D?
Minority Advancement	A?
Charitable Giving	C?
Community Outreach	B
Family Benefits	N
Workplace Issues	D?
Social Disclosure	D

Northrop Grumman Corporation, headquartered in Los Angeles, California, is an advanced technology company operating in the aircraft and electronics industry segments of the aerospace industry. The aircraft segment includes the design, development and manufacturing of aircraft and aircraft assemblies. The electronics segment includes the design, development, manufacturing and integration of electronic systems for military and commercial use and the operation and support of computer systems for scientific and management information. At year-end 1996, Northrop Grumman had sales of $8 billion and 46,600 employees. In July 1997, Lockheed Martin announced that it would acquire Northrop Grumman Corp.

EEO: In 1996, Northrop Grumman's board totaled 11 directors, including one woman and two minorities. None of the 15 corporate officers were women or minorities.

In 1996, an ex-employee filed a $33 million complaint against Northrop Grumman in an age and gender bias suit. Louise Farrel alleged that though she had worked for Northrop for 27 years, she was denied continued employment while younger, male employees were promoted to positions for which she was qualified. Earlier in the year, a group of current and former employees filed a $100 million suit claiming they were denied promotions based on age and race. Again, in the same year, another group filed a complaint with the EEO Commission that a disproportionate number of women and African-Americans were laid off in 1994. The cases have yet to go to trial.

Community Involvement: In 1995, Northrop Grumman's contributions to various charitable institutions included cash donations totaling $3.2 million. The company's cash contributions for 1995 were equivalent to 0.78 percent of its earnings before taxes.

Northrop Grumman's High School Involvement Partnership program was one of twenty that received the Presidential Service Award in 1996 from President Clinton. The program creates job-training sites for high school students at several of its plant locations.

Students are paired with mentors and trained in fields including engineering, manufacturing, office organization, environmental management, health, and fire-fighting. Also in 1996, Northrop Grumman donated more than $72,000 in labor and materials to refurbish the Roark Elementary School in Arlington, Texas.

Northrop Grumman's volunteer program, WINGS (We In Northrop Grumman Serve), involves employees in programs dealing with AIDS, disadvantaged youth, elderly persons, environment, homelessness, persons with disabilities, and violence.

Workplace Information: The records of the Occupational Safety and Health Administration indicate that Northrop Grumman underwent one health and safety inspection from 1994 to 1996. The violations reported by OSHA as a result of the inspection include two classified as "serious." The company was required to pay $10,375 as a result of its violations. In comparison, the median amount of fines per inspection for other companies in similar manufacturing industries was $2,412.

Weapons Contracts: In 1996, Northrop Grumman was the fourth largest defense company in the world with defense revenue of $6.7 billion. This represented 82.7 percent of its total business. That year, Northrop ranked as the sixth-largest military contractor to the U.S. Department of Defense with $2.6 billion in prime contracts. It is the manufacturer of aircraft such as the B-2 bomber as well as electronics and communications systems, space systems, armored vehicles and other military equipment.

Norwest Corporation

STOCK SYMBOL: NOB
STOCK EXCHANGES: NY, B, C, CH, PH, P

Environment	N
Women's Advancement	B?
Minority Advancement	C?
Charitable Giving	B
Community Outreach	A
Family Benefits	N
Workplace Issues	A?
Social Disclosure	C

Norwest, headquartered in Minneapolis, Minnesota, is a diversified financial services company with 4,087 stores in all 50 states, Canada, the Caribbean, Central America and elsewhere internationally. Its subsidiaries are engaged in banking, mortgage, consumer finance, and a variety of related businesses providing retail and corporate banking services to customers. At year-end 1997, the corporation had assets of $88 billion, becoming the United States' 11th largest bank holding company. In 1997, Norwest had income of $1.4 billion and 57,000 employees.

Environment: Recycling programs exist throughout Norwest's banking system. A heat recovery system, which is located at its operations center in Minneapolis, eliminates the need for 800,000 gallons of heating oil each year.

EEO: In 1996, Norwest Corp.'s 16-member board of directors included two women and two minorities. Three women served among the company's 26 corporate officers at the company, but no minorities were employed at that level.

During the holiday season of 1996, Norwest decided to develop its holiday decorations with a theme of diversity. Decorations included references to the Chinese, Vietnamese, Japanese, and Hmong New Years as well as Christmas, Hanukkah, and Kwanzaa.

Community Involvement: Norwest reports that its banks have received numerous "outstanding" ratings from bank regulators for their Community Reinvestment performance. Norwest banks have made over $500 million in mortgage loans to low-income families and small business lending reached nearly $500 million in 1996.

In Minnesota, the primary focus of Norwest's philanthropy is the area of job training for adults of economically disadvantaged families. However, the giving priorities vary according to the differing needs of the many communities where Norwest maintains operations.

The Norwest Mortgage Housing Foundation makes grants to projects that work to improve access to housing for families making less than 80 percent of the median income common in the operating area. Ten or more Norwest employees must volunteer for the project in order for the company to provide the grant. Norwest provided more than 30,000 mortgages to minorities. Norwest Mortgage offers specialized services to operators of group homes for the mentally and physically disabled. In 1996, Norwest Corp.'s charitable giving totaled $19 million in cash, which was equal to 1.07 percent of the company's pretax earnings for that year. In terms of the actual dollar amount donated by the company, the level of cash contributions in 1996 represented a decrease of 21 percent from that of 1995.

Workplace Information: According to the Occupational Safety and Health Administration's records, Norwest Corp. was inspected once from 1994 to 1996. OSHA inspectors cited the company only for violations classified as "other," which is the least egregious type of violation. The company did not receive any financial penalites as a result of its violations. In comparison, the median amount of fines per inspection for other companies in the service industry, such as entertainment and communications companies, was $573.

In 1996, *Business Ethics* magazine named Norwest the sixth most ethical company with headquarters in the United States. The sixth place position also made Norwest the highest rated of all domestic banks.

Occidental Petroleum

STOCK SYMBOL: OXY

STOCK EXCHANGES: NY, TO, B, C, CH, PH, P

Environment	C
Women's Advancement	F?
Minority Advancement	C?
Charitable Giving	F?
Community Outreach	N
Family Benefits	N
Workplace Issues	A?
Social Disclosure	B

Occidental Petroleum, headquartered in Los Angeles, California, had $10.6 billion in sales in 1996, split about evenly between chemical and oil and gas operations. The company employs about 14,200 people.

Environment: Occidental Petroleum has a written environmental policy and an annual corporate environmental report, available on the Internet. Occidental has a pollution prevention policy and program, which establishes reduction goals for point sources, fugitive emissions, and solid waste. Occidental has a policy on community involvement and has 26 community advisory panels. The company has a HES group dedicated to product stewardship.

Occidental Petroleum's average toxic releases and transfers during the years 1993–1994 were the highest compared to an industry sample. However, its emissions decreased by about a fourth during those years, an above average performance.

Canadian Oxy Chemicals, its subsidiary, was convicted of charges in October, 1997, relating to a December 1992 chemical spill at the company's plant in Squamish, B.C., and fined $25,000. About 73,000 liters of sodium chlorate escaped from a barge loading pipe into the environment. The first trial resulted in the dismissal of the charges. An appeal found the company responsible because employees were not properly instructed in their duties; the communications systems and transfer monitoring procedures were inadequate; and, there was no containment system at the facility.

Occidental Petroleum has faced opposition to exploration activity in Colombia by the U'Wa tribe, which asked the company to stay away from their tribal lands. Although Occidental Petroleum had full governmental backing for its work, U'Wa leaders said Occidental Petroleum violated the tribe's constitutional rights and failed to meet legal requirements for consulting with U'Wa communities before engaging in seismic work. After a long legal battle, the Interior Ministry's Decree 1397 in 1996 required "approval" and assent of third parties, including nongovernment environmental organizations, for environmental permits. The company remains in Colombia and is now conducting seismic work outside the U'Wa reservation.

EEO: In 1996, Occidental's board totaled 14 directors, including one woman and one minority. None of 22 corporate officers were women or minorities.

A 1997 shareholders' resolution proposing that Occidental Petroleum implement greater efforts to diversify its board was withdrawn. In the majority of cases, a proposal is withdrawn when an agreement has been reached with management.

Community Involvement: In 1995, Occidental Petroleum's contributions to various charitable institutions included cash donations totaling $725,361. Cash contributions for 1995 were 0.08 percent of its earnings before taxes.

Preliminary approval was granted by a Texas judge in June 1995, for a $65.7 million settlement of a toxic exposure class action suit against OxyChem, stemming from a 1992 leak of several thousand pounds of butadiene at a Texas facility that allegedly spread to a nearby Hispanic neighborhood. The jury in the case found OxyChem "grossly negligent." Of the 12 plaintiffs, the jury awarded compensatory damages ranging from $300 to $1,000 to five and none to the other seven.

Workplace Information: OSHA records indicate that Occidental Petroleum underwent one health and safety inspection from 1994 to 1996. The company received only incidental violations for $150 in fines.

International: Occidental has been involved in oil and gas operations in Ecuador since the 1980s. According to the company, an audit conducted by the European Community Commission praised Occidental's operations there for "reinjection of fluids, sanitary landfill and recycling and disposal of effluents." In June 1995, Occidental began exploratory oil drilling in Northeastern Peru on indigenous lands. The Candoshi people rejected oil development activities on its land and are demanding negotiation on the social and environmental terms of Oxy's operations.

Oryx Energy

STOCK SYMBOL: ORX
STOCK EXCHANGES: NY, P

Environment	N
Women's Advancement	C?
Minority Advancement	D?
Charitable Giving	F
Community Outreach	C
Family Benefits	N
Workplace Issues	N
Social Disclosure	C

Oryx Energy Company engages in the exploration and production business. The company, headquartered in Dallas, Texas, has a strong base of reserves and production in the U.S., the U.K., North Sea and around the world. It also has exploration projects in the Gulf of Mexico, the U.K., North Sea, Ecuador, Australia, Kazakhstan, and Algeria. Oryx became an independent oil and gas company in 1988 with operations in the U.S., when it was spun off from Sun Company, Inc. Effective January 1990, Oryx went overseas with a major acquisition of producing properties and development projects. Revenues for the year ended December 31, 1996 totaled $1.2 billion. Oryx employs 976 people.

Environment: The company does not publish a corporate environmental report, but does have a written environmental policy. Oryx provides environmental health and safety (EH&S) training to field employees and has a policy committed to full disclosure of health, safety, or environmental risk to employees and communities where facilities are located, sometimes working with communities to make contingency plans. Oryx plans an array of pollution prevention and remediation measures including a revegetation project and environmental awareness training for contractors. Oryx has implemented an environmental audit program. Internationally, Oryx states that it follows U.S. environmental regulations in the U.S. and local regulations abroad. The company is working actively with government representatives, in countries in which it is involved, to help develop laws, regulations, and rules for environmental protection.

Oryx received the Conservation Award for Respecting the Environment in 1997 from the Minerals Management Service for its operations in the Gulf of Mexico. The agency cited Oryx for its commitment to instill an environmental ethic throughout the company, its "extraordinary" commitment to pollution prevention and its leadership as an independent operation seeking to improve industry practices. The agency was most impressed by Oryx's willingness to go beyond minimum standards and common practices and to test new technology to protect air and water quality. Noteworthy accomplishments include the company's support and stewardship of the Flower Garden Banks National Marine Sanctuary, its cooperation with the Coast Guard in area-wide oil-spill contingency planning and its "hands-on" environmental action through the Texas General Land Office's Adopt a Beach program.

EEO: In 1996, Oryx Energy's 11-member Board of Directors included one woman and no minorities. Of eight corporate officers at the company, one was a woman and none were minorities.

Community Involvement: In 1996, Oryx Energy's charitable giving totaled $299,000 in cash, which was equal to 0.11 percent of the company's pre-tax earnings for that year. In terms of the actual dollar amount donated by the company, the level of cash contributions in 1996 represented an increase of 7 percent from that of 1995. The company's in-kind giving — the donation of products or services — came to $25,000 in 1996.

Oryx Energy states that it focuses its charitable efforts to "encourage long-term solutions to educational, social, economic, and environmental needs, with special emphasis on public policy and programs that promote educational and economic self-sufficiency and independence." The company also reports that it encourages "volunteerism among Oryx Energy Company employees, family, and friends."

Workplace Information: According to the Occupational Safety and Health Administration's records, Oryx Energy was not inspected from 1994 to 1996. Consequently no violations or fines were assessed to the company.

Pacific Enterprises

STOCK SYMBOL: PET

STOCK EXCHANGES: NY, B, C, CH, P, PH

Environment	B
Women's Advancement	A
Minority Advancement	A
Charitable Giving	B
Community Outreach	C
Family Benefits	D
Workplace Issues	B
Social Disclosure	A

Based in Los Angeles, Pacific Enterprises is a utility holding company engaged primarily in supplying natural gas to most of Southern, and portions of Central, California. The company's primary subsidiary, Southern California Gas Co. (SCG), is the nation's largest natural gas distribution utility, serving 535 communities with a population of about 16 million. Pacific Enterprises is also engaged in interstate and offshore natural gas transmission and in marketing a wide range of unregulated energy products and services. In 1996, the company had revenues of $2.6 billion and 7,600 employees.

Environment: PET has a public policy committee of the Board of Directors. Its SCG subsidiary in 1993 constructed an inner-city plant in Los Angeles to build natural gas–fueled vehicles in an effort to become a major player in the alternative-fueled vehicles market.

In 1994, SCG won a certificate of distinction for its participation in EPA's Green Lights program. The company invested in environmentally friendly technologies for its Energy Resource Center near Los Angeles.

From 1990 to 1994, only 14,400 pounds of toxic materials were reported released, lower than the industry average.

EEO: In 1996, Pacific Enterprises achieved a higher than average rating in both diversity categories, placing it easily in the top third of S&P 500 companies. Two women and two minorities served on Pacific Enterprises' 8-member Board of Directors. Of 13 corporate officers, two were women and two were minorities. Five of the top 24 paid employees were women and four were minorities.

Pacific Enterprises has an Employee Diversity Council that addresses gay and lesbian issues as well as other employee concerns.

Community Involvement: In 1996, Pacific Enterprises' charitable giving totaled $3.7 million in cash, which was equal to 1.05 percent of the company's pretax earnings for that year. Cash contributions in 1996 represented a decrease of 2.2 percent from 1995.

Pacific Enterprises makes direct cash contributions to support the arts, education, and cultural programs in the greater Los Angeles area.

Family Benefits: Pacific Enterprises offers flexible work arrangement options to its employees.

Workplace Information: According to the Occupational Safety and Health Administration's records, Pacific Enterprises was not inspected from 1994 to 1996. Consequently no violations or fines were assessed to the company. In comparison, the median amount of fines per inspection for other companies in the utility business in 1996 was $2,625.

More than half of Pacific Enterprises' employees are represented by the Utility Workers Union of America and the International Chemical Workers Union.

Legal Proceedings: In 1994, Pacific Enterprises agreed to pay $45 million to settle shareholder lawsuits stemming from a failed diversification effort. The lawsuits claimed that the company's ventures into drug and sports equipment retailing, and oil and gas operations (all since abandoned), breached the company's fiduciary duty to its shareholders. Pacific Enterprises' contribution to the settlement was $17 million; the additional $28 million was paid by its auditors and insurers.

Pacific Gas & Electric Company

STOCK SYMBOL: PCG
STOCK EXCHANGES: NY, B, C, Cн, P, Pн, Vc

Environment	A
Women's Advancement	B?
Minority Advancement	D?
Charitable Giving	C
Community Outreach	C
Family Benefits	N
Workplace Issues	N
Social Disclosure	C

Pacific Gas & Electric Company, headquartered in San Francisco, is one of the largest investor-owned gas and electric utilities in the United States, serving 4.1 million electric and 3.4 million gas customers in its 94,000-square-mile service territory in Northern and Central California. In 1996, the company had revenues of $9.6 billion and 22,000 employees.

Environment: PG&E announced in 1991 that it would spend more than $2 billion over ten years on programs designed to dramatically increase energy efficiency and cut energy use. The company offers cash incentives to builders and customers to encourage installation of energy-efficient technologies. PG&E generates 47 percent of its electricity from renewable sources, including 22 percent from hydropower, 10 percent from geothermal steam, and the rest from wind, solar, and biomass such as municipal trash. It also buys electricity from independent suppliers of wind, solar, and geothermal power.

PG&E expects that its carbon dioxide emissions will not grow at least until the year 2000. Its sulfur dioxide emissions are the lowest among utility companies CEP studied, and its rate of emission for nitrogen oxides is lower than average.

In April 1995, PG&E announced it would pay between $50 and $400 million to settle a lawsuit filed by a group of San Bernadino residents. The plaintiffs alleged that the utility had polluted their drinking water supplies, causing a variety of cancers and numerous birth defects.

Nuclear Power: PG&E's Diablo Canyon Nuclear Power Plant generates about 30 percent of the utility's energy. The Diablo Canyon reactor has had six leaks of radioactive steam or water in the last several years, but no radioactivity has escaped the plant during any of the incidents. Critics of the plant have voiced concerns, however, because it lies near an earthquake fault line. The company has paid well below the industry average in penalties to the Nuclear Regulatory Commission.

EEO: In 1996, Pacific Gas & Electric's Board of Directors totaled 16, including two women and one minority. Five of a total of 35 corporate officers were women and none were minorities.

Pacific Gas & Electric was one of very few companies to publicly oppose California's proposition 209, the passage of which ended affirmative action in state government practices. As a result of taking a public position, the company faced picket lines. PG&E was also the only public company to testify before Congress in support of the 1990 Civil Rights Act.

The company was also one of 83 cited in the Glass Ceiling Commission's March 1995 report for implementing "employment practices that help break the glass ceiling." PG&E was cited, for its "Accelerated Development Program." Ten slots are available in the two-year program, which started in 1988. The Commission writes that through 1993, 16 of 21 participants "were successful, including one woman who now manages a power plant."

Community Involvement: PG&E giving priorities include organizations that promote employment and economic self-sufficiency. The company funds job training and retraining programs, career mentoring programs, precollege tutoring, and youth programs that teach decision-making and develop values.

PG&E's charitable contributions totaled $9.1 million in cash in 1996, the equivalent of 0.69 percent of the company's pretax earnings, and a decrease of 9.9 percent from its cash contributions in 1995.

Workplace Information: OSHA records indicate that PG&E was not inspected from 1994 to 1996. Consequently no fines or violations were assessed to the company. In 1993, the company cut 11 percent of its workforce.

PG&E opened a new $1.3 million day care at its headquarters in 1992. The company's chairman, Richard Clarke—named Family Champion of the Year in 1992—has pledged additional sites if employees desire them.

182

PacifiCorp

STOCK SYMBOL: PPW
STOCK EXCHANGES: NY, B, C, CH, PH, P

Environment	B
Women's Advancement	A
Minority Advancement	F
Charitable Giving	D?
Community Outreach	A
Family Benefits	N
Workplace Issues	D?
Social Disclosure	A

PacifiCorp, the number one bulk power trader in the West, owns Pacific Power & Light and Utah Power & Light, which sells electricity to 1.4 million customers in seven western states. The company also owns Powercor, an Australian electric distribution utility, and a minority stake in The Hazelwood powerstation in the state of Victoria, Australia. Pacificorp is based in Portland, Oregon. At year-end 1996, the company had revenues of almost $4.3 billion and employed approximately 8,750 people in North America.

Environment: While PacifiCorp's fuel mix is dominated by coal (77 percent), the company does have plans to significantly increase its use of renewable resources. The utility has already integrated hydro-electric power and some geothermal power into its generation mix. It is developing a $60 million wind project in Wyoming, the second largest wind facility in the West, and is a partner in the Solar II central station solar tower that will add about 135 MW of new capacity. The company has also installed three $100,000 photovoltaic systems in Oregon, Utah, and Wyoming to monitor the extent to which solar technology can supplant power lines.

During the period from 1989 through 1992, PacifiCorp performed better than the industry average in terms of sulfur dioxide and nitrogen oxide emissions, but worse than average for emissions of carbon dioxide. The company is already in compliance with Phase II of the Clean Air Act due to its use of low-sulfur coal and its early installation of pollution controls. Since 1992, the company has been planting trees, protecting rain forest acreage, and reducing emissions from the energy sector to offset carbon dioxide (CO_2) emissions even though such actions are not mandated or controlled. The utility submitted a Climate Challenge Program that focuses on the integration of renewable resources and the expansion of demand-side management programs (DSM).

In 1993, PacifiCorp spent $41 million on its 14 DSM programs, saving about 20 MW of energy. From 1994 through 1998, the company plans for DSM to handle 20 percent of the expected 2 percent increase in demand during that period. The utility is a participant in the EPA's Green Lights program to promote energy efficient lighting.

EEO: In 1996, PacifiCorp's board totaled 12 directors, including two women and no minorities. Three of a total of 26 corporate officers were women and none were minorities. Additionally, three women and no minorities were among the 25 employees with the highest salaries at the company.

PacifiCorp does not have any separate gay and lesbian employee groups, but its Diversity Advisory Panel includes representation/input from gay and lesbian employees.

Community Involvement: The majority of the PacifiCorp Foundation's support for social services goes towards united funds and youth organizations. Colleges and universities receive most of the education funding from the foundation, which places emphasis on electrical and computer engineering departments.

In 1996, Pacificorp's contributions totaled $2.7 million in cash, the equivalent of 36 percent of the company's pretax earnings.

Workplace Information: The records of the Occupational Safety and Health Administration indicate that Pacificorp underwent nine health and safety inspections from 1994 to 1996. The violations reported by OSHA as a result of the inspections include three classified as "willful" or "repeat" and 34 classified as "serious." The company was required to pay $10,301 as a result of its violations, or about $1,145 per inspection. In comparison, the median amount of fines per inspection for other companies in the utility business in 1996 was $2,625.

Sixty-four percent of PacifiCorp's workforce is represented by collective bargaining agreements. Principal unions include the International Brotherhood of Electrical Workers, the Utility Workers Union of America, and the United Mine Workers of America.

PECO Energy

STOCK SYMBOL: PE
STOCK EXCHANGES: NY, B, C, CH, PH, P

Environment	N
Women's Advancement	A?
Minority Advancement	C?
Charitable Giving	D?
Community Outreach	N
Family Benefits	N
Workplace Issues	A?
Social Disclosure	D

PECO Energy Company is an operating utility which provides electric and gas service to the public in southeastern Pennsylvania and buys and sells power in the wholesale generation market throughout North America. Retail electric service is supplied to a population of about 3.6 million, including 1.6 million in the city of Philadelphia. Natural gas service is supplied to a population of 1.9 million. Revenues for fiscal year 1996 were $3.85 billion. PECO employed approximately 7,200 people in 1996.

Environment: PECO Energy does not currently publish a corporate environmental report.

PECO has been criticized in the past by environmentalists for building nuclear power plants and a water-diversion project despite public opposition. However, a study released in April 1997 by the Natural Resources Defense Council, Public Service Electric & Gas Co. and Pace University School of Law found PECO and four other companies among those utilities emitting pollution at rates up to 10 times below that of the worst polluters. The study, "Benchmarking Air Emissions of Electric Utility Generators in the Eastern U.S.," summarizes data on emissions from fossil fueled steam, hydro and nuclear facilities collected by the 50 largest utility generating companies in the 37 eastern states.

In October 1997, Pennsylvania's governor presented PECO Energy, Waste Management Inc. and USX with an Environmental Excellence Award for their joint project to capture landfill gas for power generation. This award identifies business strategies that positively affect the environment and share information with others about ways to reduce waste, pollution and energy.

EEO: In 1996, PECO Energy's 17-member Board of Directors included two women and two minorities. Of 30 corporate officers at the company, six were women and none were minorities.

Community Involvement: In 1995, PECO Energy's contributions to various charitable institutions included cash donations totaling $3 million. The company's cash contributions for 1995 were 0.3 percent of its earnings before taxes for the same year.

The Taft Corporate Giving Directory reports that PECO Energy Co. "supports traditional funding categories across the board" and restricts its funding primarily to its service area of five counties in Pennsylvania.

Workplace Information: According to the Occupational Safety and Health Administration's records, PECO Energy was inspected once from 1994 to 1996. OSHA inspectors cited the company only for violations classified as "other," the least egregious type of violation. A total of $2,625 in fines was assessed to the company following the inspections. In comparison, the median amount of fines per inspection for other companies in the utility business in 1996 was $2,625.

J.C. Penney

STOCK SYMBOL: JCP
STOCK EXCHANGES: NY, B, C, CH, PH, P

Environment	N
Women's Advancement	B
Minority Advancement	B
Charitable Giving	A
Community Outreach	A
Family Benefits	N
Workplace Issues	A?
Social Disclosure	B

Dallas, Texas–based J.C. Penney is America's largest department store. It operates over 1,200 department stores and 2,800 Eckerd drug stores in all 50 states, Puerto Rico, Mexico, and Chile. Established in 1902, the company employs 250,000 people and, in 1997, had sales of $30 billion.

Environment: J.C. Penney has reduced energy consumption in its stores by half through its ongoing energy conservation program. The company has utilized clean burning natural gas as a means of cooling some of its facilities, and has phased out the use of thousands of pounds of CFC refrigerants. Penney is a partner in the EPA's Green Lights program, and is working to increase the volume of corrugated cardboard and plastic being recycled, and to reduce packaging.

EEO: In 1996, two women and one minority served on J.C. Penney's 12-member Board of Directors (10 in 1997). Of 66 corporate officers at the company, seven were women and two were minorities. Two of the top 25 paid employees were women and one was a minority. In 1997, eight women and four minorities were among 59 officers, and a third woman joined the ranks of the highest 25 paid employees.

In 1996, Penney purchased $676 million in goods and services from minority- and women-owned businesses. It does business with 14 minority-owned banks and one women-owned bank, and continues its $1 million investment with the Business Consortium Fund of the National Minority Supplier Development Council. The company does not have a written policy explicitly banning sexual orientation discrimination.

Community Involvement: J.C. Penney Company's charitable contributions totaled $25 million in cash in 1996, or 2.75 percent of its pretax earnings, and $5.7 million in in-kind donations.

Workplace Information: The Department of Labor (DOL) stated in 1996 that J.C. Penney bought garments from three companies that maintained sweatshop conditions in their factories. The DOL said that Penney had been informed in the last year that it had purchased goods produced under sweatshop conditions. Labor officials requested that Penney use only contractors that monitor the suppliers with whom they work. Penney reports that it has a comprehensive and effective program for promoting compliance with labor and other laws in its suppliers' factories.

A federal appeals court ruled in August, 1997, that J.C. Penney's 1977 policy of removing union materials from company property in a Lenexa, Kansas, facility violates federal labor laws. Employees trying to unionize with the Teamsters said that managers at the catalog facility repeatedly removed union notices from bulletin boards and removed union stickers from work carts. Also in August, Penney offered an early retirement plan in an attempt to reduce its workforce by 5 percent, or approximately 1,500 workers who are employed as managers. From 1994 to 1996, Penney had one OSHA inspection, receiving incidental violations and $450 in fines.

International: The company operates two department stores in Mexico and one in Santiago, Chile. Through licensed J.C. Penney Collections stores, private brand merchandise is sold in the Middle East, the Philippines and Indonesia. J. C. Penney also maintains supplier liaison and quality inspection offices in 16 countries in Asia, Europe, and South America.

According to reports by the National Labor Committee and the Union of Needletrade, Industrial and Textile Employees (UNITE), Nicaraguan workers for a J.C. Penney supplier face conditions of forced overtime, 12-hour shifts, strip searches, and blacklisting for trying to defend themselves. Nicaraguan workers producing clothes under the Arizona label for J.C. Penney have reportedly been subjected to abusive and dangerous conditions. Workers in some production facilities in the Nicaraguan Free Trade Zone have started efforts to unionize. Labor activists have accused the Ministry of Labor and foreign investors of collaborating to obfuscate the process of labor organization.

185

Pennzoil Corporation

STOCK SYMBOL: PZL
STOCK EXCHANGES: NY, TO, B, C, CH, PH, P

Environment	C
Women's Advancement	C
Minority Advancement	B
Charitable Giving	N
Community Outreach	C
Family Benefits	F
Workplace Issues	D
Social Disclosure	A

Pennzoil, headquartered in Houston, Texas, markets the nation's best-selling motor oil and derives more than half its income from automotive products. The company also owns Jiffy Lube International, the world's largest quick-lube outlet operator, and is active in oil and gas exploration, production and marketing. In 1994, Pennzoil announced it would sell its sulfur business to Freeport-McMoran. Total revenue for 1996 was $2.5 billion. Pennzoil has approximately 10,000 employees.

Environment: Pennzoil Corporation has an environmental policy, but does not currently publish a corporate environmental report. The company has implemented an integrated environmental management system. Pennzoil does not have a written pollution prevention policy and it has not initiated a companywide pollution prevention program. The company does not have a corporate policy on community involvement relating to local environmental concerns, but currently has community advisory panels at three of its facilities. Pennzoil has a written policy on product stewardship, but does not evaluate its products with the objective of reducing their life-cycle impacts on the environment. The company participates in EPA's WasteWi$e, 33/50, and Green Lights programs.

Pennzoil's average toxic releases and transfers during the years 1994 –1995 were just less than the industry sample average. However, its emissions increased by almost a fourth during those years, one of the worst performances within the industry sample.

EEO: Pennzoil turned in an average overall performance in workforce diversity for S&P 500 companies in 1996. The company's nine-member board included no women and one minority, compared with the average of 10.8 percent women and 7.6 percent minorities for S&P 500 companies. One woman and no minorities served among the company's seven corporate officers.

In August, 1996, a lawsuit was filed by eleven plaintiffs alleging that Pennzoil discriminated against African-American employees, seeking actual damages of $75 million. The plaintiffs claim that they were discriminated against on the basis of their race in areas of employment, promotions, transfers, and pay. They are seeking $300 million in damages, and will attempt to have the case certified as a class action in July. Pennzoil vigorously denies the allegations and will oppose the plaintiffs' efforts to have the case certified as a class action suit. Larkin C. Eakin, Jr., a Houston lawyer involved in the case, claims that there are no minorities among Pennzoil's top managers, and that out of several hundred employees making $100,000 or more, only one is African-American.

Community Involvement: In 1996, Pennzoil's charitable giving totaled $2.8 million in cash, equal to 1.7 percent of the company's pretax earnings. The company's in-kind giving—the donation of products or services—came to $1,800 in 1996.

In 1995 and 1996, Pennzoil took several measures in an effort to cut general and administrative expenses from $250 to $175 million, including reducing contributions to charitable and arts programs. The company also reduced the size of its employee matching gift program from a three-to-one to a one-to-one ratio.

Workplace Information: OSHA records indicate that Pennzoil was inspected four times from 1994 to 1996. Violations included one classified as "serious" and 27 as "unclassified" for a total of $1.5 million in fines, stemming largely from a single accident. Not including the inspection of the accident, the average fines per inspection for the company was $2,900. In comparison, the median amount of fines per inspection for other companies in the extractive business was $2,941.

186

Peoples Energy Corporation

STOCK SYMBOL: PGL

STOCK EXCHANGES: NY, B, C, CH, P, PH

Environment	N
Women's Advancement	D?
Minority Advancement	A?
Charitable Giving	B?
Community Outreach	D?
Family Benefits	N
Workplace Issues	N
Social Disclosure	F

Peoples Energy Corporation, headquartered in Chicago, Illinois, is the holding company with principally two utility subsidiaries, Peoples Gas Light and Coke Co. and North Shore Gas Co. These utility subsidiaries are engaged primarily in the purchase, storage, distribution, sale, and transportation of natural gas in Northeastern Illinois and the City of Chicago. For the fiscal year ending September 30, 1996, Peoples Energy had revenues of $1.2 billion and approximately 3,000 employees.

Environment: Peoples Energy Corporation does not currently publish a corporate environmental report.

EEO: In 1996, Peoples Energy's board totaled 11 directors, including one woman and four minorities. One of 14 corporate officers was a woman and one was a minority.

Community Involvement: In 1995, Peoples Energy's contributions to various charitable institutions included cash donations totaling $944,931. The company's cash contributions for 1995 were equivalent to 1.04 percent of its earnings before taxes for that year.

Peoples Energy matches employee donations to all eligible organizations, and matches donations to primary and secondary schools and hospitals at a two-to-one ratio. Donations towards health and welfare are largely made through united funds; selected public and private colleges and universities receive annual contributions as the focus of the company's giving to education. Additionally, the company supports educational television and community outreach programs in North Shore and Chicago, Illinois, public school systems. Peoples Energy sponsors a volunteer program in cooperation with the United Way of Metropolitan Chicago.

Workplace Information: The records of the Occupational Safety and Health Administration indicate that Peoples Energy was not inspected from 1994 to 1996. Consequently no fines or violations were assessed to the company. As an inspection can frequently be called in response to a complaint about the health and safety conditions or practices at a company or facility, a lack of inspections may indicate that the company operates under relatively healthy and safe working conditions. However, it is not particularly unusual for a company to have no OSHA inspections over the course of several years.

187

PepsiCo, Inc.

STOCK SYMBOL: PEP
STOCK EXCHANGES: NY, B, C, CH, P PH

Environment	B
Women's Advancement	A
Minority Advancement	A
Charitable Giving	B
Community Outreach	A
Family Benefits	A
Workplace Issues	B
Social Disclosure	A

PepsiCo, Inc. is the second largest softdrink maker in the world (Pepsi, Mountain Dew, Slice) and the largest maker of snack chips (Fritos, Doritos, Lay's, Ruffles). In 1997, the company completed the spin off of its fast-food division, including Taco Bell, Pizza Hut and KFC chains as TRICON Global Restaurants. In 1997, PepsiCo had sales of $20 billion and 140,000 employees.

Environment: Pepsi's major environmental concerns are product packaging and water quality. Though Pepsi has a corporation-wide environmental policy, issues are primarily addressed at the subsidiary level. Pepsi's beverage business, for instance, has improved treatment of its wastewater and reduced or recycled much of its soft drink packaging through participation in EPA's WasteWi$e program. Pepsi's snack food business conducts environmental audits at manufacturing plants and has a number of innovative programs to reuse its waste.

EEO: In 1996, one woman and one minority served on PepsiCo's 13-member Board of Directors. Of eight corporate officers, one was a woman and one was a minority. Two of the top 19 paid employees were women, and two were minorities.

188

In 1994, a bottling unit of PepsiCo was required to pay $1.6 million to a former employee in a sexual harassment suit. The plaintiff complained of lewd remarks and unwanted physical contact. PepsiCo suspended two of the employees involved in the incident for a month without pay. In 1996, 4.06 percent of PepsiCo shareholders voted to update the company's Code of Conduct.

Community Involvement: In 1996, PepsiCo's charitable giving totaled $14 million in cash, which was 0.68 percent of the company's pretax earnings. Contributions in 1996 were identical to 1995. The company's in-kind giving—the donation of products or services—came to $26 million in 1996.

Over the past decade the PepsiCo Foundation has committed nearly $20 million to 26 institutions of higher learning for building projects and endowed scholarships and fellowship funds.

Workplace Information: PepsiCo facilities were inspected 52 times from 1994 to 1996 by OSHA.

Violations included 106 classified as "serious" for a total of $95,491 in fines, an average of $1,836 per inspection. In comparison, the median amount of fines per inspection for companies making food, beverages, or household products was $1,515.

Taco Bell Corp., while still part of PepsiCo, was found to have systematically violated Seattle wage and hour laws by forcing employees to work before and after their shifts with no pay and work over forty hours without getting overtime pay. Taco Bell was found to have exhibited "a pattern or practice of violating the state's wage and hour laws," through actions that were "willful and intentional." Taco Bell intends to appeal, claiming that these instances were isolated cases of managers not adhering to Taco Bell policy, and the managers in question are no longer employed by Taco Bell.

International: Pepsi has been criticized for its investments in countries known for human rights violations (i.e., Burma, Guatemala, Indonesia, China, Saudi Arabia, Turkey, and Thailand). In 1996, when concerned shareholders demanded that Pepsi review and address its involvement in these countries, the Board of Directors responded that "it is neither prudent nor appropriate for us to establish our own country-by-country foreign policy." In May, 1997, production and distribution of all Pepsi products in Burma ceased.

In 1995, a PepsiCo plant in China was heavily fined for noise and waste pollution, while a foods plant in India was cited for violations of the Water and Air Act in 1996.

Animal Testing: A contractor conducts nutritional tests of Pepsi products on animals.

Perkin-Elmer Corporation

STOCK SYMBOL: PKN
STOCK EXCHANGES: NY, B, CH, P, PH

Environment	C
Women's Advancement	D?
Minority Advancement	B?
Charitable Giving	A?
Community Outreach	N
Family Benefits	C
Workplace Issues	C
Social Disclosure	B

Perkin-Elmer, headquartered in Norwalk, Connecticut, is the world's leading producer of live science and analytical instrumentation systems with applications in environmental technology, genetic engineering, pharmaceuticals, petrochemicals, and agriculture. In 1997, Perkin-Elmer had approximately $1.3 billion in revenues and employed over 6,000 people.

Environment: Perkin-Elmer has an environmental policy, but does not publish a corporate environmental report. Perkin-Elmer has implemented an integrated environmental management system and provides environmental health and safety (EH&S) training to its employees as required. It also considers contribution towards EH&S goals in the job performance reviews of all employees and presents awards to employees for their contributions to environmental issues. Perkin-Elmer has a written pollution prevention policy and has initiated a companywide pollution prevention program, which establishes annual reduction goals for point sources, secondary emissions, fugitive emissions, and solid waste. The company also has a corporate policy on community involvement relating to local environmental concerns and has community advisory panels at two facilities. In the selection of suppliers, Perkin-Elmer determines whether suppliers have necessary permits. The company has an environmental audit program; it does not have worldwide standards and applicability. In 1996, 50 percent of U.S. facilities were audited. Internationally, Perkin-Elmer states that it follows U.S. regulations in the U.S. and local regulations abroad.

Perkin-Elmer's toxic releases and transfers were below average for both 1993 and 1994 compared to its industry sample, but emissions quadrupled in that period, one of the largest increases of the companies in the sample. The company increased its emissions by 328 percent between 1993 and 1994, the fourth largest percentage increase in the industry sample; a trend from 1993 to 1996 shows emissions doubling.

EEO: In 1996, Perkin-Elmer Corp.'s board totaled 12 directors, including one woman and one minority. One of a total of 11 corporate officers were women and none were minorities. In 1997, one woman and two minorities joined the ranks of corporate officers.

Perkin-Elmer has recruitment and apprenticeship programs to promote diversity, and minority purchasing and banking arrangements. The company assesses diversity goals in management performance reviews, and bars discrimination based on sexual orientation.

Community Involvement: In 1994, Perkin-Elmer made $600,000 in cash contributions to charitable institutions, the equivalent of 1.7 percent of the company's earnings before taxes that year. The company also made in-kind donations totaling $200,000 in 1994.

Perkin-Elmer product donations include donations of equipment for research purposes in such areas as forensic science, biotechnology, and the Human Genome project. The company's "We Care, Foster Care" program is intended to increase awareness of the foster care issue, and encourages employees to be advocates for foster care.

Workplace Information: OSHA records indicate that Perkin-Elmer Corp. was not inspected from 1994 to 1996. Consequently no fines or violations were assessed to the company. The company has introduced several programs in recent years to minimize injuries. None of its employees are unionized.

Legal Proceedings: In 1993, Perkin-Elmer paid the U.S. government $15 million to settle potential claims related to the Hubble Space Telescope. The company sold its Optical Lithography Operations (maker of the focusing system in the Hubble Space Telescope) in 1990; with its sale, Perkin-Elmer ended its military contract work.

Pfizer, Inc.

STOCK SYMBOL: PFE
STOCK EXCHANGES: NY, B, C, CH, P, PH

Environment	C
Women's Advancement	B
Minority Advancement	B
Charitable Giving	A
Community Outreach	B
Family Benefits	B
Workplace Issues	A
Social Disclosure	A

Pfizer, headquartered in New York City, is a global health care company with four business segments: health care, consumer health care, food science, and animal health. In 1996, Pfizer had revenues of $11.3 billion and 46,500 employees.

Environment: Pfizer has an environmental policy, but does not currently publish a corporate environmental report. Pfizer has implemented an integrated environmental management system and provides environmental health and safety (EH&S) training to its EH&S and facility staff. It also considers contribution towards EH&S goals in job performance reviews for senior management and EH&S staff. Pfizer has a written pollution prevention policy and has initiated a company-wide pollution prevention program. Its facilities and operating groups set annual reduction goals for point sources, secondary emissions, fugitive emissions, and solid waste. The company does not have any community advisory panels. Pfizer has a written policy on product stewardship and evaluates its products with the objective of reducing their life-cycle impacts. It utilizes the following criteria in selection of its suppliers: 1) conducting or reviewing environmental audits on suppliers' facilities, and 2) determining whether suppliers have necessary permits.

Pfizer's average total toxic releases and transfers during the years 1994 to 1996 were slightly less than the industry sample average. Emissions decreased by an average of one-third annually during those years, a better than average performance.

EEO: In 1996, Pfizer achieved a higher than average rating in both diversity categories, placing it easily in the top third of S&P 500 companies. Two women and two minorities served on Pfizer's 12-member Board of Directors. Of 23 corporate officers, one was a woman and none were minorities. One of the top 25 paid employees was a woman and none were minorities. Pfizer is on the DOL's Working Women Count Honor Roll.

Community Involvement: In 1996, Pfizer, Inc. made $21.6 million in cash contributions to charitable institutions, the equivalent of 0.93 percent of the company's earnings before taxes. The company also made in-kind donations of products and services totaling $63.9 million in the same year.

Pfizer supports efforts on the part of health organizations to increase access to high-quality health care for those in need. Pfizer donates medical products through "Sharing the Care," which provides 25,000 prescriptions per month to over 350 health care centers serving the urban and rural poor. In 1996, the company received CEP's Corporate Conscience Award for Community Involvement in recognition of the program. Pfizer encourages volunteerism by paying for a limited amount of employee volunteering time.

Workplace Information: OSHA records indicate that Pfizer was inspected two times in 1996. Pfizer received only incidental violations and no fines. In comparison, the median amount of fines per inspection for other companies in the drugs, cosmetics, and medical supplies industries was $2,266. In recent years, Pfizer has improved its environmental safety policy to insure safer handling and use of chemicals in the workplace.

International: Pfizer has operations in Europe, Latin America, Africa and Asia. The company's code of conduct for suppliers includes detailed information on environment and health and safety issues, but does not address child labor, forced labor, prison labor, and minimum wage.

Product Issues: Pfizer's Procardia, approved by the FDA to treat angina, has been criticized by the *Journal of the American Medical Association (JAMA)* for its serious and sometimes fatal side effects when prescribed in some hypertensive emergencies. *JAMA* argues that the drug should be prohibited for use in the treatment of high blood pressure emergencies. Pfizer notes that Procardia is approved only for angina and should not be used for indications such as hypertension.

Pharmacia & Upjohn

STOCK SYMBOL: PNU
STOCK EXCHANGES: NY, P

Environment	D
Women's Advancement	B?
Minority Advancement	C?
Charitable Giving	B?
Community Outreach	N
Family Benefits	C
Workplace Issues	F
Social Disclosure	B

Pharmacia & Upjohn, headquartered in Kalamazoo, Michigan, is among the largest pharmaceutical companies in the world. The company has franchises in metabolic diseases, ophthalmology, oncology, inflammation, infectious diseases, central nervous system diseases, women's health and consumer healthcare. At year-end 1996, Pharmacia & Upjohn had revenues of $7.17 billion and more than 30,000 employees.

Environment: Pharmacia & Upjohn has an environmental policy and a corporate environmental report. The company has implemented an integrated environmental management system and provides environmental health and safety (EH&S) training to all its employees. It also considers contribution towards EH&S goals in job performance reviews for all its employees. Pharmacia & Upjohn has a written pollution prevention policy and has initiated a companywide pollution prevention program. Components of its pollution prevention program include source reduction, treatment, recycling, materials substitution, reuse, and use of recycled commodities. The company also has a corporate policy on community involvement relating to local environmental concerns.

Pharmacia and Upjohn's average total toxics releases and transfers during the years 1993–1994 were higher than the industry sample average. Emissions increased by about a half during those years, a below average performance.

EEO: In 1996, Pharmacia & Upjohn's board totaled 15 directors, including two women and one minority.

Community Involvement: In 1995, Pharmacia & Upjohn's contributions to various charitable institutions included cash donations totaling $8.3 million, and a total of $14.6 million in in-kind giving, which is the donation of products or services by the company. The company's cash contributions for 1995 were equivalent to 0.73 percent of its earnings before taxes.

The Pharmacia & Upjohn Foundation concentrates its donations in the areas of healthcare and academic education. Through a collaboration with International Aid Inc., Pharmacia & Upjohn employees work with local groups to provide medicine to Third-World countries, free of charge. Funding is also available from the foundation for the arts and cultural organizations and community-enhancing groups in locations where Pharmacia & Upjohn has major operations. In 1995, $1 million was granted to the Kalamazoo, MI United Way.

191

Workplace Information: According to the Occupational Safety and Health Administration's records, Pharmacia & Upjohn was not inspected from 1994 to 1996. Consequently no violations or fines were assessed to the company. As inspections can frequently be called in response to a complaint regarding the health or safety conditions at a company, or in response to an accident, a lack of inspections may indicate a relatively healthy and safe working environment.

Philip Morris

STOCK SYMBOL: MO
STOCK EXCHANGES: NY, B, C, CH, PH, P

Environment	D
Women's Advancement	B?
Minority Advancement	A
Charitable Giving	D?
Community Outreach	B
Family Benefits	N
Workplace Issues	B?
Social Disclosure	C

Philip Morris, headquartered in New York City, NY, is the world's largest producer of tobacco products, owns the second biggest food company in Kraft Foods and is also the parent of Miller Brewing, number two behind Anheuser-Busch. In 1996, annual revenues exceeded $69 billion and the company had approximately 154,000 employees.

Environment: In 1992, Philip Morris was the sole corporate sponsor of a President's Commission on Environmental Quality project to gather case studies of effective partnerships between companies and environmental organizations. That year, Miller Brewing gave a large grant to the Nature Conservancy to preserve endangered species habitats. The company has been criticized for wasteful packaging of some products.

EEO: In 1996, Philip Morris achieved a higher than average rating in both diversity categories, placing them easily in the top third of S&P 500 companies. Two women and one minority served on Philip Morris's 13-member Board of Directors. Of 31 corporate officers, three were women and none were minorities.

In October, 1996, nine women, current and former employees of the company's Louisville plant, sued Philip Morris over charges of sexual harassment. Another woman filed suit against the company and two male employees in the same month, claiming she was sexually harassed and discriminated against from 1968 to 1994 and is now under psychiatric care. In July 1996, a woman who worked at the Louisville plant for fifteen years was awarded $2 million in compensatory damages for humiliation, embarrassment, and mental anguish following instances of sexual harassment.

Community Involvement: In 1995, Philip Morris's contributions to various charitable institutions included cash donations totaling $45 million. The company's cash contributions for 1995 were equivalent to 0.48 percent of its pretax earnings for that year.

Philip Morris pledged to give $1 million in 1997 to 25 American dance companies in celebration of the 25th anniversary of its first grants to dance. Philip Morris's support of education focuses on teachers, through programs that support and enhance the critical role of educators. The company contributes to the Helping the Helpers and Food for Thought programs.

Workplace Information: OSHA records indicate that Philip Morris was inspected once from 1994 to 1996. Violations included one classified as "serious" for a total of $4,500 in fines. In comparison, the median amount of fines per inspection for other companies in similar manufacturing industries was $2,412.

Product Issues: A proposed settlement between more than 40 state attorneys general and the tobacco industry was proposed in June, 1997; as of February 1998, it had not been approved by Congress, and prospects for an approval were uncertain. The $368.5 billion settlement over 25 years would protect tobacco companies against class-action suits, place an annual cap of $5 billion on legal payouts, and provide immunity from paying punitive damages for allegations of previous misconduct. Companies would also agree to modify their advertising and marketing practices, providing the other concessions are made to the industry.

In 1997 and 1998, Philip Morris and other leading cigarette companies agreed to settlements with Texas, Mississippi, and Florida for $14.5 billion, $3.4 billion, and $11.3 billion respectively over 25 years.

International sales have increased dramatically for Philip Morris in the last ten years under intense marketing; combined international revenues for Philip Morris and R.J. Reynolds went from $6.8 billion of $18.5 billion total in 1986 to $27.7 billion of $34.7 billion total. The World Health Organization found that 1.1 billion people, or one-third of the world's population, smoke, 72 percent of that in underdeveloped and developing nations. WHO reports that by 2020, smoking is expected to be the leading cause of death, and that half a billion people now living will die due to smoking-related illnesses.

In February 1998, Philip Morris announced that it planned to cut its U.S. tobacco workforce by almost 12 percent through voluntary early-retirement offerings.

Phillips Petroleum

STOCK SYMBOL: P
STOCK EXCHANGES: NY, To, B, C, CH, PH, P

P hillips Petroleum, headquartered in Bartlesville, Oklahoma, is one of the nation's largest oil companies, and is among the largest domestic producers of natural gas liquids. In 1997, sales were $15.4 billion and there were 17,000 employees.

Environment	REV
Women's Advancement	B?
Minority Advancement	C?
Charitable Giving	D
Community Outreach	N
Family Benefits	N
Workplace Issues	N
Social Disclosure	B

Environment: Phillips Petroleum Company has an environmental policy and publishes a corporate environmental report, which is updated annually and is available on the Internet. Phillips has implemented an integrated environmental management system and provides environmental health and safety (EH&S) training to all employees. It also considers contribution towards EH&S goals in job performance reviews for all employees, and presents awards to employees for their contribution to environmental issues. Phillips has a written pollution prevention policy, and has initiated a companywide pollution prevention program. The company also has a corporate policy on community involvement relating to local environmental concerns, and currently has community advisory panels (CAPs) at five of its facilities. CAPs are part of a broader based program called Community Awareness and Emergency Response (CAER), which Phillips established in the late 1980s, to respond to concerns about the impact of chemicals on health, safety and the environment. Phillips has a written policy on product stewardship and evaluates its products with the objective of reducing their life-cycle impacts on the environment. It utilizes the following criteria in selection of its suppliers: 1) conducting/reviewing environmental audits on suppliers' facilities, 2) evaluating environmental management systems of suppliers, 3) determining whether supplier has necessary permits, and 4) requiring suppliers to follow the company's environmental guidelines as a contract condition. The company has an environmental audit program, which has worldwide standards and applicability. Phillips does not make the audit findings available to the public. Internationally, Phillips does not monitor SARA Title III, or equivalent emissions and in addition to complying with all applicable laws and regulations, the company maintains a set of health, environment, and safety policies and directives which define additional worldwide requirements. It also participated in EPA's WasteWi$e and Green Lights programs. Phillips also sponsors Playa Lakes Joint Venture which preserves wetland for migratory birds, and also sponsors other Wildlife Habitat Council projects.

Phillips' average total toxic releases and transfers during the years 1994–1996 were among the highest in the industry sample. Emissions decreased by an average of about a third annually during those years, one of the best performers in the sample. The company ranked 13th out of 15 in CEP's Campaign for Cleaner Corporations' (C-3) 1997 Petroleum Refining Report and was listed as a "worst" performer.

EEO: In 1996, Phillips Petroleum's board totaled 13 directors, including two women and one minority, while one of 13 corporate officers was a woman, and none were minorities (one in 1997).

A survey conducted by *The Oil Daily* in December, 1996, put Phillips Petroleum near the bottom of its list of employers of minorities. Only 18 percent of the company's employees are minorities, a statistic which may be related to the fact that the company is located in Oklahoma. However, the representation of women on the Board of Directors and among corporate officers is about average for an S&P 500 company.

Community Involvement: Phillips Petroleum's charitable contributions totaled $9 million in both 1996 and 1997; the 1996 figure was 0.41 percent of the company's pretax earnings for that year.

Most of the Phillips Petroleum Foundation's support of education, which is its largest giving priority, is directed towards fields in which the company has an interest, such as engineering and science. The next highest category of giving is safety and health.

Workplace Information: OSHA records indicate that Phillips Petroleum was not inspected from 1994 to 1996. Consequently no fines or violations were assessed to the company.

Weapons Contracts: Like many in the oil industry, Phillips provides fuel for the U.S. military.

Phillips-Van Heusen

Environment	N
Women's Advancement	A
Minority Advancement	C
Charitable Giving	A
Community Outreach	A
Family Benefits	D
Workplace Issues	C
Social Disclosure	A

Founded in 1881, Phillips-Van Heusen is a leading manufacturer and marketer of apparel whose Van Heusen dress shirts are the best-selling brand in the U.S. The company, headquartered in New York City, NY, also produces sweaters, shoes, neckwear, furnishings, and accessories under such names as Bass, Izod, Geoffrey Beene, and Gant. In 1996, PVH's sales were $1.4 billion. The company has 9,800 employees.

Environment: PVH has few environmental policies or programs.

EEO: Two women serve on PVH's 12-member board, and two women are among top officers—including Margaret Lachance, who heads the company's Geoffrey Beene subsidiary. Minorities are present on both the board and among corporate officers. Seventy percent of PVH's officials and managers are women; 9 percent are minorities. PVH's diversity initiatives appear limited in scope. The company does not explicitly prohibit discrimination based on sexual orientation.

Community Involvement: In 1995, PVH made cash contributions of approximately $1.3 million, or a generous 2.6 percent of the company's average pretax earnings. Giving is directed to social service agencies, hospitals, educational programs, and Jewish organizations. The company also donates an unspecified amount of clothing and shoes to organizations serving the homeless. PVH maintains an active listing of volunteer opportunities and pays employees for up to four hours per month for voluntary community service.

Family Benefits: PVH's work/family programs are not extensive but include flexible work arrangements, dependent care seminars, and the guarantee of returning to one's own job following family leave.

Workplace Information: PVH offers a defined benefit pension plan to all employees who meet age and service requirements. These funds are supplemented by a savings plan through which the company matches 50 percent of employee contributions. Other benefits include tuition reimbursement and fitness/wellness programs.

A small portion (5 percent) of PVH's workforce is unionized. The company has a formal complaint resolution process for nonunionized employees.

In December 1995, PVH closed three factories and 200 stores. The restructuring resulted in the elimination of 1,200 positions. PVH reports that affected employees were offered "a substantial severance package."

International: PVH manufactures a portion of its product at facilities in the U.S., Puerto Rico and the Caribbean Basin. The company also sources production overseas, principally in the Far East. For these suppliers, the company has developed a code of conduct addressing such issues as wages, health and safety, child and forced labor, environmental protection, and harassment and discrimination. The code contains strong provisions related to workers' rights and working hours, and includes a reference to PVH's willingness to pay wages that meet industry averages (i.e., occasionally higher than local minimum wage). It also includes specific references to monitoring provisions.

Following the considerable political and social turmoil that racked Central America during the 1980s, PVH launched a five-year, $1.5 million program of comprehensive community development and primary education in 1993, concentrating on a village just outside Guatemala City (where the company has manufacturing facilities). The program, "New Educational Opportunities" or Project NEO, targets seven public elementary schools serving about 3,500 children.

Specific components of the initiative include improving existing school facilities, enhancing curriculum design and teaching strategies, increasing access to basic teaching materials, and bettering the children's overall nutrition and health conditions. Overall, the program seeks to have a measurable impact on enrollment and retention, while also reducing educational disparities between boys and girls. Parents and other family members are directly involved and ownership of the program will transfer to local communities after its final phase has concluded.

Pitney Bowes

STOCK SYMBOL: PBI
STOCK EXCHANGES: NY, B, CH, P, PH

Environment	A
Women's Advancement	A
Minority Advancement	B
Charitable Giving	C
Community Outreach	C
Family Benefits	N
Workplace Issues	B?
Social Disclosure	B

Pitney Bowes, headquartered in Stamford, Connecticut, is a multinational manufacturing and marketing company, which provides mailing, logistics, and office systems. In 1996, the company had 28,600 employees and revenues of $3.9 billion.

Environment: Pitney Bowes has an environmental policy and a Corporate Environmental Report (CER), which is updated biennially and is available on the Internet. Pitney Bowes provides Environmental Health and Safety (EH&S) training to all employees. The company also considers contribution towards EH&S goals in the job performance reviews of EH&S staff and presents awards to employees for their contribution to environmental issues. Pitney Bowes has a written pollution prevention policy and a company-wide pollution prevention program, which establishes goals for point sources, fugitive emissions, secondary emissions, and solid waste. In the selection of suppliers, Pitney Bowes evaluates environmental management systems of suppliers and determines whether suppliers have necessary permits. Pitney Bowes also has a corporate policy on community involvement relating to environmental concerns. Pitney Bowes has an environmental audit program with worldwide standards/applicability. Internationally, the company follows U.S. regulations in the U.S. and local regulation abroad, but goes beyond compliance to address pollution prevention and product stewardship in all operations.

Pitney Bowes' average toxic releases and transfers during the years 1994–1996 were among the lowest compared to an industry sample. However, although its emissions decreased by an average of about a seventh annually during those years, its performance was still below average within the industry sample.

EEO: In 1996, two women and two minorities served on Pitney Bowes' 12-member board. Of eight corporate officers at the company, two were women and none were minorities, while three of the top 25 paid employees were women, and none were minorities. Pitney Bowes was one of 83 cited in the Glass Ceiling Commission's March 1995, report for its Pairing System Program, and its Minorities Resource Group and Women's Resource Group.

Community Involvement: Pitney Bowes' charitable contributions totaled over $3.2 million in cash in 1996, and almost $3.8 million of in-kind donations. The $3.4 million cash-giving figure represented the equivalent of 0.5 percent of the company's pretax earnings for the same year.

Workplace Information: OSHA records indicate that Pitney Bowes underwent three health and safety inspections from 1994 to 1996. Violations include one classified as "serious" and a total of $6,000 in fines, an average of $2,000 per inspection. In comparison, the median amount of fines per inspection for other companies in the industries manufacturing electronic equipment was $1,347.

Pitney Bowes has held annual employees' meetings since 1947 at which workers get a chance to ask senior managers questions. Since 1987, a corporate ombudsman has been available on a confidential basis to any employee who feels he or she has been treated unfairly.

Animal Testing: Pitney Bowes uses a minimal number of animals in research through outside contractors to test inking products and toners.

⚙ Polaroid Corporation

STOCK SYMBOL: PRD
STOCK EXCHANGES: NY, B, C, CH, PH, P

Environment	B
Women's Advancement	B
Minority Advancement	A
Charitable Giving	N
Community Outreach	B
Family Benefits	A
Workplace Issues	A
Social Disclosure	A

Headquartered in Cambridge, Massachusetts, Polaroid Corporation designs, manufactures and markets a variety of products primarily in the instant image recording fields. 1997 revenues amounted to $2.2 billion. Worldwide employees totaled about 10,000, including 4,000 outside the United States.

Environment: In 1994 Polaroid endorsed the CERES Principles. Polaroid's Toxic Use and Waste Reduction (TUWR) program and Environmental Accounting and Reporting System are the key company efforts driving pollution prevention. Polaroid is currently in the second phase of its TUWR program. Polaroid's U.S. SARA Title III releases were 10 million pounds in 1994, a 12.5 percent increase from 1993. However, the company has reduced Title III emissions by 2.3 million pounds since 1987. In 1995, Polaroid exceeded its annual five percent reduction TUWR goal by achieving a six percent overall reduction in chemical waste. Polaroid also achieved a nine percent reduction in its chemical use and waste per unit of production from 9.97 million to 9.07 million pounds in 1995. Polaroid's most recent "Report on the Environment" was published in 1995 and contained information for 1994. An annual environmental report has been issued since 1988; however, the report containing information for 1995 is not available yet.

Polaroid states that it follows U.S. regulations in the United States and local regulations abroad. The company monitors SARA Title III emissions in non-U.S. operations. Polaroid's "Guide to Business Conduct" includes an environmental affairs section, outlining ethics and compliance standards for record-keeping, reporting, waste treatment processes and disposal of wastes.

EEO: In 1996, one woman and one minority served on Polaroid Corp.'s 14-member board. Of 26 corporate officers at the company, two were women and four were minorities, while three of the top 25 paid employees were women, and four were minorities.

Although the company has no formal programs for banking with minority-owned banks, it indicates that it has banked with the Boston Bank of Commerce, a minority owned bank, for over 15 years.

Community Involvement: In 1996, Polaroid made cash contributions of $3.8 million, or 2.3 percent of the company's pretax earnings for that year. In 1995, the company registered a loss, and the high contribution percentage may reflect relatively low earnings for the company in 1996.

All grants given by the Polaroid Foundation support the development of skills for the disadvantaged, including covering the tuition costs of low-income adults in training as day care teachers and school-to-work programs. The Product Donation Program gives photographic products to organizations that help the disadvantaged. Product donations are also given to disaster relief efforts and animal humanity programs. In 1996, Polaroid's charitable conributions totaled $3.79 million in cash.

Workplace Information: According to OSHA records, Polaroid Corp. was not inspected from 1994 to 1996. Consequently no violations or fines were assessed to the company.

International: In 1995, Polaroid adopted a "Supplier Principles of Conduct" covering areas such as environment and safety, and work practices and compensation.

Additional Information: Because the company continually develops new chemicals, it is required to conduct extensive toxicity testing in Europe using animals. In the U.S., animal testing is also conducted for consumer and worker protection reasons. Overall, measures are taken to minimize animal testing, which is dependent on the amount of new chemicals developed per year.

Potlatch Corporation

STOCK SYMBOL: PCH

STOCK EXCHANGES: NY, B, CH, P, PH

Environment	C
Women's Advancement	A?
Minority Advancement	N
Charitable Giving	C?
Community Outreach	D?
Family Benefits	N
Workplace Issues	D?
Social Disclosure	C

Potlatch, headquartered in San Francisco, California, is a diverse manufacturer of such forest products as wood building materials, paper and pulp, kraft containers, and tissue paper. The company also owns approximately 1.5 million acres of timber in the United States, which supplies less than one half its need for raw materials. Most of the remaining timber has traditionally been supplied by cutting on government land, though that has recently been scarce because of restrictions on cutting. Potlatch President John Richards assumed the additional titles of CEO and Board Chairman in May 1994, succeeding the retiring Richard B. Madden. In 1996, Potlatch had $1.6 billion in revenues and 6,700 employees.

Environment: The company publishes a brief corporate environmental report and has a written environmental policy. Potlatch provides environmental health and safety training to facility staff. There is no written pollution prevention policy, but the company has initiated a pollution prevention program, which establishes reduction goals for point source emissions. Potlatch is in compliance with the American Forest & Paper Association's Sustainable Forestry Initiative.

Potlatch was the second highest emitter of toxic releases and transfers in 1993 and the fourth highest in 1994, compared to a 12-company industry sample. Emissions increased by nearly half between the two years, a below average performance within the sample.

Potlatch and the U.S. Forest Service are sponsoring a detailed study of migratory songbirds in northern Idaho. Scientists claim that knowing facts about songbird populations, habitat, and nesting sites would allow Potlatch and the Forest Service to work the birds into its forest management plans. In 1996, the company joined with the Rocky Mountain Elk Foundation in an effort to improve elk habitat on Potlatch lands in North Central Idaho. The company is engaged in cooperative stream habitat enhancement work and is sponsoring a long-term water quality study in North Idaho, and will make the results publicly available.

Potlatch's Lewiston, Idaho, pulp and paper complex expects to obtain 20 percent of its wood from poplar plantations within the next few years. Planted as eight-inch long twigs, the genetically engineered trees grow 10 feet or more every year. Potlatch plans to harvest its first crop of hybrid poplar trees in 1999 and currently plants 4,000 acres a year. The company states that 22,000 acres of intensively managed tree farm provides as much wood fiber as 400,000 acres of forest.

EEO: In 1996, Potlatch Corp.'s board totaled 15 directors, including two women and no minorities, while three of a total of 16 corporate officers were women, and none were minorities.

Community Involvement: In 1995, Potlatch's contributions to various charitable institutions included cash donations totaling over $1.2 million ($1.6 million in 1997). The company's cash contributions for 1995 were equivalent to 0.73 percent of its earnings before taxes for the same year.

The Potlatch Corp. gives primarily through its two foundations—the Potlatch Foundation for Higher Education and the Potlatch Foundation II, with the majority of funding from both going towards education. The company also makes regional contributions.

Workplace Information: OSHA records indicate that Potlatch underwent five health and safety inspections from 1994 to 1996. Violations included 29 classified as "serious" for a total of $22,085 in fines, an average of $4,417 per inspection. Two of the company's plants were recognized by OSHA through its Voluntary Protection Program, which designates sites meeting specific safety criteria.

Potlatch laid off approximately 200 workers at the Lewiston, Idaho, pulp mill after completing a $400 million technological upgrade there in 1994. Lewiston is the home of Potlatch's largest sawmill, pulp mill, and tissue facilities.

In 1990, Potlatch's Warren, Arkansas, facility opened a learning center, which offers literacy, math, and computer programs for company employees.

PP&L Resources

STOCK SYMBOL: PPL
STOCK EXCHANGES: NY, B, C, CH, PH, P

Environment	N
Women's Advancement	A?
Minority Advancement	N
Charitable Giving	F?
Community Outreach	A
Family Benefits	B
Workplace Issues	B
Social Disclosure	A

P P&L, headquartered in Allentown, Pennsylvania, is the holding company for PP&L, Inc., PP&L Global, Inc., PP&L Spectrum, Inc., and H.T. Lyons, Inc. Through its subsidiaries, PP&L provides electricity, generates and sells electricity in 22 states and Canada; develops, owns, and operates electric generation and distribution companies in the U.K., Chile, Argentina, Bolivia, Peru, Spain, and Portugal; and operates a heating, ventilating, and air-conditioning firm. At year-end 1996, the company had revenues of $2.9 billion and employed 6,428 people.

Environment: PP&L, Inc., publishes a corporate environmental report. The company is a member of CERES. The company received a National Land Management Award for its land management practices and environmental education programs, sponsored by the Edison Electric Institute.

PP&L was also chosen as a participating utility in a two-year program that will allow 1,000 motorists to test drive General Motors Corp.'s new two-seat electric "Impact" as part of a "PrEView Drive." The company was chosen as a participant due to its long-term support of electric vehicles.

EEO: In 1996, PP&L Resources' board totaled 12 directors, including three women and no minorities, while two of a total of 23 corporate officers were women, and none were minorities.

Community Outreach: In 1996, PP&L's charitable giving totaled $1.5 million in cash and in-kind contributions totaled $25,000. The cash giving figure represented 0.27 percent of the company's pretax earnings for 1996. PP&L reports that, including customer service programs for low income citizens, total philanthropic contributions are $13 million. PP&L operates economic development partnership programs, and reports that they have frequently been recognized as model efforts. The Community

Partnership Program that focuses on neighborhood and small business development won the EEI Common Goals Award in 1997. The program is funded at $3 million annually.

Family Benefits: PP&L Resources makes a resource/referral service for child care available to employees with children. A full 26 weeks is offered for maternity or paternity leave, well above the 12 week minimum required under the Family and Medical Leave Act. The first eight weeks of maternity leave are paid by the company.

The company also offers such flexible scheduling options as a compressed work week, work-at-home arrangements, flextime, and part-time return to work following leave.

Workplace Information: The records of the Occupational Safety and Health Administration (OSHA) indicate that PP&L Resources was not inspected from 1994 to 1996. Consequently no fines or violations were assessed to the company. As inspections can frequently be called in response to a complaint regarding the health or safety conditions at a company, the lack of inspections may indicate a relatively strong workplace in terms of health and safety issues. However, it is not unusual for OSHA to report that a company was not inspected over the course of several years. The company has seen a reduction in incidents rates for the last two years of approximately 45 percent.

PPG Industries

STOCK SYMBOL: PPG
STOCK EXCHANGES: NY, B, CH, P, PH

Environment	A
Women's Advancement	F?
Minority Advancement	C?
Charitable Giving	D
Community Outreach	D
Family Benefits	N
Workplace Issues	B?
Social Disclosure	B

A s the nation's leading glass manufacturer and the world's largest producer of optical resins, PPG Industries' products range from windshields for autos and jets to fiberglass and caustic soda. The company is also a leading producer of chlorine. PPG Industries, headquartered in Pittsburgh, Pennsylvania, has continued to expand globally with the 1994 opening of its second silica manufacturing plant in China. In 1997, PPG had revenues of $7.4 billion and 32,000 employees worldwide.

Environment: PPG Industries has an environmental policy and a corporate environmental report, which is verified by Responsible Care and is available on the Internet. PPG Industries has an environmental health and safety (EH&S) training program and considers contributions towards EH&S goals in the job performance reviews of executives and managers. PPG Industries has a written policy on product stewardship. In the selection of suppliers, the company conducts or reviews environmental audits on suppliers' facilities. The company conducts compliance audits of industrial facilities. Internationally, PPG Industries states that it follows U.S. regulations in the U.S. and abroad unless local regulations are stricter. PPG Industries' average total toxic releases and transfers during the years 1993–1994 were less than the industry sample average. Emissions decreased by about a third during those years, a better than average performance.

PPG's Ohio plant reduced hazardous waste by more than 9 million pounds, a 64 percent reduction, while increasing plant production by 42 percent. In 1995, PPG's Ohio plant won the Governor's Award for Outstanding Achievement in Pollution Prevention for its waste-reduction efforts.

PPG was fined $522,000 by the EPA for filing late substantial risk reports about its products, a requirement of the Toxic Substances Control Act.

EEO: In 1996, PPG's 12-member Board of Directors included one woman and one minority. Of 31 corporate officers at the company, one was a woman and none were minorities. In 1997, one additional minority was elected to the Board of Directors and two minorities joined the corporate officers.

In addition to its corporate Manager of Affirmative Action, PPG has formed diversity teams, mentoring programs, and support groups to improve the quality of life for minority employees. The company has internships and scholarships for minority students and supports minority community organizations.

Community Involvement: In 1996, PPG Industries' charitable giving totaled $4.6 million in cash ($4.8 million in 1997), which was equal to 0.37 percent of the company's pretax earnings for that year. PPG developed a local agent system of 32 managers to ensure company sensitivity to local needs in its plant communities. Agents recommend a budget once a year for contributions in their communities. The company also operates a seven-year old Public Education Leadership program in 55 communities, and includes the participation of employee volunteers, as well as teacher and student internships.

Workplace Information: OSHA records indicate that PPG was inspected eight times from 1994 to 1996. Violations included 24 classified as "serious" for a total of $10,087 in fines, an average of $1,261 per inspection. In comparison, the median amount of fines per inspection for other companies in the extractive business was $2,941.

In 1992, the company opened a training center to help employees improve basic reading and math skills necessary for a GED. In 1991, PPG received the Pennsylvania Large Employer of the Year Award for People. Despite these programs, union relations at PPG have at times been contentious. In 1993, more than 1,000 employees represented by the Aluminum, Brick, and Glass Workers struck at four PPG plants when negotiations broke down. PPG later closed two of the plants, citing long-term negative market forces.

Weapons Contracts: In 1994, PPG had $10.3 million in contracts with the Department of Defense (0.1 percent of total revenues).

199

Procter & Gamble

STOCK SYMBOL: PG

STOCK EXCHANGES: NY, B, C, CH, P, PH

Environment	N
Women's Advancement	B
Minority Advancement	C
Charitable Giving	D
Community Outreach	B
Family Benefits	A
Workplace Issues	A
Social Disclosure	A

Procter & Gamble, headquartered in Cincinnati, Ohio, markets more than 300 brands, including soaps, cosmetics, detergents, disposable diapers, and beverages. In 1996, the company reached sales of $35.3 billion and was the world's leading household products company. It has 103,000 employees.

Environment: P&G has a comprehensive environmental policy with high-level corporate executives reporting to the Board of Directors on environmental issues. In 1996, the company reported TRI emissions had declined to 4.5 million pounds in 1995, a 75 percent decrease since 1991. In 1996, P&G and the EPA agreed to a settlement concerning an EPA investigation of permits, reports, and excess methanol emissions at its Sacramento industrial chemicals plant.

By 1995, through increased use of recycled plastic in detergent bottles (some use 100 percent postconsumer recycled plastic), composting programs, and improvements in disposable diaper materials, the company reduced total waste per unit of production by 51 percent worldwide. It also eliminated the use of elemental chlorine in the manufacture of pulp for personal care products.

EEO: In 1996, P&G's 17-member Board of Directors included two women. Of 30 corporate officers at the company, one was a woman. There were no minorities in either group.

In March 1997, a Federal Court ruled that a group of former Max Factor employees could proceed with their suit claiming they were subject to age discrimination by Procter & Gamble. The eight sales representatives alleged that Procter & Gamble did not offer them jobs after it acquired Max Factor in 1991 primarily because each of them was over 40 at the time.

In November, 1996, Procter & Gamble was the first recipient of the Corporate Affirmative Action Award from the NAACP Legal Defense Fund. John Pepper, Chief Executive Officer of Procter & Gamble, was lauded by the NAACP Legal Defense Fund committee for his commitment to diversity. In 1996, P&G was awarded the National Council of Negro Women's Corporate Partnership award. In 1994, the U.S. Department of Labor gave P&G the Opportunity 2000 award, its highest recognition, for the company's efforts to promote diversity. In 1994 and 1995, P&G

was one of the 50 companies recognized by VISTA magazine for its leadership role in offering career opportunities to Hispanic women.

Community Involvement: The *Corporate Giving Watch* ranked P&G among the top ten corporate contributors in the areas of civic & public affairs, education, and international interests for the fiscal year ending June 1996. P&G awarded $2.8 million, $19.7 million, and $9.7 million respectively in those areas. P&G created the Sycamore Investment Company in 1984 to lend money to minority businesses, and invested $250,000 with Blue Chips Venture Capital Fund which provides loans to small, minority/women-owned businesses. The National Alliance of Business named P&G its 1995 Distinguished Company of the Year for education and training opportunities for disadvantaged youth.

In 1996, P&G's contributions to various charitable institutions included cash donations totaling $38.6 million, and $7 million in in-kind donations.

Workplace Information: P&G was inspected once in 1996, receiving only incidental violations and no fines. In comparison, the median amount of fines per inspection for other companies in the food, beverage, and household products industries was $1,515.

Animal Testing: P&G conducts tests on animals for both its medical and consumer product operations. P&G has invested $64 million to develop and use alternative test methods.

Product Issue: Olestra, a synthetic fat substitute, approved by the FDA for use only in certain snack foods, has been controversial and is not without risk, according to the government. Critics of the product claim that the label does not warn consumers of possible consequences such as cancer and digestive problems.

Quaker Oats

STOCK SYMBOL: OAT
STOCK EXCHANGES: NY, To, B, CH, P, PH

Environment	B
Women's Advancement	N
Minority Advancement	N
Charitable Giving	C
Community Outreach	C
Family Benefits	N
Workplace Issues	F?
Social Disclosure	C

Quaker Oats, headquartered in Chicago, Illinois, is a worldwide marketer of consumer grocery products, including such brands as Quaker Oats, Life Cereal, Aunt Jemima, Gatorade, and Rice-a-Roni. In 1994, the company added Snapple to its line-up, which proved to be a costly venture and may have led to the resignation of Philip Marineau, president of Quaker Oats in October 1995. That year, the company shed its U.S. and European pet food operations, Van Camp beans, and a Mexican chocolate business. It also cut its workforce and consolidated divisions. Quaker has 14,800 employees. Sales were $5.2 billion in 1996.

Environment: Quaker participates in the Buy Recycled Business Alliance and spends more than $22 million a year expanding its line of products containing recycled materials. Within the company, recycling and waste minimization programs are run at the plant level.

In 1989, when U.S. cornfields were being flooded with aflatoxin (a highly toxic carcinogen), Quaker implemented comprehensive testing measures to guard against contamination and adopted anticontamination standards 25 percent stricter than those of the Food and Drug Administration (FDA).

The company has low toxic releases and hazardous waste generation. However, its accidental spills — 272,470 pounds — are twice as high as the food industry average. Between 1991 and 1995, total penalties paid for EPA and local compliance citations were less than $100,000.

EEO: Quaker Oats was one of ten companies recognized by the National Minority Business Council in February 1997 for its efforts to further minority businesses and its support for council initiatives. It was also one of three companies that formally supported a 1995 bill that would have made discrimination on the basis of sexual orientation illegal in Illinois if it had passed. In 1995, Quaker Oats' 10-member Board of Directors included one woman. Of 24 corporate officers at the company, five were women.

Community Involvement: In addition to Quaker Oats' focus on nutrition and hunger relief, the company provides grants to minority education and programs. In 1996, the company sponsored the Susan G. Komen Foundation's Race For a Cure, donating 10 cents from every Quaker Rice Cakes item sold. Quaker is also a major sponsor of the Women's Sports Foundation.

Quaker Oats' charitable contributions totaled almost $1.5 million in cash in 1996, and almost $7.2 million in in-kind donations. The $1.5 million cash-giving figure represented the equivalent of 0.36 percent of the company's pretax earnings for the same year, and a decrease of 16.7 percent from the company's cash contributions in 1995.

Workplace Information: OSHA records indicate that Quaker underwent seven inspections from 1994 to 1996. Violations included one classified as "willful" or "repeat" and 68 classified as "serious" for a total of $33,187 in fines, an average of $4,741 per inspection. In comparison, the median amount of fines per inspection for other companies in the food, beverage, and household products industries was $1,515.

The QuakerFlex benefit program allows employees to use flex credits or cash to buy up to five annual vacation days or sell up to 10 days.

Quaker's medical plan, which is close to cost-free for workers, won a 92 percent satisfaction rate from employees in a 1995 survey of benefit plans conducted by *Money* magazine. Quaker came in second in a list of the top ten. The company also offers a confidential basic health screening, which has helped reduce health risks such as smoking and hypertension (and related medical costs) over a 13-year period. Quaker received the C. Everett Koop National Health Award in 1995. Fitness and wellness programs are also available.

At the time they are hired, employees are enrolled in a 401(k) and the employee stock-ownership plan (ESOP) through which Quaker gives workers company stock, valued at an average 12 percent of annual earnings.

The Bakery, Confectionery, & Tobacco Union (BCT) reports that Quaker opposed its organizing drives in Jackson, Tennessee, and at its Liqui-Dri unit.

Ralston Purina Group

STOCK SYMBOL: RAL
STOCK EXCHANGES: NY, B, C, CH, P, PH

Environment	N
Women's Advancement	D
Minority Advancement	F
Charitable Giving	D?
Community Outreach	N
Family Benefits	N
Workplace Issues	C?
Social Disclosure	C

The Ralston Purina Group, headquartered in St. Louis, Missouri, is the world's largest producer of dry dog food and dry and soft-moist cat foods, marketed under the Purina brand name. Ralston is also the world's largest manufacturer of dry cell battery products, including Eveready and Energizer brand products. The company is a major producer of dietary soy protein, fiber food ingredients, and polymer products. In 1996, Ralston had sales of $6.1 billion and employed 29,300 workers worldwide.

Environment: Ralston does not publish an environmental progress report or a corporate environmental policy. Ralston's hazardous waste (both real and adjusted for size) was worse than the food industry average for companies studied by CEP.

The company's battery production most likely accounts for the difference. Eveready and Energizer market an ultra-low mercury alkaline battery aimed at environmentally conscious consumers.

Ralston's accidental spill record is also higher than the food industry average from 1991 through 1995. Toxic releases, however, have shown a 32 percent decline from 1990 through 1994. By 1997, the Purina C.A.R.E.S. Fund—formerly the Purina Big Cat Survival Fund—donated $3.4 million to help zoos across the country save endangered species.

EEO: Ralston Purina turned in a below average performance in the area of diversity in 1996, compared to other S&P 500 companies. Among the companies surveyed by CEP, the average representation of women and minorities on S&P corporate boards was 10.8 percent and 7.5 percent, respectively. In comparison, Ralston Purina had one woman and one minority on its ten-member Board of Directors. Additionally, the company's total of 11 corporate officers included two women and no minorities.

Community Involvement: In 1995, Ralston Purina's contributions to various charitable institutions included cash donations totaling almost $1.8 million. The company's cash contributions for 1995 were equivalent to 0.35 percent of its earnings before taxes.

Half of Ralston Purina's total giving is done through the Ralston Purina Trust Fund, primarily to support the United Way. In 1995, it gave $1.05 million to the United Way in St. Louis.

Workplace Information: According to the Occupational Safety and Health Administration's records, Ralston Purina was inspected three times from 1994 to 1996. The OSHA inspectors' citations included six violations classified as "serious." A total of $10,000 in fines was assessed to the company following the inspections, an average of $3,333 per inspection. In comparison, the median amount of fines per inspection for other companies in the food, beverage, and household products industries was $1,515.

Animal Testing: Ralston conducts nutritional testing at its Purina Pet Care Center. According to the company, testing does not harm the animals in any way.

Legal Proceedings: In January 1993, the company was served with the first of nine substantively identical actions currently pending in the United States District Court of New Jersey. The now consolidated proceeding is a certified class action on behalf of all direct purchasers of baby foods, alleging that the Beech-Nut baby food business—owned by Ralston from 1989 to 1994—together with Gerber Products and the Heinz Company conspired to fix prices of

Raychem Corporation

STOCK SYMBOL: RYC
STOCK EXCHANGES: NY, B, CH, PH, P

Environment	C
Women's Advancement	F
Minority Advancement	D?
Charitable Giving	B
Community Outreach	C
Family Benefits	N
Workplace Issues	D?
Social Disclosure	C

Raychem, headquartered in Menlo Park, California, is a global manufacturer of electronics and electrical equipment. The company serves customers in many markets, including the automotive, commercial electronics, computer, construction, and defense industries. In 1996, Raychem had 8,697 workers worldwide, and revenues reached $1.6 billion.

Environment: Raychem Corp. has an environmental policy but does not currently publish a corporate environmental report. The company's pollution prevention measures include source reduction, process recycling, and use of recycled commodities. The company evaluates its products with the objective of reducing their life-cycle impacts on the environment.

Raychem's toxic releases and transfers were above average in 1993 and just below average in 1994, compared to an industry sample. During that period, emissions decreased slightly, a better than average performance, and from 1993 to 1995, emissions showed a trend of decreasing by about half.

EEO: Raychem was one of 83 companies cited in the Glass Ceiling Commission's 1995 report for implementing "employment practices that help break the glass ceiling." The Commission cited the company specifically for its Women's Network, which was developed in 1991 to address the needs of female employees in a heavily male-dominated workplace.

However, Raychem was below the average of women and minority representation for S&P 500 companies in 1996. The company had no women or minorities on its nine-member Board of Directors. Two of its 19 corporate officers were women.

Community Involvement: The Raychem Foundation provides support to any graduating high school seniors from schools in the Sequoia Union High School District in California who have been accepted at a four-year college or university.

Raychem's charitable contributions totaled $1 million in cash in 1996, the equivalent of 0.73 percent of Raychem's pretax earnings for that year, and $15,000 of in-kind donations.

Family Benefits: Raychem covers 100 percent of medical insurance premiums for individuals and 80 percent coverage for families. The company offers flexible spending accounts and work schedules, as well as referral services for child care and reference materials for elder care. Raychem has a worldwide scholarship program for its employees' children.

Workplace Information: OSHA records indicate that Raychem Corp. underwent three health and safety inspections from 1994 to 1996. Violations include six classified as "serious" for a total of $9,235 in fines, an average of $3,078 per inspection. In comparison, the median amount of fines per inspection for other companies in the industries manufacturing electronic equipment was $1,347.

Raychem offers its non-unionized workforce a noteworthy benefits package, including profit-sharing, stock purchase plans, 401(k) plan, life insurance, and disability. The company also offers tuition reimbursement and training programs in career enhancement, literacy, and skills building.

Weapons Contracts: In 1994, Raychem received Department of Defense contracts worth $1.3 million. In 1991, sales of electronics to the Department of Defense accounted for 17 percent of Raychem's revenue. The company manufactures components or provides support equipment for such military hardware as the M1 Tank; F-14, F-16, and B-2 planes; and various helicopter programs.

Legal Proceedings: In January 1995, Raychem settled a lawsuit for $8.5 million for property damage and personal injury (a death) caused by a heat-tracing product.

Raytheon Company

STOCK SYMBOL: RTNA, RTNB
STOCK EXCHANGES: NY, B, C, CH, PH, P

Environment	N
Women's Advancement	F
Minority Advancement	F
Charitable Giving	C
Community Outreach	N
Family Benefits	N
Workplace Issues	D?
Social Disclosure	B

Raytheon, based in Lexington, Massachusetts, is a defense and aerospace company. There are four different segments within the company: electronics, aircraft, engineering and construction, and appliances. Its largest segment is electronics, with products such as environmental monitoring systems; global broadcast systems; Patriot missile, Trident missle, and other defense systems, and marine electronics. Raytheon is one of the top manufacturers of small passenger aircraft. In 1997, the company acquired the defense businesses of Texas Instruments and GM's Hughes Electronics. At year-end 1997, Raytheon had sales of $20 billion and approximately 120,000 employees.

Environment: Raytheon has an environmental policy that commits to going beyond regulatory compliance with environmental laws. The company published a white paper in 1996, highlighting and describing its environmental progress. Raytheon has implemented an integrated environmental management system and provides environmental, health and safety (EH&S) training to all its employees. Raytheon hosts an annual EH&S conference for its employees to provide a forum for information exchange.

The company has a written commitment to pollution prevention and has implemented a companywide pollution prevention program, which requires each site to establish waste minimization goals and report to management on an annual basis. By the end of 1992, the company eliminated the use of two ozone depleting cleaning solvents, methyl chloroform and Freon 113, and shared its study results at hundreds of forums throughout the U.S. Raytheon also eliminated virtually all its use of suspected carcinogenic solvents in 1990. The company has a corporate policy on community involvement relating to local environmental concerns.

As part of its product stewardship program, Raytheon embarked on a Design for the Environment Initiative (DfE), committing to minimize the volume of hazardous raw materials used in its manufacturing process. The company has taken a leadership role in the formation of Massachusetts Watershed Awareness and Policy Initiative, and maintains an active involvement with local watershed associations such as Merrimack River Watershed Council, Save the Bay, Charles River Watershed Association, and Massachusetts Water Watch Partnership. Raytheon also has a partnership with the Nature Conservancy. The company was an early voluntary participant in EPA's Industrial Toxics Program, and was selected by EPA as a case study for exemplary emission reductions in the program.

Raytheon's toxic emissions have been on the decline, as has its hazardous waste generation, and its ozone depleting emissions have been virtually eliminated.

EEO: In 1996, one woman sat on Raytheon's 15-member Board of Directors. The company's total of 39 corporate officers included one woman and one minority. One woman and no minorities were among the 25 highest paid employees.

Community Involvement: In 1995, Raytheon Co.'s contributions to various charitable institutions included cash donations totaling $65,000. The cash contributions for 1995 were equivalent to 0.01 percent of its earnings before taxes for the same year.

Workplace Information: OSHA records indicate that Raytheon was inspected 20 times from 1994 to 1996. Violations included 70 classified as "serious" for a total of $45,635 in fines, or an average of $2,281 per inspection. In comparison, the median amount of fines per inspection for other companies in similar manufacturing industries was $2,412. Raytheon is a member of the Department of Labor's Working Women Count Honor Roll, specifically for its benefits program. The program includes immunizations for children, annual pap smears, and baseline mammograms.

Raytheon was the ninth-largest defense contractor in the world in 1996 with $4 billion in defense revenue, representing 32.8 percent of its total business. With its 1997 acquisitions of Hughes and TI's defense businesses, Raytheon joined Boeing and Lockheed Martin as one of the three largest aerospace companies; now $14.5 billion of its $20 billion in revenue is defense-related.

Reebok International

STOCK SYMBOL: RBK
STOCK EXCHANGES: NY, B, CH, P, PH

Environment	N
Women's Advancement	F
Minority Advancement	B
Charitable Giving	C
Community Outreach	C
Family Benefits	C
Workplace Issues	A
Social Disclosure	A

Reebok, headquartered in Stoughton, Massachusetts, is a major designer and marketer of footwear and apparel. Reebok does not manufacture any of its own shoes, nor does it own any of the facilities in the Pacific Rim that make them. In 1996, the company had 6,900 employees and sales of $3.5 billion.

Environment: Reebok uses vegetable-based dyes for gloss on its shoe boxes. The boxes themselves are made from at least 90 percent recycled material, with the filler of 100 percent recycled material. Its catalogues, promotional material, and posters are also made entirely of recycled materials.

EEO: In 1996, Reebok International's board totaled ten directors, including two minorities. One of its seven corporate officers was a minority. Additionally, two women and one minority were among the 25 employees with the highest salaries at the company.

Though Reebok does not currently offer diversity training to all its employees, it is developing a program to be offered in 1998. In 1997, the *New York Times* described Reebok as one of few American companies with high representation of women among company executives. However, in 1996, there were no women among corporate officers or board members at the company.

Community Involvement: The Reebok Foundation priorities are human rights, Out-of-School Time programs, and organizations that promote Hispanic and Black American pluralism. In 1988, Reebok launched an annual Human Rights Award, which gives a $25,000 prize to four individuals under the age of 30 who help promote human rights in their communities.

Reebok International's charitable contributions totaled $2.1 million in cash in 1996 and $304,845 in in-kind donations. The $2.1 million cash-giving figure represented the equivalent of 0.89 percent of the company's pretax earnings for the same year, an increase of 7.4 percent from the company's cash contributions in 1995. In 1995, the company contributed 0.8 percent of its pretax earnings to charity.

Family Benefits: Reebok offers back-up day care, a prenatal/postnatal care program, lactation room, reduced summer hours, and an on-site cooperative food program and dry-cleaner. The company also provides domestic partner benefits.

International Operations: In late 1992 Reebok instituted Human Rights Production Standards, which include fair wages and freedom of association, limiting work weeks to 60 hours, and avoiding contractors who use forced or child labor. In addition, the company seeks contractors who agree to on-site inspection of production facilities.

Over 70 percent of Reebok's shoe production is in China, Indonesia, and Thailand. The human rights group Press for Change notes that although Reebok's code calls for compliance with local laws on minimum wages, the minimum legal wage in these countries is far below subsistence level.

A new central facility has been built to keep Reebok soccer balls from being made in rural villages, where monitoring is more difficult. In February 1997, Reebok joined with more than 50 sporting goods manufacturers, three major sporting goods associations, and international child advocacy groups to eradicate child labor in the soccer ball industry in Pakistan. The group established a $1 million fund to hire independent monitors and support educational efforts.

Workplace Information: OSHA records indicate that Reebok International underwent one health and safety inspection in 1996. The only violations reported by OSHA were classified as "other," the least serious kind of violation, and the company was not fined.

205

Reynolds Metals Company

STOCK SYMBOL: RLM
STOCK EXCHANGE: NY

Environment	C
Women's Advancement	C?
Minority Advancement	D?
Charitable Giving	D
Community Outreach	B
Family Benefits	D
Workplace Issues	D
Social Disclosure	A

Based in Richmond, Virginia, Reynolds Metals is the world's third largest aluminum company. In 1997, the company had $7 billion in sales and 25,500 employees.

Environment: Reynolds Metals has an environmental policy, but does not publish a corporate environmental report. Reynolds Metals has implemented an integrated environmental management system and provides environmental health and safety (EH&S) training to all employees. It also considers contribution towards EH&S goals in the job performance reviews of senior management. Reynolds Metals has a written pollution prevention policy and has initiated a companywide pollution prevention program, which establishes annual reduction goals for point sources, secondary emissions, fugitive emissions, and solid waste. Reynolds Metals does not have a written policy on product stewardship, but states that it evaluates its products with the objective of reducing their life-cycle impacts. Internationally, Reynolds Metals does not monitor SARA Title III, or equivalent emissions. The company states that it follows U.S. regulations in the U.S. and local regulations abroad. The company will apply U.S. technology standards where appropriate or for new ventures.

Reynolds Metals' average toxic releases and transfers during the years 1993–1994 were the highest compared to an industry sample. However, its emissions decreased by almost 10 percent during those years, an above average performance.

In October 1996, Reynolds Recycling, a division of Reynolds Metals Co., received the Virginia Governor's Environmental Excellence Award for Manufacturers. Reynolds won in the "environmental programs— larger manufacturer" category. The company recycles more than 1 million pounds of aluminum cans per day.

EEO: In 1996, Reynolds Metals' 14-member board of directors included two women and no minorities (one minority of 12 directors in 1997). Of 30 corporate officers at the company (22 in 1997), two were women and none were minorities. The company has special recruitment programs for women and minorities. It also assesses progress toward affirmative action goals in management job reviews.

Community Involvement: In 1996, Reynolds Metals' charitable giving totaled $940,000 in cash, which was equal to 0.61percent of the company's pretax earnings for that year. Giving increased to $1.1 million in 1997.

Reynolds seeks specifically to encourage precollege and higher education institutions to place special emphasis on business, engineering, and science core curriculums "in order to attract more of the best students and to train them for the workplace." Reynolds reports that one of its "annual corporate goals, as part of its social responsibility value is community involvement. Each business unit and plant is expected to develop a plan each year— appropriate to the interests of its employees—and report on accomplishments twice yearly."

Family Benefits: Reynolds offers job sharing, flextime, work-at-home, part-time work arrangements, and adoption expense reimbursement.

Workplace Information: According to the Occupational Safety and Health Administration's records, Reynolds was inspected 19 times from 1994 to 1996. Violations included 75 classified as "serious" for a total of $144,825 in fines, an average of $7,622 per inspection. In comparison, the median amount of fines per inspection for other companies in the extractive business was $2,941.

In June 1996, the company successfully negotiated a six-year contract with the United Steelworkers of America and the Aluminum, Brick and Glass Workers International Union. The new contract includes wage increases and improved benefits. A cooperative partnership agreement gives all levels of the company and union joint decision-making responsibility on safety issues, information-sharing, training, and changes in the workplace. It also guarantees employment security and joint decision-making prior to employee layoffs.

Rockwell International

STOCK SYMBOL: ROK

STOCK EXCHANGES: NY, TO, B, C, CH, P

Environment	N
Women's Advancement	D
Minority Advancement	A
Charitable Giving	B
Community Outreach	B
Family Benefits	A
Workplace Issues	C
Social Disclosure	A

Rockwell International is engaged in research, development and manufacture of many diversified products (electronics and automotive). The company was incorporated in 1996 and is the successor to the former Rockwell International Corp. as the result of a tax-free reorganization completed on December 6, 1996. As part of the reorganization, the company divested its former aerospace and defense businesses to Boeing for approximately $3.2 billion by means of a merger in which the company's predecessor corporation became a wholly owned subsidiary of Boeing. Total revenues for the fiscal year ended September 30, 1996 (before the company completed reorganization) totaled $10.5 billion. In 1996, Rockwell had 58,600 employees, of whom 18,000 were employed outside the U.S.

Environment: Rockwell International has an environmental policy that covers goals, policies and programs, compliance, operations, management practices, community relations, and public policy development. The policy has been translated into six languages and distributed to all employees worldwide. The company publishes a comprehensive corporate environmental report that displays extensive environmental impact data including toxic emissions, ozone-depleting substances, hazardous waste, and fuel and energy.

Rockwell conducts an annual training program through a consultant for training environmental professionals. Various in-house and off-site training programs are attended by environmental and safety professionals, handlers of hazardous materials and wastes, and employees involved with transportation of hazardous materials and wastes. A program has been initiated to ensure that significant environmental and chemical safety risks are addressed throughout the corporation. Rockwell has a written commitment on product stewardship and evaluates its products with the objective of reducing their life-cycle impacts on the environment, mostly through concentrating on the substitution or elimination of materials used in numerous manufacturing processes. Rockwell is a member of the WasteWi$e program and participated in EPA's "Common Sense Initiative."

EEO: In 1996, Rockwell International's 13-member Board of Directors included one woman and one minority. Of 15 corporate officers at the company, none were women and one was a minority. Two minorities were among the 25 highest paid employees.

In 1997, Rockwell added two minorities and one woman to its ranks of vice presidents. Rockwell states that it has three offices responsible for implementing and monitoring Affirmative Action and EEO programs, handling complaints, developing guidelines, acting as a liaison between the company and government agencies, and preparing reports. Rockwell also distributes a sexual harassment handbook, a report on its diversity management program, and a report on company ethics.

Community Involvement: In 1996, Rockwell International's charitable giving totaled $10.2 million in cash ($8.9 million in 1997, a relative increase when company restructuring is taken into account), which was equal to 1.14 percent of the company's pretax earnings for that year. The company's in-kind giving came to $500,000 in 1996.

Workplace Information: OSHA records indicate that Rockwell was inspected ten times from 1994 to 1996. Violations included one classified as "willful" or "repeat" and 17 classified as "serious" for a total of $257,780 in fines, largely resulting from a 1994 explosion at one of the company's former Rocketdyne division's labs. The average fine per inspection in 1996 was $2,085. The median amount of fines per inspection for similar manufacturing companies was $2,412.

Following the 1996 divestment of its aerospace and defense businesses, defense revenue fell from $2.24 billion or 17.3 percent of total revenue in 1995 to $600 million or 5.8 percent of total revenue in 1996. While Rockwell is no longer directly involved in manufacturing defense systems, it continues to build computers for use in defense electronics, avionics and aerospace.

In 1997, Rockwell was faced with a lawsuit over its allegedly poor management of the Rocky Flats nuclear weapons power plant in Colorado between 1975 and 1989. Allegations include overbilling the Department of Energy and failing to solve environmental problems.

207

Rohm & Haas Company

STOCK SYMBOL: ROH
STOCK EXCHANGES: NY, B, CH, P, PH

Environment	B
Women's Advancement	C
Minority Advancement	A
Charitable Giving	B
Community Outreach	A
Family Benefits	N
Workplace Issues	C?
Social Disclosure	A

R ohm & Haas, based in Philadelphia, Pennsylvania, is a specialty chemical manufacturer that produces polymers, resins, acrylic plastics (Plexiglas), insecticides, and other biologically active compounds used in industry and agriculture. In 1996, the company had 11,600 employees and revenues close to $4 billion.

Environment: Rohm and Haas has an environmental policy and a corporate environmental report, which is available on the Internet. Rohm and Haas has implemented an integrated environmental management system and provides environmental health and safety (EH&S) training to all employees. Rohm and Haas has a written pollution prevention policy and has initiated a companywide pollution prevention program, that establishes annual reduction goals for point sources and solid waste. Twelve facilities have community advisory panels. Rohm and Haas has a written policy on product stewardship.

Rohm and Haas's average total toxic releases and transfers during the years 1994–1996 were less than the industry sample average. Emissions decreased by an average of about a quarter annually during those years, a slightly better than average performance.

Rohm and Hass was honored as a 1997 Environmental Champion (for the second time) and received the EPA's Presidential Green Chemistry Challenge Award for their redesign of Sea-Nine 211 marine antifoulant (a ship paint coating). The company's biocides business team, which developed the environmentally friendly coating, continues to produce products that provide positive environmental alternatives.

R&H has formed a working committee of CAP members in the Bridesburg section of Philadelphia to resolve an issue related to styrene groundwater contamination in the area. The group will work on an economic protection package for 60 homes that are affected, and could involve the purchase of homes by the company and restitution for some homeowners whose property values have been affected. The committee will work to minimize the impact on those affected and will address health concerns and remediation at the site.

EEO: In 1996, Rohm & Haas Co.'s board totaled 14 directors, including two women and two minorities.

Three of 30 corporate officers were women and two were minorities. Additionally, two women and two minorities were among the 25 employees with the highest salaries.

In 1994, Rohm and Haas was awarded the Exemplary Voluntary Efforts (EVE) award, from the U.S. Department of Labor, in recognition of its programs designed to encourage minorities and women to consider careers in chemistry. Such programs at Rohm and Haas include programs to track the career development of women and minorities and recruiting efforts that allow the company to hire more than ten percent of the available female and minority Ph.D. candidates in chemistry and chemical engineering in the U.S.

Community Involvement: Rohm & Haas Co.'s charitable contributions totaled $4.5 million in cash in 1996, or 0.8 percent of the company's pretax earnings for the same year.

Workplace Information: OSHA records indicate that Rohm & Haas underwent five inspections from 1994 to 1996. Violations included 17 classified as "serious" for a total of $23,425 in fines, an average of $4,685 per inspection. In comparison, the median amount of fines per inspection for other companies in the extractive business was $2,941.

International: R&H has production facilities in 21 countries, including China, the Philippines, Singapore, Taiwan, Mexico, Colombia, and Brazil.

Animal Testing: R&H, which conducts chemical toxicity tests on animals, is one of 12 corporate sponsors of the Center for Alternatives to Animal Testing. In 1994, it donated software for a program to use computer modeling to replace animal tests.

208

Safeway Inc.

STOCK SYMBOL: SWY
STOCK EXCHANGES: NY, CH, PH

Environment	N
Women's Advancement	C
Minority Advancement	D
Charitable Giving	A
Community Outreach	B
Family Benefits	C
Workplace Issues	B
Social Disclosure	C

Safeway, headquartered in Oakland, California, operates 1,052 stores in the U.S. and Canada. In support of its retail operations, Safeway has an extensive network of distribution, manufacturing and food processing facilities. In April 1997, Safeway merged with Vons Companies, Inc., making Safeway the second largest grocery chain in North America, with sales in excess of $22.5 billion, and 135,000 employees.

Environment: Safeway was the first supermarket to refuse to sell Alar-treated apples in 1986, the first of its size to require all tuna products be certified dolphin-safe, and among the first not to sell milk or milk-based products from cows treated with genetically engineered bovine growth hormones (BGH). Safeway educates consumers on environmental issues.

By the end of 1995, Safeway had paid a total of $121 million to residents affected by a 1988 fire at its Richmond, California, warehouse. The fire released toxic fumes and resulted in 18 deaths.

EEO: There are no women on Safeway's nine-member Board of Directors; three women are senior vice presidents responsible for retail operations, human resources, and finance/public affairs. In 1995, company shareholders rejected requests to supply information on its promotion of women and minorities. In 1997, women constituted 36 percent of officials and managers, and minorities totaled 21 percent. Safeway is a participant in the NAACP's Fair Share program.

In June 1994, Safeway paid $7.5 million to settle a sex discrimination suit brought on behalf of 20,000 women. In 1991, the company settled similar charges (brought by the EEOC five years earlier) for a total of $900,000. Safeway was recently ordered to pay $3 million in punitive damages and $450,000 in compensatory damages in a sexual harassment case brought by a former delicatessen clerk in Mill Valley, California. The company is seeking a new trial.

In 1995, Safeway reached a settlement with the Department of Justice regarding store access for disabled individuals.

Community Involvement: Safeway's charitable giving consists primarily of product and equipment donations valued at about $15 million annually.

Its modest cash contributions support job training and other community programs. Since 1985, the company has sponsored the National Easter Seal Society, raising an estimated $50 million for the organization through 1996.

In 1994, Safeway supported a 14-city initiative aimed at expanding supermarket presence in the inner cities. In 1997, Safeway developed a 95,000 square foot shopping center in the District of Columbia as an inner-city project to revitalize an economically depressed area in D.C. Safeway agreed to and has recently sold the property to the Anacostia Economic Development Corp., a nonprofit community organization which will oversee its continued operation.

209

Workplace Information: Safeway is party to 400 union contracts covering nearly 90 percent of its workforce. A representative for the United Food and Commercial Workers (UFCW) reported generally favorable relations with Safeway. In recent years, the company faced a nine-day strike in northern California and a 44-day strike in Denver. Each dispute involved contracts covering multiple grocers.

In 1997, Safeway signed an agreement with the United Farm Workers to support basic worker rights for more than 20,000 strawberry workers in California. Though the agreement does not require Safeway to take any action, UFW President Arturo Rodriguez described the agreement as "the first time in three decades that Safeway and the UFW are working together."

Product Information: In May 1995, Safeway agreed to pay $125,000 to settle charges of alleged pricing violations in Mendocino County stores. Safeway paid $93,500 in 1989 for similar charges at stores in Oakland.

Sara Lee Corporation

STOCK SYMBOL: SLE

STOCK EXCHANGES: NY, C, B, CH, P, PH

Environment	B
Women's Advancement	A
Minority Advancement	A
Charitable Giving	B
Community Outreach	C
Family Benefits	B
Workplace Issues	N
Social Disclosure	B

Sara Lee Corporation, based in Chicago, Illinois, is a large diversified global manufacturer and marketer of brand-name products including Sara Lee Packaged Foods, Champion Jogbra, Coach leatherware, Hanes, and personal care products. Sales in 1996 were $18.6 billion, a 5 percent increase over fiscal 1995. About 40 percent of Sara Lee's sales are outside the United States. The company employs 135,300 people worldwide.

Environment: Sara Lee has a brief environmental policy and educates its employees on environmental issues and regulations that affect the facilities in which they operate.

The company states that it does not irradiate food, a controversial practice. Its Environmental Packaging Council annually assesses the company's U.S. operations with the intent to minimize packaging.

The company's toxic releases have declined to approximately half the food industry average. The Kiwi division participates in EPA's 33/50 toxics reduction program and reached the 50 percent reduction goal on schedule.

EEO: In 1996, Sara Lee Corp. achieved a higher than average rating in both diversity categories. Two women and two minorities served on Sara Lee's 19-member board. Of 40 corporate officers, six were women and two were minorities. Three of the top 25 paid employees were women and one was a minority.

In November 1996, Sara Lee was awarded the first Corporate Affirmative Action Award by the NAACP Legal Defense Fund. Sara Lee was recognized for its aggressive affirmative action programs, including its employee mentoring and minority vendor purchasing programs as well as its initiatives and scholarships for minority students. The company is also on the Department of Labor's Working Women Count Honor Roll, for its pledge to make middle- and senior-management levels more diverse through the establishment of goals for promotion, lateral development, and hiring.

Community Involvement: Sara Lee Corp.'s charitable contributions totaled $14.7 million in cash in 1996, and $8 million in in-kind donations. The $14.7 million cash giving figure represented 1.07 percent of the company's pretax earnings for that year.

the *Corporate Giving Watch* listed Sara Lee as one of the top ten corporate contributors in the area of arts and humanities in 1995, awarding almost $5 million. Approximately 50 percent of its cash grants go to those organizations that enhance the lives of disadvantaged people, especially those affected by poverty, hunger, and homelessness. The company's annual Chicago Spirit Award of $50,000 is designed to honor one Chicago-based organization that demonstrates leadership in improving the lives of disadvantaged people. Sara Lee maintains the "Employee Volunteer Committee" which is responsible for organizing volunteer programs. It also sponsors the "Board Placement Program" which recruits company executives to serve on nonprofit boards.

Workplace Information: OSHA records indicate that Sara Lee underwent seven inspections from 1994 to 1996. Violations included one classified as "willful" or "repeat" and 16 classified as "serious" for a total of $67,275 in fines, an average of $9,611 per inspection. In comparison, the median amount of fines per inspection for other food, beverage, and household products companies was $1,515.

In 1996, Sara Lee was on *Working Mother*'s "100 Best Companies for Working Mothers" list.

The Bakery, Confectionery and Tobacco Workers International Union reports that Sara Lee has explicitly pursued a "union-avoidance" strategy.

International: According to an article in *The Economist*, Sara Lee insists on applying American safety and environmental standards at all its factories worldwide. The company has a strong code of conduct for labor rights which includes workplace safety, child labor (16 year minimum), workweek, and wages. While the guidelines do not mention monitoring, Sara Lee states that it internally monitors all its facilities annually, using a standardized questionnaire.

SBC Communications

STOCK SYMBOL: SBC
STOCK EXCHANGES: NY, B, CH, PH, P

Environment	N
Women's Advancement	A
Minority Advancement	A
Charitable Giving	A?
Community Outreach	C
Family Benefits	N
Workplace Issues	F?
Social Disclosure	B

S outhwestern Bell, based in San Antonio, Texas, is among the smallest of the Baby Bells, with over nine million customers in five states (Arkansas, Kansas, Missouri, Oklahoma, and Texas). By 1996, revenues were almost $14 billion, and there were 61,540 employees.

Environment: Southwestern Bell does no manufacturing. It undertakes programs in a number of communities to collect and recycle used telephone directories into toilet paper, paper towels, insulation and shingles. There is a Corporate Public Policy and Environmental Affairs Committee of the Board of Directors that meets several times annually.

EEO: In 1996, Southwestern Bell achieved a higher than average rating in both diversity categories, placing it easily in the top third of S&P 500 companies. One woman and two minorities served on Southwestern Bell's 14-member board. Of 53 corporate officers, ten were women and five were minorities. Eight of the top 42 paid employees were women, and five were minorities.

Southwestern Bell received a "Pacesetter Award" in October 1996 from the Dallas Together Forum for goals the company achieved in 1995. Dallas Together is a coalition of area businesses, chambers of commerce, and non-profit organizations created as a means to help overcome racial barriers. Member companies set hiring, promotion, and purchasing goals and disclose their progress in reaching the goals. In 1996, Southwestern Bell purchased over $290.3 million in goods and services from women- and minority-owned businesses.

Southwestern Bell operates recruitment programs, support networks, maintains diversity goals, and gives special consideration for management training to both women and minorities

Community Involvement: In 1995, Southwestern Bell's contributions to various charitable institutions included cash donations totaling $20.2 million. The company's cash contributions for 1995 were equivalent to 0.72 percent of its earnings before taxes. Most of the SBC Foundation's funding allocated to education goes to strengthening kindergarten through high school programs. Organizations that promote economic stability, business retention, or job training receive funding from the economic development allocation.

Southwestern Bell encourages employee involvement in the community through the Volunteer Involvement Program, which provides grants to organizations where employees or retirees regularly volunteer. Over 4000 employees participate on 130 Community Relations Teams. Teams meet monthly to set objectives and plan activities. The company provides formal training (motivation, fundraising, team organization, etc.) for volunteers.

As a major producer and distributor of the paging devices often most heavily used by drug dealers, Southwestern Bell decided to impose a $1 surcharge on every page over 1,000 per month, and to donate proceeds from the surcharge to TARGET, a nonprofit group that works with young drug addicts.

Workplace Information: The records of the Occupational Safety and Health Administration indicate that Southwestern Bell underwent eight health and safety inspections from 1994 to 1996. The violations reported by OSHA include three classified as "willful" or "repeat" and 39 classified as "serious." The company was required to pay $13,250 as a result of its violations, an average of $1,656 per inspection. In comparison, the median amount of fines per inspection for other companies in the service industry, such as banks and communications companies, was $573.

211

Schering-Plough

STOCK SYMBOL: SGP
STOCK EXCHANGES: NY, B, C, CH, P, PH

Environment	D
Women's Advancement	C
Minority Advancement	A
Charitable Giving	F
Community Outreach	C
Family Benefits	N
Workplace Issues	N
Social Disclosure	A

Based in Madison, New Jersey, Schering-Plough is a leading international pharmaceuticals company. In 1996, the company had sales of $5.7 billion and 20,600 employees.

Environment: Schering-Plough has an environmental policy and a corporate environmental report (CER). Compared to its industry, however, the company's policy and CER are below average in substance. The company provides environmental health and safety (EH&S) training to employees responsible for implementing environmental control measures. Again, compared to its competitors, Schering-Plough's EH&S training program was below average. Schering-Plough has a written pollution prevention policy and has initiated a companywide pollution prevention program. The company has a written policy on product stewardship and evaluates its products with the objective of reducing its life-cycle impacts. The company has an environmental audit program which has worldwide standards and applicability.

Schering-Plough's average total toxic releases and transfers during the years 1993–1994 were less than the industry sample average. Emissions decreased slightly during those years, a better than average performance.

EEO: In 1996, Schering-Plough's board totaled 13 directors, including two women. One of 15 corporate officers was a woman and two were minorities. The company added an African-American to the Board of Directors in 1997. Additionally, four minorities were among the 25 employees with the highest salaries.

In November 1996, Schering-Plough fired a supervisor at its Kenilworth, New Jersey, plant after a black employee claimed he was the victim of discriminatory remarks made by the supervisor. Several employees and a civil rights activist threatened a boycott and demanded $20 million in damages for the employee and other alleged victims, as well as immediate policy changes. The company reached a settlement with the original claimant in June 1997. Two lawsuits are still pending.

Schering-Plough works with groups such as the United Cerebral Palsy Association and the New Jersey Business and Rehabilitation Alliance to improve recruitment, training, and accommodation of people with disabilities. In 1996, Schering-Plough purchased over $19 million in goods and services from women- and minority-owned businesses.

In February, 1995, a jury awarded $8.4 million to a former Schering employee who charged that he was fired because of his age. In June 1997, an appellate court dismissed this judgment and awarded only $435,000 for compensatory damages. A March 1998 re-trial on punitive damages has been granted.

Community Involvement: Schering-Plough's charitable contributions totaled $5.5 million in cash in 1996, and $304,000 in in-kind donations. The cash-giving figure represented the equivalent of 0.34 percent of the company's pretax earnings, an increase of 2.17 percent from the company's cash contributions in 1995.

Family Benefits: *Working Mother* magazine has recognized Schering-Plough over the last few years as one of the 100 best companies for working mothers. The company sponsors an on-site day care center at one facility and near-site day care centers at four other locations. Schering also offers work-at-home, job sharing, flextime, compressed workweeks and part-time options, and resource and referral services for child care, elder care, and adoption are available.

Workplace Information: OSHA records indicate that Schering-Plough was not inspected from 1994 to 1996. Consequently no fines or violations were assessed to the company.

Seagram Company Ltd.

STOCK SYMBOL: VO
STOCK EXCHANGES: NY, To, B, CH, PH, MO

Environment	N
Women's Advancement	D?
Minority Advancement	N
Charitable Giving	A
Community Outreach	N
Family Benefits	N
Workplace Issues	N
Social Disclosure	F

Though known primarily for its beverage business, Canada-based Seagram acquired an 80 percent interest in MCA Holding Corp. on June 5, 1995, just two months after selling its $9 billion interest in DuPont. Seagram acquired the Dole juice business the same year. During 1996, Seagram changed its fiscal year to end on June 30; reported revenues for the period between February 1 and June 30, 1996, were just over $5 billion. There were approximately 30,000 employees.

Environment: A participant in EPA's Green Lights program, Seagram has installed low energy equipment/bulbs. The company saves additional energy by the use of cogeneration equipment. Seagram's Tropicana processors dry orange pulp and peels for cattle feed, but its products have been noted for wasteful packaging. In 1993, Seagram's vice-president of legal affairs was named chief environmental officer, reporting directly to the company president.

EEO: In 1996, Seagram Company Ltd.'s 17-member Board of Directors included one woman and no minorities. Of 14 corporate officers at the company, two were women and none were minorities. Seagram includes sexual orientation in its antidiscrimination policy and its diversity training, supports gay and lesbian events, and extends health coverage and bereavement leave to employees with same-sex partners.

Community Involvement: In 1996, Seagram Company Ltd.'s charitable giving totaled $7.5 million in cash, which was 6.58 percent of the company's pretax earnings for that year. In terms of the actual dollar amount donated by the company, the level of cash contributions in 1996 was identical to that of 1995, which was 2.07 percent of the company's earnings for that year.

Workplace Information: The records of the Occupational Safety and Health Administration indicate that Seagram Company Ltd. was not inspected from 1994 to 1996. Consequently no fines or violations were assessed to the company.

In response to a drop in revenues in its wine and spirits business, Seagram announced plans in November 1995 to cut jobs and close some facilities. Though Seagram has been doing well overall, industrywide sales of hard liquor have slumped in recent years.

After three months of negotiations and the threat of a strike, Seagram's Tropicana Dole subsidiary signed a three-year contract in January 1996 with 2,000 employees represented by the Teamsters. The new contract protects employees from layoffs, provides raises, and increases company contributions to employee pension plans. The company won more flexibility to decrease job classifications, initiate cross-training, and freeze some entry-level salaries.

International: Though Seagram does not own any facilities in Burma, its beverages are distributed there by businessman U Thein Tun. Mr. Tun had participated in a joint venture with PepsiCo until that company came under enormous pressure from human rights activists and sold its interest to Tun.

Legal Proceedings: MCA is one of several defendants named in a class-action suit brought in May 1995 on behalf of buyers of compact discs in 14 states and the District of Columbia. The suit accuses MCA's Uni Distribution, together with Polygram, BMG, and divisions of Sony, Time Warner, and Thorn/EMI, of illegally fixing the price of CDs when the companies began refusing to pay for the current and future advertisments of low-price CD retailers. A Federal Trade Commission investigation was launched in September, 1997, specifically into the companies' policies on paying for retailers' advertisiing and the enforcement of minimum advertised price policies. Music companies typically pay for retailers' advertising costs when CD's are advertised at a minimum price.

Additional Information: In February 1997, MCA bought 50 percent of Interscope Records, the company that Time Warner sold after being publicly attacked for selling "gangsta rap." Seagram has reserved the right not to distribute records of its choosing.

Sears, Roebuck & Company

STOCK SYMBOL: S
STOCK EXCHANGES: NY, B, C, CH, P PH

Environment	N
Women's Advancement	B?
Minority Advancement	A?
Charitable Giving	D?
Community Outreach	C
Family Benefits	N
Workplace Issues	F?
Social Disclosure	F

In 1995, Sears, Roebuck & Company (Sears) spun off its Allstate division to Sears shareholders, completed its sale of Homart, and acquired more auto-related businesses. Sales in 1996 reached $38.2 billion, making four consecutive years of income growth. Sears employed 335,000 persons.

Environment: Sears issued its latest environmental policy statement in May 1994. The company's environmental committee assists management in the promotion of environmental policies and safety.

EEO: In 1996, two women and three minorities served on Sears, Roebuck & Co.'s 12-member Board of Directors. Of 13 corporate officers, one was a woman and none were minorities. Sears is involved in a three year study, showing accommodation of the mentally ill at the workplace has a relatively low cost.

Members of the NAACP and the Nation of Islam have asked that workers at a Sears store be fired and charged with assault for accusing an African-American woman of shoplifting. Witnesses claim that Sears security employees used excessive force on the woman and allege that she was targeted as a shoplifter because of her race.

Community Involvement: In 1995, Sears, Roebuck & Co.'s contributions to various charitable institutions included cash donations totaling over $12.3 million. The company's cash contributions for 1995 were 0.72 percent of its earnings before taxes.

Workplace Information: According to OSHA's records, Sears, Roebuck & Co. was inspected 56 times from 1994 to 1996. Violations included two classified as "willful" or "repeat" and 118 classified as "serious" for a total of $102,718 in fines, or an average of $1,834 per inspection. In comparison, the median amount of fines per inspection for other companies in the retail industry was $694.

Sears, Roebuck and Co. has been restricted by a U.S. Bankruptcy Court in Delaware from recruiting salaried managers from stores Montgomery Ward has publicly stated it will close. Montgomery Ward claimed Sears was trying to hire away its management in an attempt to damage the retailer as it reorganizes under bankruptcy protection.

Sears is among seven major retailer chains that the Sweatshop Watch coalition accused in early 1996 of ignoring evidence that some of their goods were manufactured in sweatshop conditions. Sears had been named by federal labor investigators as a possible recipient of garments produced by a sweatshop in El Monte, California that had been raided six months earlier. All the retailers bought goods from contractors that purchased garments from the El Monte sweatshop. Sears denied any wrongdoing, and said that products suspected of being produced under sweatshop conditions were taken out of stores if they made it there at all. The El Monte facility housed 72 Thai workers, and eight of its operators pleaded guilty to federal civil rights violations and other charges in 1996.

International: Sears has thousands of vendors and subcontractors in the U.S. and abroad supplying its stores. While Sears' business code requires the facilities, business and labor practices, and merchandise of suppliers to comply with all applicable local and U.S. laws, the code contains no mention of child labor, working hours, wages, or monitoring provisions.

Shell Oil Company, USA

Royal Dutch/Shell Group

STOCK SYMBOL: RD
STOCK EXCHANGES: NY, B, C, CH, P

Environment	C
Women's Advancement	D
Minority Advancement	C
Charitable Giving	REV
Community Outreach	A
Family Benefits	N
Workplace Issues	N
Social Disclosure	A

Based in The Hague, Netherlands, Royal Dutch Petroleum has no operations of its own and virtually all of its income is derived from its 60 percent share in The Royal Dutch/Shell Group of Companies, held jointly with London-based Shell Transport and Trading Company PLC since 1907. Oil and gas production generates 90 percent of the group's earnings, though it also manufactures chemicals and has interests in coal and nonferrous metals. Royal Dutch/Shell had 110,000 employees at the end of 1996, a year in which it had $156.5 billion in revenue. The ratings are primarily based on the company's U.S. operations, Shell Oil Company, USA.

Environment: Shell has an environmental policy and publishes a corporate environmental report, which is updated annually and is available on the Internet. Shell has implemented an integrated environmental management system and provides environmental health and safety (EH&S) training to EH&S and facility staff. It also considers contribution towards EH&S goals in job performance reviews for appropriate employees, and presents awards to employees for their contribution to environmental issues. Shell does not have a written pollution prevention policy, and has not initiated a companywide pollution prevention program. The company has a corporate policy on community involvement relating to local environmental concerns, and currently has community advisory panels at five of its facilities. Shell has a written policy on product stewardship and evaluates some of its products with the objective of reducing their life-cycle impacts on the environment. Internationally, Shell monitors SARA Title III, or equivalent emissions and follow U.S. regulations in the U.S. and abroad, unless local regulations are stricter. Shell has formed a partnership with the National Fish and Wildlife Federation project to undertake a five-year, multifaceted marine initiative to support conservation projects in the Gulf of Mexico. The company participated in EPA's WasteWi$e, 33/50, Green Lights, and Common Sense Initiative programs.

Adjusted for worldwide company sales, Shell's average total toxic releases and transfers during the years 1994–1996 were less than the industry sample average. Emissions decreased slightly on average annually during those years, a below average performance. The company was ranked 9th out of 15 in CEP's Campaign for Cleaner Corporations (C-3) 1997 Petroleum Refining Report.

According to RAG, Newsletter of the National Oil Refinery ACTION! Network, Margie Richards, leader of the Concerned Citizens of Norco in Louisiana, is spearheading a lawsuit against Shell to force them to buy out some 300 of her Norco neighbors, who can no longer tolerate the toxic pollution, noise, and frequent accidents caused by the Shell Oil Norco Refinery and Shell Chemical plants between which they are sandwiched. Residents of this community, once a part of the Diamond Plantation on the Mississippi, were already evacuated twice in 1996 due to Shell-related accidents.

Residents of Ogoniland (the most heavily polluted area of Nigeria) complain that Shell pollutes the environment, occupies scarce farming land, and fails to ensure that the benefits of the region's vast oil wealth flow back into local communities. Furthermore, Shell has been under public scrutiny over its environmental and human rights policies, especially in Nigeria. Shell has yet to publicly call for the release of 19 Ogoni in Nigeria, still being held in inhumane conditions on the same charges for which Ken Saro-Wiwa, an activist who fought Shell and the government for environmental cleanup and Ogoni rights, was executed. Shell claims to have taken steps to lessen the criticism by establishing regular contacts with representatives of several groups including Greenpeace, Amnesty International, and the World Wide Fund for Nature. Shell claims that the Group no longer operates in Ogoniland, had removed its staff five years ago, and currently has no production there. The company also claims that it has made efforts to encourage the Nigerian government to put more oil revenues back into the producing communities of Ogoniland.

215

Continued on next page

Rainforest Action Network and Project Underground (a human rights group) calls to attention the gap between the rhetoric of the public relations department of Shell and the reality of its operations. In addition to criticizing Shell for its activities in Nigeria, it claims that in Peru, Shell failed to consult indigenous communities before beginning operations in their territory just a few months ago. It claims Shell's plans also include drilling in an Amazon reserve set aside for isolated and nomadic peoples, which will damage one of the most biologically diverse places on Earth and threaten the existence of the indigenous people. Shell claims that this allegation is simply not true; in fact, it has an agreement with Red Ambiental Peruana, a Peruvian social and environmental network comprising 35 NGOs, to monitor the social and environmental performance of the project. The company states, "Shell Peru is committed to openness and transparency and is determined that the development will become an example of sustainable development to the benefit of Peru, the Inca Region and local peoples."

Greenpeace released internal Shell company documents showing a 20-year policy of pumping toxic production waters into an aquifer that provides drinking water for the residents of the Turkish city of Diyarbakir. Shell apparently pumped nearly 490 million barrels of wastewater into the Midyat aquifer between 1973 and 1994, and had plans to inject another 172 million barrels there through 2001. Turkey has been aware of the pollution and has demanded that Shell monitor it, but the company did not agree to do so until the release of the documents. The documents also show that "Shell officials willfully flouted Turkish regulations that called for the company to use a more expensive option for managing the wastewater."

EEO: In 1996, Shell's board totaled 11 directors, including one woman and one minority; two of 37 corporate officers were women.

In early 1997, soon after the Texaco settlement, Shell was named as the defendant in two separate suits alleging racial discrimination. The two suits, one in California on behalf of ten plaintiffs and one in Texas on behalf of five, are each seeking damages of $100 million. The plaintiffs allege that Shell practiced racial discrimination in its retail and marketing operations. Shell claims that there is no system of discrimination against African-Americans or any other group of employees at the company. Shell ranked towards the bottom of oil companies surveyed by *The Oil Daily* in December, 1996, for its employment of minorities. Minorities make up 18 percent of the Houston–based company's workforce. Shell provides diversity-awareness training for all its employees in management positions.

Community Involvement: In 1996 Shell made a $5 million grant to establish the Shell Center for Gene Therapy, where research will focus on treatment strategies to correct defective genes or replace missing genes. Shell's support of education includes a $10 million commitment towards the Shell Youth Training Academy, created following the 1992 riots in Los Angeles, California. The first Shell Academy provides supplemental education and arranges part-time work at local offices for high school students in South-Central Los Angeles. Shell has since opened an Academy in Chicago, Illinois, and plans to open another one in Oakland. Shell is also the first oil company to create a minority financing program, arranging 10 $2 million loans for new African-American and Hispanic station owners in California. At the time of the riots, approximately 12 of nearly 700 stations in Los Angeles were owned by African-Americans.

The company manages its own coordinated in-house retiree volunteer program for the Houston, Texas, area, and actively recruits employees to serve as members of non-profit boards. Approximately 15 percent of employees are involved with the 20 year-old Houston program. The company's CEO is involved as a participant and recruiter.

Workplace Information: The records of the Occupational Safety and Health Administration indicate that Shell was not inspected from 1994 to 1996. Consequently no fines or violations were assessed to the company.

Silicon Graphics

STOCK SYMBOL: SGI
STOCK EXCHANGES: NY, CH, PH, P

Environment	B
Women's Advancement	N
Minority Advancement	N
Charitable Giving	N
Community Outreach	C
Family Benefits	B
Workplace Issues	C
Social Disclosure	B

Silicon Graphics, based in Mountain View, California, is a leading manufacturer of visual computer systems and multimedia servers targeted for a wide range of technical, scientific, corporate, and entertainment applications. Recently, Silicon Graphics entered joint ventures with Disney, AT&T, Time Warner, and Nintendo. With operations worldwide, the company in 1996 reached sales of $2.9 billion and employed 10,500 persons.

Environment: Silicon Graphics has an environmental policy and a corporate environmental report, which is updated biennially and is available on the Internet. Silicon Graphics has implemented an integrated environmental management system and provides environmental health and safety (EH&S) training to all employees. It also considers contributions towards EH&S goals in the job performance reviews of all employees and presents awards to employees for their contribution to environmental issues. Silicon Graphics has a written pollution prevention policy and has initiated a company-wide pollution prevention program. The company also has a corporate policy on community involvement relating to local environmental concerns; however, it does not have any community advisory panels. Silicon Graphics has a written policy on product stewardship and evaluates its products with the objective of reducing their life-cycle impacts on the environment. In the selection of suppliers, Silicon Graphics conducts or reviews environmental audits on suppliers' facilities. The company has an environmental audit program, which does not have worldwide standards and applicability. Internationally, Silicon Graphics states that it follows U.S. regulations in the U.S. and abroad unless local regulations are stricter.

EEO: Silicon Graphics is listed as one of the five most gay-friendly companies, according to Ed Mickens in his 1994 book, *The 100 Best Companies For Gay Men and Lesbians* (Pocket Books, 1994).

Community Involvement: The company supports local magnet schools that provide community mentoring, Junior Achievement, and literacy training. The 40 percent figure listed as Silicon Graphics' giving to the arts and humanities also includes its giving towards science.

Family Benefits: In 1993, Silicon Graphics appeared on *Working Mother*'s list of 100 top firms with family-friendly policies. The company has a resource and referral program for child and elder care, and it subsidizes 75 percent of sick child care at an approved health care facility. Silicon Graphics offers a variety of flexible work arrangements, including job-sharing, flextime, and work-at-home. Its family-friendly benefits provide up to $4,000 for adoption assistance and a paid sabbatical every four years.

Workplace Information: According to the Occupational Safety and Health Administration's records, Silicon Graphics was not inspected from 1994 to 1996. Consequently no violations or fines were assessed to the company. The lack of any inspections frequently indicates that few or no complaints have been lodged with OSHA regarding the company's health and safety practices.

In 1994, the company won the sixth annual Business Ethics Award.

Weapons Contracts: In 1994, Silicon Graphics had $21.4 million in contracts with the Department of Defense—$299,000 of this amount for nuclear weapons-related systems.

Sonat, Inc.

STOCK SYMBOL: SNT
STOCK EXCHANGES: NY, B, C, CH, PH, P

Environment	N
Women's Advancement	F?
Minority Advancement	D?
Charitable Giving	C?
Community Outreach	D?
Family Benefits	N
Workplace Issues	N
Social Disclosure	F

Birmingham, Alabama–based Sonat is engaged in exploration and production, natural gas transmission, and energy marketing systems. The exploration and production segment is involved in exploration, development and production of domestic oil and natural gas. The natural gas transmission segment is primarily engaged in the interstate transmission of natural gas; it is the major natural gas pipeline in the Southeast. The energy marketing segment is primarily engaged in the marketing of natural gas and electric power. At year-end 1996, Sonat had revenues of $3.4 billion and 1,900 employees.

Environment: Sonat, Inc. does not currently publish a corporate environmental report. The company has used, and continues to use, gas meters containing elemental mercury; it plans to remove all remaining mercury meters during scheduled facility upgrades.

Sonat has determined that its pipeline meters may in the past have been the source of small releases of elementary mercury during the course of normal maintenance and replacement operations.

EEO: Sonat, Inc. turned in a below average performance in the area of diversity in 1996, compared to other S&P 500 companies. Among the companies surveyed by CEP, the average representation of women and minorities on S&P corporate boards was 10.8 percent and 7.5 percent, respectively. In comparison, Sonat, Inc. had no women and one minority on its 14-member Board of Directors. The company's total of nine corporate officers included one woman and no minorities.

Community Involvement: In 1995, Sonat, Inc.'s contributions to various charitable institutions included cash donations totaling almost $1.9 million. The company's cash contributions for 1995 were 0.66 percent of its earnings before taxes.

Sonat operates a volunteer program for current and retired employees, through which participants volunteer at Alabama organizations. Sonat reports that its "scholarship programs have been established to assist students pursuing degrees that meet the company's recruiting needs." The company matches contributions made by employees, retirees, and directors to educational institutions, arts and cultural institutions, and the United Way. In its funding of organizations outside its regular giving, Sonat gives priority to organizations supported by major customers, directors, officers, or other employees.

Workplace Information: The records of the Occupational Safety and Health Administration indicate that Sonat, Inc. was not inspected from 1994 to 1996. Consequently no fines or violations were assessed to the company. As inspections can frequently be called in response to complaints about the health or safety conditions at a company, a lack of inspections may be an indicator of good health and safety conditions.

218

Southern Company

STOCK SYMBOL: SO
STOCK EXCHANGES: NY, B, C, CH, P, PH

Environment	REV
Women's Advancement	C
Minority Advancement	B
Charitable Giving	F?
Community Outreach	B
Family Benefits	N
Workplace Issues	N
Social Disclosure	B

Southern Company, based in Atlanta, Georgia, is the nation's largest producer of electricity. It is a holding company for five utilities in the Southeast: Alabama Power, Georgia Power, Gulf Power, Mississippi Power, and Savannah Electric. These operating affiliates generate, transmit, and sell power to about 3.4 million customers in the region. In 1996, Southern and its operating units employed 29,200 people and had revenues of $10.4 billion.

Environment: In 1994 and 1995, Southern was on CEP's Campaign for Cleaner Corporations (C-3) list of companies with poor environmental performance relative to industry peers. The company rated worse than average in terms of emissions of carbon dioxide and sulfur dioxide, and about average in regard to penalties paid to the Nuclear Regulatory Commission. In 1994, Southern generated 75 percent of its energy from coal, 19 percent from nuclear, 5 percent from hydroelectric, and 1 percent from oil and gas.

As part of the C-3 process, CEP recommended that Southern promote demand-side management, identify and implement ways of reducing CO_2 emissions, and investigate the potential of renewable resources more aggressively. The company was taken off the list in 1996, when it committed to a goal of reducing (by the year 2000) projected carbon dioxide emissions by 15 percent. Southern also improved its environmental management systems and developed demand-side programs to offset more than 11 percent of estimated increase in demand.

As part of its demand-side management program, Southern has developed a power management service that allows customers to closely monitor their energy costs and program appliances/equipment to operate when such costs are lowest. Widespread use of this service enables Southern to better manage its production capacity and lower peak demand.

EEO: In 1996, Southern Company's 14-member Board of Directors included one woman and one minority. Of 16 corporate officers at the company, one was a woman and none were minorities. The company explicitly prohibits discrimination based on sexual orientation.

In 1996, Southern Company purchased over $52 million in goods and services from women- and minority-owned businesses. The company also offers mentoring programs, recruitment programs, support networks, maintains diversity goals, and gives special consideration for management training to both women and minorities

Community Involvement: In 1995, Southern Company's contributions to various charitable institutions included cash donations totaling $330,000. The company's cash contributions for 1995 were 0.01 percent of its earnings before taxes for the same year.

Georgia Power operates a statewide mentoring program and has participated with donations and loaned employees in former President Jimmy Carter's Atlanta Project aimed at rehabilitating 20 inner-city communities. Other units are also involved in local improvement efforts.

Family Benefits: Southern allows for flexible work schedules and telecommuting, and offers day care discounts, emergency child care, and elder care referrals.

Workplace Information: According to the Occupational Safety and Health Administration's records, Southern Company was not inspected from 1994 to 1996. Consequently no violations or fines were assessed to the company.

Less than half of Southern's workforce is unionized, virtually all of which is represented by the International Brotherhood of Electrical Workers. CEP is not aware of any labor disputes at the company.

219

Springs Industries

STOCK SYMBOL: SMI
STOCK EXCHANGES: NY, CH, PH

Environment	C
Women's Advancement	A?
Minority Advancement	D?
Charitable Giving	B
Community Outreach	C
Family Benefits	N
Workplace Issues	C?
Social Disclosure	B

Springs Industries, based in Fort Mills, South Carolina, is the largest U.S. sheet manufacturer and one of the top producers of home furnishings and specialty fabrics. In 1995, the company restructured along its primary product lines: bath fashions, bed fashions, and diversified products. That year it acquired Dawson Home Fashions and Dundee Mills, and in 1996, it sold its Clark-Schwebel subsidiary. Springs has 53 domestic manufacturing plants, most located in the Southeast. The company has 20,700 employees and, in 1996, had sales of $2.2 billion.

In 1989, Springs launched the Springs of Achievement program, a new corporate philosophy focusing on quality, service, creativity, education, personal and family well-being, respect for history, and planning for the future.

Environment: In 1992, Springs became one of 25 charter members of the Encouraging Environmental Excellence program sponsored by the American Textile Manufacturers Institute (ATMI). Participants adopt a ten-point plan, including the development of a corporate environmental policy, conducting environmental audits, establishing company goals, expanding employee and community education programs, and creating outreach programs to suppliers and customers to encourage recycling and more environmentally sound processes.

Renew America honored Springs Industries with its Christopher Reeves Award for Environmental Excellence in 1997.

In 1995, Springs spent approximately $4.8 million for environmental, health, and safety projects. It has currently accrued $15 million for environmental liabilities, much of it for anticipated remediation expenditures at a hazardous waste disposal site near Beaufort, South Carolina.

EEO: In 1996, Springs Industries's board totaled 12 directors, including two women and no minorities, while three of a total of 17 corporate officers were women, and none were minorities.

Community Involvement: Springs Industries's charitable contributions totaled $883,448 in cash in 1996. The $883,448 cash-giving figure represented 0.85 percent of the company's pretax earnings for the same year, and a decrease of 18 percent from the company's cash contributions in 1995. In 1995, the company contributed 0.80 percent of its pretax earnings for that year to charity.

Half of Springs Industries' annual charitable giving goes towards education. The donations support improvements in higher education, adult education, business and economic education, elementary and high schools, and public and private education organizations. The company sponsored employee volunteer program, has partnerships with twenty public schools and works in coordination with New York Cares.

Workplace Information: The records of the Occupational Safety and Health Administration indicate that Springs Industries underwent two health and safety inspections from 1994 to 1996. The violations reported by OSHA as a result of the inspections include eight classified as "serious." The company was required to pay $4,050 in fines, or an average of $2,025 per inspection. In comparison, the median amount of fines per inspection for other companies in similar manufacturing industries was $2,412.

The company operates a management feedback system. It also offers worker literacy programs at most of its plants and an employee wellness program that includes health fairs, cholesterol and blood pressure screenings, and safety instruction. Springs has periodically closed plants and cut corporate staff. Where possible, the company has offered transfers and early retirement packages in an effort to limit layoffs.

Sprint Corporation

STOCK SYMBOL: FON
STOCK EXCHANGES: NY, B, C, CH, PH, P

Environment	C
Women's Advancement	B
Minority Advancement	D
Charitable Giving	B
Community Outreach	B
Family Benefits	N
Workplace Issues	N
Social Disclosure	A

Sprint Corporation, based in Kansas City, Missouri, is the nation's third largest long-distance services provider. In March 1993, the company completed its merger with Centel Corporation. In 1996, Sprint had 48,000 employees and revenues of $14 billion.

Environment: Sprint has an environmental policy, but does not publish a corporate environmental report. Sprint has not implemented an integrated environmental management system, but provides environmental health and safety (EH&S) training to EH&S, and facility staff. It also considers contribution towards EH&S goals in the job performance reviews of EH&S staff.

In June 1997, The EPA fined Sprint's Central Telephone Co. unit $21,600 for using an unacceptable refrigerant, HC-12a, also known as Freon-12. Central Telephone used HC-12a as a replacement for a banned stratospheric ozone-depleting chemical, chlorofluorocarbon-12 or CFC-12. HC-12a is a flammable refrigerant and is prohibited for use as a CFC replacement in car, truck, and bus air conditioners.

EEO: In 1996, Sprint Corporation's 12-member Board of Directors included two women and no minorities. Of 34 corporate officers at the company, three were women and none were minorities. Three women and one minority ranked among the company's 25 highest paid employees.

In 1996, ICCR sponsored a shareholder resolution proposing that Sprint diversify its board of directors. It then withdrew the resolution, which generally indicates that an agreement has been reached with management. In 1997, ICCR sponsored and withdrew another resolution asking Sprint to distribute an EEO report.

Community Involvement: In 1996, Sprint gave over $8.8 million in cash, which was 0.46 percent of the company's pretax earnings for that year. The level of cash contributions in 1996 represented a decrease of 34 percent from that of 1995, which was 0.60 percent of the company's earnings for that year.

In 1996, Sprint sponsored the Alzheimer's Association Memory Walk. The Sprint Foundation supports education by making grants to programs that work to renew and reform public schools. In its commitment to the arts and culture, Sprint contributes to programs intending to provide access to cultural events for the impoverished. Sprint gives to the area of youth development by supporting organizations that work with issues like drug and alcohol education, minority youth endeavors, and business and economic education for youth. Ten percent of Sprint employees are involved in the company volunteer program, called the Community Relations Team Program.

Workplace Information: According to the Occupational Safety and Health Administration's records, Sprint Corporation was not inspected from 1994 to 1996. Consequently no violations or fines were assessed to the company. As inspections can be called in response to complaints about safety or health conditions, a lack of inspections may indicate a relatively healthy and safe workplace.

In 1997, the National Labor Relations Board demanded that Sprint Corp. rehire and pay back wages to 177 workers, mostly Hispanic women, who lost their jobs when Sprint closed its San Francisco telemarketing center due to what it described as financial losses. The termination of the workers came just a week before a vote was to be held on unionization by the Communications Workers of America, and the NLRB claimed that the organizing was the impetus for the closing of the center. In November 1997, the U.S. Court of Appeals for the District of Columbia Circuit overturned an NLRB decision, finding that there was no substantial evidence linking the closure to the CWA's organizing campaign, and that Sprint closed the center for legitimate business reasons. Sprint owes no back pay to the former employees, and is not required to rehire any of those who had worked at the center.

Stride Rite

STOCK SYMBOL: SRR
STOCK EXCHANGES: NY, CH, PH, P

Environment	N
Women's Advancement	A
Minority Advancement	C
Charitable Giving	A
Community Outreach	B
Family Benefits	A
Workplace Issues	C
Social Disclosure	A

Stride Rite, based in Lexington, Massachusetts, is the leading U.S. marketer of children's footwear and a major marketer of athletic and casual shoes for children and adults. It manufactures products in the U.S. and in the Dominican Republic, and in addition, imports a significant portion of its products from other locations outside the United States. Stride Rite also operates approximately 124 Stride Rite Bootery stores, 58 leased children's shoe departments, and 19 outlet stores. At the end of 1997, the company employed approximately 2,700 full-time and part-time workers. In 1997, Stride Rite's sales were $515 million.

Environment: Stride Rite has a thorough office recycling program; however, only 5 percent of paper used by the company contains recycled fibers. According to the company, almost all of its shoeboxes are made of low-grade recycled material.

EEO: In 1996, Stride Rite's board totaled eight directors, including two women and no minorities, while four of a total of 14 corporate officers were women, and none were minorities. Additionally, four women and two minorities were among the 25 employees with the highest salaries.

Although Stride Rite did not have special programs for purchasing from minority- or women-owned businesses in 1996, the company reports that it has hired a Purchasing Manager who has "implemented a formal effort to target and track the business we do with women and minorities." Stride Rite has a written policy on equal employment opportunity, which covers sexual harassment and the hiring and accommodating of persons with disabilities.

Community Involvement: Stride Rite's charitable contributions totaled $1.9 million in cash in 1996, and $500,000 in in-kind donations. In 1995, the company experienced a loss.

Stride Rite gives primarily to organizations in the cities of Boston and Cambridge that affect underprivileged inner-city children and families through after-school,

recreational, and educational programs. Stride Rite gave $437,00 to the Stride Rite Children's Centers in Lexington, Mass. and Louisville, Kentucky in 1997. Also that year, the company gave $200,000 to Harvard University's Scholars Program, and $100,000 to Northeastern University in Boston. Some other organizations receiving grants are the Families First Parenting Program, Cambridge Partnership for Public Education, Partners for Youth with Disabilities, and Adolescent Consultation Services. Stride Rite has a mentoring program with two Boston-area inner city schools in which employees participate on company time.

Workplace Information: The records of the Occupational Safety and Health Administration indicate that Stride Rite underwent one health and safety inspection from 1994 to 1996. The violations reported by OSHA as a result of the inspection include four classified as "serious." The company was required to pay $3,375 as a result of its violations. In comparison, the median amount of fines per inspection for other companies in similar manufacturing industries was $2,412.

In 1995, declining revenue forced Stride Rite to cut its labor force by 600.

International: Stride Rite maintains a staff of approximately 98 professional and technical personnel in South Korea, Taiwan, Thailand, and mainland China to supervise "a substantial portion" of its canvas and leather footwear production.

⭐ Sun Company

STOCK SYMBOL: SUN
STOCK EXCHANGES: NY, B, CH, PH

Environment	A
Women's Advancement	B
Minority Advancement	B
Charitable Giving	A
Community Outreach	N
Family Benefits	C
Workplace Issues	B
Social Disclosure	A

Sun Company, Inc., based in Philadelphia, Pennsylvania, is one of the largest oil companies in the U.S. and the largest independent U.S. oil refiner/marketer. The company has five domestic refineries, sells gasoline under the Sunoco brand (mainly in the Northeast), markets petrochemicals and lubricants worldwide, and operates pipelines and terminals in the U.S. In 1996, the company employed 12,100 people and had revenues of $11.2 billion.

Environment: Sun Company, currently the only signatory of the Coalition for Environmentally Responsible Economies (CERES) in the petroleum industry, has an environmental policy and publishes a corporate environmental report (CER) that is updated annually and adheres to CERES reporting guidelines. Sun Company was also the first Fortune 500 company to endorse the CERES principles. Sun is planning to make its 1997 CER available in the internet. The company ranked first out of 15 for CEP's Campaign for Cleaner Corporations' 1997 Petroleum Refining Report. The company has implemented an integrated environmental management system. Sun has a written pollution prevention policy, and has initiated a company-wide pollution prevention program. The company also has a corporate policy on community involvement relating to local environmental concerns, and currently has community advisory panels (CAPs) at three of its facilities. The company states that its other refineries are engaged in dialogues with surrounding communities about the establishment of CAPs. Sun has a written policy on product stewardship and evaluates its products with the objective of reducing their life-cycle impacts on the environment. Sun has a performance standard—Product Stewardship Distribution—and as part of this standard a New Product Approval Process was developed to address limiting the environmental impacts of products. Sun participates and is involved in the Wildlife Habitat Enhancement Council, Nature Conservancy, and the Tidal Wetlands Restoration Project along the Schuykill River. The company also participated in EPA's Green Lights and 33/50 programs, and is currently participating in the Petroleum Refinery Sector of the Common Sense Inititative.

For just its refinery operations, Sun's environmental impact performance was favorable compared to its industry sample's refinery operations. Its toxic emissions were just lower than the industry average; benzene emissions were far less than average. Both categories of emissions experienced a decreasing trend from 1993 to 1995. In 1995, Sun's refinery emissions of sulfur dioxide were below average; VOC emissions were above average.

In 1997, the federal government named Sun Refining and Marketing as one of 16 companies in significant violation of air quality control standards.

During 1996, Sun continued its efforts to develop environmentally sound products, including a zinc-free hydraulic fluid and vegetable oil based lubricant primarily used for irrigation pumps in farming operations.

EEO: In 1996, Sun Company's 12-member Board of Directors included one woman and one minority. Of 13 corporate officers at the company, two were women.

Community Involvement: In 1996, Sun Company's contributions to various charitable institutions included cash donations totaling $3.2 million. The company registered losses for 1996.

The Sun Company's contributions program focuses on needs of the company's operating locations; however, due to recent budget reductions, it is not encouraging new grant applications. The company reinstated employee matching gifts in 1994.

Workplace Information: OSHA records indicate that Sun was inspected 12 times from 1994 to 1996. Violations included 27 classified as "serious" for a total of $27,600 in fines, or an average of $2,300 per inspection. In comparison, the median amount of fines per inspection for other companies in the extractive business was $2,941. No strikes or NLRB charges have been upheld against the company in the last few years.

223

Sun Microsystems, Inc.

STOCK SYMBOL: SUNW
STOCK EXCHANGES: NNM, CH, PH

Environment	C
Women's Advancement	N
Minority Advancement	N
Charitable Giving	D?
Community Outreach	B?
Family Benefits	N
Workplace Issues	A?
Social Disclosure	B

Sun Microsystems, headquartered in Mountain View, California, is the world's largest manufacturer of computer workstations. With manufacturing sites in California and Scotland, Sun has international sales and services in 38 countries and distributors in nearly 150 countries. In 1996, the company employed 17,400 people and reached revenues of $7.1 billion.

Environment: Sun Microsystems has an environmental policy and a corporate environmental report, which is only available on the Internet and is updated quarterly. Sun Microsystems has implemented an integrated environmental management system and provides environmental health and safety (EH&S) training to its employees upon request. Training for facility staff is specialized. Sun Microsystems does not have a written pollution prevention policy, but has initiated a company-wide pollution prevention program, which establishes annual reduction goals for solid waste through the WasteWi$e Program.

Sun Microsystems has a written policy on product stewardship, a division dedicated to product stewardship review and development, and evaluates its products with the objective of reducing their life-cycle impacts on the environment. The company participates in several EPA Energy Star Programs.

EEO: Highlighted in *The 100 Best Companies for Gay Men and Lesbians* (Pocket Books, 1994), Sun provides excellent domestic partner benefits to its gay and lesbian employees, including health and dental, as well as bereavement and sickness leave. Health coverage even extends to children of partners. Relocation assistance, counseling, and all company events and facilities are open to domestic partners.

Community Involvement: Approximately 15 percent of employees are involved with the Sun Microsystems' volunteer program, which contracts with local volunteer centers near its four largest sites to coordinate its volunteer efforts. Sun also operates an international Sun Volunteer Week.

In 1995, Sun Microsystems' contributions to various charitable institutions included cash donations totaling over $1.4 million. The company's cash contributions for 1995 were equivalent to 0.28 percent of its earnings before taxes for the same year.

Sun Microsystems Foundation places a special emphasis on the development of emerging communities throughout its contribution program. Projects funded in education (grades 7-12) must investigate the role of the individual in the community and enhance student motivation and skills for higher education. Through its focus on leadership development, Sun seeks to promote leadership in emerging communities and augment the capabilities of established community leaders. The company's support of job development requires that programs assist individuals from emerging communities through job training, placement, and counseling programs.

Workplace Information: OSHA records indicate that Sun Microsystems was inspected once from 1994 to 1996, receiving only incidental violations and $270 in fines. In comparison, the median amount of fines per inspection for other companies in the industries manufacturing electronics equipment was $1,347. In the previous five years, the company received just two citations and no fines.

Sun's workforce is not unionized. In 1995, the company published a benefits manual, which won the 1995 Business Insurance Employee Benefits Communication Award.

Weapons Contracts: In 1994, Sun had $35 million in contracts with the U.S. Department of Defense. The contracts were for computer systems and services that were not weapons related.

Legal Proceedings: In 1994, a former employee charged Sun with breach of employment, breach of promise, and sexual discrimination. The court concluded that the employee was not a victim of sexual harassment, but found the company guilty of breach of contract and awarded the employee $500,000.

Tandy Corporation

STOCK SYMBOL: TAN
STOCK EXCHANGES: NY, B, CH, C, P

Environment	N
Women's Advancement	F
Minority Advancement	C
Charitable Giving	N
Community Outreach	C
Family Benefits	N
Workplace Issues	B?
Social Disclosure	A

Tandy Corporation, headquartered in Fort Worth, Texas, is a retailer of consumer electronics, computers and related services. The company's principal retail operations include the Radio Shack and Computer City store chains. The company adopted a plan to exit the Incredible Universe and McDuff retail business in December 1996. At year-end 1996, Tandy Corp. had sales of $6.28 billion and approximately 40,000 employees.

EEO: In 1996, Tandy Corp.'s ten-member Board of Directors included no women and one minority. Of 15 corporate officers at the company, two were women and none were minorities. As of February, 1998, four women are corporate officers

In 1996, the company purchased over $140 million in goods and services from women- and minority-owned businesses. The company's total purchasing for that year was almost $3.8 billion. Tandy maintains diversity goals for both women and minorities, and has recruitment programs intended to meet those goals. The company reports that 72 Diversity Awareness Workshops have been conducted for field sales management, and a series of similar workshops is being conducted for headquarters and support operations management.

Several suits have been brought against Tandy regarding discrimination and harassment at some of its Radio Shack and Incredible Universe retail outlets. In October, 1996, a U.S. District Court jury awarded $650,000 to Shannon Lovett, a former employee at Radio Shack, finding that she had been sexually harassed while working at Radio Shack stores. Lovett contended that she had been harassed by supervisors, then demoted and fired when she complained. She also contended that a corporate officer pressed a room key into her hand at a 1989 managers' meeting, and introduced the key as evidence in the trial.

In December 1995, a jury found that a Radio Shack store in a Chicago mall refused to serve a Hispanic teenager on the basis of his race. The teen was given $55,000 in damages, and the company was ordered to pay $275,000 in punitive damages. Tandy is appealing the decision, and stated that discrimination "is not our practice or our policy."

In the same month, Michael V. Webster, an employee, brought a $2.5 million discrimination and wrongful-termination suit against the company, claiming he had been discriminated against after co-workers learned of his sexual orientation. Tandy reports that it won the case on summary judgment.

Community Involvement: One of Tandy's community involvement initiatives is its Tandy Technology Scholars program, which awarded $350,000 in stipends and scholarships to high school math, science, and computer science teachers and students nationwide. The company reports that since 1995, it has provided over 1,000 class sessions of free computer training to children from Boys & Girls Clubs of America.

Workplace Information: According to the Occupational Safety and Health Administration's records, Tandy was inspected 24 times from 1994 to 1996. The OSHA inspectors' citations included 14 violations classified as "serious." A total of $5,407 in fines was assessed to the company following the inspections, an average of $225 per inspection. In comparison, the median amount of fines per inspection for other retail companies was $694.

Tektronix, Inc.

STOCK SYMBOL: TEK
STOCK EXCHANGES: NY, B, C, CH, P, PH

Environment	B
Women's Advancement	A?
Minority Advancement	N
Charitable Giving	B?
Community Outreach	N
Family Benefits	N
Workplace Issues	A?
Social Disclosure	C

Designer of the first oscilloscope (in the 1940s), Tektronix is a leading producer of electronics equipment, including other measurement products, color printers, video, and networking systems. The company is based in Wilsonville, Oregon. In 1996, Tektronix had total revenues of close to $1.8 billion and 7,929 employees.

Environment: Tektronix has a written environmental policy, but does not publish a corporate environmental report. The company has initiated an integrated environmental management system and provides training to all employees and considers contribution towards EH&S goals in the job performance reviews of all employees. Employees are also presented awards for their contribution to environmental issues. Tektronix has a written pollution prevention policy and a company-wide pollution prevention program. The company also has a corporate policy on community involvement relating to environmental concerns and a written commitment to product stewardship. The company has an environmental audit program with worldwide standards and applicability, but does not make audit findings available to the public.

Tektronix's toxic releases and transfers were well below average in 1993 and in 1994, compared to its industry sample. Emissions decreased by over nine tenths from 1993 to 1994, one of the best performances in the industry. However, from 1993 to 1996, the average trend was an increase of about two fifths a year.

In May 1997, Tektronix was fined $23,137 by the Oregon Department of Environmental Quality for hazardous waste management violations. The company was cited for its failure to examine the structural soundness of five hazardous waste storage tanks during the 1994–95 biennium as required under Tektronix's permit.

EEO: In 1996, Tektronix, Inc.'s Board of Directors totaled 11 directors, including two women and no minorities, while two of a total of 15 corporate officers were women, and none were minorities. Former vice president Deborah Coleman was chosen to head Merix, which Tektronix spun off in 1994. In 1995, 21 percent of the firm's officials and managers were women.

Tektronix maintains that its minority representation in management positions is in line with the percentage of minorities in Oregon. Tektronix's minority purchasing program was recently commended by the Defense Department. The company has also been recognized for its support of people with disabilities and for its fair treatment of employees with AIDS. Tektronix prohibits discrimination based on sexual orientation.

Community Involvement: In 1995, Tektronix, Inc.'s contributions to various charitable institutions included cash donations totaling $1 million. The company's cash contributions for 1995 were equivalent to 0.91 percent of its earnings before taxes for the same year.

The Tektronix Foundation's funding of education provides major support for colleges and universities emphasizing technical, business, and computer science education. Support for social services is nearly all in the form of donations to the United Way. Other major grants include over $70,000 to the Oregon Museum of Science and Industry in Portland, and $20,000 each to the Oregon Symphony Association and Oregon Public Broadcasting, which received an additional $9,000 from the foundation in matching grants.

Workplace Information: OSHA records indicate that Tektronix was inspected twice from 1994 to 1996, and received only incidental violations for $500 in fines, an average of $250 per inspection. In comparison, the median amount of fines per inspection for other companies in the industries manufacturing electronic equipment was $1,347.

Weapons Contracts: Sales to the Department of Defense have steadily declined in recent years. In 1995, this business was approximately $20.8 million, or 1.4 percent of total revenues. The company reports that all sales are of off-the-shelf products.

Texaco, Inc.

STOCK SYMBOL: TX
STOCK EXCHANGES: NY, TO, B, C, CH, PH, P

Environment	B
Women's Advancement	D
Minority Advancement	F
Charitable Giving	C
Community Outreach	N
Family Benefits	D
Workplace Issues	C
Social Disclosure	A

Texaco, the nation's fourth largest petrochemical concern, is involved in the worldwide exploration, production, refining, transportation and marketing of crude oil and its products. In 1996, the White Plains, New York–headquartered company employed approximately 28,000 people and had sales of $45.5 billion.

Environment: Texaco, Inc. has an environmental policy and publishes a corporate environmental report, which is updated biennially, follows the Public Environmental Reporting Initiative (PERI), and is available on the Internet. The company ranked 10 out of 15 for CEP's Campaign for Cleaner Corporations 1997 Petroleum Refining Report. Texaco has implemented an integrated environmental management system and provides environmental health and safety (EH&S) training to all employees. It also considers contribution towards EH&S goals in job performance reviews for all employees. Texaco has a written pollution prevention policy, and has initiated a companywide pollution prevention program which establishes annual reduction goals for fugitive emissions. The company does not have a corporate policy on community involvement relating to local environmental concerns, nor any community advisory panels at its facilities.

Texaco has a written policy on product stewardship and evaluates its products with the objective of reducing their life-cycle impacts on the environment. The company has an environmental audit program, which has worldwide standards and applicability. In 1996, 100 percent of U.S. facilities and 100 percent of International facilities were audited.

Internationally, Texaco does not monitor SARA Title III, or equivalent emissions. The company has Worldwide EH&S Standards and Guidelines and it monitors adherence to these standards through its 3-tiered EH&S Auditing Program. Texaco sponsors the Cawelo Water District Conservation Program (CA), and has participated in EPA's 33/50, WasteWi$e, and Green Lights programs.

Texaco's average total toxic releases and transfers during the years 1994–1996 were among the lowest in the industry sample. Emissions decreased by an average of about a quarter annually during those years, a better than average performance.

An August, 1997, oil spill of 685 tons at Texaco's Captain Field in the North Sea was reported by the British government to be the worst spill from an offshore installation in nearly ten years.

A 1996 national report found that five of the largest water polluters in Washington, of which Texaco was one, were located on Puget Sound. Texaco was fined for not meeting permit conditions, for violations of their permit limit, and for oil spills, and was among companies criticized for not meeting their responsibility to protect the Sound's diverse ecosystem from their pollution.

EEO: In 1996, Texaco Inc. had one woman and one minority on its 16-member Board of Directors. Additionally, the company's total of 19 corporate officers included one woman and no minorities, while the company counted one woman and no minorities among the 25 highest paid employees.

In November, 1996, Texaco settled a race discrimination law suit for $176.1 million. The suit, which was filed in 1994 on behalf of six African-American officials in Texaco's finance department, alleged that members of Texaco's "good old boy" network treated blacks dismissively, calling them "orangutans" and "porch monkeys," and kept the biggest raises and promotions for whites. Though the suit was not classified as a class action, the settlement will apply to the 1,400 current and former employees who would have been part of the class. Peter Bijur, Texaco's CEO, decided to settle after the audio-tape recordings of managers belittling black employees' grievances were made public on November 4, 1996. As a result of the incident, some retirement benefits were cut for two executives, one was suspended, and one was dismissed.

227

Continued on next page

Texaco, Inc. (continued)

As a part of the settlement, Texaco is required to establish a seven-member "equality and tolerance task force," which will be authorized to help shape personnel policies and practices. The company expects the funding for the task force to be as much as $35 million over its five-year existence, during which the EEOC will likely monitor its efforts.

Shortly afterward, Texaco outlined a variety of programs in the areas of recruitment and hiring, workplace, purchasing and contracting, and account-ability and oversight that were not required under the settlement. New programs include an Alternative Dispute Resolution process which would include mediation and arbitration of employee complaints, a closer link between managers' compensation and their "performance in creating openness and inclusion in the workplace," a mentoring process, and a partner-ship with INROADS. Among other initiatives, the company expects to expand the "scope and focus of programs with minority- and women-owned" businesses and "is already increasing the number of women and minority banks with which it does business from 21 to 50 and increasing deposits in those banks." A proposed boycott of Texaco was called off after the company announced its plan to promote diversity.

228

Texaco had increased total minority employment at the company from 16 percent in 1991 to 23 percent at the time of the settlement. However, the plaintiffs'[o] attorneys say a survey that was prepared by Mobil Corp. indicates that African-Americans make up only 0.4 percent of employees at Texaco earning more than $128,000, compared with 1.8 percent on average for other major oil companies in the United States.

Community Involvement: Texaco Inc.'s charitable contributions totaled $12 million in cash in 1996. The $12 million cash-giving figure represented the equiva-lent of 0.40 percent of the company's pretax earnings for the same year, and a decrease of 7.50 percent from the company's cash contributions in 1995. In 1995, the company contributed 1.22 percent of its pretax earnings for that year to charity.

The Texaco Foundation is currently "conducting a major review of the entire contributions and community relations program." The review will be completed later in 1997, and the new priorities will be established by early 1998. The company itself will evaluate "its level of support for all programs… that complement its business focus and further promote community improvements."

In January, 1997, Texaco announced that it was estab-lishing a program that will "develop minority students for management careers in disciplines important to Texaco, such as engineering, the physical sciences, information systems and international business." The announcement came shortly after the company's November, 1996, settlement of a $176 million racial discrimination case.

Workplace Information: The records of the Occupational Safety and Health Administration indicate that Texaco Inc. underwent 26 health and safety inspections from 1994 to 1996. The violations reported by OSHA as a result of the inspections include 49 classified as "serious." The company was required to pay $72,860 as a result of its violations. In comparison, the median amount of fines per inspection for other companies in the extractive business was $2941.44.

Additional Information: Texaco is among a con-sortium of oil companies operating in Burma. Their presence there is opposed by human rights advocates for providing financial support to Burma's military regime, which has held Nobel Peace Prize Laureate Aung San Suu Kyi under house arrest since 1989.

Weapons Contracts: Texaco supplies fuel to the U.S. military.

Texas Instruments

STOCK SYMBOL: TXN
STOCK EXCHANGES: NY, B, C, CH, P

Environment	B
Women's Advancement	D
Minority Advancement	A
Charitable Giving	D
Community Outreach	B?
Family Benefits	A
Workplace Issues	D
Social Disclosure	B

Inventor of the integrated circuit, Texas Instruments (TI) is the sixth largest manufacturer of semiconductors and is a leading supplier of computer systems and peripherals, defense electronics, industrial services, and consumer electronics. Texas Instruments is based in Dallas, Texas. In 1996, the company had 59,574 employees and revenues of $9.9 billion.

Environment: Texas Instruments has an environmental policy and a corporate environmental report, which is updated annually and is available on the Internet. An integrated environmental management system has been implemented by the company. TI has a written pollution prevention policy and has initiated a companywide pollution prevention program, which establishes annual reduction goals for point sources, secondary emissions, fugitive emissions, and solid waste. TI also has a corporate policy on community involvement relating to local environmental concerns; however, it does not have any community advisory panels. TI does not have a written policy on product stewardship, but has a products stewardship review board and evaluates its products with the objective of reducing their life-cycle impacts on the environment.

Texas Instruments' toxics releases and transfers were below average in 1993, but after almost tripling emissions, the company became the fourth highest emitter in 1994 compared to its industry sample.

EEO: In 1996, TI's nine-member Board of Directors included one woman and no minorities. Of 148 corporate officers at the company, 11 were women and 25 were minorities. Four minorities also ranked among the 25 highest paid employees at the company.

TI won the 1996 Catalyst award for its efforts to promote women. Catalyst reports that Texas Instruments' program has evolved with women's advancement and has developed ways to measure results. In 1996, five percent of domestic goods and services were purchased from minority- and women-owned businesses.

Community Involvement: In 1995, TI's cash contributions totaled $2.3 million, or 0.16 percent of its pretax earnings.

Workplace Information: According to OSHA's records, TI was inspected two times from 1994 to 1996. Violations included 20 classified as "serious" for $4,700 in fines, an average of $2,350 per inspection.

The median amount of fines per inspection for other electronic equipment manufacturers was $1,347.

TI charges smokers an additional $10 per month in health insurance premiums. TI increasingly uses self-directed work teams and has retained Merex Corporation to develop workplace literacy programs and train supervisors to be more effective communicators. The company estimates it will have eliminated 5,000 defense electronics positions from 1993 to 1997.

International: TI is the largest exporter in the Philippines, where it established a semiconductor assembly plant in 1980. In 1989, the plant was recognized by the Manila government for excellence in employee and community relations.

Weapons Contracts: In 1997, TI's defense operations were purchased by Raytheon. In 1996, TI ranked 21st in the list of worldwide defense firms, with nearly $1.8 billion in defense-related business, or 17.8 percent of revenue. TI was the 23rd largest military contractor to the U.S. Department of Defense with prime contracts worth $528 million.

Product Quality: Like many of its peers, TI implemented Total Quality Management in the mid-1980s. TI established nearly 5,000 employee teams involving over 30,000 individuals and sent managers to quality leadership training classes. In 1992, TI's defense electronics division received the Malcolm Baldrige Award.

Legal Proceedings: In August 1994, TI paid $5.2 million to settle allegations that its defense electronics group overcharged the government for contracts for guided missiles sold to the Navy.

Additional Information: In 1987, TI established one of the strongest corporate ethics programs. The $700,000 program includes management training and ethics pamphlets.

229

Texas Utilities

STOCK SYMBOL: TXU
STOCK EXCHANGES: NY, B, C, CH, P, PH

Environment	REV
Women's Advancement	B
Minority Advancement	A
Charitable Giving	N
Community Outreach	B
Family Benefits	N
Workplace Issues	C
Social Disclosure	A

Texas Utilities (TU), headquartered in Dallas, Texas, is a holding company for TU Electric Company and Southwestern Electric Service Company, both in Texas, and TU Australia Pty. Ltd. Seven other subsidiaries provide support services related to TU Electric's activities. In 1996, the company had revenues of $6.6 billion and 11,451 employees.

Environment: TU was named to CEP's Campaign for Cleaner Corporations (C-3) in 1993 but was removed from the list in 1994 after improving its environmental performance. The company postponed closing six natural gas plants and delayed construction of two coal burning facilities, lowering projected growth in CO_2 emissions. These emissions are nevertheless expected to increase 7.5 percent through 2000 from a 1990 baseline.

TU now expects to exceed its goal of offsetting 20 percent of capacity growth through DSM programs, such as the company's thermal cool storage program, the largest of its kind in the U.S. It provides cash incentives to larger customers who install equipment that chills water at night when system demands are low. The chilled water and ice is then used for air conditioning during the day. This program was named one of the country's best load management initiatives in 1994 by the Results Center, an environmental consulting firm.

TU has integrated renewable energy sources into its generation mix with the purchase of 40 MW of wind generation. In addition, the company is testing and evaluating photovoltaics, solar thermal, wind, fuel cells, and alternative fuel vehicles.

TU has reclaimed the land it mined since its operations began in 1971, developing wildlife habitat features on about 20 percent of it and planting millions of trees.

EEO: In 1996, one woman and one minority served on TU's ten-member Board of Directors. Of 41 corporate officers, three were women and four were minorities.

TU Electric was recognized by the Dallas Together Forum for its promotion of minority purchasing in October, 1996. Dallas Together is a coalition of area businesses, chambers of commerce, and nonprofit organizations created as a means to help overcome racial barriers. Member companies set hiring, promotion, and purchasing goals and disclose their progress in reaching the goals, though the companies are not required to provide the purchasing figures in the context of total purchasing.

A company response from Texas Utilities states that it "maintains Affirmative Action Programs" and has several committees, the goals of which are to diversify the work force population and provide support and promotion opportunities for women, minorities, and people with disabilities. The statement indicates that in 1996, 21.4 percent of employees promoted were minorities and 29.4 percent were women at its operations located in Dallas County. Of total hiring, 52.7 percent were ethnic minority and 43.2 percent were women. The committees and programs developed as part of the Diversity Advancement Initiatives include the Diversity Steering Committee, the Employee Diversity Advisory Council, an employee diversity task force, and focus groups.

Community Involvement: No recent information is available on TU's charitable giving. Its 1996 annual report cites community activities in which employees helped clean and repair elderly people's homes, schools, and parks. The commune also was instrumental in preserving a Caddo Indian Village at its Martin Lake mining site. Past philanthropic efforts focused on youth education and leadership training, primarily through collaborative programs with such organizations as 4-H, FFA, Business Professionals of America, and Future Business Leaders of America.

Workplace Information: OSHA records indicate that TU was not inspected from 1994 to 1996. Consequently, TU received no violations or fines. About 24 percent of TU's workforce is represented by the International Brotherhood of Electrical Workers.

Nuclear Power: TU's Comanche Peak power plant generates about 15 percent of the company's energy.

The Timberland Company

STOCK SYMBOL: TBL
STOCK EXCHANGES: NY, CH, P

Environment	B
Women's Advancement	B
Minority Advancement	D
Charitable Giving	A
Community Outreach	A
Family Benefits	B
Workplace Issues	B
Social Disclosure	B

Timberland, based in Stratham, New Hampshire, manufactures and distributes footwear, apparel and accessories for work and outdoor use. Until 1995, Timberland owned most of its factories and operated in the U.S., Puerto Rico, and the Dominican Republic. That year, it closed manufacturing facilities in Boone, North Carolina, and Mountain City, Tennessee, and cut back operations in the Dominican Republic, increasing the amount of work sourced to outside suppliers. In 1996, the company had sales of $796.5 million and approximately 6,000 employees.

Environment: A strong promoter of environmental awareness, Timberland supports such programs as the Earth Conservation Corps, Student Conservation Association, American Forest Foundation, and the Society for the Protection of New Hampshire Forests. The company is a member of the Outdoor Industry Conservation Alliance, a collection of 32 outdoor companies that pool resources to assist grassroots environmental causes.

Timberland endorsed the CERES Principles in April 1993. The company states that it applies the same environmental standards to all of its facilities, regardless of location, and monitors its suppliers for use of Class I ozone-depleting chemicals. Recycling of paper, cardboard, leather, and used office equipment is done at its major facilities. Environmental criteria such as recycled content of paper is specified for bulk purchases.

EEO: As of February 1998, Timberland's General Counsel, Vice President of Human Resources, and Vice President of Licensing are women. There are no women or minorities among its seven-member Board of Directors. There are 22 women and three minorities among the company's 86 officials and managers.

Community Involvement: Timberland won CEP's Corporate Conscience Award for Community Involvement in 1995. In 1992, Timberland committed $1 million over three years to Boston-based City Year, which allowed the youth volunteer effort to expand beyond Boston and Providence, Rhode Island, to several other cities. The program, which brings together young adults to participate for a year in community service efforts, served as a model for President Clinton's national service initiative. In 1994, Timberland announced a second investment, this time of $5 million over five years. In 1997, Timberland announced an additional $1 million challenge grant to City Year, to begin in 1998.

To encourage civic involvement among its employees, Timberland provides up to 40 hours paid time off for volunteerism and special volunteer opportunity days. In conjunction with America's Promise, Timberland also committed to serve 40,000 hours by the year 2000. In 1997, Timberland employees performed 17,128 hours of community service.

Family Benefits: Timberland's employees are paid for at least two weeks of parental, dependent care, and family illness leaves. Generous adoption benefits range from $4,000 to $8,000 (more for a special-needs child). Many benefits are extended to domestic partners, including health coverage and bereavement leave.

Workplace Information: In 1995, laid-off employees in North Carolina and Tennessee complained that the company did not help with retraining and was not active in their communities. A Timberland representative said that laid-off workers received one week's pay for each year worked, as well as outplacement services.

International: Timberland manufactures and markets men's and women's footwear, apparel, and accessories under the Timberland brand name. The company operates in the U.S., Europe, Middle East, Asia Pacific and South America (with the bulk of its manufacturing done in Puerto Rico and the Dominican Republic). The company has strong sourcing guidelines which cover child labor, workweek, wages, prison/forced labor and other issues. While the policy defaults to the local required age for children, it does indicate the company's support of apprenticeship programs. Moreover, Timberland limits regularly scheduled workweeks to 48 hours and one day off in seven. The company has not been subject to public or media attention regarding labor rights issues.

Time Warner, Inc.

STOCK SYMBOL: TWX
STOCK EXCHANGES: NY, B, CH, P, PH

Environment	B
Women's Advancement	B
Minority Advancement	C
Charitable Giving	N
Community Outreach	B
Family Benefits	N
Workplace Issues	C?
Social Disclosure	A

Time Warner, the world's largest media and entertainment conglomerate, was formed in 1989, through the merger of Time Inc. and Warner Communications. In 1997, the New York City–based company had 72,000 employees worldwide and total revenues of $24 billion dollars.

Environment: TWX reports that it has no toxic or *de minimus* releases at any of its facilities. The company has developed a written environmental policy. Chemical-based inks are being replaced with vegetable-based inks, and publishing subsidiaries use some recycled and chlorine-free paper. The company participates in the Paper Task Force of the Environmental Defense Fund. Time Warner developed the Eco-Pak for compact discs as an alternative to the longbox. The Eco-Pak container generates no waste other than the shrink-wrap plastic in which it is delivered.

EEO: In 1996, Time Warner's board totaled 13 directors, including two women and one minority. Nine of a total of 33 corporate officers were women and two were minorities. Additionally, four women and one minority were among the 25 employees with the highest salaries.

Time Warner has launched a companywide diversity program in partnership with public schools across the country. The program promotes appreciation and understanding of cultural, racial and ethnic diversity among students in the public school system. Time-Warner is also a member of the Center for Women's Policy Programs, a multiethnic and multicultural feminist policy research and advocacy institution.

Community Involvement: Time Warner's charitable contributions totaled $11.5 million in cash in 1996; $10 million in 1997. In addition, Time Warner divisions contributed an additional $7 million in 1997.

Time Warner devotes particular attention to education and literacy. The company's main funding objective is education and dispersing educational experiences more equitably. In terms of direct financial aid, more than 45 percent of Time Warner's corporate contributions goes to educational institutions. This includes a pledge of $5 million to the Annenberg Challenge Grant for School Reform to set up Time Warner media labs in public schools throughout New York City.

Time Warner pledged to expand its Time To Read volunteer literacy program (already the largest such corporate program in the U.S.) to provide one million volunteer hours of tutoring by the end of 1998; it had reached 900,000 hours by October, 1997. The program provides 4,000 tutors for 14,800 adults and children. The company won CEP's 1991 Corporate Conscience Award for community involvement.

The company also pledged the largest single corporate commitment to the Virtual Y, the largest extended school day program in New York City. Time Warner and the Upper Manhattan Empowerment Zone are funding 19 new Virtual Y after-school sites at public schools located throughout the empowerment zone.

Family Benefits: The company's work and family program includes an emergency drop-in child care center at company headquarters, child care and elder care resource referral services, emergency child care services, and bi-weekly information workshops on child, elderly, and individual care. Employees can take up to four months of family-care leave for the care of a spouse, child, or elderly relative. Time Warner was also among the first companies to extend healthcare benefits to same-sex partners of employees.

Workplace Information: OSHA records indicate that Time Warner underwent six inspections from 1994 to 1996. Violations include seven classified as "serious" for a total of $13,050 in fines, an average of $2,190 per inspection. In comparison, the median amount of fines per inspection for other companies in the service industry, such as banks and communications companies, was $573.33.

The Timken Company

STOCK SYMBOL: TKR
STOCK EXCHANGES: NY, B, CH, PH

Environment	D
Women's Advancement	N
Minority Advancement	N
Charitable Giving	D?
Community Outreach	N
Family Benefits	N
Workplace Issues	F?
Social Disclosure	F

Based in Canton, Ohio, the Timken Company is one of the world's largest manufacturers of bearings and alloy steels. In 1996, the company had revenues of $2.4 billion and 19,000 employees.

Environment: The Timken Company has an environmental policy and currently publishes a corporate environmental report (CER). Timken has in place a comprehensive training program for its employees, which attempts to reach nearly every associate in the company's U.S. manufacturing plants. The company pledges to continue with the effort of training new and reassigned associates and give refresher courses to those previously trained. The company also sponsored its first internal environmental conference to provide a forum for all employees who handle environmental coordinator duties to exchange information. As reported in its 1995 CER, Timken's steel plants recently became free of polychlorinated biphenyls (PCBs) with the removal of the last three PCB transformers. Timken addresses its waste minimization by pledging to "purchase supplies and materials with minimal environmental impact, minimizing waste in operations, recycling waste where possible, and disposing of any remaining waste in an environmentally responsible manner." Timken has in place an environmental audit program with worldwide standards/applicability, and has audited all of its U.S. facilities. The company is in the midst of completing audits for its international facilities.

Timken's toxic emissions have been declining over the last few years, especially for its steel business; however, emissions from its bearing business have been on the increase.

In December 1997, the Timken Company received the Ohio Governor's annual award for Outstanding Achievement in Pollution Prevention. The award is presented to those companies, organizations and individuals who have made exceptional efforts in reducing pollution through source reduction and recycling waste. Timken is a leadership member of Ohio Prevention First, a voluntary planning initiative that urges Ohio companies to incorporate pollution prevention and waste minimization into their operations.

EEO: In 1996, Timken Co.'s 12-member board and 13 corporate officers included no women or minorities.

A shareholder proposal in Timken's 1997 proxy statement states that the shareholders urge the company to enlarge its search for qualified board members by selecting the best people regardless of race, gender, or physical challenge.

Community Involvement: In 1995, Timken Co.'s contributions to various charitable institutions included cash donations totaling $500,000. The company's cash contributions for 1995 were equivalent to 0.28 percent of its earnings before taxes for the same year.

Timken's giving priorities include United Way agencies in Ohio, food distribution organizations, education reform, Junior Achievement, business education, colleges and universities, art funds, and economic development programs.

Workplace Information: OSHA records indicate that Timken was inspected nine times from 1994 to 1996. Violations included two classified as "willful" or "repeat" and 53 classified as "serious" for a total of $42,375 in fines, an average of $4,708 per inspection. In comparison, the median amount of fines per inspection for other companies in similar manufacturing industries was $2,412.

In 1993, the company announced a restructuring program that would cut 12 percent of its workforce by 1997. Most of the reductions were achieved through retirements and attrition.

Through its employee stock ownership program, currently more than 50 percent of employees collectively own 10 percent of the company's shares. Timken has an awards program for teams of employees who develop initiatives to save the company money.

Weapons Contracts: In 1994, the company had $6.2 million in Department of Defense contracts, $4.8 million of which were military related and $1.3 million of which were nuclear related.

233

TJX Companies

Stock Symbol: TJX
Stock Exchanges: NY, B, Ch, Ph, P

Environment	N
Women's Advancement	B
Minority Advancement	B
Charitable Giving	A
Community Outreach	C
Family Benefits	N
Workplace Issues	B?
Social Disclosure	B

TJX, headquartered in Framingham, Massachusetts, emerged in 1989 as the successor to general merchandiser Zayre's specialty retailing operations. TJX quickly grew to become the nation's largest retailer of off-price clothing. In November 1995, it acquired its leading competitor, Marshalls, for $550 million, adding 450 stores to its 660 T.J. Maxx, Winners Apparel, and HomeGoods outlets. In August 1995, TJX announced the sale of its Hit or Miss women's apparel chain to 10 company executives. In early 1996, it decided to spin off its Chadwick's of Boston mail order catalogue. TJX had sales of almost $6.7 billion for the year ending January 25, 1997. The company has approximately 56,000 employees.

Environment: TJX has not joined the EPA's Green Lights program or adopted other noteworthy environmental policies.

EEO: In 1996, TJX Companies achieved a higher than average rating in both diversity categories, placing them easily in the top third of S&P 500 companies. Two women and two minorities served on TJX Companies' ten-member Board of Directors. Of 18 corporate officers at the company, one was a woman and one was a minority, while one of the top 25 paid employees were women, and none were minorities.

TJX offers mentoring programs and maintains diversity goals for both women and minorities. It also operates a recruitment program for minorities. In 1996, TJX Companies purchased over $15 million in goods and services from women- and minority-owned businesses.

Community Involvement: TJX Companies' charitable contributions totaled $1.3 million in cash in 1996, and $3 million in in-kind donations. The $1.3 million cash-giving figure represented the equivalent of 0.36 percent of the company's pretax earnings for the same year, and a decrease of 39 percent from the company's cash contributions in 1995. In 1995, the company contributed 1.46 percent of its pretax earnings for that year to charity.

The TJX Foundation seeks "to help needy families with children" through initiatives concerning education and job training, housing, and community development. As part of its commitment to arts and culture, the company supports programs that encourage diverse art, especially by handicapped, young or disadvantaged people.

In 1996, TJX Companies pledged to create 2,000 jobs for persons leaving the federal government's welfare program by the year 2000.

Workplace Information: The records of the Occupational Safety and Health Administration indicate that TJX Companies underwent two health and safety inspections from 1994 to 1996. The violations reported by OSHA as a result of the inspections include one classified as "serious." The company was required to pay $470 as a result of its violations, an average of $235 per inspection. In comparison, the median amount of fines per inspection for other companies in the retail industry was $694.

TJX's 3,700 distribution facility employees are members of the Union of Needle Trades, Industrial and Textile Employees (formerly the International Ladies Garment Workers Union). While new contracts at three centers were agreed to in January 1995, in May 1996 1,300 workers at the Evansville, Indiana, facility struck the company after narrowly rejecting a company proposal that would have offered annual 50 cent per hour wage increases.

The consolidation of TJX's T.J. Maxx and Marshall's headquarters staff resulted in about 100 layoffs in February 1996.

TJX has sourcing guidelines for labor rights, but has not disclosed them to CEP.

Toys "R" Us

STOCK SYMBOL: TOY

STOCK EXCHANGES: NY, B, CH, P, PH

Environment	N
Women's Advancement	A
Minority Advancement	B
Charitable Giving	A
Community Outreach	C
Family Benefits	N
Workplace Issues	C?
Social Disclosure	B

The largest retailer of toys in America, Toys "R" Us operates more than 600 toy and clothing (Kids "R" Us) stores in the U.S. and more than 300 abroad. The toy retailer's philosophy of offering huge selection and affordable prices brought its sales to $9.4 billion by 1996. The company has 60,000 employees.

Environment: Toys "R" Us conducts comprehensive environmental audits at just 10 percent of its U.S. and international facilities. The company is not a member of any voluntary initiatives, but it has a companywide energy conservation program. Toys "R" Us has a central energy management system and plans gradual replacement of heating, ventilation, and air conditioning equipment with highly efficient units.

EEO: In 1996, two women and one minority served on Toys "R" Us's ten-member Board of Directors. Of corporate officers at the company, none were women and none were minorities.

A 1996 ICCR-sponsored shareholder resolution addressing board inclusiveness at Toys "R" Us was withdrawn by its proponents, as was a 1997 resolution proposing that the company conduct a Glass Ceiling Review. The withdrawal of a resolution usually indicates that an agreement with management has been reached regarding the issue.

Community Involvement: In 1996, Toys "R" Us's charitable giving totaled $4 million in cash, which was equal to 0.59 percent of the company's pretax earnings for that year.

The corporate giving program of Toys "R" Us focuses on improving the health care needs of children. The company has sponsored kids' playrooms in hospitals. It consults with therapists and doctors on design and equipment, taking into account the specific needs of resident patients. A total of 35 playrooms in hospitals in 16 states have now been sponsored. Toys "R" Us continues to pay for the labor and upkeep at all sites.

Toys "R" Us is also a national sponsor of the Juvenile Diabetes Foundation. In 1996, the company's annual Children's Benefit Fund dinner raised $2.8 million.

Workplace Information: According to the Occupational Safety and Health Administration's records, Toys "R" Us was inspected 17 times from 1994 to 1996. The OSHA inspectors' citations included 13 violations classified as "serious." A total of $12,907 in fines was assessed to the company following the inspections. In comparison, the median amount of fines per inspection for other companies in the retail industry was $694.

Many Toys "R" Us managers meet several times annually with employees for a free interchange of ideas, questions, and suggestions. The company has implemented a number of employee suggestions, including the all-inclusive stock option plan and the hospital playrooms mentioned above. Though the company is not unionized, it has three ombudspersons to hear and mediate grievances. In 1996, Toys "R" Us introduced a peer review program, which allows employees to resolve grievances by meeting with a panel of three fellow employees and two managers. The company abides by the majority decision of the panel.

Product Information: Toys "R" Us has agreed to carry only rated video games in its stores following consumer pressure on the toy industry to label toys suitable for children. After police shootings in New York City, where police officers mistook toy guns for real weapons, in 1994 the company announced that it would stop selling certain realistic toy guns.

International: In 1996, Toys "R" Us adopted an extremely thorough Code of Conduct for Suppliers, addressing basic workers' rights, child labor, working hours, and wages. The code refers to collective bargaining and expresses the company's preference for vendors who pay fair wages. Toys "R" Us was instrumental in the development of SA8000, the first international standard on labor rights for companies subcontracting their manufacturing.

Tyson Foods, Inc.

STOCK SYMBOL: TYSNA
STOCK EXCHANGE: NNM

Environment	D
Women's Advancement	C
Minority Advancement	F
Charitable Giving	B
Community Outreach	N
Family Benefits	N
Workplace Issues	D
Social Disclosure	F

Tyson, based in Springdale, Arkansas, is the world's largest fully integrated producer, processor, and marketer of fresh and frozen poultry-, beef-, pork-, and fish-based food products, and convenience foods. The company's distribution network reaches 80 percent of the nation's fast-food restaurants. In 1996, Tyson had $6.5 billion in sales and 58,300 employees.

Environment: Tyson publishes a small brochure that discusses the company's efforts to make its production less environmentally damaging. Its toxic releases were better than the food industry average in 1994, despite having doubled since the previous year. Between 1990 and 1994, TRI adjusted for size increased 47 percent. Tyson's accidental spills between 1991 and 1995 were among the highest in the food industry, resulting in 22 injuries and 1,484 evacuations.

In 1992, Tyson redesigned its frozen dinner package to eliminate over one million pounds of packaging annually. The company invested $14 million to expand its byproducts recycling operations, which convert scrap parts (bones, etc.) into pet feed and other usable products. Tyson substitutes poultry litter for chemical fertilizer and limits its usage to prevent runoff, which might lead to eutrophication of nearby waters. It also invested $43.2 million for water quality programs and facility upgrades. Such expenditures, however, may have been prompted by past compliance problems under the Clean Water Act. Water resources and effluents are one of the most environmentally impactful aspects of chicken farming.

EEO: There is one woman (a family member) on the 11-member Board of Directors and one woman among 16 corporate officers; an African-American man has served on the board since 1991.

Community Involvement: In 1995, the Tyson Foods, Inc. Foundation donated $900,000, or 0.35 percent of the company's average pretax income, to charitable organizations, while the company makes $2 to $3 million annually in direct corporate contributions. The foundation focuses primarily on organizations in Arkansas and communities in close proximity to Tyson operating facilities. Tyson also donates approximately 2 million pounds of food a year to hunger relief organizations.

Workplace Information: Tyson states that its lost-time injury rate is far below the U.S. manufacturing average: 1.4 compared with 5.3 hours per 100 workers per year. In 1996, a Tyson plant in Pennsylvania received recognition for surpassing one million man-hours of work without a lost-time accident; since 1994, over 30 Tyson plants have matched that achievement, some of them several times. In late 1995, Tyson formed National Comp Care Inc. as a wholly owned subsidiary to handle workers' compensation for itself and other Arkansas companies in reaction to a new state regulation. Tyson's workers hold approximately 60 percent of the company's stock.

Employees of the former Henry House Inc. in Michigan, now owned by Tyson, sued the company, alleging pension shortfalls in the aftermath of the takeover. In 1995, the U.S. Fourth Circuit Court of Appeals ruled that Tyson broke federal labor laws when it used threats and other fear tactics to keep its employees from joining unions in Virginia and Texas. The court rejected Tyson's appeal of a National Labor Relations Board Court ruling that the company was guilty of unfair labor practices.

Additional Information: The Tyson political action committee and company employees contribute about $200,000 a year to various federal, state, and local candidates. The company is reportedly a big contributor to interest groups, associations, and causes that further its agenda. Tyson workers have been involved with the Justice Department's criminal investigation of Mike Espy, the Clinton administration's former Agriculture Secretary.

UAL Corporation

STOCK SYMBOL: UAL
STOCK EXCHANGES: NY, B, C, CH, P, PH

Environment	B
Women's Advancement	B
Minority Advancement	B
Charitable Giving	C
Community Outreach	A
Family Benefits	C
Workplace Issues	B
Social Disclosure	A

United Airlines, principal unit of the UAL Corporation, was reborn as a 55 percent employee-owned company in July 1994 after years of corporate losses and controversy over the extent of wage concessions traded for the buyout. This makes Chicago-based UAL the largest U.S. company to be majority-owned by employees. In 1996, the company had 87,628 employees and revenues of $16 billion.

Environment: In 1995, United totally eliminated ozone-depleting chemicals from its aircraft-related processes. From 1992 through 1994, the company reduced usage of CFCs for aircraft maintenance by about 90 percent. United Airlines recycles cardboard, cans, glass, and paper on most domestic flights and seeks new ways to reduce waste and increase recycling. On-board menus and napkins are manufactured from recycled paper.

EEO: Five of 41 officers are women, one of whom is Hispanic. There are no female directors. In the early 1990s, United employed more African-American airline pilots—144—than any other airline. There were few members of any minority group in management, however. By 1995, there were four minority corporate officers, and two divisions were headed by minorities.

UAL promotes multicultural training and provides focus groups for its minority employees. More than a quarter of those in its management development program are minorities. The company also has a thriving minority vendor program.

Community Involvement: United Airlines Foundation contributed approximately $2.8 million to charitable causes in 1995. The United Believers Program promises inner-city fifth graders at Johnson Elementary (Chicago) a four-year state university scholarship if they graduate from high school. Employee volunteers act as mentors and tutors, and the relationship between company and child continues for ten years. The Friendly Skies program helps critically ill children and their families when travel is needed for treatment (and for whom travel expenses would be a hardship).

Workplace Information: In 1994, the directors of UAL agreed to sell a majority stake in United Airlines to its two major unions (pilots and machinists) in exchange for significant wage and work-rule labor concessions. Employees agreed to more than five years of wage cuts and changes in work rules that would save the company $5 billion. The workers also won the right to choose a new CEO and to fill three seats on the 12-member board. In March 1997, the pilots and mechanics reached tentative agreements calling for two 5-percent wage increases, one in July 1997 and one in July 1998. In 2000, wage rates are to go back to the levels that were in place when employees became owners of the company.

In January 1994, three UAL shareholders requested that a Delaware judge strike down the plan to transfer majority ownership, claiming that UAL failed to consider the best interest of the shareholders when approving the agreement. In January 1995, six United Airlines workers filed suit in an effort to rescind the wage concessions of 24,000 nonunion workers, charging that negotiations were primarily carried on between the company and the two major unions, without input from the unorganized sector. The 18,000 members of the flight attendants' union never agreed to the buyout; they did not make wage concessions or become shareholders.

237

Unicom Corporation

STOCK SYMBOL: UCM
STOCK EXCHANGES: NY, B, C, CH, P, PH

Environment	B
Women's Advancement	C
Minority Advancement	A
Charitable Giving	D
Community Outreach	C
Family Benefits	C
Workplace Issues	C
Social Disclosure	A

Unicom Corp. (formerly Commonwealth Edison Co.), headquartered in Chicago, Illinois, generates, transmits, and sells electricity to 3.3 million customers in Chicago and northern Illinois. In 1996, the company employed 16,871 persons and had revenues of $6.9 billion.

Environment: Named to CEP's Campaign for Cleaner Corporations (C-3) list in November 1994, Unicom was removed the following year. At the time of the listing, Unicom projected that its CO_2 emissions would increase nearly 50 percent by the year 2000—the greatest percent increase of the companies studied by CEP. On a pruduction unit basis, in 1991 Unicom emitted 20 percent more SO_2 and 30 percent more nitrogen oxide than the industry average. Revised construction plans and enhanced demand-side management programs significantly lowered the utility's projected CO_2 increases (which were among the highest in the industry). In addition, the company's acid rain program is expected to reduce SO_2 and nitrogen oxide emissions.

Unicom owns the intellectual rights to a massive frictionless flywheel. With this technology, energy is stored during off-peak times and then drawn off again when demand is greatest.

In October 1994, Unicom agreed to pay a $10,000 fine and make a $90,000 contribution to the Illinois Chapter of the Nature Conservancy to settle EPA charges that it illegally destroyed two acres of wetlands in order to build a road and electrical towers.

EEO: In 1996, Unicom Corp./ComEd's 13-member Board of Directors included two women and three minorities. Of 24 corporate officers at the company, one was a woman and two were minorities. One woman and two minorities also ranked among the 25 highest paid employees at the company.

In December 1993, Unicom agreed to a $3.3 million settlement of a discrimination case filed by the Equal Employment Opportunity Commission (EEOC) in 1988. Women who applied for meter-reader jobs in the 1980s but were not hired received $3 million; the remainder went to training programs for women seeking positions in nontraditional fields. Unicom paid $1.5 million as part of a 1989 settlement with the EEOC for alleged discrimination against women at its Waukegan, Illinois, power plant.

Community Involvement: Unicom's charitable contributions totaled $3.9 million in cash in 1996, and $29,000 in in-kind donations. The $3.9 million cash-giving figure represented the equivalent of 0.35 percent of the company's pretax earnings for the same year.

The Power House is an educational facility created by ComEd to educate children and the general public about energy and conservation. In 1995, ComEd initiated its voluntary Stewardship Program as well as various prairie planting projects.

Workplace Information: OSHA records indicate that Unicom underwent six health and safety inspections from 1994 to 1996. Violations included 16 classified as "serious," and resulted in $81,482 in fines, an average of $13,580 per inspection. In comparison, the median amount of fines per inspection for other utilities was $2,625. In a 1995 ranking of 109 nuclear plants in the U.S., Lehman Brothers gave three of Commonwealth Edison's plants a below-average or poor performance rating in safety.

Nuclear Power: Nuclear power plants are the company's main power source (roughly 70 percent). From 1990 through July 1994, Unicom received $1.9 million in fines from the Nuclear Regulatory Commission (NRC). In 1995, the NRC announced a $100,000 fine against the company; its Braidwood nuclear plant left disconnected for three months a system used to detect hydrogen gas leaks.

In September 1993, Unicom agreed to pay a $1.3 billion customer refund and extend a $339 million annual rate reduction to settle lawsuits filed by consumer groups. The lawsuits charged the utility with building multibillion-dollar reactors that were deemed largely unnecessary.

Union Camp

STOCK SYMBOL: UCC
STOCK EXCHANGES: NY, B, CH, P, PH

Environment	C
Women's Advancement	C
Minority Advancement	C
Charitable Giving	C
Community Outreach	C
Family Benefits	N
Workplace Issues	F?
Social Disclosure	B

New Jersey-based Union Camp manufactures fine paper, packaging, wood products, and chemicals. One subsidiary engages in land sales and development, and another is a paper and office supply merchant distributer. The company has a strong overseas presence, especially in corrugated container and chemical manufacturing. In 1997, revenues were $4.5 billion, and the company had 18,000 employees.

Environment: Union Camp has a publicly available environmental policy, but does not publish a corporate environmental report. Union Camp provides environmental health and safety (EH&S) training to employees and considers contributions towards EH&S goals in the job performance reviews of executives and managers. As stated in their environmental policy, Union Camp has a policy on product stewardship and evaluates products with the objective of reducing their life-cycle impacts on the environment. Union Camp is in compliance with the American Forest & Paper Association's Sustainable Forestry Initiative.

Union Camp's toxic releases and transfers were below average in both 1993 and 1994, compared to a 12-company industry sample. Emissions decreased by about one seventh between the two years, the second best performance in the sample.

Union Camp's forestry-related research includes seeking lab-engineered species as a solution to environmentally responsible future fiber production needs. One of the company's "experimental trees" has the potential to grow 40 feet in five years. Use of this technology could reduce the company's reliance on traditional forest harvesting practices.

Union Camp encourages conservation and environmental education through two award programs; The Alexander Calder Conservation Award, which recognizes individuals who conserve wildlife habitat thought a partnership of business and conservation, and the Gene Cartledge Award for Excellence in Environmental Education.

EEO: In 1996, Union Camp's 12-member Board of Directors included one woman and no minorities. One woman served among the company's 25 corporate officers and the company's 25 highest paid employees.

In addition to special programs for purchasing from minority- and women-owned businesses, Union Camp has developed a program for purchasing from companies owned by people with disabilities.

Community Involvement: In 1996, Union Camp's charitable giving totaled $2.4 million in cash, equal to 0.3 percent of the company's pretax earnings for that year.

Teams of employees at Union Camp facilities are instrumental in recommending how donations are directed in the local communities where the company has plants. According to the May 1997 issue of Corporate Philanthropy Report, Union Camp "has yet to develop a specific strategy in its funding of environmental causes," but it does support some national environmental groups, and gave 50,000 acres of swamp land to the Nature Conservancy, donating 84,000 acres overall through its Land Legacy Program.

Workplace Information: OSHA records indicate that Union Camp was inspected 11 times from 1994 to 1996. Violations included 44 classified as "serious" for a total of $83,891 in fines, an average of $7,626 per inspection. Union Camp reports impressive safety records; five facilities have acheived Star status under OSHA's VPP Star Site program. Less than 400 of the 6 million U.S. workplaces have Star status.

It has been more than 20 years since Union Camp has had a strike at one of its mills, an impressive feat when one considers that about 40 percent of the company's 19,000 employees are represented by one of 66 unions.

Legal Proceedings: A subsidiary of Union Camp remains a defendant (with scores of others) in more than 7,000 cases concerning workers' alleged exposure to asbestos while working on Union Camp premises. About 13,100 cases have been resolved from 1994 to 1997, with Union Camp's insurance company funding the cost of the settlements.

Union Carbide

Environment	B
Women's Advancement	C
Minority Advancement	B
Charitable Giving	C
Community Outreach	B
Family Benefits	B
Workplace Issues	D
Social Disclosure	A

Union Carbide, based in Danbury, Connecticut, is a worldwide chemicals and polymers company. It operates two business segments: Specialties & Intermediates, and Basic Chemicals and Polymers. For the past decade it has undergone a massive restructuring that involved selling numerous businesses, resulting in a 90 percent reduction in its workforce. In 1997, the company had 11,800 employees and revenues of $6.5 billion.

Environment: Union Carbide has an environmental policy and a corporate environmental report, which is updated annually and is available on the Internet. The company has implemented an environmental management system. The company's Responsible Care Standards covering Health, Safety, Medical, Product Stewardship and other areas are mandatory at the corporation's sites worldwide.

Union Carbide was named to CEP's worst performer list in the 1994 Campaign for Cleaner Corporations for its poor spills and worker accident records, in addition to its apparent reluctance to committing to a concrete timetable for the establishment and maintenance of a hospital in Bhopal, India. (In 1984, 2000 people were killed by a chemical release from a Union Carbide plant. Thousands more subsequently died from the accident's after effects. The company has also received criticism for delays in relief effort and compensation for the victims.) In 1995, Union Carbide was removed from the list for funding the construction of a 260 bed hospital in Bhopal, taking measures to prevent and reduce spills, and an improved worker safety record.

Union Carbide's average total toxic releases and transfers during the years 1994–1996 were higher than the industry sample average. Emissions increased slightly during those years, a better than average performance.

A team from Union Carbide and the EPA received Vice President Al Gore's Hammer Award for its partnership role in the EPA's Environmental Technology Initiative for Chemicals. The team was recognized for efforts to manage the risks of a new chemical (Triton SP surfactants), without burdensome regulatory controls.

EEO: In 1996, Union Carbide's 12-member Board of Directors included one woman and one minority. Of ten corporate officers, none were women or minorities. Two women ranked among the top 25 paid employees.

The company and its subsidiaries actively participate in the National Minority Supplier Development Council. Union Carbide has prohibited discrimination based on sexual orientation for more than a decade.

Community Involvement: Union Carbide's charitable contributions totaled $2.7 million in cash in 1996, or 0.32 percent of its pretax earnings, and $200,000 in in-kind donations. The Company reports that it increases its contributions by 3 percent annually.

Workplace Information: OSHA records indicate that Union Carbide underwent four inspections from 1994 to 1996. Violations included 16 classified as "serious." One inspection resulted in $11,475 in fines, and the other in $125,000. Union Carbide instituted a behavior-based safety program at its South Charleston, West Virginia, facility in 1992.

Weapons Contracts: In 1994, Union Carbide had $2 million in non-weapons-related contracts with the Department of Defense.

Legal Proceedings: Union Carbide is one of a number of defendants named in cases brought by former and current IBM workers who allege occupational exposure to chemicals while working at IBM's Fishkill, N.Y. and Essex Junction, Vt. facilities. The plaintiffs claim the chemical supplier defendants failed to warn and to adequately test their products. As of this date, no specific Union Carbide product has been identified by plaintiffs as an alleged cause of any injuries. Union Carbide denied all charges as has IBM and the other defendants and is vigorously defending the case.

Union Carbide joined a multibillion-dollar silicone breast implant litigation settlement agreement, with an estimated share under $138 million. The company provided bulk silicone materials to breast implant manufacturers, and owned the stock of a supplier of intermediate materials briefly.

Union Electric

STOCK SYMBOL: UEP
STOCK EXCHANGES: NY, B, C, CH, PH, P

Environment	C
Women's Advancement	C?
Minority Advancement	N
Charitable Giving	C
Community Outreach	C
Family Benefits	N
Workplace Issues	N
Social Disclosure	C

In August 1995, Union Electric announced it would join the flurry of merger activity in the electric utility industry by joining with CIPSCO Inc. (Central Illinois Public Service Co.). This widespread movement toward consolidation is viewed as necessary to compete in an increasingly deregulated market. The joint company will serve approximately 1.7 million customers in Missouri, Illinois and Iowa. Union Electric is based in St. Louis, Missouri. For the fiscal year ending December 1996, the utilities had revenues totaling $2.3 billion and approximately 6,000 employees.

Environment: Union Electric estimates it will spend $300 million on compliance at its fossil fuel plants, which account for about 70 percent of its electric generation. To meet Clean Air Act requirements, Union Electric will increase its use of low-sulfur coal and bank its emission credits for future use. In addition, the utility has six demand-side management (DSM) pilot programs that it hopes will offset some of its estimated growth in demand. As part of its DSM agenda, the company conducts audits of its business customers, buys back inefficient refrigerators and appliances, encourages efficient lighting through rebates, offers weatherization kits, and provides grants for affordable, energy-efficient housing.

Union Electric's recycling efforts include the recovery of 2.5 million pounds of scrap wire, 2,000 gross tons of steel, and 1,000 batteries each year. The company is experimenting with using chipped tires in its coal burners and has replaced old growth trees with laminated cross-arms for its utility poles. Due to a source reduction program, Union Electric's annual production of low-level waste has steadily declined in recent years — in 1992 alone, it dropped 40 percent.

CIPSCO derives virtually all of its energy from coal-fired plants. CEP is not aware of any significant compliance concerns involving the company.

EEO: In 1996, Union Electric's Board of Directors totaled ten, including one woman and no minorities, while two of a total of 22 corporate officers were women, and none were minorities.

Community Involvement: In 1996, Union Electric's charitable giving totaled $2.6 million in cash, which was equal to 0.52 percent of the company's pretax earnings for that year. In terms of the actual dollar amount donated by the company, the level of cash contributions in 1996 represented a decrease of 15.38 percent from that of 1995, which was 0.50 percent of the company's earnings for that year. The company's in-kind giving — the donation of products or services — came to a total of $119,000 in 1996.

In November 1996, Union Electric dedicated five $200,000 donations in recognition of the volunteer efforts of four St. Louis, Missouri–area citizens. Donations were made to the Missouri Historical Society, St. Louis Science Center, St. Louis Zoo, St. Louis Art Museum, and Forest Park Forever. The company's current giving priorities include education, services for the elderly and youth, and the environment.

Workplace Information: According to the Occupational Safety and Health Administration's records, Union Electric was inspected six times from 1994 to 1996. The OSHA inspectors' citations included two violations classified as "serious." A total of $1,100 in fines was assessed to the company following the inspections, an average of $183 per inspection. In comparison, the median amount of fines per inspection for other utilities was $2,625.

Most employees of Union Electric and CIPSCO are represented by collective bargaining agreements. While relations at Union Electric have generally been amiable, CIPSCO locked out 1,500 workers in May 1993 during contract negotiations. A company spokesperson stated the action was taken in response to an alleged work slowdown by union employees. Union officials denied the allegations, stating that the company had not negotiated in good faith with the union. The parties agreed to settle the matter through arbitration.

Unisys Corporation

Environment	C
Women's Advancement	C?
Minority Advancement	B?
Charitable Giving	F?
Community Outreach	N
Family Benefits	N
Workplace Issues	F?
Social Disclosure	C

Unisys, headquartered in Blue Bell, Pennsylvania, is an information management company providing computer systems, software, and services to 50,000 clients in 100 different countries. After suffering three years of losses in the early 1990s, Unisys has concentrated on four areas of growth: telecommunications, financial services, airlines, and the public sector. In 1996 Unisys had $6.4 billion in revenues and 37,400 employees.

Environment: Unisys has an environmental policy and a corporate environmental report. The company has implemented an integrated environmental management system and provides environmental health and safety (EH&S) training to all employees. Unisys has a written pollution prevention policy and has initiated a companywide pollution prevention program. The company also has a corporate policy on community involvement relating to local environmental concerns and has community advisory panels at all facilities. Unisys has a written policy on product stewardship and evaluates its products with the objective of reducing their life-cycle impacts on the environment. In the selection of suppliers, Unisys requires suppliers to follow the company's environmental guidelines as a contract condition. The company has an environmental audit program.

Unisys' toxic releases and transfers were below average for both 1993 and 1994 compared to its industry sample. The company decreased its emissions by over 90 percent between 1993 and 1994, one of the best performances in the sample. The average yearly change from 1993 to 1996 was also over 90 percent.

EEO: In 1996, Unisys Corp.'s Board of Directors totaled ten, including one woman and one minority.

Ten former Unisys employees filed age bias suits claiming that workers at the Roseville, Minnesota–based plant were illegally laid off based on their ages in a workforce reduction procedure. Unisys laid off 68 employees, at least 70 percent of whom were over 40 years old.

Community Outreach: Unisys' first priority in its contributions towards education is developing literacy in science and technology, which it works to accomplish through educational exhibits and programming at science museums. The company reports that "key

activities include a multi-year sponsorship of the Philadelphia Liberty Medal." Recipients of the medal include Vaclav Havel for his role in ending Communist rule in what was then Czechoslovakia.

In 1995, Unisys Corp.'s contributions to various charitable institutions included cash donations totaling $2.6 million.

Workplace Information: According to the Occupational Safety and Health Administration's records, Unisys Corp. was inspected three times from 1994 to 1996. The OSHA inspectors' citations included one violation classified as "willful" or "repeat" and 22 violations classified as "serious" for a total of $20,065 in fines, an average of $6,688 per inspection. In comparison, the median amount of fines per inspection for other companies in the industries manufacturing electronic equipment was $1,347.

Since 1992, Unisys has reduced its workforce by nearly 25 percent. Only 3 percent of Unisys' 46,300 employees are unionized, and the company has no grievance procedures for nonunionized workers.

In 1993, Unisys announced that it would phase out health insurance for retirees, affecting 25,000 retirees over three years. Unisys retirees filed a series of class action suits, but the court ruled that the company had the legal right to change medical plans.

Weapons Contract: Unisys, a provider of communications systems and defense electronics for anti-submarine warfare and other defense needs, was 32nd in the list of prime contractors to the U.S. Department of Defense in 1996. Its contracts totaled $381.6 million. The company sold its Unisys Defense division to Loral Corporation in 1995; Loral was subsequently acquired by Lockheed Martin.

Unocal Corporation

STOCK SYMBOL: UCL
STOCK EXCHANGES: NY, B, C, CH, PH, P

Environment	D
Women's Advancement	D?
Minority Advancement	D?
Charitable Giving	F
Community Outreach	N
Family Benefits	N
Workplace Issues	C?
Social Disclosure	B

Founded in 1890 as Union Oil of California, Unocal is an integrated energy company principally engaged in the exploration for and production and distribution of oil and natural gas and related products. The company is also the world's largest producer of geothermal energy. The company, based in El Segundo, California, has approximately 11,650 employees. Sales equaled $5.1 billion in 1996.

Environment: Unocal has a written environmental policy and a corporate environmental report which follows the guidelines established by the Public Environmental Reporting Initiative. The environmental report is updated annually and is available on the Internet. Unocal has implemented an integrated environmental management system and provides EH&S training to managers. The company considers contribution towards EH&S goals in the job performance reviews of senior management and operating personnel. Unocal's Loss Control Program System requires employees and contractors to comply with all EH&S and company policies and procedures. Unocal has a corporate policy on community involvement relating to local environmental concerns and an environmental audit program.

Unocal's average total toxic releases and transfers from 1993 to 1994 were among the highest in the industry sample. Emissions increased by about a sixth during those years, among the sample's worst performances.

In July 1997, Unocal and four other companies were sued by Communities for a Better Environment (CBE) for swapping pollution credits to avoid installing equipment that would keep hazardous fumes out of minority neighborhoods in southern California. The suit attacks a program that allows the companies to buy and scrap high-polluting cars in exchange for not having to prevent emissions that escape from tanks when gasoline is loaded onto ships for transport. CBE claims that people living and working near the loading docks said fumes have caused a variety of health problems.

Unocal's Yadana natural gas development project in Burma is a major cross-border energy project, involving construction of a pipeline from the offshore Yadana field to the Thai border. The project will begin in 1998.

In May 1997, the EPA said Unocal's Union Oil unit must pay $375,000 in penalties for failing to notify federal and state authorities about releases of hazardous substances from its refinery in Rodeo, California.

Unocal's Thailand facility was awarded certification for ISO 14001, an international environmental standard, in 1997. Unocal's Alaska facility was presented with the National Health of the Land award from the U.S. Department of the Interior for environmental excellence at the Swanson River Field, located in the Kenai National Wildlife Refuge.

EEO: In 1996, Unocal had one woman and no minorities on its 12-member Board of Directors. The company's total of 34 corporate officers included two women.

According to a survey of oil companies conducted by *The Oil Daily* in December, 1996, Unocal ranked last as an employer of women, but employs "relatively large numbers of minorities."

Community Involvement: Unocal Corp.'s charitable contributions totaled $2 million in cash in 1996. The cash-giving figure represented the equivalent of 0.26 percent of the company's pretax earnings for the same year. In 1997, Unocal increased the rate at which it matches employee contributions from one-to-one to two-to-one. The company only matches gifts to education; in 1996, contributions totaled $200,000.

Workplace Information: OSHA records indicate that Unocal Corp. underwent 28 inspections from 1994 to 1996. Violations included 65 classified as "serious" for a total of $78,752 in fines, an average of $2,813 per inspection. The median amount of fines per inspection for other extractive companies was $2941.

Additional Information: Unocal is among a consortium of oil companies operating in Burma. Their presence there is opposed by human rights advocates for providing financial support to Burma's military regime, which has held Nobel Peace Prize Laureate Aung San Suu Kyi under house arrest since 1989.

243

US Airways Group

STOCK SYMBOL: U
STOCK EXCHANGES: NY, B, C, CH, PH, P

Environment	N
Women's Advancement	D
Minority Advancement	C
Charitable Giving	F
Community Outreach	D
Family Benefits	C
Workplace Issues	A
Social Disclosure	A

U S Airways, based in Arlington, Virginia, is the nation's sixth largest airline. As with others in the industry, in the last ten years US Airways has been plagued with heightened competition and multiple annual losses (six consecutive years). Revenues for 1996 were $8.14 billion; the company has 43,500 employees.

Environment: US Airways reports that it maintains Department of Environmental Programs which monitor corporate compliance with environmental statutes. The company provides environmental awareness training, though its recycling program appears to cover only aluminum cans. In 1993, the company received the Forsyth County (North Carolina) Commendation for Achieving Air Quality Excellence. From 1990 to 1994, US Airways reported spills of 1,206 gallons of jet fuel. This was below industry averages.

EEO: In 1996, US Airways' board totaled 15 directors, including one woman and two minorities, while four of a total of 30 corporate officers were women, and one was a minority. Additionally, no women and one minority were among the 25 employees with the highest salaries at the company.

The Equal Employment Opportunity Commission and other fair employment practice agencies are investigating US Airways regarding charges by certain job applicants, employees and former employees of its subsidiaries involving allegations of employment discrimination. US Airways participates in the Pittsburgh Minority Purchasing Council.

Community Involvement: In 1996, US Airways' charitable giving totaled $45,910 in cash, which was equal to 0.02 percent of the company's pretax earnings for that year. In terms of the actual dollar amount donated by the company, the level of cash contributions in 1996 represented an increase of 3.7 percent from that of 1995, which was 0.04 percent of the company's earnings for that year. The low percentages may reflect the multiple years of losses experienced by the company in the past decade.

Workplace Information: According to OSHA's records, US Airways was inspected 12 times from 1994 to 1996. Violations included one classified as "willful" or "repeat" and 35 classified as "serious" for a total of $48,787 in fines, an average of $4,066 per inspection.

In November, 1997, US Airway pilots overwhelmingly approved a five-year contract agreement. The agreement, which was initially established October 2, provides for the creation of US2, a low-cost carrier the airline had long wanted. Pilots for US2 will be paid two thirds of what pilots currently earn at the company, and the low-cost airline will operate at up to 25 percent of the company's flying capacity. The company's proposals of a year ago sought greater reductions in pay and operating US2 at up to 40 percent of the company's capacity. Pilots forced to work at US2 would receive current wages for 18 months, followed by parity with other US2 pilots plus 10 percent for an additional 18 months, while those employed in the mainline will receive compensation one percent higher than the average of American, Delta, Northwest, and United pilots. An early retirement package was developed for 325 pilots over 45 to eliminate higher-paid pilots and so allow younger pilots to advance and furloughed pilots to be reinstated. By December 15, the 103 pilots laid off in 1997 were to be recalled, and 42 additional furloughs that were to take place October 1 were canceled. Recalls of pilots laid off earlier than 1997 will go into effect by the end of 2001. The new contract includes a no-furlough clause and guarantees continued growth of the airline at the minimum of 2 percent annually, starting at a level five percent below that of 1997. Also included in the agreement were stock options valued at $350 million, $50 million of which will be part of the early retirement package.

Flight Safety: In 1992, a federal judge found US Airways negligent in a jet crash that killed 27 people. Federal investigators concluded the crew failed to detect ice on the wings that led to the crash. Plaintiffs were to be awarded compensatory damages on an individual basis. In a 10-year study of airline safety commissioned by *Newsweek*, US Airways had the poorest risk rating of eight major airlines (1 death in 2 million).

US West Inc.

STOCK SYMBOL: USW
STOCK EXCHANGES: NY, B, CH, PH, P

Environment	N
Women's Advancement	A
Minority Advancement	A
Charitable Giving	D
Community Outreach	C
Family Benefits	N
Workplace Issues	B?
Social Disclosure	B

US West provides local telephone services to residential and business customers in 14 Western and Midwestern states, publishes telephone directories, and is in the cable television business. In 1996, revenues were $9.8 billion, and the company had over 69,000 employees.

Environment: US West does no manufacturing and produces no process wastes. In 1993, the company collected and recycled 3,242 tons of old phone books in Arizona as part of a 14-state effort to recycle 40 million pounds of paper. Its annual reports are printed on recycled paper.

EEO: In 1996, US West Inc. achieved a higher than average rating in both diversity categories, placing them easily in the top third of S&P 500 companies. Two women and two minorities served on US West's nine-member Board of Directors. Of seven corporate officers at the company, two were women and none were minorities. US West is a member of the National Minority Supplier Development Council. Its Minority/Women Business Enterprise Program makes at least 10 percent of total purchases from minority and women suppliers.

US West was one of 83 companies listed in the Glass Ceiling Commission's March, 1995 fact-finding report for implementing "employment practices that help break the glass ceiling." US West was cited for three programs it instituted. Through its "Women of Color Project," which had just completed its five-year duration at the time of the report, all 36 participants were provided developmental opportunities and 83 percent were offered one or more promotional opportunities. The company established its "Pluralism Performance Menu" which tracks the performance of the officers' qualitative and quantitative efforts to develop and advance women and minorities, and offers feedback and suggestions after semi-annual reviews.

US West is the defendant in a suit filed by 38 employees who claim that company supervisors ignored harassing and intimidating behavior by Robert Harlan, a former employee who was ultimately sentenced to death in 1995 for the murder of Rhonda Maloney, a cocktail waitress. The plaintiffs contend that US West knew for seven years that Harlan had raped an employee and had been disciplined for three other sexual harassment incidents, yet did not fire him or report the incidents to the police. Harlan is also the prime suspect in the 1988 murder of Jessica Arredondo, a co-worker of Harlan's at US West. In March 1997, the company settled a civil suit brought by the family of Maloney and Jacquie Creazzo, who was shot and partially paralyzed by Harlan when she tried to help Maloney. Details of the settlement were not released, and the presiding judge ordered the entire case file to be sealed.

Community Involvement: US West's charitable contributions totaled $20.9 million in cash in 1996. This figure represented the equivalent of 1.14 percent of the company's pretax earnings for the same year, and an increase of 21.48 percent from the company's cash contributions in 1995. In 1995, the company contributed 0.97 percent of its pretax earnings for that year to charity.

Organizations that work with education reform, multicultural diversity, and economic development receive support from the US West Foundation. One program funded by the company is "Connecting Teachers with Technology," which promotes the implementation and utilization of communications technology in the classroom.

Workplace Information: The records of the Occupational Safety and Health Administration indicate that US West Inc. underwent 18 health and safety inspections from 1994 to 1996. Violations included one classified as "willful" or "repeat" and 19 classified as "serious." The company was required to pay $7,755 as a result of its violations, an average of $431 per inspection. In comparison, the median amount of fines per inspection for other companies in the service industry, such as banks and communications companies, was $573.

USX Marathon Group

Environment	D
Women's Advancement	B
Minority Advancement	A
Charitable Giving	B
Community Outreach	B
Family Benefits	B
Workplace Issues	B
Social Disclosure	A

USX Marathon is engaged in worldwide exploration, production, transportation and marketing of crude oil and natural gas; and domestic refining, marketing and transportation of petroleum products. At year-end 1996, USX Marathon had sales of $13.56 billion and employed approximately 20,468 people.

Environment: USX Marathon Group has an environmental policy and publishes a corporate environmental report, which is updated annually. The company provides environmental health and safety (EH&S) training to all employees. The company also has a corporate policy on community involvement relating to local environmental concerns, and most of Marathon's operating facilities participate on Citizen Advisory Panels and Local Emergency Planning Committees. Marathon also evaluates its products with the objective of reducing their life-cycle impacts on the environment. Internationally, Marathon does not monitor SARA Title III, or equivalent emissions and follows U.S. regulations unless host country's laws and regulations dictate otherwise. Marathon participated in EPA's Green Lights and 33/50 programs.

USX Marathon's average total toxic releases and transfers during the years 1993–1994 were among the lowest in the industry sample. Emissions decreased by about a third during those years, a better than average performance. The company ranked 7th out of 15 for CEP's Campaign for Cleaner Corporations' 1997 Petroleum Refining Report.

In 1996, under EPA's new environmental audit policy, Marathon self-reported nearly a decade of unpermitted produced water discharges in Alaska's Upper Cook Inlet, and settled with nominal penalties. The National Oil Refinery ACTION! Network reports that the oil industry in the area has opposed regulations and environmentally-protective practices for over 40 years.

In August, 1997, EPA tests found that the fluid catalytic cracker at Marathon's Robinson, Illinois, refinery emitted particulate matter at a rate 1,456 percent higher than the legal limit. Marathon faces a maximum fine of $200,000, and possible civil suit for the Clean Air Act violation, which was the refinery's fourth in three years. A 350,000 gallon pipeline spill along six miles of the Blind River in 1996 killed an undetermined number of fish, alligators, birds, and other wildlife according to Florida officials.

EEO: In 1996, USX achieved a higher than average rating in both diversity categories, placing them easily in the top third of S&P 500 companies. One woman and one minority served on the company's 15-member board. Of seven corporate officers at the company, one was a woman and one was a minority, while one of the top 25 paid employees was woman, and one was a minority.

USX Marathon Group offers mentoring programs, recruitment programs, support networks, maintains diversity goals, and gives special consideration for management training to both women and minorities. It also provides diversity training.

Community Involvement: In 1996, USX's foundation grants totaled $6.4 million in cash, which was equal to 0.46 percent of the company's pretax earnings for that year. In terms of the actual dollar amount donated by the company, the level of cash contributions in 1996 represented a decrease of 17.21 percent from that of 1995, which was 2.36 percent of the company's earnings for that year.

Over 100 Marathon Oil employees volunteer on programs that augment learning and social development at the predominantly Hispanic Browning Elementary in an inner-city area of Houston. The employees serve as tutors and pen pals to the students; the foundation provides $20,000 annually to support the partnership with the school.

Workplace Information: According to the Occupational Safety and Health Administration's records, USX Marathon Group was not inspected from 1994 to 1996. Consequently no violations or fines were assessed to the company; 1996 was a record year for safety at the company.

Wachovia Corporation

STOCK SYMBOL: WB
STOCK EXCHANGES: NY, B, PH

Environment	N
Women's Advancement	C
Minority Advancement	B
Charitable Giving	B
Community Outreach	B
Family Benefits	N
Workplace Issues	N
Social Disclosure	B

Wachovia Corporation is an interstate holding company with dual headquarters in Atlanta, Georgia (Wachovia Bank of Georgia), and Winston-Salem, North Carolina (Wachovia Bank of North Carolina). In 1996, its assets were nearly $47 billion, and net interest income was $1.4 billion. Wachovia employed 16,208 people.

Environment: Wachovia participates in EPA's Green Lights program and has upgraded equipment to ensure maximum efficiency, including installation of low-energy computer systems. The company recycles paper and aluminum cans and provides bike racks for employees. It implemented a waste minimization program in 1996.

EEO: In 1996, Wachovia Bank's 14-member Board of Directors included one woman and one minority. Of nine corporate officers at the company, all were white men. One woman ranked among the 25 highest paid employees at the company. The company has correspondent relationships with minority-owned banks, operates a small purchasing program, and provides diversity awareness training to its employees. In 1996, Wachovia purchased over $4.4 million in goods and services from women- and minority-owned businesses.

Wachovia Bank offers mentoring programs, apprenticeship programs, recruitment programs, maintains diversity goals, and gives special consideration for management training to both women and minorities.

Wachovia has a written policy expressly prohibiting discrimination on the basis of sexual orientation.

Community Involvement: In 1994, Wachovia Bank made $12.3 million in cash contributions to charitable institutions, the equivalent of 1.3 percent of the company's earnings before taxes that year.

The Wachovia Corporation matches employee gifts to education, the arts, and health organizations. Wachovia's charitable allocation to social services goes to youth organizations, child welfare, community service and religious charities. The company supports education by contributing to colleges, universities and student aid.

Wachovia's Advantage program seeks out low- to moderate-income applicants across the state and offers higher loan-to-value ratios and lower closing costs. It also uses flexible credit guidelines, such as taking into account unusual circumstances that may have affected an applicant's payment record and allowing rent or utility payments records to establish creditworthiness for first-time borrowers.

Workplace Information: The records of the Occupational Safety and Health Administration indicate that Wachovia Bank was not inspected from 1994 to 1996. Consequently no fines or violations were assessed to the company. Inspections can often be called as a result of a complaint, suggesting that no complaints were filed in reference to Wachovia; however, it is not unusual for a company not to be inspected over several years.

Walgreen Company

STOCK SYMBOL: WAG
STOCK EXCHANGES: NY, B, CH, P

Environment	N
Women's Advancement	C?
Minority Advancement	N
Charitable Giving	C
Community Outreach	D
Family Benefits	N
Workplace Issues	F?
Social Disclosure	B

Walgreen Company, headquartered in Deerfield, Illinois, is the leading drugstore chain in the United States, with 2,403 stores operating in 34 states and Puerto Rico. Committed to moving into more new markets, the company has been opening new stores. In fiscal year ending in August of 1997, the company reached $13.4 billion in sales and employed 85,000 persons.

EEO: In 1996, Walgreen's Board of Directors totaled nine, including one woman and one minority, while none of a total of 14 corporate officers were women, and none were minorities.

In 1993, a former employee's suit against Walgreen Co. was dismissed when the judge determined that racial discrimination was not a factor in his firing. The judge indicated that the plaintiff may have had a more compelling case if he had sued over earlier incidents of discrimination he testified to, including being assigned to a store in a black neighborhood and being shunned by white managers at district-wide meetings.

Community Involvement: In 1996, Walgreen's charitable giving totaled $4 million in cash, which was equal to 0.66 percent of the company's pretax earnings for that year. In terms of the actual dollar amount donated by the company, the level of cash contributions in 1996 was identical to that of 1995, which was 0.76 percent of the company's earnings for that year.

Walgreen contributes charitably to the area of social services through programs that work with issues like healthcare programs, drug and alcohol rehabilitation, underprivileged children, emotionally disturbed children, youth service, and race relations. The company also supports symphonies and theatre as part of its commitment to the arts and culture.

Walgreen funds and participates in "One-on-One," a volunteer program that tutors and provides role models for inner-city children in fourth through sixth grades.

Workplace Information: According to the Occupational Safety and Health Administration's records, Walgreen Co. was inspected ten times from 1994 to 1996. The OSHA inspectors' citations included one violation classified as "willful" or "repeat" and 38 violations classified as "serious." A total of $154,937 in fines was assessed to the company following the inspections, an average of $15,494 per inspection. In comparison, the median amount of fines per inspection for other companies in the retail industry was $694.

As is the case of many establishments that are family-run for generations--in this case for 97 years—there is a strong sense of "family" and being part of the community at Walgreen, which makes a point of avoiding malls, seeking instead to locate near focal points in the neighborhood.

Process Quality: Walgreen's Strategic Inventory Management System, fully operational in 1994, will allow instant checking of inventory, and let warehouses know when stores are running low.

Wal-Mart Stores

Stock Symbol: WMT
Stock Exchanges: NY, B, Ch, P

Environment	N
Women's Advancement	A
Minority Advancement	B
Charitable Giving	C?
Community Outreach	D?
Family Benefits	N
Workplace Issues	C?
Social Disclosure	B

Arkansas-based Wal-Mart Stores, Inc., has approximately 2,265 stores in the U.S. and over 230 stores internationally. Wal-Mart also owns more than 430 Sam's Wholesale Clubs. The company has been the most profitable and fastest-growing in the retail industry, with $93.6 billion in sales and 675,000 employees in 1996.

Environment: In 1995, Wal-Mart provided approximately $1 million to its Green Teams to spearhead such community environmental programs as Adopt-a-Highway, educational field trips, and recycling. The same year, Wal-Mart opened its third "environmental store," which showcases solar power, skylights, and energy-efficient heating and cooling systems and reduces electric energy consumption in half.

EEO: In 1996, Wal-Mart Stores achieved a higher than average rating in both diversity categories. Two women and one minority served on Wal-Mart Stores' 13-member Board of Directors. Of 38 corporate officers, eight were women and two were minorities.

According to a brief article in *Hispanic* Magazine, Wal-Mart is the "number one employer of Hispanics," and is implementing a campaign to recruit 200,000 employees by 2000, focusing on Hispanic, African-American, and women candidates.

In 1996 sponsors withdrew their proposals for shareholder resolutions asking for a "glass ceiling" report and Board inclusiveness. Withdrawal of a proposal generally indicates that the sponsors reached an agreement with company management.

Company policy dictates that managers and supervisors "shall take action to ensure" that women and minorities "are hired and that these associates are encouraged to aspire for advancement and are considered as promotional opportunities arise."

Community Involvement: Wal-Mart's annual community service project in Dallas consisted of planting trees along major roads. The company asked for volunteers from the surrounding community to participate. Wal-Mart is a strong supporter of the United Way and the Children's Miracle Network. Educational programs and industrial development programs are funding priorities of the foundation.

In 1995, Wal-Mart's contributions to update charitable institutions included cash donations totaling $23.7 million. The company's cash contributions for 1995 were equivalent to 0.56 percent of its earnings before taxes for the same year.

Workplace Information: OSHA records indicate that Wal-Mart Stores underwent 134 health and safety inspections from 1994 to 1996. Violations include one classified as "willful" or "repeat" and 167 classified as "serious" for a total of $105,986 in fines, an average of $791 per inspection. In comparison, the median amount of fines per inspection for other companies in the retail industry was $694.

Wal-Mart has been cited by the National Labor Relations Board for threatening to close one of its stores rather than allow its employees to unionize. The store has been ordered to stop its threats and post a notice stating adherence to the labor laws. The store was also found guilty of unlawfully censuring an employee who was one of five initial employees to accept a union card.

International: Wal-Mart internally monitors its sourcing guidelines for labor rights, and does not involve outside auditors or non-governmental organization in the process. Wal-Mart has strong sourcing guidelines, which reference basic workers' rights, child labor (under 15), wages that match industry standard, and a 60-hour workweek. In 1996, Wal-Mart was linked to U.S. sweatshops in the production of the Kathie Lee Gifford line of clothing. More recent allegations state that Wal-Mart has been using both U.S. and offshore subcontractors who employ children and abuse their workers. Wal-Mart is working with Business for Social Responsibility and the Interfaith Center on Corporate Responsibility to develop a poster which will list their sourcing guidelines in English, Spanish and Mandarin, and will describe how to report violations through the company's 800 number.

Warner-Lambert

STOCK SYMBOL: WLA
STOCK EXCHANGES: NY, B, C, CH, PH, P

Environment	B
Women's Advancement	N
Minority Advancement	N
Charitable Giving	C?
Community Outreach	N
Family Benefits	N
Workplace Issues	A?
Social Disclosure	C

Warner-Lambert, headquartered in Morris Plains, New Jersey, develops, manufactures, and markets health care and consumer products on a global basis. In 1996, the company had 38,000 employees worldwide and $7.2 billion in sales. Warner-Lambert has 72 production facilities in 34 countries.

Environment: Warner-Lambert has an environmental policy, but does not currently publish a corporate environmental report. The company has implemented an integrated environmental management system. Warner-Lambert has a written pollution prevention policy and has initiated a companywide pollution prevention program, which establishes annual reduction goals for point sources, secondary emissions, fugitive emissions, and solid waste. The company also has a corporate policy on community involvement relating to local environmental concerns, and has some community advisory panels. Warner-Lambert has a written policy on product stewardship and evaluates its products with the objective of reducing their life-cycle impacts on the environment. All of Warner-Lambert's pharmaceutical and over-the-counter products are evaluated in this manner. Warner-Lambert was also a participant in EPA's Green Lights, Energy Star Buildings, Energy Star Computers, and WasteWi$e Program.

Warner-Lambert's average total toxic releases and transfers during the years 1994–1996 were slightly higher than the industry sample average. Emissions increased by an average of about a fifth annually during those years, a below average performance.

The Justice Department reported that Warner-Lambert pleaded guilty in September 1997 to falsifying reports on pollutants released from a waste-water treatment plant in Puerto Rico, and was fined $3 million. Department officials reported that Warner-Lambert will pay an additional $670,000 civil penalty for releasing excessive levels of pollutants from 1992 to 1995, violating its waste-water discharge permit 347 times. The plant's supervisor, who is no longer employed by the company, pleaded guilty to similar charges and could be sentenced to up to 27 months in jail.

EEO: In 1996, one minority sat on Warner-Lambert's Board of Directors. In the same year, Warner-Lambert purchased over $35.6 million in goods and services from women- and minority-owned businesses. ICCR has submitted a shareholder resolution to Warner-Lambert seeking publication of the company's EEO-1 data, which must be filed annually with the Department of Labor.

Community Involvement: In 1995, Warner-Lambert's contributions to various charitable institutions included cash donations totaling $7.8 million. The company's cash contributions for 1995 were 0.68 percent of its earnings before taxes for that year. The majority of Warner-Lambert's charitable contributions go to the areas of higher education, medical research, community, hospitals, civil rights, and youth agencies.

Workplace Information: OSHA records indicate that Warner-Lambert Co. underwent three health and safety inspections in 1996 and received only incidental violations for $4,725 in fines, an average of $1,575 per inspection. In comparison, the median amount of fines per inspection for other companies in the industry sample was $2,266.

At Warner-Lambert, all full-time, nonunion workers — not only top executives — are eligible to join a stock option program after one year of service.

Legal Proceedings: Warner-Lambert was named to the Multinational Monitor's ten worst corporations list in 1995 because of the company's criminal conviction for failing to notify the federal government about problems with company drugs that did not maintain stable dosages. The company pled guilty to criminal charges late that year and was fined $10 million.

In June 1996, Warner-Lambert settled a federal class-action conspiracy lawsuit for $15.1 million. Retail pharmacies sued Warner-Lambert and several other pharmaceutical manufacturers, claiming that the companies practiced price discrimination in concert with one another, favoring institutions, managed care entities, mail order pharmacies, and other buyers with lower prices than those charged to the plaintiffs. An appeal is pending.

Wells Fargo & Company

STOCK SYMBOL: WFC
STOCK EXCHANGES: NY, B, C, CH, P, PH

Environment	N
Women's Advancement	B?
Minority Advancement	B?
Charitable Giving	F?
Community Outreach	B?
Family Benefits	N
Workplace Issues	A?
Social Disclosure	D

Established in 1852 and based in San Francisco, California, Wells Fargo is the holding company for Wells Fargo Bank. The company's operations include commercial real estate, corporate services, small business lending and consumer credit. It has more than 600 branch offices and serves nearly 3.5 million California households. As of December 1996, it had income of $8.7 billion and almost 35,000 employees. Wells Fargo's total assets in 1996 were nearly $109 billion.

Environment: In 1990, Wells Fargo set out to adopt recycling wherever possible through its "Recycle — It Makes Sense" program. The company's internal newsletter, corporate stationary, business cards and deposit slips have incorporated recycled content. As of 1993 the company had spent $4 million on energy reduction projects.

EEO: In 1996, Wells Fargo & Co. achieved a higher than average rating in both diversity categories, placing them easily in the top third of S&P 500 companies. Two women and three minorities served on Wells Fargo & Co.'s 18-member Board of Directors. Of 14 corporate officers at the company, two were women and none were minorities. Additionally, the company's vice president in charge of corporate computer systems is a person with disabilities.

Wells Fargo, known to be the largest lender to small businesses, has linked up with the National Association of Women Business Owners in an attempt to secure loans for small women-owned businesses. The company made a $1 billion lending pledge in 1995, and extended the pledge to $10 billion over ten years after the initial pledge was exhausted in a single year. Wells Fargo received a Working Women Honor Roll certificate from the U.S. Department of Labor Secretary as a result of this program.

Community Involvement: In 1995, Wells Fargo & Co.'s contributions to various charitable institutions included cash donations totaling $1.2 million. The cash contributions for 1995 were equivalent to 0.35 percent of its earnings before taxes for the same year.

Wells Fargo has established a goal of making $45 billion in small business and community loans from 1996 to 2006 following its merger with First Interstate. Wells Fargo's giving focuses on education, economic development and community. It also pledged $300 million in charitable giving and $500 million for economic development. But Wells did not set targets for community reinvestment in states other than California. Wells Fargo's record of creating and implementing special lending programs to meet community credit needs is validated with an outstanding community reinvestment rating by the Office of the Comptroller of the Currency. Wells Fargo is active with K–12 education and social services for the disadvantaged. Wells Fargo received the certificate of Honor from the City of San Francisco Board of Supervisors for promoting job opportunities for youth.

Workplace Information: According to the Occupational Safety and Health Administration's records, Wells Fargo & Co. was inspected two times from 1994 to 1996. OSHA inspectors cited the company only for violations classified as "other," the least egregious type of violation. A total of $760 in fines was assessed to the company following the inspections, an average of $380 per inspection. In comparison, the median amount of fines per inspection for other companies in the service industry, such as banks and communications companies, was $573.

Wells Fargo offers employees the opportunity to take a paid sabbatical to work for a non-profit organization.

251

Westvaco Corporation

STOCK SYMBOL: W
STOCK EXCHANGES: NY, B, CH, P, PH

Environment	C
Women's Advancement	D?
Minority Advancement	C?
Charitable Giving	B?
Community Outreach	N
Family Benefits	N
Workplace Issues	B?
Social Disclosure	C

Headquartered in New York but operating primarily in the Southeast, Westvaco is a major producer of paper and paperboard in the U.S. and abroad. It makes paper products for catalogues, packaging, envelopes, and other business clients. The company's primary international operations are in Brazil, where the wholly-owned subsidiary Rigesa, Ltd., operates. The company also owns nearly 1.5 million acres of timberland, though less than one-third of all raw timber used by Westvaco is harvested on company lands. In 1996, sales were $3 billion, and the company had 13,430 employees.

Environment: Westvaco has an environmental policy and a corporate environmental report, which is updated annually. Westvaco is in compliance with the American Forest & Paper Association's Sustainable Forestry Initiative.

Westvaco Corp.'s average total toxic releases and transfers during the years 1993–1994 were the highest compared to an industry sample. However, its emissions decreased by almost a fourth during those years, indicating the best performance within the industry sample. Westvaco was named to CEP's worst performer list in the 1994 Campaign for Cleaner Corporations for emitting the most toxic releases — adjusted for size and absolute — among 21 industry competitors. In addition, the company had refused to submit timber harvesting plans to CEP. The following year Westvaco was removed from the list for its progress in reducing toxic emissions under the 33/50 program; creating the new position of Vice President for Environmental Affairs; and committing $140 million for an initiative to eliminate the use of elemental chlorine in the company's paper bleaching mills.

Westvaco received the North American Waterfowl Management Committee's Great Blue Heron Award in 1995 for setting up a research forest to study the effects of forestry on ecosystem elements. The American Forest and Paper Association awarded the company the Environmental and Energy Achievement Award, in the solid waste management category, for its undeliverable bulk mail recycling program. Westvaco was presented the 1995 Corporate Award by the Ecological Society of America for the company's use of ecosystem-based, multiple use forestry management. Westvaco was honored with a total of 14 environmental awards from 1990 to 1995.

In May 1997, Westvaco Corp.'s paper mill at Covington, Virginia was identified as the top polluter in the state, according to EPA's Toxic Release Inventory. The company announced in March 1997 that it plans to invest $150 million in environmental controls in the next few years at the mill.

EEO: In 1996, Westvaco Corp.'s board totaled 11 directors, including one woman and one minority, while three of a total of 43 corporate officers were women, and none were minorities. The company has a diversity program and bans discrimination based on sexual orientation.

Community Involvement: In 1995, Westvaco Corp.'s contributions to various charitable institutions included cash donations totaling $6.8 million. The company's cash contributions for 1995 were equal to 1.45 percent of its pretax earnings for the same year.

Donations are earmarked for areas in which the company has operations. New York recipients of Westvaco support include Lincoln Center, the New York Public Library, and the Central Park Conservancy.

Family Benefits: Westvaco operates an education center in South Carolina that is open to both employees and their families. The Westvaco Learning Center provides classes ranging from basic reading and writing education and skills training to advanced education.

Workplace Information: OSHA records indicate that Westvaco was inspected 17 times from 1994 to 1996. Violations included 30 classified as "serious" for an average of $1,968 in fines per inspection. The median amount of fines per inspection for other companies in the extractive business was $2,941.

Weyerhaeuser

STOCK SYMBOL: WY
STOCK EXCHANGES: NY, B, C, CH, P, PH

Environment	C
Women's Advancement	C?
Minority Advancement	F?
Charitable Giving	B
Community Outreach	D?
Family Benefits	N
Workplace Issues	D?
Social Disclosure	B

Weyerhaeuser is one of the world's largest manufacturers of wood products, including building materials, paper, and packaging. Sales in 1996 surpassed $11 billion. The company has 39,700 employees.

Environment: Weyerhaeuser has an environmental policy and a corporate environmental report, which is available on the Internet. Weyerhaeuser provides environmental health and safety (EH&S) training to its management and production staff. It also considers contribution towards EH&S goals in the job performance reviews of all employees. Weyerhaeuser has initiated a company-wide pollution prevention program, which establishes reduction goals for point sources, fugitive emissions, and solid waste. The company also has a corporate policy on community involvement relating to local environmental concerns and holds community forums at facility locations. The company has an environmental audit program, which is evaluated by a third party. Internationally, Weyerhaeuser follows U.S. regulations in the U.S. and abroad unless local regulations are stricter. Weyerhaeuser is in compliance with the American Forest & Paper Association's Sustainable Forestry Initiative.

Weyerhaeuser Co.'s average total toxic releases and transfers during the years 1993–1994 were the lowest compared to an industry sample. However, its emissions increased by about a third during those years, a below average performance.

In May 1997, the Oregon Department of Ecology fined Weyerhaeuser $40,000 for leaking 8,700 gallons of turpentine and condensate from one of its paper mills that caused temporary illnesses in the local community.

In April 1997, Weyerhaeuser became the first participant in the EPA's Project XL, a program designed to achieve greater company flexibility in environmental regulations in exchange for greater protection of public health and the environment. The company's Flint River, Georgia, pulp mill agreed to reduce water usage, enhance wildlife habitats in its forests, update the mill's environment management system and facilitate greater protection of the Flint River.

In January 1997, Weyerhaeuser agreed to pay $178,000 in fines resulting from a July 1994 chlorine release at its Longview, Washington mill. The settlement is the largest that the EPA has extracted from a Northwest company under EPCRA.

EEO: In 1996, Weyerhaeuser Co.'s nine-member board of directors included one woman. Of eight corporate officers at the company, none were women or minorities. As of February 1998, Weyerhaeuser's board includes one minority, and one of eight senior corporate officers is a minority.

Community Involvement: According to the company, Weyerhaeuser has two purposes in awarding grants: "to improve the quality of life in areas where Weyerhaeuser Co. has a major presence, and to increase understanding of the importance and sustainability of forests and the products they provide that meet human needs."

Workplace Information: OSHA records indicate that Weyerhaeuser Co. underwent 57 health and safety inspections from 1994 to 1996. Violations included five classified as "willful" or "repeat" and 174 classified as "serious" for a total of $186,326.75 in fines. Fines were slightly above the median amount per inspection for other extractive companies.

Relations with unions have been good since a difficult six-week strike in 1986 resulted in pay cuts. More than one half of Weyerhaeuser's U.S. work force is unionized, and competition for Weyerhaeuser jobs tends to be high because of a better-than-average pay scale.

In 1994, an outside investment manager hired by Weyerhauser embezzeled two percent of the company's pension funds (the full amount for which he was responsible). The investment manager was subsequently convicted and spent time in prison; the company restored the missing $22 million to the fund.

Whirlpool Corporation

STOCK SYMBOL: WHR
STOCK EXCHANGES: NY, B, C, CH, P, PH

Environment	B
Women's Advancement	D
Minority Advancement	C
Charitable Giving	B
Community Outreach	A
Family Benefits	N
Workplace Issues	D?
Social Disclosure	B

Whirlpool is the world's largest manufacturer of home appliances. The company is expanding aggressively into international markets. In 1996, its revenues were $8.7 billion. Whirlpool employs 48,000 people.

Environment: Whirlpool has a formal environmental vision and policy statement for its worldwide operations that addresses such issues as product development, resource conservation, waste reduction, chemical releases, and community relations. The company conducts environmental audits at all manufacturing and distribution facilities.

In October 1989, Whirlpool became the first appliance manufacturer to establish a recovery process for CFCs previously lost to the atmosphere during repairs. In June 1993, Whirlpool was named the winner of a $30 million "green carrot" prize in the Super-Efficient Refrigerator contest sponsored by 24 utilities to develop a more efficient and environmentally friendly refrigerator. The new refrigerators contained no CFCs and were 25 percent more energy-efficient than required by then current government standards. Whirlpool has broken industry ranks by testifying in support of the government's energy-efficiency standard setting for appliances. Whirlpool participates in EPA's 33/50 reduction of targeted chemicals program and Green Lights program to retrofit spaces with energy-efficient lighting.

In 1993, two environmental organizations and the California attorney general sued faucet manufacturers, including Whirlpool, alleging that the faucets were allowing high levels of lead to be leached into drinking water. In September 1995, Whirlpool was among seven major producers that reached an agreement with the Natural Resources Defense Council to embark on a lead reduction program that will make their products virtually lead-free by 1999.

EEO: In 1996, Whirlpool Corp.'s board totaled 12 directors, including two women and one minority. All eight corporate officers were white men. The 25 highest paid employees included one minority. In November 1995, Whirlpool received the National Women's Political Caucus Good Guy Award for its "commitment to cutting-edge child care and diversifying [its] employee base."

Community Involvement: In 1996, Whirlpool Corp.'s charitable giving totaled over $4.9 million in cash, equal to 2.1 percent of the company's pretax earnings. Cash contributions in 1996 represented an increase of 22.9 percent from that of 1995.

Nearly one-third of Whirlpool Foundation's budget supports contemporary family life, cultural diversity, and lifelong learning issues. The foundation launched two global research programs in 1995 to study women's views on work, family, and society. A grant of $100,000 was given to the Family Violence Prevention Fund that year to help raise awareness of domestic violence issues. The foundation also awarded a three-year grant to the 9 to 5 Working Women Education Fund to support a career advancement training program for non-management women workers.

Workplace Information: According to OSHA's records, Whirlpool Corp. was inspected nine times from 1994 to 1996. Violations included two classified as "willful" or "repeat" and 38 classified as "serious" for a total of $64,430 in fines, an average of $7,158 per inspection.

About 30 percent of Whirlpool's domestic workforce is unionized. Though recent negotiations have occurred without major conflict, the company's relations with organized labor have at times been contentious. In the early 1990s, the company was placed on union boycott lists related to a stalemate with members of Allied Industrial Workers at its Fort Smith, Arkansas, plant. The conflict ended in July 1993 with the signing of a new five-year contract.

International: Whirlpool has formed four joint manufacturing ventures in China, and has 13 plants in Mexico, Brazil, Argentina, and India.

Winn-Dixie Stores, Inc.

STOCK SYMBOL: WIN
STOCK EXCHANGES: NY, B, CH, PH

Environment	N
Women's Advancement	D?
Minority Advancement	B?
Charitable Giving	B?
Community Outreach	N
Family Benefits	N
Workplace Issues	B?
Social Disclosure	D

Founded in 1925 by William Davis, Table Supply Stores was renamed Winn-Dixie in 1955 to reflect its owners' growing interest in dominating the Southeast. The chain, headquartered in Jacksonville, Florida, is the primary food retailer in the region and the fifth largest in the U.S. It operates 1,178 stores and has dozens of manufacturing and distribution facilities. Private label sales represent nearly 20 percent of total revenue, which in 1996 totaled nearly $13 billion. In 1995, the company purchased the 25-store Thriftway chain, its largest acquisition in two decades. Winn-Dixie has 126,000 employees, about 60 percent of whom work part-time. The Davis family controls approximately 40 percent of the firm's stock.

Environment: Winn-Dixie pledges to promote environmentally safe packaging, waste reduction, recycling and resource recovery in the most efficient and cost-effective manner possible, yet maintaining the high quality of products as they travel from the manufacturer to its customers' tables. The company is very active in its recycling and reuse efforts, including the recycling of grocery bags, corrugated cardboard, fluorescent lamps, pallet plastic shrink wrap, motor oils from its fleet maintenance operations, paper, aluminum cans, and single use camera empty bodies. Winn-Dixie also reuses its plastic crates, wooden pallets in its distribution centers, and returns reusable produce crates to its growers and farmers. In its efforts to reduce waste, the company has reduced packaging for its produce and private label paper products, and orders equipment and parts for retail maintenance in bulk. Winn-Dixie also has implemented an energy conservation program, monitoring its utility bills and watching for excessive use, as well as redesigning its buildings and appliances to conserve energy. The company also utilizes natural gas fleet vehicles to reduce air pollution.

EEO: In 1996, Winn-Dixie Stores' 11-member Board of Directors included one woman and one minority. Of 27 corporate officers, none were women or minorities.

Winn-Dixie is the defendant in two separate suits filed by former employees, one alleging sexual harassment and the other racial discrimination. In the latter case, in November 1996, a Native American woman who had worked at the company's store in Lakeland, Florida, claims that she was the victim of crude comments and ethnic jokes almost immediately after she was hired.

She alleges that her manager fired her when she told him she was going to complain to the district manager, and is seeking damages in excess of $25,000. Another woman formerly employed at the St. Petersburg store filed suit in May 1996, charging she was sexually harassed by one of her managers.

Community Involvement: In 1995, Winn-Dixie Stores' contributions to various charitable institutions included cash donations totaling more than $3.3 million. The company's cash contributions for 1995 were equivalent to 0.94 percent of its earnings before taxes for the same year. Winn-Dixie funds Hope Lodges in Miami and Gainesville, Florida, which provide a nurturing residence for patients undergoing treatment for cancer at a nearby medical center.

Workplace Information: OSHA records indicate that Winn-Dixie was inspected 24 times from 1994 to 1996. Violations included 38 classified as "serious" for a total of $22,258 in fines, an average of $927 per inspection. In comparison, the median amount of fines per inspection for other companies in the retail industry was $694.

In November 1993, Winn-Dixie agreed to pay $175,000 in fines for federal child labor law violations in five states. The company is alleged to have employed a significant number of minors, allowed minors to operate hazardous equipment, and allowed 16-year-olds to work during prohibited times and in excess of permissible hours.

Product Issues: In October 1995, Winn-Dixie was fined $28,000 for food safety violations at 22 stores in Georgia. State inspectors found out-of-date produce, meat, and other foodstuffs on shelves. The stores were also cited for sanitary violations such as unclean equipment.

William Wrigley Jr. Company

STOCK SYMBOL: WWY
STOCK EXCHANGES: NY, CH, PH, P

Environment	B
Women's Advancement	B?
Minority Advancement	D?
Charitable Giving	D
Community Outreach	N
Family Benefits	N
Workplace Issues	N
Social Disclosure	F

Headquartered in Chicago, Illinois, William Wrigley Jr. Company's (WWY) principal business is the manufacture and sale of chewing gum, both in the United States and internationally. During 1996, WWY employed 7,800 people worldwide and generated $1.83 billion in net sales.

Environment: The company states that it has a long legacy of environmental consciousness. WWY does not publish an environmental progress report and did not disclose its environmental policy. WWY utilizes natural and synthetic raw materials blended to make chewing gum base. WWY states that the manufacture of chewing gum produces virtually no air or water pollution. The company reuses its waste sugar by developing initiatives such as supplying it to animal feeders or local beekeepers. WWY maintains universal environmental, safety and health policies at all factories worldwide. In addition, worldwide environmental compliance audits are conducted at WWY offices and factories annually. Audits include waste disposal vendors. While not providing specifics, WWY claims it has aggressive energy conservation, passive and active recycling and waste reduction programs. Since the company's primary waste reduction goal is to divert waste from landfills, company policy dictates that every shipping case used throughout the U.S. be made from a minimum of 50 percent recycled materials, and all vending machine trays be made of 100 percent recycled materials. To date, recycling efforts at WWY's printing plant has resulted in a 65 percent reduction of solid waste landfills. WWY's commitment to clean air is exemplified by the company's provision of subsidies for public transportation at its Chicago headquarters.

EEO: In 1996, Wrigley's Board of Directors totaled ten, including two women and no minorities, while one of a total of 25 corporate officers was a woman, and none were minorities.

WWY operates recruitment programs to identify qualified minority and female candidates for specific job openings and is developing a physical demands analysis to determine the ability of disabled individuals to perform essential job functions. WWY cooperates with the INROADS program to provide professional guidance and summer employment for students and offers of employment upon graduation.

Community Involvement: In 1996, Wrigley's charitable giving totaled $1.6 million in cash, which was equal to 0.45 percent of the company's pretax earnings for that year. In terms of the actual dollar amount donated by the company, the level of cash contributions in 1996 was identical to that of 1995, which was 0.46 percent of the company's earnings for that year.

A majority of Wrigley's support in the health and welfare sector goes to the United Way and dental health programs. The company also focuses on minority education, but no direct grants are given to colleges or universities. Instead, the foundation chooses to give scholarships to the children of employees and to those organizations benefiting minority advancement in higher education, such as the United Negro College Fund.

Workplace Information: According to the Occupational Safety and Health Administration's records, Wrigley was not inspected from 1994 to 1996. Consequently no violations or fines were assessed to the company. As inspections can be called in response to a complaint about the health or safety conditions, a lack of inspections may indicate relatively good safety and health conditions at a company.

International: WWY reports that it has translated and published its International Personnel Policies handbook into the local languages of its countries of operation. The company states that its principles frequently exceed the prevailing legal requirements or customs, and that a key component of its personnel policies in international locations is to recruit and develop local talent.

⬤ Xerox Corporation

STOCK SYMBOL: XRX
STOCK EXCHANGES: NY, B, C, CH, P, PH

Environment	B
Women's Advancement	B
Minority Advancement	A
Charitable Giving	A?
Community Outreach	A
Family Benefits	A
Workplace Issues	B
Social Disclosure	B

Xerox, the Document Company, is focused on being the world leader in production and servicing of a wide range of copiers, printers, scanners, and software. In 1995, the company rolled out networked color laser printers and a new assortment of software products. It also sold its Financial Service Life Insurance Company to General Americana Life Insurance. Xerox is based in Stamford, Connecticut. In 1996, Xerox had sales of $17.4 billion and employed 86,700 people.

Environment: Xerox has an environmental policy, but does not publish a corporate environmental report. Xerox considers contribution towards EH&S goals in the job performance reviews of executives and managers. The company also has an environmental audit program. Internationally, Xerox states that it follows U.S. regulations in the U.S. and abroad unless local regulations are stricter.

Xerox's toxic releases and transfers were below average for both 1993 and 1994, compared to an industry sample, during which time emissions decreased by nearly three quarters, a better than average performance within the industry sample.

EEO: In 1996, Xerox Corporation achieved a higher than average rating in both diversity categories, placing it easily in the top third of S&P 500 companies. Two women and two minorities served on Xerox's 13-member Board of Directors. Of 34 corporate officers, four were women and six were minorities. Three of the top 25 paid employees were women and three were minorities.

Xerox has developed a program in which senior executives are named as "champions" for specific minority groups of employees, and are given leeway to address their concerns. In 1996, a group of African-American employees expressed concern at the limited representation of African-American women at Xerox. Under the prompting of their "champion," the company designed an internship program for African-American female engineering students, through which interns are encouraged to consider a position at the company following graduation.

Community Involvement: In 1995, Xerox's contributions to charitable institutions included cash donations totaling $15 million. The cash contributions for 1995 were 0.81 percent of its pretax earnings.

The Xerox Community Involvement Program was created over 20 years ago, and currently involves over one third of the company's employees. The company provides paid leaves of absence to 15 employees each year to participate in volunteer projects for up to one year through the 26 year-old Social Service Loan Program.

Workplace Information: OSHA records indicate that Xerox was inspected five times from 1994 to 1996. Violations included six classified as "serious." The company was required to pay $9,150 as a result of its violations, an average of $1,830 per inspection. In comparison, the median amount of fines per inspection for other companies in the industries manufacturing electronic equipment was $1,347.

Xerox made *Working Mother* magazine's 1996 "100 Best" list for its extensive work/family programs.

Weapons Contracts: In 1994, Xerox had $187 million in contracts with the Department of Defense. Of this amount, only $28,000 was for weapons-related systems. While the company does not manufacture components used directly in weapons systems, it does provide services such as field mapping technology, which assisted in coordinating battlefield operations during Desert Storm.

Glossary

33/50 Program: Voluntary EPA program for the reduction of 17 high-priority toxic substances. Participants had to reduce the use of those toxics by 33 percent by 1992 (base year 1988) and 50 percent by 1995.

Campaign for Cleaner Corporations (C-3): CEP's annual listing (since 1992) of the most egregious polluters within particular industries. All companies listed through 1996 have met with CEP and the C-3 panel of judges to determine what steps they need to take to improve environmentally and be delisted.

CANICCOR: Caniccor is a nonprofit, independent agency that annually monitors and evaluates home mortgage lending data from every lender nationwide. This information is collected under the Home Mortgage Disclosure Act (HMDA). The group focuses primarily on lending to minority and low-income borrowers (both mortgages and small business loans). It regularly networks with institutional church investors and social screening organizations, bringing pressure to bear on lenders to improve performance in this area.

CERCLA: The Comprehensive Environmental Response, Compensation and Liability Act created a tax on the chemical and petroleum industries in 1980. The tax, called Superfund, goes toward the cleanup of abandoned or uncontrolled hazardous waste sites.

CERES Principles: The Coalition for Environmentally Responsible Economics was established in response to the *Exxon Valdez* oil spill. The principles are ten commitments to environmental ethics creating a standard by which corporate environmental practices can be judged.

CFCs: Chlorofluorocarbons are a class of highly inert organic compounds that have been used for refrigeration, aerosol propellants, foam blowing, and solvents in the electronics industry. CFCs and other ozone-depleting chemicals cause destruction of the stratospheric ozone layer, a filter for the damaging UV radiation from the sun.

Clearcutting: A practice of forestry management that cuts every tree on a site and removes the marketable timber to a mill. Critics consider clearcutting to be the most ecologically damaging form of logging.

Coal gasification: One of a number of processes for converting coal to gas by the addition of hydrogen in the presence of steam at high temperature and pressure.

CONEG: The Coalition of Northeastern Governors (CONEG) challenged more than 250 companies to use more recycled content, enhance recyclability, and reduce or eliminate use of toxic heavy metals in inks. Many companies now use more environmentally-sound packaging, and some states have passed legislation proposed by CONEG to cut down use of heavy metals.

CRA: The Community Reinvestment Act of 1977 is one of four Fair Lending Laws enacted by Congress to ensure that the credit needs of communities previously discriminated against are met. A later reform measure was passed in 1989 to strengthen the law, under which banking institutions report on their lending activities to the Federal Reserve Board, the Federal Deposit Insurance Corp., Office of Thrift Supervision, and the Office of the Comptroller of the Currency. The institutions are rated Outstanding, Satisfactory, Needs to Improve, or Substantial Noncompliance, according to their record of meeting community needs.

DBCP: Dibromochloropropane (DBCP), a pesticide used on banana plantations, was banned in the early seventies for use in the U.S. when it was discovered to cause cases of sterility in unprotected workers. However, it remained in use in some Central American countries for several more years, prompting lawsuits as new cases of sterility allegedly caused by DBCP developed.

Demand Side Management (DSM): A broad range of strategies to reduce electric power consumption in homes, offices, businesses and industry. DSM has become a major focus of utilities' efforts to balance generation capacity with consumer demand. DSM includes measures to use electricity more efficiently and to shift the use of electricity away from peak usage hours.

ECF: Designation of a facility as elemental chlorine-free.

EHS: Environment, Health and Safety department in a corporation.

EPA: The Federal Environmental Protection Agency, which sets policies and standards for the U.S.

EPCRA: The Emergency Planning and Community Right-to-Know Act of 1986 was enacted as a freestanding provision of the Superfund Amendments and Reauthorization Act of 1986. Prompted largely by the chemical release from the Union Carbide plant in Bhopal, India, which caused thousands of deaths, it is a congressional effort to compel state and local governments to develop emergency response plans for unanticipated releases of potentially hazardous substances.

ESOP: Employee stock ownership plan

FIFRA: The Federal Insecticide, Fungicide, and Rodenticide Act of 1947 requires that all these substances be registered/licensed with the EPA before they may be sold or distributed. An overall risk/benefit standard is established for each such registration.

Green Lights Program: A voluntary EPA program to encourage the use of energy-efficient lighting systems.

HCGC123: One of a family of compounds containing carbon and hydrogen in various combinations. Some of these are major air pollutants and may be carcinogenic.

HDPE: High-density polyethylene, a type of plastic used in milk jugs and shampoo bottles, that is readily recyclable (denoted by #2 on bottom of bottle).

KKR: Kohlberg Kravis Roberts & Co. is a company specializing in corporate takeovers through leveraged buyouts. KKR is perhaps best known for its orchestration of the RJR Nabisco buyout in 1988.

Life-cycle Assessment: The evaluation of a particular material or activity from raw material through to final disposal—also referred to as the "cradle-to-grave" approach.

MacBride Principles: Equal opportunity employment guidelines proposed by Dr. Sean MacBride, founder of Amnesty International, to address discriminatory corporate practices in Northern Ireland.

NPDES: National Pollutant Discharge Elimination System, a national program for issuing, modifying, revoking, terminating, monitoring, and enforcing permits; and imposing and enforcing pretreatment requirements, under the Clean Water Act.

NO_x: NO with a subscript x is a general abbreviation for nitrogen oxides.

OSHA: The Federal Occupational Safety and Health Agency, which oversees health and safety in the U.S. workplace.

PAH: Polycyclic aromatic hydrocarbons are components in organic materials that may pose a risk of cancer.

Particulates: Environmental pollution in the form of air-borne particles from industrial processes.

PCB: Polychlorinated biphenyl (PCB) refers to any of several organic compounds used in the manufacture of plastics, transformers, and capacitators. These are long-lived environmental pollutants that have a tendency to accumulate in animal tissues (such as fish in the Hudson river). In 1979, additional sales or new uses of the compounds were terminated by the Toxic Substances Control Act.

PET: Polyethylene terephthalate, a type of plastic used in soda bottles, is readily recyclable (denoted by #1 on bottom of bottle).

Potentially Responsible Party (PRP): Any individual or company considered by the Federal Environmental Protection Agency to be potentially responsible for, or contributing to, the contamination problems at a Superfund site. EPA requires PRPs — through administrative and legal actions, to clean up hazardous waste sites they have contaminated.

Project XL: A part of the "Reinventing Environmental Regulation" initiative of President Clinton, under which participants engage in projects that satisfy specific environmental objectives, and in exchange are allowed a degree of regulatory flexibility.

Superfund: see CERCLA

TCF: Totally chlorine-free facility.

TRI: Toxic Release Inventory was mandated by Section 313 of the Emergency Planning and Community Right-to-Know Act of 1986. The purpose of TRI is to provide the public and government with information about possible chemical hazards. Manufacturers are required to report annually the amounts of over 300 toxic chemicals released at their facilities.

WasteWiSe Program: EPA voluntary program designed to reduce municipal solid waste through source reduction, collection of recyclables and the increase of the use of recycled products.

Work stoppage: A strike or walkout by unionized employees of a corporation to protest and heighten awareness of unsolved workplace issues.